The Synagogue in America

Marc Lee Raphael

The Synagogue in America

A Short History

New York University Press • *New York and London*

68903160

NEW YORK UNIVERSITY PRESS
New York and London
www.nyupress.org

References to Internet websites (URLs) were accurate at the time of writing.
Neither the author nor New York University Press is responsible for URLs
that may have expired or changed since the manuscript was prepared.

Library of Congress Cataloging-in-Publication Data
Raphael, Marc Lee.
The synagogue in America : a short history / Marc Lee Raphael.
p.   cm.
Includes bibliographical references and index.
ISBN 978-0-8147-7582-0 (cl : alk. paper) — ISBN 978-0-8147-7704-6 (e-book)
1. Synagogues—United States—History. 2. Judaism—United States—
History. 3. Jews—United States—History. 4. Jews—United States—
Social life and customs.   I. Title.
BM205.R372 2011
296.6'50973—dc22   2010047146

New York University Press books are printed on acid-free paper,
and their binding materials are chosen for strength and durability.
We strive to use environmentally responsible suppliers and materials
to the greatest extent possible in publishing our books.

Manufactured in the United States of America

10 9 8 7 6 5 4 3 2 1

Contents

Acknowledgments

Lengthy conversations with Pamela Nadell, Julie Galambush, and Linda Schermer Raphael helped me organize this book. Tamara Cooper assisted me continuously with the technology needed for conveying the manuscript in the proper manner to the press. Jeffrey Gurock read the entire manuscript and made critical suggestions for improvement. And Jennifer Hammer, editor extraordinaire at New York University Press, who approached me to write a history of the synagogue in America, improved every paragraph of this book not only in style but in content.

1

Building the Synagogue Community in Colonial America

The Earliest Years

FOLLOWING THE ELECTION of George Washington as president of the United States of America in 1789, laymen from all six Jewish congregations in the new nation sent him congratulatory letters. He replied to four of them—those in Charleston, New York, Philadelphia, and Richmond—with a single letter and to the Hebrew Congregation in Savannah and to the Newport congregation with individual greetings. Thus, after more than a century of Jewish life in colonial America, the 1,500 or so Jews present at the birth of the nation proudly announced their religious institutions to the country and were recognized by its new leader.

Synagogues have a history in America almost as lengthy as the history of individual Jews in the colonies. Expelled from Spain and Portugal in the 1490s, Jews built a thriving community in tolerant Amsterdam and then in the Dutch as well as English colonies in the New World. In these European outposts, their mercantile experience and networks of friends and family throughout the Atlantic world enabled them to play a significant role in the commercial revolution and in the territorial expansion that developed the New World and established the colonial economies.

Jews came to Recife in the seventeenth century after the Dutch conquered this part of northeastern Brazil from the Portuguese in 1630 and vigorously welcomed Jews. But, with the reconquest by the

Portuguese in 1654 and the impending Inquisitions, twenty-three Jews fled on a ship, which, after being attacked at sea, made port in New Amsterdam. While they may not have been in actuality the very first Jews in North America, the Jews who stepped off this vessel are remembered as such in most histories. These Sephardic Jews—that is, Jews of Spanish and Portuguese heritage—formed the initial seeds of the community that would establish congregation Shearith Israel, the first in North America.

This book offers a history of the American synagogue. Using the records of approximately 125 Jewish congregations, it traces the emergence of the synagogue in the United States from its first appearance in the colonial period, when each of the half-dozen initial Jewish communities had just one synagogue each, to the proliferation of synagogues as the nation and the American Jewish community grew and diversified.

Promptly following the first arrival of Jews in colonial America, the synagogue became the most significant institution of Jewish life. Unlike in the twentieth and twenty-first centuries, when other institutions, such as Jewish community centers and Jewish philanthropic organizations, often claimed to be the "central address" of the Jewish community, no other organization challenged the dominance of the early synagogues. In part, this was the case for two reasons: because, well into the nineteenth century, synagogues incorporated activities that later, as the Jewish population grew, could not all be contained within the synagogue or whose leaders did not want them to be part of the synagogue, and also because the Jewish community was so small. The first federal census of 1790 counted only 1,243 Jews in America out of a total population of 2.8 million, or less than one-twentieth of one percent. The synagogue, thus, *was* the Jewish community in the seventeenth and eighteenth centuries. As American Jews slowly created philanthropic organizations, the synagogue enveloped them. As Jews ritually slaughtered kosher animals and sold the parts to coreligionists, locally and in the Caribbean, the synagogue employed the slaughterer, and its leaders routinely announced not only the time of prayer services and holiday celebrations but the availability (and price) of kosher meat.

This volume illuminates the changing role of the synagogue within the American Jewish community over the course of its history—from the sole institution in which nearly all communal functions took place to an entity focused primarily on worship and on children's education. We also explore developments in the leadership, membership, worship styles, and architecture of the American synagogue. The format of this book is largely chronological, with each of a number of subthemes receiving attention within each broad time period. Care is taken both to acknowledge differences as they evolved among the major branches of Judaism and to attend to both differences within branches and similarities across them. Divisions among different Jewish movements and heritages are addressed particularly as we move into the late nineteenth century. These later chapters are organized by Judaism's branches, sectors, or wings— what Protestants call "denominations." But, for the first two centuries of Jewish life in America, congregations generally came without labels. In our discussion of the late nineteenth and twentieth centuries and beyond, we focus particularly on rabbis, as congregants began to call the synagogue by the name of the rabbi (e.g., "Krauskopf's" or "Zelizer's") as often as they used the actual name of the synagogue. For almost the first two centuries of Jewish life in America, however, no rabbi served a synagogue; laymen (rarely laywomen), paid or volunteer, dominated synagogue leadership.

This work draws not only on secondary literature but on surveys, interviews, and other primary sources. A note on how I have used and cited these sources appears in the bibliography. Although there are some exceptions, including one in Atlanta, one in San Francisco, and one in Washington, D.C., synagogue histories to this point have been overwhelmingly written by either the rabbi of the congregation, his spouse, or an interested layperson. Each has its limitations:

the rabbi is usually primarily interested in discussing the years of his (there are as yet none by women) rabbinate; the laypeople are usually preoccupied with mentioning the good deeds of every layperson (or, in the case of *rebbetzin* histories, her husband). None devotes much attention to the issues that are of interest to a historian of American Judaism.

The answer to the question of why so many rabbis write about themselves—sometimes even in the third person—must remain in the area of psychology. But the practice has a long history. In the late nineteenth century, for example, Bernhard Felsenthal of Kehilath Anshe Ma'ariv, in Chicago, co-authored one of the earliest congregational histories, noting of himself that "Felsenthal delivered a scholarly sermon" that "was highly appreciated by the congregation." A few years later, David Philipson wrote a history of the Cincinnati synagogue he served for many years, Bene Israel, and pointed out that, "with youthful vigor," Rabbi Philipson "addressed himself to the work" and the "congregation advanced steadily onward and upward." Julius Nodel, at Portland, Oregon's Congregation Beth Israel, was a bit more discreet in the synagogue history he authored. He had a congregant write the last chapter; the collaborator made sure to note that Rabbi Nodel had an "intellectual originality all his own [*sic*]," a "sharp, uncompromising mind," and a "rare combination of scholarship, sharp wit, rhetorical polish, and uncompromising conviction." No surprise, then, that his sermons were "aesthetic gems," bringing "an average of 450 persons" to the Friday-evening services, including "a large percentage of non-Jewish visitors who come once, twice, and often many more times to listen and to learn." Rabbi Abraham Shusterman pointed out, in a history of the Baltimore synagogue he served for many years, that "Rabbi Shusterman has achieved an important role in community affairs as well as religious influence."

Those interested in the history of synagogues in America are often most interested in "firsts." But dating the precise beginning of any congregation is often difficult. Washington Hebrew Congregation of the District of Columbia, for example, celebrated its 150th anniversary in 2002, but the evidence for its origin in December 1855, not 1852, is extensive. It includes the date of founding submitted by the congregation in 1875 when it joined the national synagogue organization, the Union of American Hebrew Congregations; the date given by the congregation for the 1880 volume *Statistics of the Jews of the United States*; the date indicated in the original "Pen Written" history of the congregation, now behind a glass case in the vestibule outside the sanctuary; the date of origin noted in the *Evening Star* of June 5, 1897, and December 4, 1915; the "special citation" presented by the U.A.H.C. to the congregation for its centennial celebration in 1955; and, finally, the fact that Rabbi Abram Simon, who served the congregation for many decades as spiritual leader and (unofficial) synagogue historian, celebrated the 50th anniversary of the congregation in December 1905, the 60th anniversary in December 1915, the 70th anniversary in December 1925, and the 80th anniversary in December 1935, and that Rabbi Norman Gerstenfeld, his successor, led the 90th anniversary celebration in December 1945. But, like numerous other congregations that have used one date for a century or more and then suddenly adopted an earlier date, it is always possible that a few men began to *discuss* forming a synagogue prior to the year that they actually formed the congregation. Others may use as their date of origin the time when the first worship service—in a home or a rented room—took place or when congregational founders incorporated their institution. To judge only by synagogue websites, most congregations seem to prefer the earliest possible date. And, more and more, congregations have pushed back the date of their birth to the year that someone conceived of the future congregation, not the date of the first official meeting. Thus, for at least 100 congregations with websites, more than one date of origin appears in the print and the Web histories.

In the case of New York's Shearith Israel, there is a 1695 map of the city with the site of a "synagogue" marked, so worship certainly began no later than that year. The first native-born American to serve as a quasi-clergyman or "reader" (mostly conducting worship, not having significant pastoral duties) or hazan was Gershom Mendes Seixas, appointed by Shearith Israel in 1768. One of his tasks was to supervise the exporting of kosher meat to West Indies congregations and to Surinam, in South America; another was to administer the modest income or "treasury" for the care of the poor, sick, and elderly members of the congregation, including old-age pensions. Generally, the congregation hired an additional salaried man, as Shearith Israel did in 1762, when it brought in Abraham Abrahams to teach Hebrew, English, reading, and writing. Like many other colonial educators, Abrahams often called himself "minister" or even "rabbi." The 1790 constitution of the congregation (which begins, "Whereas in free states all power originates and is derived from the people") is obviously modeled on that of the nation; it laid out the Duties of the Rabbi, even though there was no ordained rabbi at that time.[1]

With minimal documentation, Jeshuat Israel, later known as the "Touro Synagogue," in Newport, Rhode Island, dates its beginning to 1658. Yet, we are much safer in concluding that Shearith Israel, which we can date back to 1695, was the first congregation (as distinct from synagogue building) in colonial America, as it possesses more compelling evidence. Isaac Touro, a native of Holland, was appointed hazan in 1758, becoming the congregation's first spiritual leader, and by 1763 the congregation had a synagogue building, dedicated in the presence of the Reverend Ezra Stiles, future president of Yale College. A few years before hiring Touro, the community's leaders, in 1754, appealed to the London Sephardic congregation Shaarei Shomayim for financial aid, and this appeal was so successful that by the end of the year the congregation had dedicated a building, which is still standing.

Congregation Mickve Israel of Savannah dates its origins to the year the Jews arrived there from England (1733), apparently assuming

Interior of Mickve Israel in Savannah, Georgia. Courtesy of the
Georgia Historical Society Foltz Photography Studio (Savannah,
Georgia), photographs, 1899–1960.

that the earliest Jews created a religious congregation immediately.
More realistically, its origins date from the early 1790s. Beth Elohim
of Charleston began in 1749, incorporated more than forty years later
with fifty-three families (more than 400 persons), and dedicated an
existing building as a synagogue in 1794.

Philadelphia's Mikve Israel had a Torah scroll by 1761. Its leaders
hired Ezekiel Levy in 1776 as ritual slaughterer of cattle and fowl,

hazan, and Hebrew teacher—following a common practice in which an individual assumed every "professional" role in the congregation. In Richmond, Virginia, Beth Shalome's leaders adopted a constitution and a name in 1789, just in time to write to the new U.S. president.

While the precise "origins" are often vague, we can say with certainty that three of these six congregations definitely had synagogue buildings by the time the new nation was born: New York's Shearith Israel (1730), Newport's Jeshuat Israel or "Touro" (1763), and Philadelphia's Mikve Israel (1782). Only the Touro Synagogue building still stands.

These six congregations were all Sephardic (Spanish-Portuguese) in their ritual and organization, although, already in the eighteenth century, Ashkenazic Jews immigrating primarily from Germany had become a majority. Following a pattern similar to that in the twentieth century in which many Reform congregation members became more traditional while the ritual of their congregations remained, sometimes for lengthy periods, less so, the Sephardic ritual in this early period continued to dominate in many of these congregations well after the Jews whose ancestors lived in Spain or Portugal in the fifteenth century ceased to be a majority. In fact, more Ashkenazic Jews than Sephardim served as *parnas*, or president, of "Sephardic" Shearith Israel in the colonial period, 1654–1790.

"Sephardic ritual" refers to the practices related to prayers, cantillation (ways of chanting Scripture), pronunciation, and standing-sitting patterns (and much more) that differ from those of Jews of central or east European ancestry, the Ashkenazic Jews. For Sephardic ritual, the model was the European or Caribbean Sephardic congregations (e.g., those in Holland or Curaçao), especially London's Bevis Marks and Amsterdam's 1675 magnificent synagogue, which are still standing. The early nascent U.S. synagogues looked to these older, more established synagogues for aid and counsel. In 1757, the "Elders and all the members" of New York's Shearith Israel resolved that the officers should ask the "*parnassim* [presidents] and *mamad* [*sic*; *mahamad* or trustees]" to write to the Sephardic congregation Shaarei Shamayim in London and request that its leaders send them "a proper hazan." Mordecai M. Mordecai of Philadelphia's Mikve Israel sought approval (with letters in Hebrew, a language of scripture and liturgy rarely used for correspondence or speech) from both London and Amsterdam for the Sephardic design of the synagogue's 1782 buildings—a design quite similar to those of the synagogues in Newport and New York—featuring a women's gallery upstairs, the ark against the east wall, columns (usually Corinthian) on two sides of the rectangular basilica, and podium and reader's table in the middle of the men's floor, rather than against the wall housing the ark and Torah as was common in Ashkenazic settings.

Hebrew terms dominated the designations for the officers in these Sephardic congregations; *parnas* (president), *hatanim* (vice presidents or assistants), *shamas* (sexton or beadle), *gabai* (treasurer), *mahamad* (board of directors). A member was known as a *yahid* (pl., *yahidim*). Often, members did not wish to serve, so the colonial congregations levied fines on those chosen for office if they would not accept. This practice continued in numerous American synagogues into the second half of the nineteenth century. The earliest constitution (1728) of Shearith Israel exists in parallel columns of Portuguese and English (with some Hebrew). Sephardic custom required that the officers tightly control the members, primarily because they were so dependent on the support of these small communities for survival, and the congregants frequently called themselves *kahal kodesh*, sacred community, to position themselves as the synagogue-community. The leaders determined who received honors, approved all marriages and burials, fined members who did not attend important events or who gave "any affront or abuse, either by words or action," set the order and time for worship as well as the choice of Torah readings, announced the beginning and end of the Sabbath, supervised the baking of matzah for Passover and the proper slaughtering of kosher animals, assigned and sold seats in the synagogue (what later was called "dues"), and carefully delineated precisely what the hazan and the sexton should do.

The hazan (sometimes called minister or reader or, a bit later, reverend) read and chanted the liturgy, facing the ark on the eastern wall, from a podium in the middle of the men's floor, chanted the scriptural readings, officiated at all life-cycle events (with the approval of the *parnas*), and often instructed the children. The *parnas* attended all worship and life-cycle events and made sure the hazan properly conducted religious affairs. (After the eighteenth century, most synagogue bylaws continued to require the president—or a "designated replacement"—to attend worship services.) He was extremely powerful, having supreme authority during worship services over the other officers, and over the actions of members. Rabbi Isaac Mayer Wise, a nineteenth-century immigrant from central Europe who served congregations in Albany and Cincinnati, would later claim, with only partial exaggeration, that "the *parnas* was an autocrat in the congregation. He was president, *shamas*, chazzan, rabbi. . . . He was the law and the revelation, the lord and the glory." Occasionally the officers would hire a *mohel* (circumciser), a *shochet* (slaughterer), a *melamed* (teacher), or even a *mashgiach* (supervisor of dietary observance and Passover matzah preparation). The *shamas* might make, light, and properly extinguish the Sabbath and festival candles, open and close the synagogue, and supervise life-cycle events, much as a wedding coordinator or funeral director would do at a later date. More than anything, the officers kept busy enforcing observances in general and decorum, specifically, in the synagogue, sometimes even using excommunication (prohibiting involvement with the congregation and burial in the Jewish cemetery) when desperate. When Manuel Josephson, a congregant of Mikve Israel who later was elected *parnas*, became angry at the leaders of the synagogue and said, according to a Revolutionary soldier, Benjamin Nones, "that the Parnas, the Juntas and the whole Congregation might be Damnd and that he would not send the Sophar [ram's horn blown on the Jewish new year]," he was virtually excommunicated. Usually, fines and denial of honors did the job, however; in 1746, the minutes of Shearith Israel noted that members petitioned for the officers to punish those who "disturb the devotion and quiet of our holy worship in any manner of way whatever."

As we will see, this concern for what Gershom Cohen of Charleston (1791) called "decoram [sic] and decent behaviour" would be a constant theme in synagogues over the following nearly three centuries. The constitution of Shearith Israel sought punishment, within the ritual of the worship, for public violation of the ceremonies, customs, observances, and rituals of traditional Judaism by its members. Thus, a *yehudi* (member) who violated religious laws by "eating trafa, breaking the Sabbath, or any other sacred day, shall not be called to the *sepher* [Torah]," or receive any other honor or "be elgable [sic] to any office in the congregation." The bylaws of Mickve Israel in Savannah, paralleling those of Shearith Israel, "deprived of every honor in the synagogue" a member who "violates the Sabbath or holydays." Philadelphia's Mikve Israel likewise declared that "if it is known that a person has desecrated the Sabbath, that person has no right to receive a religious courtesy in the synagogue until he hears what his sentence is to be." In 1757, the *parnassim* and other officers of Shearith Israel "received undoubted Testimony That several of our Brethren, that reside in the Country have and do daily violate the principles of our holy religion, such as Trading on the Sabath [sic], Eating of forbidden Meats and other Henious [sic] Crimes." The congregation declared that "whosoever for the future continues, to act contrary to our Holy Law," will "not be deem'd a member of our Congregation, have none of the Mitzote [sic]of the Sinagoge Confered on him and when Dead will not be buried according to the manner of our brethren." All the colonial congregations extended their radar as far as possible and felt responsible for Jews in the vicinity who did not observe Jewish ritual and who did not belong to the community. It was the strategy of these synagogue leaders, when they found Jews who did not belong and who did not observe, to warn them of the consequences of their indifference come time to be buried. This was their strongest membership pitch. As remains true in the twenty-first century, not all those who identified themselves as "Jewish" claimed interest in the synagogues of colonial America. We must remind ourselves at all times that, when we discuss the synagogue, even in the eighteenth century, we are far from discussing all the Jews in the community.

Yet, most members of the original six American synagogues—all in communities on the water and thus connected to maritime trade—were nominally observant, insisting on circumcision for male children when a circumciser could be found and celebrating holidays and festivals (including the cessation of Sabbath work) in more or less the manner of their ancestors. Samuel Hays wrote to his sweetheart, Richea Gratz, in Lancaster, Pennsylvania (1793), and noted that he would be brief so that he could finish writing before the Sabbath began in Philadelphia; in 1790, Aaron Hart of New York asked his son Moses to remove the leaven from the house to prepare for Passover in Pennsylvania. Overwhelmingly merchants, they educated their children—whether in general studies (reading, writing, and counting) or in reading the prayer book in Hebrew—themselves, with private tutors, or with an "educator" at the synagogue.

The early congregations not only turned to each other and to the mother Sephardic synagogues in Europe for assistance, especially in ritual matters, but also interacted economically and socially with Sephardic congregations in Barbados, Curaçao, Martinique, St. Eustatius, and Surinam (Dutch Guiana). Trading networks crisscrossed the Atlantic, the Caribbean islands, and the American coast. Colonial American congregations hired functionaries from the islands and Europe; for example, Newport lured Judah Touro away from the Caribbean in 1759 to be the hazan of the synagogue. Isolated synagogue communities often lacked necessary ritual objects; Rebecca Samuel wrote from Petersburg, Virginia, in the early 1790s that, for Rosh Hashanah and Yom Kippur, there was no Torah from which to read. The Jews of Petersburg used a printed Pentateuch in place of the Torah scroll, just as the Jews of San Francisco would do during the Gold Rush. Colonial Jews rarely obtained Torah scrolls until the congregation was well established. These congregations received numerous ritual objects from London, Amsterdam, and the Caribbean; London Jews, for example, sent the Savannah Jewish community a Torah scroll and a Hanukkah candelabrum. Marriages brought men and women from the far-flung Jewish communities together; Levi Sheftall of Savannah married a young woman of fourteen on the island of St. Croix in 1768 and brought his new wife home after the wedding.

Auxiliary organizations, especially those helping needy Jews in the community (and elsewhere), filled the meeting rooms of these congregations. At Shearith Israel, these included the committee to dispense acts of kindness (known by its Hebrew equivalent, *gemilut chasadim*), the Hebrew relief society, and the Hebrew benevolent society; Mikve Israel had a society for [destitute] strangers (also called by its Hebrew name, Ezrat Orechim). Sometimes the *parnas* alone distributed *tsedakah* (charity); other times a committee (or a "committee of the whole") provided aid for members unable to work because of illness, for burial expenses, for the elderly, or for itinerant Jews seeking alms.

Synagogue life and reliance on Sephardic customs and contacts changed dramatically during the first half of the nineteenth century because of an influx of immigrants and concomitant shifts in the social and economic life of the nation. Nearly 1.5 million central Europeans came to America during this time period, and at least 2 percent of these were Jews. A population explosion in Europe, coupled with the resulting economic dislocation from the beginnings of the Industrial Revolution, overwhelmed Jew and non-Jew alike, spurring mass relocation. Marcus Fechheimer, born in Bavaria in 1818 and the eldest son among thirteen siblings, felt too anxious about economic opportunity, despite the existence of a *Matrikel* giving him settlement rights or lawful residence, to remain in Bavaria. He emigrated to New York City in 1837.

Like Marcus, Jews came from the villages and small towns of Bohemia and Moravia, from Baden, Hesse-Darmstadt, Saxony, Württemberg, and the cities of Bavaria and established themselves in the small towns and, occasionally, the cities of Georgia, North Carolina, Ohio, Pennsylvania, South Carolina, Tennessee, West Virginia, Wisconsin, and elsewhere. They would become, overwhelmingly, the bulk of the membership of nearly every nineteenth-century synagogue.

It was this steady migration of European Ashkenazic Jews—Jews who did not trace their ancestry to the Iberian Peninsula—that would doom the Sephardic synagogue monopoly. Central European Jews brought their own ceremonies, customs, observances, and rituals to America and by the early 1800s began to establish their own congregations or to take over the existing ones. Even before the middle of the nineteenth century, the congregations of Central European Jews would dominate American Judaism, and Sephardic Jewry would be of little importance nationally. Shearith Israel and Mikve Israel continued to dominate the small world of Sephardic Jewish life, but the other congregations, when they played a role in the national affairs of American Jewry, did so as part of Ashkenazic Jewish institutional life. Already in the late nineteenth century, descendants of colonial Jews had become a curiosity outside the tiny but still tightly knit Sephardic community. The Ashkenazim had taken over, initiating a new chapter in the history of the American synagogue.

NOTE

1. I follow the custom I learned many years ago from Jacob Marcus and which he noted in *American Jewry* (1959): "Naturally, the faulty Hebrew and Yiddish transliterations in original texts are not changed. This, of course, may at times be confusing to the reader who finds the same word transliterated differently. . . . All foreign words in the text are italicized, save when *Webster's* accepts a Hebrew or Yiddish word (e.g., hazan) as English" (ix–x).

2

Reforming Judaism Everywhere

Ushering in Change in the Nineteenth Century

The Reforms in the Service had been gradual.
Slowly, but surely, one step was taken after another.
    —David Philipson, *The Oldest Jewish Congregation in the West*
                [Cincinnati's Bene Israel], 1924

IN THE 1790S, an increasing number of Dutch, German, Polish, and even French Jews became more outspoken about their lack of comfort with the Sephardic ritual at Mikve Israel of Philadelphia, and they began in 1795 to worship at the German Hebrew Society "according to the German and Dutch Rule"—that is, following Ashkenazic ritual customs. By 1801, the society had purchased land for a cemetery, and the following year it dedicated a "new German Shul," Rodeph Shalom, with a constitution in Yiddish. It was the first Ashkenazic synagogue in the Western Hemisphere—notwithstanding a possible short-lived Ashkenazic group in Charleston in either the 1770s or the 1780s.

During the eighteenth century, Ashkenazic Jews came to America from all over Europe. Many first gravitated to existing Sephardic congregations. Thus, nearly everywhere, congregations with Sephardic rituals and organizational patterns found Jews who traced their ancestry to Portugal and Spain increasingly becoming a minority of the membership. It was inevitable that Sephardic customs and ceremonies would give way to those of the Ashkenazim or, if leaders were not ready to do so, that members would depart and attempt to start their own congregations. This was not easy—not in the eighteenth or even in the twenty-first century—and failures occurred everywhere. But there were many success stories, and nearly every decade of the nineteenth century saw an increase in the number of new congregations initiated by Jews from (primarily) central and eastern Europe.

The increasing number of Ashkenazic Jews at synagogues with Sephardic origins and ritual reenacted a pattern from previous centuries of Jewish life. Jews who had once lived in the Iberian Peninsula had scattered throughout southern and western Europe and created congregations with rituals that made them comfortable. From time to time, Jews came from the German states or Poland or the Austro-Hungarian Empire and began to worship at these Sephardic congregations. In what generally seemed like no time at all, the Askhenazic Jews left their Sephardic brethren and formed congregations using their own ceremonies, customs, rituals, and administrative structure. With hindsight, it was inevitable that this same pattern would occur in the United States as the Ashkenazic Jewish migration increased.

Two Congregations in One City

Following the establishment of the first American Ashkenazic synagogue, Rodeph Shalom, in Philadelphia, Ashkenazic Jewish immigrants at Shearith Israel in New York who were "educated in the German and Polish minhag [ritual]" also found "it difficult to accustom [themselves] to the Portuguese minhag." Moreover, they found Shearith Israel "very far from the convenience of a considerable number of our Brethren" and the sanctuary too crowded—all complaints that would echo and reecho within various congregations in the following two centuries. They withdrew in 1825 and formed B'nai Jeshurun, with worship modeled, according to the synagogue historian, Israel Goldstein, on the Great Synagogue of London, and dedicated their first building, on Elm Street (the former meeting place of the First Coloured Presbyterian Church), in 1827. Within three years, German, Dutch, and Polish Jews who had apparently become unhappy at B'nai Jeshurun in turn left and formed the also Ashkenazic Anshe Chesed, a congregation that would soon face its own secession struggle.

The nineteenth century thus began with the splitting of the first congregation in American history, leaving two congregations in a single city for the first time. This pattern would be repeated, year after year, with no end in sight, into the twenty-first century, among all the branches of Judaism. In Milwaukee, at Congregation Imanu-Al (later, Emanu-El), divisions over ritual practice began almost immediately after the synagogue's incorporation, and by 1854 dissident members had organized Ahabath Emuno. The opponents of the new congregation claimed that "all [we] wish for is to repeat the same *piutim* [prayers] in the same order exactly, as [our] fathers did." One year later, the new congregation split over arguments connected with whether to use the German or the Polish form of ritual, and Anshe Emeth formed in 1855. In Des Moines, Iowa, Congregation B'nai Israel incorporated in 1876 as a traditional synagogue. By 1881, there was a rift, and a small group left to conduct its own services with a different style and formed Beth El Jacob, another Orthodox synagogue. Like all congregations, members purchased their own seats and paid an annual "tax"; unique to Des Moines, they could sell their seats only if, among other considerations, the members on their left and their right approved the buyers they would be sitting next to at worship! And in Manchester, New Hampshire, in the 1890s, some members broke away from Orthodox Adath Yeshurun, established Queen City Congregation, and rented their own prayer hall, while others broke away, established Anshe Sephard, bought their own land in the cemetery of Adath Yeshurun, and demanded a fence to separate the two adjacent graveyards!

Almost everywhere the Jews settled in the nineteenth century (just as in Charleston, New York, Philadelphia, and Savannah in the eighteenth century), they set about buying land for a cemetery and incorporating as a synagogue, in that order. The Jews of Atlanta secured land for a cemetery in 1860 and then founded Hebrew Benevolent Congregation in 1867. In Charlottesville, Virginia, Jewish settlers established a cemetery in 1870 and Congregation Beth Israel in 1882. In Lancaster, Pennsylvania, Jews purchased a cemetery in 1747, more than a century before they formed the first congregation, in 1855. The Jews of Wilmington, North Carolina, founded a burial society in 1852 and, in Raleigh, North Carolina, a Cemetery Society in 1870—in both cities, Jews established a congregation only many years later. In Des Moines, Jews incorporated Emanuel Burial Association in 1870 and, three years later, B'nai Yeshurun synagogue; in Ft. Worth, Orthodox Jews obtained a cemetery in 1879 and a synagogue more than a decade later. The sixteen founding members of the congregation immediately rented, as Jews would do everywhere, fourteen double and two single seats for worship services. The need for fund-raising had begun.

Everywhere, nineteenth-century synagogues required their members (i.e., adult males) to lease (usually annually) or purchase (in perpetuity) a numbered pew (often called paying "seat money" in the congregation's minutes). These were usually sold or auctioned at public gatherings when a synagogue was erected or renovated. This practice guaranteed each member a reserved seat and frequently enabled the affluent to pay more and obtain the "better" (i.e., front-row) seats, thus reflecting and supporting a class structure and also providing an important source of revenue. When a member died, a special meeting was called to sell or rent the vacant pew. Almost always, a pew had four seats (father, mother, and two children or grandparents), and the price scale (e.g. $50, $100, $150, $200, and

$250) depended exclusively on location in the sanctuary, much like ticket prices in a modern theater. In the late 1860s, Cincinnati's Bene Yeshurun raised $72,000 from such a sale; at the same time, Washington [D.C.] Hebrew Congregation, a very poor synagogue community, took in $1,920 in membership dues and $560 in seat money. In both cases, seat money constituted a significant portion of each congregation's income. And when San Francisco's Emanu-El paid $15,000 in 1864 for a lot on Sutter Street, $6,500 came from "seat money."

From Tradition to Reform

Most Ashkenazic synagogues, though without a specific label, were initially "traditional," more or less like what Jews had known in central Europe or wherever they had lived before sailing to America. Almost immediately, however, whether they would eventually become officially Orthodox or Conservative or Reform, they began to "reform." We will return shortly to the thorny question of how many reforms it takes to make a synagogue a Reform congregation. By this question, I mean to suggest that the process of "reforming" in religious institutions of all kinds is commonplace (e.g., a Catholic church switching to English from Latin), but the point at which that institution becomes identified as something else, such as a Reform congregation, either in its publicity (Anshe Emeth—A Reform Synagogue) or in the eyes of the community ("Anshe Emeth has become a Reform congregation"), is more complicated. Scores of nineteenth-century synagogues instituted "reforms," but not all became identified officially as "Reform" synagogues, a branch or wing of Judaism that would, in the twentieth century, sit alongside the sectors of Conservative, Orthodox, and Reconstructionist Judaism. In the same way, numerous synagogues in the first decades of the twentieth century, as we will see later, without labels, began to "conserve" ceremonies, customs, observances, and rituals, but which sector of Judaism this would lead to could never be predicted.

Suffice it to say, initially, that it is hard to find a congregation in the second half of the nineteenth century that did not go through a process of reform. Temple Emanu-El in Milwaukee abolished reading the *haftarah* (the prophetic books of the Hebrew Bible) following the Torah reading in 1893, two decades after it banned head covering. In Des Moines, almost immediately, the members of B'nai Yeshurun abolished the second day of several holidays, arguing that reading the liturgy once was sufficient, and shortened the Rosh Hashanah morning service considerably, contending that two hours was enough for worship and the German sermon. By 1879, the members had built a three-hour recess into the middle of the day of Yom Kippur worship (previously they had spent the entire day in the synagogue)—probably for lunch, although Yom Kippur is a fast day for many Jews—and, by 1881, this congregation had decided to make head covering for male worshipers, previously mandatory, optional. And, like so many other congregations, bar mitzvah ceremonies, common in the previous decade, were eliminated in the 1870s and 1880s as another "tradition" disappeared. These developments were hardly as radical as those at Chicago's Sinai, where Rabbi Emil G. Hirsch, after abolishing Hebrew readings and prayers as well as circumcision, announced in 1894 that "the Sepher [scroll] Torah was no longer needed," tossed out the ark, and gave the synagogue's Torah scroll to the University of Chicago Semitic Library or as strange as the reforms pushed by Rabbi Solomon H. Sonneschein at St. Louis's Shaare Emeth Temple in the 1880s. He urged the congregation to celebrate both Hanukkah and Christmas—as Rabbi Norman Gerstenfeld would do at Washington [D.C.] Hebrew Congregation sixty years later ("Xanukkah")—and both rabbis liked to call their synagogues the National Jewish Church of America, or, at the very least, the National Synagogue of America. Rabbi Sonneschein's disdain for the tradition he was rejecting was deep; once he called the Judaism

of the great medieval Jewish philosopher and legal authority Maimonides "*schmutzreligion*," or the "rottenest rot of medieval Judaism."

In Wilmington, Delaware, in 1895, one citizen simply but cogently
explained the difference between the reforming synagogues and
those that tried to remain traditional, or, as synagogues began to be
called, Orthodox:

> [The Reform] Jews believe in being comfortable when they wor-
> ship. In place of shutting off women and children in a latticed bal-
> cony, they want them in their pews. In place of keeping on their
> hats, in church, they see no problem in removing them. In place of
> a male choir and no instrumental accompaniment, they think an
> organ and good mixed choir would add to the services. Then they
> want hymns or sermons in English . . . the Orthodox which has
> numbers but not so many ducats, adheres to wearing hats, the isola-
> tion of women and children, the use of Hebrew in services, and the
> banishment of music.

Few contemporary Jews could explain the reforming trend in synagogues so succinctly.

The German sermons at B'nai Yeshurun in Des Moines were not
unusual. German either dominated or alternated at synagogues, especially in the Midwest and the East, throughout much of this period, reflecting the areas of the country to which this population had
migrated. In mid-century New Orleans, James K. Gutheim preached
fluently in both German and English. When Milwaukee's B'ne Jeshurun dedicated a new synagogue in 1872, the members placed two sets
of the Ten Commandments on the side of the ark, one in Hebrew
and one in German. The sermons, in that same decade, alternated
between German and English at Milwaukee's Temple Emanu-El;
Isaac S. Moses preached his "radical reform" sermons in English on
Friday evening and in German on Saturday mornings; by the 1870s,
Rabbi Marcus Jastrow (of Philadelphia) was asked to "deliver" his

German sermon occasionally in English. As late as 1881, the officers of Baltimore's Har Sinai insisted on German; at the same time, Liebman Adler preached exclusively in German at Detroit's Temple Beth El (1854–1861) and Chicago's K.A.M. (less well known as Kehilat Anshe Ma'arav) (1861–1872). Moses May taught both Hebrew and German in the school of Portland, Oregon's Congregation Beth Israel in 1873, and Elkan Cohn delivered German sermons at San Francisco's Emanu-El in the 1860s. At Adas Israel in Washington, D.C., German and English High Holy Day sermons alternated, unofficially, in the late nineteenth century, while in Pittsburgh, at Rodef Sholom, the 1862 dedication address was in German, and Louis Naumburg, who arrived in 1865, and Lippman Mayer, who came in 1870, preached only in German. Since much of "the general citizenry" of Indianapolis spoke German, it was not surprising that the synagogue dedication at Indianapolis Hebrew Congregation took place in German. In Lancaster, the sermon at Shaarai Shomayim's first confirmation (1878) may have been the last in German; English officially became the synagogue language the next year. One constant: wherever sermons were preached in German; they were long—not as long as the three-hour sermons of Gregory Bolstrood, founder of the Puritan sect known as the Barkers (he barked like a dog while preaching), but long. When Isidore Kalisch preached a German sermon in Milwaukee at the 1859 new temple dedication of B'ne Jeshurun (the result of a merger between Imanu-Al and Ahabath Emuno), it lasted an hour and five minutes. He introduced, into this self-proclaimed Orthodox synagogue, mixed seating, the use of an organ to accompany Sabbath services, and a choir of men and women together, as a series of reforms moved the synagogue further and further away from "orthodoxy" in the 1860s; eventually, B'ne Jeshurun became a Reform congregation.

Jews in the German states and in Holland in the second decade of the nineteenth century and then in Charleston, South Carolina, a decade later initiated what we now call Reform Judaism. They began with liturgical changes (reforms)—musical instruments accompanying choirs of men and women, Jews and non-Jews; German, Dutch, and English translations of hymns, prayers, and Scripture; the elimination of some established prayers and changes in the words of others—and developed, a bit later, an ideology that defended these changes as "shucking the husk" to preserve the "kernel" of Judaism. Underlying this transformation of Judaism was the rejection of the traditional Judaic belief in Divine revelation—that God revealed the Torah to Moses at Mt. Sinai—and thus the authority of Scripture, the commandments of the Torah, and even the ceremonies, customs, observances, and rituals of the tradition. If, as Rabbi Abraham Geiger put it in Berlin in 1848, the authority of the commandments of the Torah had been replaced by the authority of the "divinely illuminated human spirit," any change was possible. Change and choice, key words of nineteenth- and twentieth-century Reform Judaism, became the watchwords of the faith, in contrast to the fundamental word of (twentieth-century) Conservative and Orthodox Judaism, tradition.

Rabbi Isaac Mayer Wise came to America in 1846 from Bohemia. In Albany, New York, and then in Cincinnati, he began to introduce reforms in music (organ) and decorum (family pews). He visited dozens of cities and spread the gospel of reforming, which included a new and truncated prayer book and late-Sabbath-evening services held hours after required by tradition. He eliminated celebration of the second day of holidays, prayers that he called "repetitive," and much more, and he became more radical in his reform as he grew older, even prohibiting head covering on worshipers seated in the sanctuary of the temple he served as rabbi.

When Rabbi Wise sought to establish the first Jewish university, rabbinic seminary, and teachers' seminary in the United States (Zion College), he was careful to announce that the (short-lived) Zion Collegiate Association (1854) was for "American Jews" and would be the "first cornerstone of the intellectual superstructure of American

מנהג אמעריקא

THE DAILY PRAYERS,

——FOR——

AMERICAN ISRAELITES

——AS——

REVISED IN CONFERENCE.

CINCINNATI:
Bloch & Co., Publishers and Printers.

Title page of *Minhag America* (*The Daily Prayers*),
1872. Reprinted courtesy of Klau Library, Hebrew
Union College–Jewish Institute of Religion.

Judaism." When Wise used the term "American Judaism," he usually
meant an undivided Judaism in America, of the kind he practiced,
rather than a Judaism (like that which emerged in the twentieth
century) of branches and sectors and wings. When he called the
Cleveland Conference, one year later, to establish a "Union," it was
a union of "American Israel," and the conference issued "Articles"
urging a synod (that would never meet) of "American Jewish congregations." When he traveled around the country as a guest speaker,

encouraging congregations to "reform," he constantly spoke of an "American Judaism." Wise called his prayer book that emerged out of the conference *Minhag America* (1857), and he pronounced it "thoroughly American, republican and cosmopolitan—every man of any creed can now pray with us."

When a group of lay leaders from more than two dozen reforming congregations sought, in 1873, to establish an umbrella organization of synagogues, the Union of American Hebrew Congregations, the leaders were careful to use a title and a preamble as inclusive as possible. They sought traditional and reforming congregations— as well as those between the poles of tradition and "Reform"; thus their attempt to include *American* congregations and the preamble's reference to "this sacred covenant of the American Israelites." Just as the founders of what would become the umbrella organization of Conservative synagogues several decades later hoped to embrace all non-Reform synagogues when they founded their United Synagogue of America, so these lay leaders, most of whom were active in congregations that had undertaken significant reforms, hoped to unfold a giant tent. By 1879, the Union of American [reforming] Hebrew Congregations had grown to include 105 synagogues. The next decade would begin to separate those congregations on a steady path from reforming to Reform Judaism (with a new, mostly English and abridged prayer book) and those synagogues that put a rather abrupt halt to the possibility of major reforms and would become what later would be called Orthodox or Conservative.

Historians everywhere tend to apply these twentieth-century terms to "traditional" synagogues of the previous century. Israel Goldstein, looking back seventy-five years, called New York's B'nai Jeshurun a "modern Orthodox" congregation in the 1850s. The historian of the Jewish community of Newark, New Jersey, noted that B'nai Jeshurun (1847), B'nai Abraham (1855), and Oheb Shalom (1860) "all were Orthodox" at their inception, even though this word was never used by any of the congregations, and it obscures these questions: what criteria should we use to define a congregation as "Orthodox" in, say, 1855, and when does an "Orthodox" synagogue in the nineteenth century, reforming little by little (all three Newark congregations eventually became Reform or Conservative), cease to be "Orthodox"? Did Charleston's Beth Elohim "become in 1841 the first Reform congregation in the United States," as its website declares? To return to our earlier question about how many reforms it takes to make a traditional synagogue a Reform congregation, did B'nai Jeshurun become a "Reform" synagogue in 1868 when it announced, in the preamble to its constitution, that it would be "discarding antiquated forms . . . as shall further the religion of enlightened Judaism"? Or was it in 1871, when it dropped the observance of the second day of holidays such as Sukkot and Passover? Or in 1880, when it abolished the requirement for men to cover their heads in the sanctuary? Or 1892, when it "reached the same level of reform [?] that predominated in most parts of the United States"? What is the difference between what Leon Jick, the historian of nineteenth-century American Judaism, called "substantial reforms," "radical reforms," and "reforms"? It is important to note that when mid-nineteenth-century American Jews used the term "Reform," they usually meant the process of reforming a religious institution, not the (sometimes) resulting Reform congregation, officially part of a movement or branch of American Judaism.

We may begin to answer these questions by looking at the twenty most popular reforms in mid- and late-nineteenth-century (1850–1890) synagogues, as noted either in synagogue bulletins, minutes, or histories:

Adopting an organ
Reducing the number of people called to the Torah
Reducing the number of verses read from the Torah
Eliminating the second day of holidays
Permitting non-Jews in choirs

Using a cornet for a shofar
Permitting women in choirs
Positioning the reader to face the congregation
Introducing mixed seating
Eliminating the practice of head covering
Having a midday break during Yom Kippur prayers
Leaving out Chapter 9 of the Book of Esther (where the Jews get
    revenge and kill 75,000 of their enemies) during the Purim
    reading
Reading the Book of Esther only in German or English on Purim
Eliminating the selling of honors
Introducing a revised prayer book
Reading the *haftarah* (prophetic books) in English or omitting it
    altogether
Reading rather than chanting the Torah
Introducing Sunday worship services
Reading prayers in English instead of Hebrew
Adding late-Friday-evening services to those at sundown
Abolishing bar mitzvah, substituting confirmation

Most of these modifications were commonplace in many American synagogues in the last decades of the nineteenth century. Boards of directors ordered reading desks moved from the center of the sanctuary to a wall in a switch from Sephardic to Ashkenazic custom, ordered the *haftarah* "declaimed" rather than chanted, forbade the wearing of shrouds on Yom Kippur, stopped the auctioning of the honor of being called to the Torah, eliminated daily services when a minyan could not regularly be gathered, introduced an organ, installed pews (as in churches) in place of seats, demanded that the dozens of shofar sounds be greatly reduced on Rosh Hashanah, urged the use of musical instruments to accompany the choir, and invited women to sing with men in the choir.

Other trustees demanded that the hazan turn around and face

the congregation, rather than the ark (which traditionally faces Jerusalem), while reciting the Eighteen Benedictions at the heart of the worship service, prohibited both rabbi and hazan from wearing a prayer shawl, eliminated the special blessing of the congregation by *kohanim* (descendants of the biblical priests, usually considered to be those who had the last name of Cohen), and insisted that the Scriptures be read in a loud and clear voice rather than chanted to a centuries-old melody.

With reforming taking place, gradually, rapidly, or somewhere between these two poles (congregant Moses May wrote to the Portland Beth Israel board of directors in 1873 that the congregation found it "very difficult to discern whether to go to the right or to the left"), what did it mean in the second half of the nineteenth century to suggest that a synagogue was "committed to Reform Judaism"? Affiliation with the UAHC (later the national organization of exclusively Reform synagogues) did not necessarily mean commitment to Reform Judaism in the 1870s or 1880s. By 1879, the original 34 congregations that formed the Union in 1873 had been overwhelmed by more than 80 additional synagogues, and the ritual patterns of these 105 members differed significantly.

The rabbi and historian Leon Jick has suggested that "worship with uncovered head" was the "hallmark of Reform," but dozens of UAHC congregations still required men to wear hats in 1879. Both Chicago's Kehillath Anshe Maarabh and Houston's Beth Israel joined the Union in 1874 but required head covering for another decade. New York's Shaaray Tefila joined the Union in 1879, and its historian noted that it had "abandoned . . . Orthodox Judaism and took its rank among the Conservative [*sic*!] congregations." In 1868, he called it Orthodox, although the Committee on Ritual had mandated "shortening the service by omitting many [prayers]"; in 1879, it was Conservative as even more prayers (including the *mussaf*, or additional service, because it was "repetitive") disappeared from the service, the Torah was no longer chanted but read, and worshipers were no longer called to say a blessing before and after the Torah reading by their Hebrew names. One year later, this "Conservative" congregation abandoned separate seating for men and women and began to use an organ, and the historian called it Reform. Was it Orthodox in 1878, Conservative in 1879, and Reform in 1880?

Only one reform, however, as the historian Marsha L. Rozenblit has noted, definitively moved a synagogue out of the "traditional" realm and firmly, incontrovertibly, into that of Reform. Once a congregation altered the fixed liturgy, including the elimination of even one core prayer, a window had been opened that could never be closed unless the congregation committed itself to the *siddur*, the traditional liturgy, in full. So the adoption of a common truncated liturgy, such as David Einhorn's liturgy or the *Union Prayer Book*, was the mark of a full-fledged Reform congregation, though with the latter this could not occur before the volumes appeared in 1894 (High Holy Days) and 1895 (Sabbath and Festivals). When Charleston's Beth Elohim placed an organ in its new building, it did not suddenly become a Reform congregation. It merely continued on the path of reforming that, sixteen years earlier, petitioners had demanded on grounds of "decency and decorum." Indeed, a few synagogues in Europe and America introduced organs and still affirmed themselves as "traditional." The historian of Philadelphia's Rodeph Shalom got it right when he noted that, in 1895, when the congregation adopted the *Union Prayer Book*, it "definitely placed itself among the ranks of the Reform Congregations of the country." Some went even further. When a number of rabbis who felt that the radical *UPB* was not radical enough introduced their own liturgies with even less of the traditional material, they too signaled that their congregations had adopted Reform Judaism. One rabbi, Emil G. Hirsch, of Chicago Sinai, did this even before the publication of the *UPB*. In 1885, he announced that he was "the Minister of a Radical Reform congregation."

Detroit's Beth El offers a typical case study of a traditional synagogue gradually moving toward Reform over a period that began in

1856, when the poetic sections of the Sabbath and festival liturgies were dropped in order to pay "due attention to the progress of the age," and ended in 1896, when head covering was prohibited during worship and a new prayer book was adopted. Along the way, the congregation added instrumental music (melodeon) and mixed choir (1861), stopped calling men to the Torah, eliminated the women's gallery and forbade worshipers to wear a prayer shawl (1862), dropped the celebration of the second day of holidays and festivals and the wearing of a prayer shawl by the rabbi (1870), and stopped reciting the mourner's prayer (*kaddish*) during Sabbath services (1883). The only setback for those intent on making Beth El a Reform synagogue was the defeat of the motion, in 1884, to eliminate Hebrew from the religious school.

The thinking of Rabbi Louis Grossman of Beth El provides us with a representative look at a minister (as he called himself, as well as a "Jewish [*sic*] rabbi") who served a congregation (1884–1898) that had completed its reforming process and clearly presented itself as a Reform synagogue at the end of this period. He gave "lectures" on Friday evenings, having concluded that the Sunday morning service and discourse, "quite dear to radicalism," did not work. (Late-Friday-evening services, rather than or in addition to sundown services, had become regularized in Cincinnati, Cleveland, New York, and San Francisco in the 1860s). Although regularly castigating congregants' "love of generalities" ("you will look in vain for a single generality in the Bible") and convinced that "you cannot achieve much good with abstractions," he, like his Reform colleagues, was a master of generalities, rarely drawing upon a text or even an analogy in his sermons. He poked fun at the "rule in Jewish homiletics that says there must be a text for every sermon," a silly "technique of the rabbinical school," and substituted elegant rhetoric and elevated prose for simpler, text-driven sermons.

For him, as well as for his Reform colleagues, the ceremonies, customs, laws, and rituals of the Torah and the Jewish tradition were "antiquities, curious, and safely dead." Like Genesis, "a history of primitive culture" with stories of "aboriginal simplicity," the "laws, commandments, and statutes" of the Torah "represented quaint things we are told by old people [and] done in days past." So, like his Protestant colleagues, he talked about the "modern conditions of life, the modern trends" (e.g., business ethics) that demand that one discard the "obligations out of which the spirit has gone."

But he was continually as critical of the reforms of Reform Judaism as he was of the tradition. The reformers have "trimmed up ancestral things to please," rather than "respecting tradition"; they have "made the new prayer book quite readable [and] the ritual quite esthetic" but deleted "fundamental traditions." Sermons, like his, have become "models of rhetoric" rather than "models of substance," though they (like his) are "very learned," with abundant "evidence of versatility and breadth of mind." He calls all this, rightly, the "classic days of Reform." And yet, he repeats, "public worship is neglected," as none of these reforms "nurse the religious warmth of the people."

For Rabbi Grossman, the problem was not the sermon, lecture, or discourse, and not the "preoccupying influence of business or industry," that is, that work interfered with attending worship. It was —and here he anticipated a development that did not become a serious concern of Reform Judaism for another century—that people did not believe in prayer and thus did not attend. Of course, he noticed that people came to the synagogue for many reasons—to hear beautiful music, to listen to a lecture, to think private thoughts—but much of this could be accomplished by attending a concert. The vast majority of congregants did not pray regularly, and since for him Judaism must not be just theology or philosophy, why attend? He had no significant answer (aside from repeating that the essence of Judaism is that God is One) but pointed explicitly to a problem that would plague Reform (and Conservative) Judaism throughout the coming century.

No less typical was Rochester's Temple B'rith Kodesh, where

the board of directors installed an organ and hired a mixed choir in 1862; instituted mixed seating in 1869 (leading some traditionalists to resign and form their own synagogue, Elon Yerek); prohibited the wearing of head covering in the sanctuary in 1879 (or 1883) and maintained this prohibition, as in scattered synagogues across the country, until after World War II; dropped the bar mitzvah ceremony in 1882 (substituting, as was common, confirmation at age fourteen) and adopted Rabbi Max Landsberg's radical *Ritual for Jewish Worship* in 1884, continuing to use it for several decades after Landsberg's long rabbinate (1871–1915).

Landsberg's prayer book replaced the minimal amount of the liturgy it chose to retain with English translations (the Sabbath-evening service was reduced to nine pages, the evening of Yom Kippur liturgy to fifteen, with less than two pages of Hebrew in addition to the *kaddish*, or memorial prayer, and with the Kol Nidre prayer excised), and fewer than two pages of Hebrew in the twenty-page afternoon service for Yom Kippur. Maximizing decorum, Landsberg created English responsive readings and gave abundant instructions to the worshipers about when to sit and when to stand ("The Congregants resume their seats"), to the rabbi about when to speak ("Lecture"), and to the choir about when to sing. As in Protestant prayer books of the period, biblical quotations served to introduce different sections of the liturgy, and Psalms (eleven in the Sabbath morning liturgy) dominated the service.

Synagogues, whether Reform or more traditional, and even those between the two poles all had in common a continual interest in decorum. Whether this concern was spurred by the protestantization of American Judaism or was just a general response to ideas of beauty, dignity, and order that appeared in nineteenth-century culture, it was everywhere. The 1851 constitution of the newly formed Emanu-El of San Francisco, in Article IV, Section 3 (with its articles and sections, like so many others, it imitated the structure of the U.S. Constitution), required the trustees to "promote order and decorum during divine service." The decorous steps taken by congregations included prohibiting worshipers from leaving their seats during worship, the Torah reading, and the sermon; insisting that everyone rise for prayers to be read standing and only for those prayers; abolishing the practice of calling men to the Torah and instead having only the service leader read or chant from Scripture; requiring children to sit in the women's section; demanding that children who could not read (and thus were not likely to maintain discipline) stay home; abolishing the auctioning of honors at all times; imposing fines on people who conversed rather than prayed; distributing hymnals so that all could sing in unison; reciting prayers in unison that previously had been recited in a cacophony; using some German hymns to maximize participation and to include visitors; requiring the service leader and the hazan to face the congregation; instituting the reading (rather than the chanting) of the *haftarah*; using Hebrew (seen as more elegant) rather than Yiddish or even German terms when giving instructions; printing a sheet of upcoming events rather than having them announced; dividing the weekly Torah reading into thirds and covering it in a three-year cycle rather than in a single year, thus reducing the time of the Torah reading dramatically; and including English responsive readings. Several congregations in Baltimore, Chicago, New York, and Philadelphia put rules such as these in a booklet (or inside the cover of prayer books) and distributed the booklets to congregants at the High Holy Days, the beginning of the Jewish calendar year. Since most members of the synagogue attended these services, it was assumed that everyone had a copy. One of these congregations had a member who took note of the failure of the prayer book revision and instructions for decorum to achieve their goals in a letter to the rabbi: "the mere introduction of an abridged prayer book with its insertion was insufficient to establish that order and decorum essential to an intelligent [service]."

The efforts of the Orthodox synagogue Rodeph Shalom (Philadelphia) to become more and more decorous throughout the nineteenth century offer a typical case study of one of many Orthodox congregations eager to institute continual reforms with the goal (1869) of "making the services as interesting . . . as possible." They included abolishing the auctioning of the honor of being called to the Torah; substituting German (and, later, English) prayers for those in Hebrew so that "the prayers might be better understood by the members"; requiring "none but clean and perfect *Talithim* [prayer shawls]," which "must be worn in a respectful manner"; requiring that worshipers enter the synagogue quietly; requiring that praying be done "in a low voice" and congregants be "rising or sitting" only when "guided by the Rabbi"; prohibiting "reciting prayers in a loud voice as well as conversing"; preventing worshipers from exiting before the end of the service; and forbidding the presence of children under age six. All of these resolutions were intended to make worship proceed in a "a quiet and orderly manner." The trustees distributed hundreds of copies of these resolutions to worshipers.

Bernard Illowy, whom Rabbi Max Heller called a "valiant champion of orthodoxy" and who was ordained in Hungary and received a Ph.D. from the University of Budapest before serving synagogues in New York, Philadelphia, St. Louis, Syracuse, Baltimore, New Orleans, and Cincinnati—where he preached in German or English for forty-five to sixty minutes on normal Sabbaths and, according to his son Henry, "not infrequently, an hour or more"—spoke on decorum repeatedly. He insisted on "no screeching, or shouting" and demanded that "all should pray together in unison." Illowy "forbade . . . indecorous scramble and rush to get out," insisting that "no one was permitted to take off his *Talith* [prayer shawl] or to leave his seat before the last echoes of the [closing hymns] had died away." Like other traditionalists, he was influenced by reforming synagogues, working toward "a decorous, beautiful service, one that could more than vie with that of any temple in the land." At Bene Israel, in Cincinnati, resolutions kept "poor boys" in "good order" so that they would recite their prayers in "proper order," stay out of the girls' section, and create "a due respect and reverence for the precepts of our holy religion." For all but the most resistant immigrant rabbi or service leader, a decorous, traditional service was as American as the 4th of July. And from time to time, Christians took notice. The lead editorial in the *Atlanta Constitution* of September 25, 1870, noted that "the solemnity and good order which prevails during the worship in the synagogue [Hebrew Benevolent Congregation] is worthy of imitation by many of us Gentile Christians."

Ordained rabbis were rare before mid-century. The first arrived in Baltimore, in 1840, and even after they began to come over from Europe, congregations frequently used laymen or minimally trained leaders for the basic ritual services, such as reading the liturgy, providing music for worship, and chanting the Scriptures, as well as for running the synagogue or supervising the dietary regulations (especially for meat). When rabbis (or, as they were sometimes called, especially when they were not ordained, ministers or reverends) or cantors (*hazzanim*), whether trained or not, were hired by these reforming congregations, they were usually given, in writing, the synagogue's expectations about how they would lead (reading or singing or both) the liturgy, how frequently they would deliver sermons, in which language they would deliver them, their obligations with respect to life-cycle events such as confirmation ceremonies, weddings, and funerals (including compensation), their responsibilities with the choir, which ages they would teach, and even the precise order of the liturgy. At Rodeph Shalom, for example, the Ritual Committee instructed the service leader to begin the Friday-evening service with *L'chu n'ran'nan* (Come let us sing) and then gave sentence-by-sentence orders. Shaarai Shomayim, a small synagogue in Lancaster, Pennsylvania (with an 1855 German constitution), hired its first ordained rabbi, Morris Ungerleider, in 1884 as "Chasan, Minister, Teacher, and *Schocet*." Indianapolis Hebrew Congregation, in 1857, hired the Reverend S. Berman as "chasan, *Shochet, and Shammes*," and twelve years later it sought someone who "can perform the duties of Chasan, teacher, and *Shochet*," is "capable of teaching in the Hebrew, German, and English languages," and could deliver sermons. The larger the congregation, that is, the greater the budget, the more likely these roles would be divided up among a rabbi, a cantor, a ritual slaughterer, a teacher, and a sexton.

In Atlanta, Abraham Jaffa—*shochet*, *mohel*, and hazan—slaughtered chickens in the rear of his home. Washington Hebrew Congregation, in the District of Columbia, hired two salaried officials in 1867, one to serve as lecturer and the other to serve as hazan or reader and teacher. In 1871, the congregation replaced the two with one man, Michael Goldberg, "reader and teacher," and explained to him that it no longer wanted sermons. He was to "read" the service, "keep" the religious school (twice during the week and on Sunday), and "educate" a choir, but he was not to preach during the Sabbath worship service. At the same time as the congregation was steadily introducing reforms, it returned to a centuries-old European tradition of eschewing weekly sermons and, instead, hiring someone to preach on occasional festivals and holy days.

As we saw earlier, boards of directors levied fines and withheld honors from members who were perceived as misbehaving—the only discipline short of expulsion from the synagogue that they had in their control. Just as the board of Philadelphia's Mikveh Israel pressed formal charges against a member who was seen shaving (i.e., working) on the Sabbath in Baltimore, 100 miles away, in an earlier decade, throughout most of the nineteenth century, bylaws imposed fines of every kind for transgressions ranging from use of improper language to inappropriate behavior. In smaller congregations, members had to attend every worship service and every congregational meeting, visit the sick or mourners when requested, and stay away from rival synagogues or face fines. At Shaarai Shomayim, members who did not attend the congregational meeting paid a fine of twelve and a half cents. They also could be fined (sometimes expelled) for ritual violations such as using improper language, opening a store on the Sabbath or a holy day, turning in committee reports late, talking during worship, singing louder than the hazan, using snuff, "shewing" tobacco, putting away a prayer shawl before the end of prayers, and leaving services before the president dismissed the worshipers following the closing hymn. Just after the Civil War, Mr. Hart, a sexton in Indianapolis, violated Jewish law by lighting a gas lamp on Yom Kippur; the board of directors of the synagogue told him he must "Repent of his Sinful Action publicly" or be fired.

The Liturgy

Nearly all American congregations in the early decades of the nineteenth century used some version of the traditional prayer book, the *siddur*. There was no standard edition, and synagogue museums and archives contain numerous publications, all in Hebrew. By the 1860s, as we have seen, two revisions of the traditional prayer book were in wide use, one by Isaac Mayer Wise and the other by David Einhorn. Other revised versions of the *siddur* could be found, but none achieved the popularity of those by Wise and Einhorn. They included *Seder Tefilah: The Order of Prayer for Divine Service* (New York, 1855), by Leo Merzbacher, who was born in Germany but later became rabbi of Anshe Chesed and Emanu-El in New York City; this is known in many congregational records as the "Merzbacher prayer book," which was made more popular by Samuel Adler in revised editions of the 1860s. Another was Seligmann Baer's *Seder Avodat Yisrael* [*Ritual of Israel's Service*], 1868, known as the "Roedelheim prayer book" for the city, a town near Frankfurt famous for its Jewish printing presses, where it was printed in various editions. Merzbacher's *Seder Tefilah: The Order of Prayer for Divine Service* had most of the traditional Hebrew text with facing pages of English translation opening as the *siddur* from right to left. But, with a few prayers omitted (e.g., the Kol Nidre, which opens the Yom Kippur evening liturgy) and others changed (e.g., "renews everything" in place of "resurrects the dead"), it could not be a serious alternative for the most traditional worshipers, and, with only a few omissions and alterations, it had little appeal to reformers. But this was not because Merzbacher did not try hard to assemble a liturgy for American Jews. He "retained intact all essential parts," he noted in the introduction, "all that tradition, authority, and usage have sanctioned," excluding only those prayers he felt were "repetitions, incongruities, and obvious abuses."

As in most efforts to reform the prayer book in the nineteenth century, Merzbacher used Enlightenment terms like "reason," "progress," "truth," and "refined," as well as a lengthy (and intelligent) history of liturgy to justify his changes, but he could not help calling Orthodox worship "thoughtless" because it is "hurried." He noted that some of the prayers treasured by the Orthodox are examples of "dogmatic particularism" or "unintelligibility" and are "inappropriate to our present social and political condition," and he anticipated traditionalists' objections, which he calls "effete arguments." His attempt to do little more, from his perspective, than "retain Hebrew parts of the service" and add "vernacular hymns and prayers" found little audience in either the traditional or reforming synagogues. Two notable exceptions were San Francisco's Emanu-El, which began using the Merzbacher prayer book in 1864 as it "abrogated the old services," and Temple Sinai of New Orleans, which used the "Merzbacher ritual," as Sinai's worshipers called it, for decades, abandoning it only in 1895 when it adopted the new *Union Prayer Book.*

Merzbacher also published a modestly used Day of Atonement prayer book with Hebrew and English. Some traditional prayers are omitted (e.g., the Kol Nidre prayer) and some prayers are revised. The traditionalists largely rejected it because of its revisions and abridgments, and the reformers saw it as too traditional because of its very modest changes.

A successor of Leo Merzbacher at Temple Emanu-El (1868–1872) and one of New Orleans's Sinai "rabbis" (1872–1886), James K. Gutheim (never ordained), preached sermons whose rhetoric was synonymous with the goals of the Merzbacher liturgy. He used words such as progress, enlightened religion, reason, universal, beauty, and solemnity repeatedly, for he believed that the function of Judaism was to unite mankind, that it was "the banner around which all the families of man may gather," the essence of the revelation at Sinai. He preached a Judaism "stripped of ritualistic observances" so that "rational progress" would "chase away the dense clouds of superstition that darken the religious horizon." Rejecting the traditional understanding of Sinai—hundreds of ceremonies, customs, observances, and rituals revealed in the Five Books of Moses—he understood the "mission from Sinai" to be the "spirit of God," a universal monotheism of the highest ethical behavior. Mr. Gutheim took the "Merzbacher ritual" and its theology from New York City to New Orleans.

Baer's *Seder Avdoat Yisrael* [*Ritual of Israel's Service*, or, later, *Service of Israel*], reinvented itself constantly. Early editions, exclusively in Hebrew, opened from right to left and contained unabridged liturgies for weekdays, the Sabbath, High Holy Days, festivals, and life-cycle (e.g., circumcision) ceremonies. Some editions preserved in synagogue archives even have extensive commentary accompanying the prayers. Subsequent editions, although used in several congregations that did not want to be identified as "reforming," had plenty of German translations (later, English translations and paraphrases, the latter, Marcus Jastrow noted, so as to not "burden it with Oriental phraseology") accompanying the Hebrew liturgy, opened from left to right (unlike the traditional prayer book), eliminated or adapted some prayers, and appears to have a sense of dignity and decorum in its arrangement. It would become the basis of a more popular version (with the same title) edited by Benjamin Szold of Baltimore in 1863 and revised subsequently by Szold and others, including Marcus Jastrow (and then known as "Minhag Jastrow"), an outstanding Hebraist and Talmudist. With all its revisions, it became the choice of numerous reforming synagogues in the late nineteenth century. *Seder Avodat Yisrael*, in a much revised form (and truncated from its original length of more than 800 pages, which few could easily lift), would become the most widely used prayer book in Conservative synagogues in the 1920s and 1930s.

David Einhorn published *Olat Tamid* [*A Perpetual Offering*] in a Hebrew-German edition in New York and Baltimore in 1858, and it was revised several times. Opening from left to right, it was a radical alteration of the traditional liturgy, not because of its German translations (a traditional Jew could pray in any language) but because of its abbreviated services that abridged and/or eliminated prayers that had been central to Jewish worship for centuries. For example, Einhorn eliminated the words "resurrects the dead" in a central prayer of every service, leaving only a vague "renews," and he affirmed the "wandering" of the Jews as a celebration of the diaspora. Its popularity, in part, surely stemmed more from the excising than from the radical revisions, as congregations everywhere in America in mid-century eagerly shortened the lengthy worship services. Many, in fact, set strict time limits on the liturgy, especially on Rosh Hashanah and Yom Kippur. Einhorn's book would eventually become the model for the official prayer book of the Reform movement, the *Union Prayer Book*. The *UPB* was a radical and abbreviated liturgy that opened from left to right, included abundant stage directions, called the rabbi "minister," and labeled the prayers with only English titles ("Adoration").

Isaac Mayer Wise's *Minhag America: The Daily Prayers for American Israelites* (Cincinnati, 1857), or, as it was commonly called in synagogue records, the "Wise Prayer Book," appeared in two versions, a Hebrew-German edition and a Hebrew-English one. The Hebrew part (with nearly 300 pages of liturgies, with abundant Hebrew on the right and translation facing on the left) opened from right to left, the English and German parts (forty-five pages of prayers for various occasions) from left to right. This gave it an appeal to a wider constituency than Einhorn's work (its adherents often called themselves "*Minhag America* temples"), instructed worshipers (occasionally) on when to rise and when to sit and offered constant stage directions to the "Minister and Choir" (maximizing decorum), and omitted prayers Wise (like Einhorn) felt were archaic or without spirituality (e.g., resurrection of the dead). As Wise put it in his autobiography, in spite of some anxiety about liturgical radicalism, "it was out of the question to retain the old prayers unchanged," for many were "medieval rubbish." The prayer book's pagination (right to left) gave it the appearance of the *siddur* from the outside, and its title suggested that it was for all American congregations, but its abridged contents, its notice that a quorum for worship may include women, its omission of "messiah" and its substitution of "messianic age" or "redemption," the suggestion that "twenty-one verses will always suffice" for the Torah reading, and the order to read "the Prophets [*haftarah*] in the vernacular" made it recognizable as a Reform prayer book, one that fit congregations open to the process of considerable reform. Thus, the adoption of *Minhag America* was typically accompanied—as in Little Rock, Arkansas's B'nai Israel—by abolition of the women's gallery, the renting of family pews, permission to remove the head covering, elimination of the second day of holiday services, and invitations to non-Jews to sing with Jews in the choir.

Laity and Rabbis

It is not difficult to reconstruct the occupational patterns of synagogue members in the middle decades of the nineteenth century thanks to the help of membership lists and city directories. Consistently, the men who led the congregations were small merchants, usually in the areas of clothing, hardware, shoes, boots, jewelry, dry goods, furniture, groceries, or tobacco. They were overwhelmingly central European-born and married and had large families.

Immigrants as well as Jewish natives of this period had large families because of high rates of infant mortality, frequently fatal epidemics of childhood diseases, the absence of birth control, and the infrequency with which women worked outside the home. While the members who were not officers also came from the same geographical area and had wives and many children, they were more frequently clerks, salesmen, peddlers, and the like. Few members were professionals, and unskilled "industrial" jobs were uncommon—this was a petit bourgeoisie from coast to coast.

Whether in German or English (only a handful of rabbis could preach fluently in both languages in the middle decades of the century), the sermons worshipers heard were quite traditional. Even Rabbi David Einhorn, as radical a reformer as anyone in America in the 1850s, offered a traditional theology. In his inaugural sermon at Baltimore's Har Sinai, he called the customs, observances, and rituals of Judaism "dead and obsolete ceremonies" and "the decay within" and explained that the "liberation of Judaism" demanded that they "must be plucked up by the roots" so that he and his congregants, by "removing the debris," could "free ourselves from [their] authority." At the same time, Rabbi Einhorn repeatedly affirmed "the divinely revealed word" and the statement in the liturgy acknowledging that "God gave the Torah to His people Israel." Einhorn saw no contradiction—he simply sought the "spirit of the Sinaic [sic] law," which he took to be ethical monotheism; the brotherhood of man and fatherhood of God; and God's omnipotence, omnipresence, and omnibenevolence.

Like Einhorn, preachers were filled with theology, and their sermons revolved around themes such as God, revelation, covenant, good and evil, prophecy, and the Messiah. The Civil War, and the run-up to it, produced sermons linking the Bible and emancipation (e.g., Rabbi Einhorn's many sermons against slavery), as well as sermons defending slavery (e.g., Rabbi Morris J. Raphall of New York City and J. M. Michelbacher of Richmond, Virginia) and attacking abolitionists (e.g., Bernard Illowy in Baltimore), but sermons on contemporary issues were the exception, not the rule. By the last full decade of this period, a few American-born and American-educated rabbis had taken over pulpits from immigrant rabbis, and the themes began to change to those favored by men who had graduated from the Hebrew Union College (Reform) in Cincinnati. Like Rabbi Grossman, they made the subjects that Protestant ministers of the late nineteenth century favored their own, emphasizing the role of the Jew in making the world a better place for all people. Social justice programs entered Reform synagogues and became, for more than a century, one of their defining features.

Nothing characterized the nineteenth century more than change. Reforming impulses were everywhere, and it would be hard to find very many nineteenth-century synagogues that did not institute reforms, whether just one or two or many. When Jews began to arrive in staggering numbers from eastern Europe in the 1880s and 1890s, those congregations that had engaged in sustained reform overwhelmingly just ignored the mass migration in their sanctuaries, though in their meeting rooms they often engaged in charity projects for poor immigrant Jews. Their hope was that the Central European Jews and their descendants who were already the core of their congregations would suffice to maintain strong or at least viable synagogues. The synagogues that had enacted only a few reforms would find themselves more compatible with the religious sensibilities of the new eastern European immigrants. These were the Orthodox, they were the most immediately impacted by the age of immigration, to which we turn our attention next.

3

An Explosion of Immigrant Synagogues

Jewish Mass Migration to America

There are [1890] 533 Jewish religious organizations.
> —*Report on Statistics of Churches at the Eleventh Census*
> (Washington, D.C., 1894)

There are [1906] 1,769 Jewish religious organizations.
> —*Census of Religious Bodies, 1906, Part I*
> (Washington, D.C., 1908)

To secure the proper decorum in worship, Reform congregations have gone to such an extreme as to silence the worshipers and reduce them to passivity.
> —Rabbi Henry Berkowitz, Rodeph Shalom,
> Philadelphia, 1921

MORE THAN TWO million Jews, most from eastern Europe, came to the United States between the early 1880s and the end of "open" immigration, in 1924. In every community where these Jews settled in the last decades of the nineteenth century, they established synagogues. Even the smallest of communities with Yiddish-speaking Jews had multiple Orthodox "synagogues," usually very small. These were frequently just one or two rented rooms, and their sole function was prayer (and talking). There was no visible evidence from the outside that they were synagogues. In 1900, the small immigrant Jewish community of Des Moines had three orthodox synagogues, each with a section where the women sat apart from the men. They had no rabbi, though the members might have engaged a hazan to chant the prayers on the High Holy Days. In 1905, there were three Orthodox synagogues in Atlanta serving the tiny immigrant community: Ahavath Achim, Beth Israel, and Shearith Israel. Men who left Ahavath Achim after disputes established the latter two congregations. Chicago had at least fifty Orthodox synagogues in 1900, and at least twenty east European Orthodox synagogues have been identified in Baltimore in 1899. Minneapolis Orthodox Jews could choose from Ohel Jacob (Lithuanians and Poles), Bes Haidrash Hagadol (Russians), Anshei Russia (Russians), or Tiferes B'nai Israel, the Fileshter [Bessarabia] Shul. St. Louis had at least three orthodox synagogues before 1900, and more emerged in the following decade. Contemporaries called them shuls and spoke of their neighborhood as the ghetto. The *Durham South* noted in 1901 that "some of the best Hebrews in the city . . . split from the old church [Durham Hebrew Congregation]" and organized Chevre Bnay Israel. In Augusta, Georgia, a few Orthodox Jewish families formed "Mr. Steinberg's Minyan" in 1889 over a drugstore on Broad Street and hired a *shochet*. The following year, the minyan split over the credentials of the *shochet*, and, the following year, another split left three Orthodox minyans. By 1892, the three had recombined and formed Adas Yeshurun, which existed for ten years before it split into two synagogues. In the small Orthodox Jewish community of Denver in the first decade of the twentieth century, the Khatzker Shteebel began in 1900 in the private home of the founder and was reorganized the next year as Tiferas Israel in another private home; Dorshei Zion began in a private home in 1903, the "Hooker Street Shul" (Keneseth Israel) started in 1907 in a private home, members of Beth Israel Anshei Matizov Chevra Volin worshipped in a private home for a few years, and Jews from Rotno formed Keheleth Jacob in 1904 in a private home before moving to a rented store, while the Rumanian Jews organized their congregation in 1903 in a tent. These synagogues had no religious schools (*cheders*); private tutors (*melamdim*) came to the members' homes to prepare the boys for bar mitzvah. Denver was the norm in this practice, not the exception.

Of course, no neighborhood had as many Orthodox services as the Lower East Side of New York City in the late nineteenth and early twentieth centuries. In fact, they were too numerous to count, in part because most were not held at "synagogues" in any formal sense; rather, congregations held makeshift gatherings in tenements, bakeries, and storefronts or met in rented rooms, and they often gathered for the holiest holidays and festivals but not on every Sabbath. Yet, some had their own building; the Bialystoker Synagogue had its own edifice in 1905 when a group of Polish Jews converted a Methodist church into a synagogue. These synagogues were quite often packed, as were the tenements in which their worshipers lived; the uptown *Jewish Messenger* noted that "below Second Street, at one [downtown] synagogue, where there is accommodation for 2,000 people, at every [weekday!] evening service every seat was occupied." As in Baltimore, Chicago, Cleveland, Denver, and elsewhere, the Orthodox Jews who did create year-round congregations used the synagogue to organize study sessions for adults and children; to celebrate holidays, bar mitzvahs, and weddings; and to help families with funeral preparations, burial, and services at the graveside and to provide comfort to the bereaved. Synagogue Ladies Auxiliaries, on the Lower East Side and elsewhere, busied themselves with countless service projects, including aiding neighborhood organizations, Jewish institutions near and far, and the Jewish community in Palestine.

The language spoken in these synagogues for announcements, for gossip before, during, and after prayer, and for sermons, as well as the language of the minutes of the boards of trustees, was usually Yiddish, though some Central European Jews, unlike the mostly east European Orthodox, did not speak Yiddish and preferred Hungarian or the like. Immigrant rabbis preached in Yiddish—not only in all the big eastern cities but in Atlanta, Durham, and Memphis and as far West as Los Angeles and Portland. Indeed, Rabbi Bernard Drachman, with a B.A. from Columbia College (1882) and a Ph.D. from Heidelberg University (1885), noted, in 1885, that there was "no demand in America for an American-born, English-speaking rabbi who insisted on maintaining the laws and usages of Traditional Judaism." Indeed, the Orthodox synagogue Tiferes B'nai Jacob in Minneapolis, hired an "American Orthodox rabbi" (old-timers reported that, unique among Orthodox rabbis of this era, he had played football in high school) and he promptly brought the congregation into the Conservative movement.

It was the children of the immigrants, not the first generation, who began to explore synagogues where English (not Yiddish) dominated but where males (as in Orthodox synagogues) wore head covering during worship and where the congregants rejected the Reform *Union Prayer Book* because it omitted sacred prayers. These were the emerging Conservative synagogues, and they distinguished themselves from Orthodox congregations by challenging the traditional authority of Jewish law and thus developing an openness to moderating and even changing ceremonies, customs, observances, and rituals —however slowly and carefully—that remained sacrosanct (that is, unchangeable) for Orthodox Judaism. These congregations slowly identified themselves with the label "Conservative."

Rabbi Solomon Schechter, the president of the Conservative rabbinical school, the Jewish Theological Seminary of America, together with a number of seminary graduates, founded the umbrella organization of Conservative synagogues—the United Synagogue of America—in 1913 with twenty-two members (half from New York City and Philadelphia). This organization was committed to clearly distinguishing its congregations from those in the Orthodox and Reform movements. By emphasizing "Jewish tradition in its historical continuity, advancing the cause of traditional Judaism, and strengthening the conservative tendency in American Israel," these congregations signaled their commitment to tradition (unlike adherents of the Reform movement) and to history (unlike Orthodoxy, which maintained that its interpretations had not evolved historically but were present at Sinai). Conservatism immediately began to combine traditional Judaism with the values and culture of modern, urban America; Conservative synagogues flaunted their American credentials, celebrating American holidays with odes to Abraham Lincoln, George Washington, Thomas Jefferson, and even the Pilgrims.

These Conservative shuls also responded to what their members perceived as a lack of decorum in Orthodox worship among East European Jewish immigrants, who frequently held private conversations, walked around the sanctuary, and were even to be seen "passing around snuff (which always led to paroxysms of sneezing) during the allegedly solemn prayer service." Because the Conservative synagogues incorporated the minimal ingredients of tradition, though with increased decorum and openness to modernity and "Americanness," thousands of second-generation East European Jews gave them a look, and there were more than 225 Conservative synagogues by 1927. Reform synagogues, where most men did not cover their heads and family pews dominated, though they "had conquered almost the entire field of Jewish life and had been accepted by practically all the congregations of standing and importance," became choices for east Europeans only in a subsequent generation, not before World War I.

In contrast to synagogues in Vilna, Lodz, Warsaw, and Crakow at the end of the nineteenth or the beginning of the twentieth century, where the programs provided little evidence of the Polish environment in which they existed, Orthodox synagogues in the United States always demonstrated an awareness that the Orthodox worship was taking place in *America*, even before the serious Americanization efforts undertaken by Orthodox congregations after World War I, when they found themselves competing with Conservatism, the new branch of traditional Judaism. When Chicago's Orthodox Rodfei

Zedek dedicated the Forty-eighth Street Shul in an unused Baptist church in the Grand Boulevard neighborhood, in 1907, it featured a three-man band, a distinguished Reform rabbi, Emil G. Hirsch, as the guest speaker, and plenty of non-Orthodox Jews as well as non-Jews among the invited guests. In Wilmington, Delaware, at the dedication of Orthodox Adas Kodesch, in 1898, in a building that also had formerly been a church, there was a band, American flags, a prayer for President McKinley, a prayer for the success of American soldiers in the Spanish-American War, and plenty of non-Jewish townspeople in attendance. Carefully planned efforts to raise funds included selling the honor of carrying the American flag from the previous place of worship to the site of the dedication ($10), as well as selling the honor of opening the door of the former church ($25) and selling the honor of opening the curtain where the Torah scroll would lodge ($25). In a few places we can find English sermons, late-Friday-evening services, congregational singing, a mother's club, Daughters of Zion (a Zionist women's organization), Boy Scouts and Girl Scouts (synagogue-sponsored units of the national movement were open also to non-Jews, who rarely, if ever, joined), and numerous other organizations that imitated the activities at established Reform synagogues, as well as at churches.

Many Orthodox synagogue constitutions from the first decade of the twentieth century show the extent to which the emphasis on the "dignity and decorum" of Reform synagogues influenced the orthodoxy emerging in America. The Orthodox synagogue Ohave Sholom Mariampol, in Chicago, noted in its constitution that "the members must behave orderly in the synagogue and keep their seats during prayer." Members were also warned against the indecorous acts of removing their prayer shawls before the closing hymn and allowing children to disturb adults who were praying. At Agudas Achim, an Orthodox synagogue in Columbus, Ohio, the constitution required worshipers to remain in their seats throughout the service.

In most of these synagogues, the *shames*, like the executive director in a later period, kept the congregation functioning. He collected dues, did the work of a custodian inside and outside the building (or hired people to do it), kept records, and often supervised the membership application process, since membership was never automatic. Sometimes a "blackball" from one "brother" (terms adopted from the Masonic Order) could prevent an applicant from joining, though in most synagogues it took two or three such negative responses. Even when the community was small, an applicant for membership had to gain acceptance through a vote by members.

Most of these Orthodox synagogues—composed of peddlers, tailors, petty merchants (retailers of notions, clothing, tobacco), and the like—had no rabbis; they were too poor, so laymen everywhere led Orthodox prayers. Someone with the ability to chant was much more important than a rabbi or even a service leader, as the worshipers were not unhappy without a sermon from the rabbi and read the prayers without anyone other than another worshiper in charge. When they could, they would rather pay for a visiting cantor (hazan) than for a visiting rabbi, choosing chanting over a sermon. And, while there were often synagogues without someone skilled enough to chant or read the Torah, laymen everywhere struggled the best they could to prepare for the task.

And it was a struggle. There were usually worshipers, raised in Europe, who were familiar with the order of prayers, the chants, and the prayers that were added or subtracted for special occasions. This was even more necessary at a time when there was no standard Orthodox prayer book—each worshiper read from his own version. But finding someone to read the Torah was more difficult. If someone in the congregation could not prepare adequately—after all, the Torah was read every week of the year—and the community was sufficiently large, the leaders would hire someone for this task. Often, as in Denver, where, by the end of World War I, more than twenty shuls could be counted on the West Side, it was a man who had read the Torah at another synagogue and rushed over to a second synagogue to do it again. But, in the main, it fell to the members of the congregation to prepare the Scriptural reading.

Orthodox synagogues, in towns and cities with more than one, divided by *landsleit* and kinship networks. There were Litvak shuls (mostly Lithuanian and Latvian), shuls of Galizianers, or Hungarians, or Poles, or Rumanians, or Ukrainians. In the tiny community of Fall River, Massachusetts, the Litiwishe Shul (Lithuanians) stood two blocks away from the Russishe Shul (Agudas Achim) of Ukranian Jews. In Richmond, Virginia, Orthodox Jews attended the "Polish shul," the "Russian shul," or Etz Chaim. In New Orleans prior to 1900, several Orthodox synagogues (Chevra Mikve Israel, Chevra Thilim, Agudath Achim, Temene Derech) divided along regional lines (Hungarians, Galitzianers, Poles, Litvaks, and even western [Posen] Poles). Philadelphia had a Russian, a Hungarian, a Galitzianer, a Rumanian, a Ukrainian, and a Polish synagogue—all listed in city directories (at one time or another) by name and nationality. In Los Angeles in the early twentieth century, Orthodox Jews had their choice of the Russian shul, the Hungarian shul, the Austro-Galician shul, and the Rumanian shul. As was the case with more than half of the twenty-eight synagogues that formed the Federation of Orthodox Jewish Congregations in Baltimore in 1908, many (e.g., the Russische shul, the Bialystoker shul, the Pekroer shul) grew out of earlier *landsmanschaften* societies (such as the Bialystoker loan society and the Pekroer mutual aid society), which were set up to aid those from their shared places of origin. These synagogues frequently offered a number of necessary services and functions, providing a source for the purchase of kosher meat, imported from a larger community if there was no slaughterer in town; offices that allowed the borrowing of small amounts of money (free loan associations); centers for visiting the sick; gathering places to get news of Jewish communities overseas; places to arrange a proper Jewish burial, including preparation of the body, the obtaining of a permit, and recitation of the Jewish memorial prayer for the deceased for eleven or twelve months; and, occasionally, a mikveh (ritual bath). Disputes over the proper slaughtering of animals and kosher meat emerged everywhere, no matter the size of the community; in Charlotte, North Carolina, seven of the nine synagogue bylaws governed kosher meat distribution.

The emerging Conservative movement of the second decade of the twentieth century challenged Orthodox congregations in various ways. Whereas some Orthodox synagogues had mixed seating, few laymen or rabbis embraced it, in contrast to startup Conservative synagogues, which advertised mixed seating. When the Conservative synagogue used the same liturgy and separated the sexes, it posed significant competition to Orthodox synagogues, as improved decorum (e.g., eliminating solicitation on Yom Kippur and the public announcement of gifts), the inclusion of some English alongside the Hebrew prayers, Americanization (a hazan who faced the congregation instead of the ark), the use of English-language sermons and American-educated rabbis, and a religious school offered much that was desirable to the children of the immigrants. For immigrants "tenaciously clinging to old habits," as the Indianapolis Hebrew Congregation *Temple Fair Journal* noted in describing dissension over the "mode of worship," a synagogue modeled on the old world was satisfying, but, for children of Yiddish-speaking Jewish immigrants, an English sermon made much more sense as they focused on moving up the ladder of American respectability.

More than anything else, it was decorum that worshipers pointed to as the primary factor in moving them from an Orthodox to a Conservative synagogue and that moved Orthodox congregations toward reforms that made them Conservative. Typical is the reminiscence of Hyman Goldman, a member of a Conservative synagogue, Adas Israel of Washington, D.C., as he recalled the worship in 1906:

> People did not come to pray. Some brought along their newspapers, or the racing sheet. The women, although they were not as yet

sitting with the menfolks, came there to display their new dresses
and spent most of the time on the street outside the synagogue.

As Conservative Judaism established itself during and after World
War I, it explicitly responded to situations such as Goldman describes with its emphasis on what the president of Los Angeles's
Temple Sinai called "tradition with decorum." By the 1930s, Orthodox synagogues everywhere had begun to compete with Conservative congregations for the children and grandchildren of immigrants,
and decorum became a high priority.

Following the practice of nineteenth-century synagogues before
the wave of Orthodox immigrants from eastern Europe, many of
these Orthodox synagogues and, later, Conservative congregations,
too, allowed members to rent specific seats. Whether they were First
Class, Second Class, Third Class (the most common terms) or identified as just A, B, or C, members rented seats in the main sanctuary (with a corresponding seat for the wife in the balcony) as a way
to raise operating funds. These seats were not transferable; when
Emeritus Rabbi Mayer Messing of Indianapolis Hebrew Congregation, who served the synagogue for forty years and had "free seats
for life," tried to pass them on to his children, the board refused and
demanded that his children rent the seats like other members. IHC
did not cease renting seats until 1958, when, as in most post–World
War II synagogues, seating became open and free for members.

Artists of all kinds decorated synagogue sanctuaries in this period
with representations that surprised many Jews. Many worshipers had
forgotten that the commandment in Exodus 20 prohibited representations only of the Deity, not humans. Elaborately carved wooden
arks, ark decorations, stained-glass windows, and magnificent wall
paintings—many modeled on Orthodox European synagogues such
as the Dohany Street synagogue in Budapest—filled sanctuaries
of both Orthodox and Reform synagogues. Heroes from the Genesis narratives dominated, as at the Baron Hirsch Congregation in

Memphis; the Wilshire Boulevard Temple in Los Angeles; Shearith Israel in San Francisco; Ohev Shalom in Washington, D.C.; and Temple Israel and Agudas Achim of Columbus, Ohio, along with animals, birds, ritual objects, landscapes, Israelite kings, and, here and there, signs of the zodiac. The latter, as in the Bialystoker and Eldridge Street synagogues of New York City, represented the months in the Jewish calendar.

One constant, whether we peek into Orthodox, Reform, or, in the second decade of the century, Conservative synagogues, was the role of women—or the nonrole of women. While they served as Sunday school teachers, organizers of social events, creators of wall decorations throughout the synagogue, providers of food for celebrations, and staffers of gift shops, they had little power. They had few rights in any synagogues, and even reforming congregations rarely stretched to change their role. They were not members; they did not vote; they could not hold office; they could not sit on the board of directors; they were usually prohibited from participating in the discussions (e.g., about hiring a rabbi) at annual meetings mandated by synagogue constitutions; and, in non-Reform synagogues, they sat in the balcony, at best with a seat number matching that of their husband, who was seated below. At Rodfei Zedek in Chicago in 1924, the sisterhood—despite contributing more than $5,000 annually to the synagogue treasury—tried without success to place two members on the board of trustees. The officers agreed to permit them to attend meetings but not to vote. At Indianapolis Hebrew Congregation, eventually a Reform synagogue, women did not receive the right to vote until 1944. The first battle women fought was to gain full membership status if their husband died or if they were a single dues-paying member. Not until the decades between the world wars would they begin to effect significant change.

While the status of women was quite similar from branch to branch, the salaries of rabbis were not. Generally, with very few exceptions, rabbis of Reform synagogues received salaries, paid monthly, which provided a reasonable standard of living for them and their families. In contrast, rabbis of Orthodox synagogues everywhere struggled to make ends meet. Many of these rabbis, in the 1890s and early 1900s, earned less than $1,000 a year in salary, and they were forced to sometimes collect the money themselves and to charge Jews for each rabbinical service. They frequently supplemented their small salary by overseeing *kashruth* (especially supervising animal slaughter); serving as an arbitrator in questions of Jewish law; performing marriages, divorces, and other life-cycle ceremonies; selling wine for ritual purposes (including later, during Prohibition, legally, because of provisions that allowed the sale of wine for religious use); and selling collections of their sermons. For example, Rabbi Gedaliah Silverstone, of Orthodox Tifereth Israel in Washington, D.C., claimed to have sold 4,000 copies total of three of his privately printed books. Rabbi Abraham Schapiro, of Portsmouth, Ohio's Orthodox B'nai Abraham, was paid $600 annually in 1896 (he was offered $500 additional salary if he would close the bookshop he owned for supplemental income on Jewish holy days), while Rabbi Abraham S. Braude of Chicago, in 1916, received the same salary from his synagogue. Baltimore's Chizuk Amuno hired Rabbi Henry W. Schneeberger in 1876 at $1,200 annually; when he sought a raise after nine years, his appeal was rejected ("no way of increasing revenue," he was told); after sixteen years of service, the trustees raised his salary to $1,600, but, when there were "not enough" funds, they reduced it to $1,500. In contrast, when Portland, Oregon's Reform Beth Israel hired the newly minted rabbi Stephen S. Wise in 1899, they paid him $5,000 a year.

An 1898 description of how an Orthodox rabbi's salary was collected and paid did not by any means describe only that period. In many communities, and for many years, especially during the early 1930s, the pattern did not change. "The salary of the rabbi in the Russian and Polish congregations is between six and ten *shekalim* per week, and it originates from the 'beggary.' Every Friday or Saturday two people go about the doorways of all the congregants with their kerchief in hand to beg small coin to small coin." In contrast, at many of these Orthodox synagogues, good cantors commanded salaries much greater than those paid to the rabbis. Orthodox congregants everywhere, as many old-timers in Columbus, Ohio, have reminisced, preferred to listen to good singing than to hear adequate sermons.

The poor peddlers and tailors of Orthodox immigrant synagogues who predominated in 1900 yielded, by 1920, to a different demographic. The leaders, as well as a substantial number of members of what was by now the second generation, had moved into the lower-middle or middle class. They were now salesmen, clerks, and, abundantly, owners of small shops offering tailoring, shoes, jewelry, clothing, notions, dry goods; they were the employers of the workers, not the workers as a generation earlier. Following World War I, because of their members' increasing affluence, many of these tiny immigrant congregations were able to build their own synagogue buildings.

By the time the United States joined the war effort, synagogues of every kind instituted programs of support. Many raised and lowered American flags to show their solidarity; others had special Sabbath services and dances for Army and Navy men, sewed for the Red Cross, and offered soldiers complimentary tickets to High Holy Day services. Bond drives appeared everywhere, including the Second Issue of 1917, the Third Issue of 1918, numerous Liberty Loan Bond rallies in 1918, and Fourth Issue sales toward the end of that same year. Bulletins included news of soldiers from the congregation who were in Europe, and, eventually, soldiers who died during World War I were memorialized at special services and their names engraved on plaques that hung on the synagogue walls.

What was Orthodox synagogue life in 1908? We will look at sixteen Orthodox synagogues in seven cities to help to answer this question: Atlanta (Ahavath Achim), Baltimore (B'nai Israel, Chizuk Emuno, Eden Street), Chicago (Anshe Kneseth Israel, Beth Hamedrosh Hagodol—"the oldest Orthodox congregation in the Midwest," according to its website—First Hungarian, Agudath Achim, Ohave Sholom Mariampol, Ohave Zedek, Rodfei Zedek), Denver (Beth Hamedrosh Hagadol), Memphis (Baron Hirsch), Philadelphia (Ahavas Achim Anshei Nezhin Nusach Ho-Ari, B'nai Abraham, Emunath Israel—Oheb Shalom), and Pittsburgh (Beth Hamedrosh Hagadol). They offer us a more or less representative look at the daily activities at east European Orthodox congregations early in the twentieth century.

It is quickly apparent that many of these synagogues emerged out of *landsleit* groups, as they were also known as the "Hungarian shul," the "Russische shul," and the like. In one case, Ohave Sholom Mariampol, a group of worshipers from the town of Mariampol in southern Lithuania split off from Beth Hamedrosh Hagodol in about 1870 and formed their own synagogue, this time representing a specific locale rather than a general area such as "Galicia." Even when congregations were known simply by the street on which they were located (e.g., the Eden Street Synagogue and the Lloyd Street Shul in Baltimore), they frequently had a large core of worshipers from the same region or town in eastern Europe.

These synagogues were made up of hardworking, poor immigrants who were at work at least five days a week and whose wives were either at home with children (mostly) or themselves working. Few members of these synagogues spent time at the shul on weekday mornings or afternoons, unless they came for brief morning worship before work or brief afternoon worship after work. And weekday evenings were not spent at the synagogue, unless there was critical business to take care of (burials, loan society meeting, discussion about hiring a rabbi or cantor, an officers' meeting). Ironically, the day of "rest," Saturday, was the busiest day of the week, and Sunday, when few worked, was also a day of abundant synagogue activity.

Most of these Orthodox synagogues held study sessions, with the rabbi if there was one or else with an educated layman, on Saturday afternoons or Sundays. Sometimes called *Chevra Shas, Talmud To-rah,* or *Chevra Mishnayot,* these classes consisted of men who stud-ied sacred Hebrew texts together. At the same time, some of these members sent their sons (rarely their daughters) to something like a religious school (often called *Talmud Torah*), which met on Sundays, though most sons were educated in liturgy and Torah by private tu-tors, for schools lacked proper teachers and proper meeting rooms. The basement of a small synagogue, in the rare case that a congre-gation owned its own building rather than rented rooms, hardly en-couraged serious pedagogy.

Rabbi Sidney K. Mossmann of Atlanta's Shearith Israel pointed out, as late as 1958, that most of the Orthodox synagogues with Or-thodox rabbis in the Midwest still had mixed seating. This was in contrast to the decades after about 1980, when orthodoxy became rigorous rather than lax. In the earlier days, while male worship-ers sometimes sat in sections separated from those for women, es-pecially when there was a balcony for women, more frequently (at least in the first decade of the century) the sexes were mixed in the sanctuary (by the second decade, this was changing in many Or-thodox synagogues, as rabbis began to vigorously push for separate seating); at Chicago's Rodfei Zedek, for example, women sat either in the women's gallery or in the center of the sanctuary with their husbands. While Orthodox synagogues maintained the traditional full liturgy (thus distinguishing themselves from many Conservative and all Reform congregations), as with seating, ritual requirements —with some notable exceptions—were lax during the immigrant era, as Orthodox worshipers would generally carry ritual objects to the synagogues, handle coins before and after worship, and head off to their shops to work after worship, all of which are prohibited ac-cording to Jewish law. But an occasional group of leaders rejected as members Jews who violated the Sabbath or committed a crime and levied fines (sometimes heavy) on officers who did not dem-onstrate consistent attendance, refused an honor (which required a contribution), failed to visit the sick or the bereaved, or did not dress in a dignified manner for worship.

Nearly every congregation had a women's group, most frequently called a ladies auxiliary, which met on Sunday afternoons after the women's husbands came home from their morning activities at the synagogue. They primarily engaged in activities (e.g., Purim fairs, dances, picnics) that raised badly needed funds for the synagogue. For men and women who were active synagogue members, most of their free time was consumed by activities—sacred and less sacred —at the synagogues. The men might meet to discuss helping poor congregants with short-term loans; wrestle with the problem of the lack of a standard prayer book and the resulting diverse collection of liturgies with different pagination; assign bereavement visits after a funeral or for a member who was ill; talk about events in eastern Europe; or just *shmoos* (chat). For the members of East European Orthodox synagogues who attended worship regularly—not those who bought a ticket only for High Holy Day services—the synagogue was their life beyond work.

Reform Judaism

In this period of mass migration of Central and East European traditional Jews to America, we often forget that Reform Judaism also responded to these new Jews on the block. As we have seen, the new immigrants did not generally gravitate to Reform synagogues upon their arrival; it was not so much that new Reform synagogues emerged in response to orthodoxy but that orthodoxy moved many reforming synagogues to clarify for themselves what Reform Judaism meant and, in the process, to move them further and further away from all similarities with their Orthodox co-religionists. We call this "classical" Reform—it is marked by rabbis who saw themselves more or less as Protestant ministers, not just in dress but liturgies without Hebrew; festivals without traditional ceremonies, customs, observances, and rituals favored by the Orthodox; pipe organs and professional—often non-Jewish—choirs that led worshipers to listen rather than participate (Birmingham Alabama's Temple Emanu-El boasted, in 1882, of a choir with "one Methodist, one Roman Catholic, one Baptist, two Episcopalians, and one Hebrew"); sermons (drawing on the language of the 1885 Reform platform: "extend the hand of fellowship to all who cooperate with us in the establishment of the reign of truth and righteousness among men") that stressed what Jews and Christians had in common; and the wearing to services of fancy dress, for women and men, resembling Sunday finest often worn by Christians in churches. Whereas in Orthodox synagogues each section of the Torah reading was frequently sold by auction, radical reformers responded not by stopping such bidding but by eliminating Torah readings completely. A generation of Reform Jews—inarticulate in the synagogue and unobservant at home —came from these congregations.

Few Reform rabbis in this period were more successful than Joseph Krauskopf, of Philadelphia's Congregation Keneseth Israel, a rabbi who served the synagogue from 1887 to 1923. In 1888, he edited a book with thirty brief Sunday-morning services (fewer than ten pages each) containing one or two Hebrew sentences, English readings, and two hymns with words by non-Jewish authors. In bold type, each service included the word "Lecture," the event that the readings and singing (there were virtually no "prayers") surrounded. For years, the doors were locked before and unlocked after his lectures. It is unclear whether this was to prevent listeners from leaving during the talk or to prevent people from entering and interrupting Rabbi Krauskopf. The authors of the hymns included in the first ten services read like the line-up in a Protestant service of the same period: Grace Aguilar, Robert Burns, Johann Wolfgang von Goethe, F. L. Hosmer, William Knox, James Russell Lowell, Charles MacKay, Thomas Moore, William B. O. Peabody, Bryan Proctor,

Charles Swain, Anna L. Waring, and J. G. Whittier. At roughly the same time (1894–1911), Rabbi Charles Fleischer, as his predecessor, Solomon Schindler, had done, promulgated a "religion of humanity" at Boston's Adath (Temple) Israel. A fusion of Judaism, liberal Christianity, and the Transcendentalism of Theodore Parker and Ralph Waldo Emerson, it included, by 1908, Fleischer asking his congregants to acknowledge Jesus as the greatest of all Jewish prophets.

There were, to be sure, classical reformers with ambivalence, as indicated in their sermons, bulletins, and correspondence. Isaac S. Moses, rabbi of New York City's Ahavath Chesed-Shaar Hashomayim, was typical. He conducted radical worship services almost entirely in English, with organ and trained choir and no head covering and no bar mitzvah, and yet he eventually concluded that "fine poems and melodies, culled from the hymnals of the different churches," had "no place in the Synagogue" and that "the voices of young and old [worshipers] should be encouraged to sing." His widely used turn-of-the-century hymnal contained 191 hymns—187 in English —but he included transliterations of all the Hebrew he read, and the choir (modest though it was) sang to maximize participation in all the Sabbath, festival, and Sunday school services, rather than just to be heard.

At Rabbi Krauskopf's congregation and at many others even before 1881, confirmation (actually, preconfirmation, confirmation, and postconfirmation) had replaced the bar mitzvah as the ceremony for which young men (and women) diligently prepared. Theater-style seats in the sanctuary were assigned to confirmands, their families, and their guests (unlike Sabbath worship), students were elected as officers, the classes were taught by rabbis, homework was assigned and graded, and the confirmation ceremony was very elaborate and formal. Worship services took place on Saturday and Sunday morning, the latter because "Saturday is a working day of the week," Eli Mayer, assistant rabbi, explained, and "Sunday is a national day of rest." The rabbis did worry that "large a [sic] number of gentiles attend," primarily because of the fame of Rabbi Krauskopf as a preacher; scores of non-Jews came to his sermons, which were advertised to be offered at a precise time, though they did not attend the worship before or after. Despite poor attendance by Jews year after year, Rabbi Krauskopf felt certain that more and more Jews would attend in the future. A mid-twentieth-century rabbi of the congregation, Bertram W. Korn, would say of Rabbi Krauskopf in 1955 that "Keneseth Israel became the largest Jewish congregation in the country and built this immense Temple to contain the throngs of Jews and Gentiles who came to hear his Sunday morning sermons." Already in 1906, Henry M. Fisher, assistant rabbi, claimed that "we have published and distributed more than one million and a half copies of our Sunday discourses (26 annually) during the past eighteen years." While attendance at services was not generally strong, numerous auxiliary organizations made the synagogue their home in 1916, including the 1,100-member sisterhood, the sewing circle (women made clothes for poor immigrants supported by the United Hebrew Charities), a singing class (to teach the hymns used at worship), the lyceum (Thursday evening lectures), Boy Scouts and Girl Scouts, and the men's temple fellowship ("the club").

Krauskopf's schedule, like that of so many of his colleagues, exhausts the reader who follows him through the bulletins and minutes as he preaches, teaches, officiates at life-cycle events, gives lectures outside the synagogue, attends meetings of communal organizations, and visits the ill and the bereaved. Krauskopf's Philadelphia Reform colleague, for almost the identical years, Henry Berkowitz of Rodeph Shalom, told rabbinic students (and faculty) at his alma mater, the Hebrew Union College, that "the rabbi . . . is apt to be consulted daily on questions that refer to the training of the young, the problems of the adolescent, the determination of a career, intimate matters of domestic relations, questions on the distinctively Jewish topics of the day, and all the educational, civic, and philanthropic problems that confront the community at large." William Rosenau, rabbi of Oheb

Shalom Congregation (the Eutaw Place Temple) in Baltimore, gave 56 sermons, delivered 20 public lectures (in and out of Baltimore), married 34 couples, conducted 35 funerals, and made 637 "calls" with Mrs. Rosenau and 1,122 calls by himself—all from the fall of 1903 to the spring of 1904. One wonders if Rosenau would have agreed with Berkowitz's conclusion that "the practical task of preparing sermons will tax your energies as a rabbi more than will any other effort you will be called upon to make."

Classical Reform rabbis of this period preached and wrote vigorously against orthodoxy in general and Orthodox rabbis in particular. Jacob Voorsanger of San Francisco's Emanu-El called the language of Orthodox immigrants, Yiddish, an "unintelligible German tongue" (other Reform rabbis called it "jargon"), described Orthodox rituals as "senseless" and "irrational," and referred to an Orthodox spokesman of weekday Jewish parochial education as a "doddering idiot." Max Heller of New Orleans's Temple Sinai noted that Bernard Illowy, an Orthodox Jew, with his "reverence for petty injunctions" (i.e., ceremonies, customs, observances, and rituals), opposed "the spirit of the times."

In many of these Reform synagogues, Sunday worship either replaced Saturday services, as occurred at Lancaster, Pennsylvania's Shaarai Shomayim, or, more often, took place in addition to poorly attended Friday evening and Saturday morning prayers and became, as at Boston's Adath Israel and Atlanta's Hebrew Benevolent Congregation, the main weekly worship service. When the members of Rochester's Temple B'rith Kodesh voted in 1911 (110 for, 46 against) to add Sunday services, they also voted decisively to continue Saturday morning worship. The leaders knew that most members arrived home late on Friday and worked on Saturday, but none did so on Sunday, and attendance was regularly much greater then than on the Jewish Sabbath. Nearly every classical Reform rabbi, at one time or another, justified the Sunday services by saying that hardly anyone attended Friday evening or Saturday morning worship and that the emphasis on the "fatherhood of God and the brotherhood of man" (a central tenet of German and American classical Reform) led to efforts to preach to non-Jews. Adolph Moses, leader of Louisville's Adas Shalom, explained this perfectly: "On Friday night we usually address about the sixth part of our congregation, at times outnumbered by the Gentiles present. On Saturday morning we preach to women, children, and a few old men. But the great mass of even those Jews that belong to a congregation goes from year's beginning to year's end without religious and moral instruction. The fact is, Saturday morning is the busiest and, commercially, the most profitable day of the week."

Louis Marshall, a Syracuse layman, put it well in the Rochester *Jewish Tidings* of May 2, 1890: "I know of no good reason why supplementary religious services on Sunday should not be encouraged," for "if properly conducted, would attract many people who find it now impossible to attend their spiritual wants on any other day." The rabbis who served such congregations delivered lengthy "addresses," lectures, or discourses—carefully prepared and edited—in the midst of a brief liturgy, and all over the country not only Jews but also non-Jews in the community came to hear these learned lectures, which the congregation published and distributed. Before radio and television, Jews and non-Jews hungered for learned analyses of current events and advice on the moral life, and if an articulate, charismatic rabbi or minister could perform this service, townspeople, irrespective of their religion, came to hear him. In fact, frequently—as at Beth Ahabah in Richmond, Virginia, and at Beth Israel in Portland, Oregon—ministers from liberal Protestant churches replaced the rabbi in the pulpit when he was away. Yet, some synagogues eschewed the lecture. At Temple Beth El in Helena, Arkansas, the ritual committee told Rabbi Aaron Weinstein in 1909 that his sermons would be timed and limited to fifteen minutes.

Little by little over time, these Sunday services disappeared or yielded to Jewish Sabbath liturgies and "sermons" in many synagogues. Max Heller "confessed" in 1922 that Sunday services at New Orleans's Temple Sinai were "a failure," and Edgar Magnin at Los Angeles's Wilshire Boulevard Temple did the same. But at many Reform synagogues with celebrated preachers such as Rabbi Abba Hillel Silver of Wheeling, West Virginia, and, later, Cleveland, Ohio, the lengthy Sunday lecture remained an important part of the intellectual life for Jews and Christians in the community.

By the end of the period of mass migration to America, a new branch, Conservative Judaism, had emerged and was growing rapidly. Orthodoxy was gearing up to challenge Conservatism for the allegiance of the children and grandchildren of the east European immigrants, and Reform Judaism was steadily moving away from its radical phase to prepare to receive those same immigrant descendants who found Conservative Judaism still too traditional. The years following World War I would further solidify the distinctions among these branches of Judaism as they each worked to find their place in America.

4

Conservative and Orthodox Judaism Define Themselves

Between the Wars

The synagogue shall remain conservative (Jewish orthodox).
—Articles of Agreement, St. Louis' Brith Shalom, 1908

Conservative Reform High Holy Day Services at the Society for Jewish Culture with Rabbi Jacob Sonderling.
—*Los Angeles Times*, 1935

Are we an Orthodox or Conservative congregation?
—Sermon title, Temple Beth Israel, Phoenix, Arizona,
May 1935

THE MOST STRIKING fact about American synagogues between the World Wars, not only with hindsight but also evident at the time, is the confusion between Conservative and Orthodox, as these two branches of American Judaism sought to define themselves internally and in contrast to each other. By the subsequent period—the postwar America of the 1950s—this confusion was generally sorted out, but it took decades, and the result was never totally predictable. Who could have foreseen that three synagogues of Roxbury and Dorchester, Massachusetts, Adath Jeshurun, Beth El, and Beth Hamidrash Hagadol, described as "modern Orthodox" immediately after World War I, would become members of the mostly Conservative United Synagogue of America within ten years but then, after the early 1930s, would never again be served by a Conservative rabbi? In 1942, Rabbi Ferdinand Isserman of St. Louis's Temple Israel wrote that Rabbi Abraham E. Halpern, also of St. Louis, "has been a staunch, courageous, and out-spoken champion of Orthodox Judaism." But Rabbi Halpern belonged to the association of Conservative rabbis, and the synagogue he served, B'nai Amoonah, with Sabbath eve services at 8 P.M., belonged to the umbrella organization of Conservative synagogues!

This phenomenon should not come as a surprise when we consider the early years of Conservative Judaism during and in the immediate years after World War I. Solomon Schechter, the head of the Conservative Jewish Theological Seminary, and Cyrus Adler, the president of the United Synagogue of America, soon to be the umbrella organization of Conservative synagogues, did not think of creating a "Conservative" movement any more than Isaac Mayer Wise intended for his Cleveland Conference of Rabbis and Laymen (1855) to serve only Reform synagogues. Wise spoke repeatedly of "Israelitish congregations" and sought a union of "American Israel"—all American synagogues. Similarly, Schechter and Adler spoke repeatedly of "organizing the Orthodox-Conservative forces of *American Israel*," and by this they meant every synagogue that did not call itself Reform—or, as Schechter once put it, much less elegantly, every synagogue that has not "accepted the Union prayer-book nor performed their religious devotions with uncovered heads."

With this description Schechter was referring to the 165 congregations in America (out of 1,800 total) that he and Adler had tabulated and labeled as "Reform" before the 1913 meeting that led to the founding of the United Synagogue. This left, by their count, 1,635 congregations ripe for organizing (see the appendix for a note on the challenges of counting synagogues). Schechter sought to create what he called a "union for promoting traditional Judaism" to identify such synagogues. So, just as the later Reform Union of American Hebrew Congregations, in its early years, included a group of synagogues that were widely diverse in their ritual practices, Schechter welcomed the inability to precisely delineate what constituted a Conservative synagogue. Thus, B'nai Amoonah could have much to "appeal to the younger and modern element of Orthodox Jewish folk," affirm "respect, dignity and decorum, grace and charm in Orthodox Jewish life," and, as did many Orthodox synagogues, sell honors in the middle of services on the High Holy Days, separate men and women during prayers, refuse to count women in making a quorum for worship, and refuse to permit women to read from the Torah, while joining the (mostly) Conservative United Synagogue and steadily making more and more of the sanctuary available to men and women seated together. Denver's "leading Orthodox synagogue" also joined the United Synagogue at its inception. And Rabbi Elias Solomon, ordained at the Jewish Theological Seminary in 1904 and the rabbi at staunchly Orthodox Kehilath Jeshurun in New York City (1917–1923), was elected president of the United Synagogue in 1919, and he steadily developed enduring roots in the emerging Conservative movement.

Adler continually spoke of "minimizing the differences between Conservative and Orthodox congregations," abetting the constant confusion. He and Schechter demanded decorum (cease, they ordered, the "constant chattering during the prayers") and the elimination of Yiddish sermons, instituting a late-Friday-evening service ("Hebrew and English") and instituted other practices that would come to constitute the essence of Conservative Judaism in America, but they rejected the word "Conservative." Most observers remained confused as they tried to sort out the Conservative movement in its first decade or two (the United Synagogue of America, the umbrella organization of Conservative Judaism, was established in 1913). If you had attended the Orthodox "Blue Hill Avenue Shul" (aka Adath Jeshurun) in 1914 for the late-Friday-evening service, you would have observed men and women praying together as in many Conservative synagogues, but if you had come into the sanctuary the next morning, you would have noticed a complete separation of the sexes, as in many Orthodox synagogues. The (mostly) Conservative Beth El of Phoenix, Arizona, did much the same throughout the 1930s and 1940; its bulletin, the *Echo*, listed "Orthodox Religious Services Daily [e.g., December] at 8 and 5 and on Saturday at 9 and 4:45" and "Conservative Worship Services Every Friday at 8:15pm." On the High Holy Days, Orthodox and Conservative services ran concurrently, differentiated (primarily) by the length of the liturgy, the seating arrangements, and the inclusion in the Orthodox service of a Yiddish sermon. Sometimes the same rabbi preached on Yom Kippur in English at 11 A.M. at one service and in Yiddish at 11:30 at the other. Brith Sholom of St. Louis crafted Articles of Agreement at the time of its incorporation in 1908 and in them noted that the synagogue shall "remain Conservative (Jewish Orthodox)"! Indeed, as the United Synagogue entered its 15th year of existence in 1927, its 227 member congregations could scarcely be held together by anything more than a term such as "traditional"—that is, not Reform. Near the end of World War II, Kehillath Israel of Brookline, Massachusetts, could claim that it was viewed concomitantly as a "Progressive Orthodox and right wing Conservative" congregation by many, highlighting again the thin line between what we might call, at the time, modern Orthodox and traditional Conservative synagogues.

A good example of confusion between an Orthodox and Conservative identity is Adath Israel of Cincinnati in 1930, the "Avondale Synagogue." Alternately identifying itself, in the minutes of the board of trustees, as Conservative and Orthodox (its application of incorporation committed the congregation "to worship according to the Orthodox forms adopted by the Polish Jews"), it moved, bit by bit, but not inevitably, toward Conservative Judaism. But, along the way, one could never be sure of its identity. It belonged to the Conservative movement in 1930, but men sat separately from women without complaint; indeed, every seat in the men's section (rows 1–10, $250 each; rows 11–21, $150; the rest, $100) had been sold—yet Sabbath-eve services were exclusively late, as in Reform (but not most Orthodox) congregations, with the full Conservative liturgy (not a brief addition to an earlier—sundown—service) and a lecture. And, most confusing of all, in an appreciation of Louis Feinberg, who served the synagogue for three decades after his arrival in 1918, Rabbi Emanuel Gamoran noted that Rabbi Feinberg, "a graduate of the Jewish Theological Seminary, was, nevertheless, Orthodox."

It was not always easier to make sense of identity or affiliation by asking about the background of the rabbi, for the "identity" of rabbis at mainstream Conservative synagogues affiliated with the larger movement was frequently complex. Irving Lehrman came to Montclair, New Jersey's Shomrei Emunah in 1936. The son of Abraham Lehrman, rabbi of one of the largest Orthodox synagogues in New York City, he attended Manhattan public schools and City College of New York, had early Hebrew training at the Orthodox rabbinical school of Yeshiva University (Rabbi Isaac Elhanan Theological Seminary), and was ordained at the (mostly) Reform Jewish Institute of Religion by a Reform rabbi, Stephen S. Wise. Dozens of rabbis ordained at the Jewish Theological Seminary went directly to Orthodox congregations after ordination. In most cases, such rabbis eventually moved the synagogue from orthodoxy to the United Synagogue of America, the (eventual) Conservative umbrella organization. And, in the process—just as we saw in traditional synagogues in the nineteenth century that "reformed" continuously and often became officially Reform Jewish congregations—these Orthodox congregations, step by step, often "reformed" on their way to Conservative Judaism. At least one rabbi, Israel Goldstein of New York's B'nai Jeshurun, reflecting on the struggle in the 1920s to move from orthodoxy to conservatism, viewed the transition as so successful that he claimed, in an extraordinary anachronism, in 1930, that his was "the only Congregation in which the Conservative Service, as distinguished both from the Orthodox and Reform, was already a tradition of nearly half a century."

All over the country, rabbinic biographies and institutional attachments confused rather than explained. Adas Israel of the District of Columbia hired a graduate of the Jewish Theological Seminary in 1898 and immediately joined the Union of Orthodox Jewish Congregations of America. Rabbi Jacob R. Mazur came to St. Louis's Orthodox Brith Sholom in 1930 and combined his Orthodox observance with civic involvement and social activism (rare for Orthodox rabbis, who rarely stretched the boundaries of social action or civic involvement beyond the Jewish community) for three decades. He initiated mixed seating, and, eventually, in 1959, the congregation joined the United Synagogue. B'nai Amoonah was the first Orthodox synagogue in St. Louis to join the United Synagogue (1917); one of its earliest reforms was the mixing of the sexes in the balcony, though not on the main level below, for a few years before it joined the Conservative movement.

Building New Synagogues

Notwithstanding confusion of identity outside of Reform, the 1920s was a period called at the time "synagogue-building boom-days." All over the country, cathedral-like synagogues and temples (these terms remain largely interchangeable) were built, often combining the Byzantine-Romanesque and the Alhambra-Moorish styles in new ways. The Byzantine-Moorish-Romanesque style dominated the largest synagogues from west to east. This style did not emerge for the first time during and after World War I; there were plenty of synagogues in the nineteenth century designed in this manner, usually either in imitation of churches in the same city (as Beth Elohim's 1840 Colonial Revival synagogue in Charleston copied a nearby Episcopal church) or of European synagogues. As early as 1858, St. Louis's

Laying of cornerstone of Sephardic Temple Etz Ahayem, Montgomery, Alabama, May 19, 1927. PC 3078. Courtesy of the American Jewish Archives, Cincinnati, Ohio.

Orthodox B'nai El, which possessed a rare mikveh and an even rarer organ, erected an octagonal building topped by a domed cupola and squared crenellated battlements. Not to be outdone, the neighboring Orthodox synagogue United Hebrew, one year later, put up a two-story Romanesque structure with a reading table in the middle and a preaching pulpit against the wall of the sanctuary.

Such buildings, which looked like mosques, were rare in the 1850s but were found everywhere for decades following 1858. The synagogue constructed in 1866 for Philadelphia's Rodeph Shalom was one of the finest examples of Moorish (and Romanesque) Revival architecture in America, and in that same year Cincinnati's B'nai Yeshurun (the "Plum Street Temple") dedicated what its rabbi, Isaac Mayer Wise, called an "Alhambra temple" with thirteen domes and plenty of Byzantine-Romanesque features. In 1868, Temple Emanu-El in New York City dedicated a Moorish Revival building; New

York's Ahavath Chesed (Central Synagogue), dedicated in 1872, was Moorish (and Gothic) in style, as was Kansas City's B'nai Jehudah ("the Oak Street Temple"), with twin towers, built in 1885. In 1887, Congregation Adas Jeshurun (the "Eldridge Street Shul"), also in Manhattan, completed a Moorish Revival building (horseshoe arches, keyhole-shape doorways, window openings) with Gothic

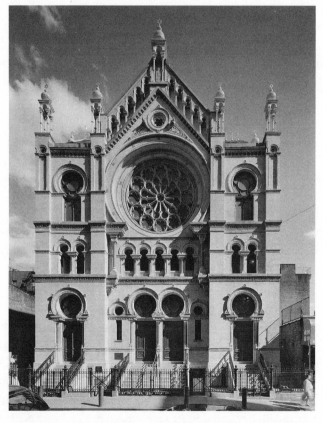

Moorish-style exterior of Congregation Adas Jeshurun (the "Eldridge Street Shul"), on the Lower East Side of Manhattan, New York. Photograph by Kate Milford. Photo courtesy of Museum at Eldridge Street.

(twin towers) and Romanesque (masonry) elements, as well. In 1891, B'nai Israel in Salt Lake City dedicated a Moorish-style building with a dome that was eighty-eight feet tall (frequently found in mosques), and, in 1899, Temple Emanuel in Denver dedicated a modified, two-story Moorish building, with a sanctuary that could seat 1,000 and two minarets, each 150 feet tall and capped by a copper dome.

But no decade of the nineteenth century matched the Byzantine Revival movement of the 1920s. There was a Classical Revival movement, as well, which was highlighted by the eight-column Ionic portico at Detroit's Beth El and the four-column Greco-Roman portico at the synagogue of Ahavath Zion in Newark, New Jersey (1922); the six-column, pedimented portico of Temple Emanu-El of Greensboro, North Carolina (1925); and the classical Temple Emanu-El of Providence (1927). But Byzantine was the key word in almost every architect's description of his 1920s synagogues. In Cleveland, The Temple (Tifereth Israel), a domed synagogue "derived from Byzantine models," was dedicated in 1924. New York City's B'nai Jeshurun "beautified" the sanctuary in 1924–1925 with an "architectural conception" that was Byzantine.

The K.A.M. (Isaiah Israel) Congregation in Chicago completed a domed synagogue, with a minaret-like tower, in 1924, inspired by the sixth-century churches of San Vitale in Ravenna and Hagia Sofia in Istanbul, the latter a masterpiece of Byzantine architecture. In 1926, Emanu-El of San Francisco dedicated a synagogue with Byzantine columns of antique marble and a 150-foot-tall high dome, also inspired by Hagia Sophia. The same churches served as inspiration for Ohabei Shalom in Brookline, Massachusetts, Buffalo's Beth Zion Temple, and St. Louis's United Hebrew Congregation (1928), all built at the heart of the Byzantine Revival craze. Kehillath Israel, also in Brookline, referred to its 1925 synagogue building as "Byzantine in character." The next building constructed for Rodeph Shalom, on North Broad Street in Philadelphia, a Byzantine-Moorish style synagogue remarkably like the Great Synagogue in Florence,

Exterior of Wilshire Boulevard Temple, Los Angeles, California. Courtesy of Wilshire Boulevard Temple. Photograph by Laszlo Regos.

was completed in 1928. In Los Angeles, Wilshire Boulevard Temple, with its monumental and ornate domed Romanesque style, including a three-arch portal on the façade, was completed in 1929, as was New York City's Emanu-El, which followed a basilica plan (based on the Ravenna model), with two domes and Byzantine-Romanesque motifs (as well as Gothic flying buttresses). As with synagogues designed by Albert Kahn in Detroit at the same time, Charles Butler, one of the architects of Emanu-El, noted the influence of the "basilica type common in Italy," the domes "reminiscent of Byzantine churches of the Near East," and "an adaptation of very early Romanesque in Syria, the East, Sicily and [especially] southern Italy," where it was "influenced by the Eastern and Arab invasions." This Byzantine Revival style, usually with both Moorish-inspired and Romanesque elements, was everywhere in the 1920s and became known as "the Jewish style of architecture"!

Neighborhood buildings served repeatedly as models for synagogues in the 1920s; the architectural critic Lewis Mumford criticized Detroit's Temple Beth El by noting that it "might as well be the Public Library or the County Courthouse." But the neighborhood church most influenced numerous synagogue architects in the 1920s. In almost every city, if not neighborhood, where a synagogue was built, one finds churches in the same, or similar, style. Orthodox Ahavath Achim's Classical Revival synagogue (1921), the "Big Shul," was modeled on the nearby First Church of Christ, Scientist. One historian noted that only the Star of David on its roof distinguished the cathedral-like Durham Hebrew Congregation's building of 1921, with Romanesque arches, a Classical pediment, and stained-glass windows, from several churches built at the same time. The other dominant influence on synagogue architects, as they noted in their public statements, was European synagogues, which were well known in the United States. Notwithstanding the fact that, in many places, especially in central Europe, synagogues were permitted only if they did not resemble synagogues (!) or if they were hidden behind or inside a building or off a main street, they were widely studied by American architects who designed synagogues. Of course, it was not hard to find a European synagogue with a mishmash ("Eclectic") of styles— Baroque domes coupled with Moorish cupolas, turrets, and crenellations; Romanesque portals, arches, and windows; and Gothic ribs —and these, especially, were the models for synagogue design.

Conservative Judaism

Many, if not most, synagogues that joined the United Synagogue of America in the 1920s had previously identified with orthodoxy. While sometimes a group of Jews, as in Rochester in 1915, sought to organize "a new Conservative congregation along modern lines," most often an Orthodox synagogue adopted one "reform" after another and eventually identified itself as "Conservative" in its bulletin and joined the Conservative movement. This was, of course, a repetition of a nineteenth-century phenomenon in which most congregations that declared themselves Reform had moved, little by little, away from orthodoxy. In the twentieth century, the reforms were often the same—just more moderate, less radical. They included the introduction of family pews (that is, mixed seating) rather than the practice of having a women's section separate from the men; the use of prayers in English, not just Hebrew; services led by the rabbi rather than a prayer leader or the cantor; the delivering of sermons in English rather than Yiddish; and the introduction of late-Friday-evening services. Rabbi Israel H. Levinthal, a rabbi with an undergraduate degree from an American university, even edited a song book, *Zemirot Vetishbahot LeLeil Shabbat: Songs and Praise for Sabbath Eve*, in 1920, that contained music to accompany the liturgy and his popular sermons at the Brooklyn Jewish Center's "Friday Evening Service," and soon the synagogue newsletter announced "The New Modern Conservative Congregation, with a Conservative Service." When Philadelphia's Orthodox B'nai Jeshurun, with women behind a curtain in the balcony (1916), erected open, elevated platforms for women on each side of the central seating provided for men (1924), it left the national Orthodox union and joined the national Conservative organization. Or, as the Orthodox Beth Israel in Phoenix, Arizona, asserted in 1930, "we want a Conservative rabbi and strictly Conservative rituals." Rabbi Israel Goldstein of B'nai Jeshurun in New York City, writing about the 1920s at the end of the decade, described the adoption of Conservative ritual (mixed seating, organ, and a late-Friday-evening service—usually with uniform prayer books, responsive readings in English, and a discourse on contemporary topics—replacing the sundown worship) as the addition of "dignity and decorum and beauty" to the services.

The transition was not always a smooth one, especially when a significant part of the congregation had a background of orthodoxy and little experience with reforming and another significant portion of the membership had already been worshiping in an environment of some reforms. There are examples everywhere. One is Philadelphia after World War I, where a group from Beth Israel Congregation, where men and women worshiped together while an organ played, joined a group from Ohel Jacob Congregation, where men and women were rigorously separated and no instrumental music accompanied the worship, to create Beth Sholom, an "emerging Conservative" congregation. Rabbi Mortimer J. Cohen would later describe the 1920s as "Beth Sholom Battles: The Battle of the Location; the Battle of the Spittoons; the Battle of the Mixed Seating; the Battle of the Mixed Choir and Organ; the Battle of Language of the Service (all Hebrew or mixed Hebrew and English)."

As congregations that we would identify, unofficially, as Orthodox when they originated in the nineteenth century reformed so much that they became, officially, Conservative in the twentieth century, reformers frequently confronted traditionalists—opponents of reforming—with synagogue constitutions that contained ambivalent language about definitions of ritual. In a large number of synagogues, constitutions had been approved that prohibited, usually explicitly, the type of ritual changes that moved a congregation from Orthodox to Conservative. Generic constitutions—"this synagogue will adhere to the fundamental principles of Judaism" or even the wording of New Haven's B'nai Jacob's 1882 constitution, which stated that "this congregation shall worship according to the Polish-Jewish ritual"—could be challenged, as words such as "fundamental" proved too vague. But not at all ambivalent was Woonsocket, Rhode Island's constitution ("The rituals of this Congregation shall be those of traditional Judaism in the Conservative manner") or the constitution of Washington, D.C.'s Adas Israel, an Orthodox congregation for many decades, which stated unequivocally that "no alteration or amendment, or modification shall ever at any time be made to those articles of the constitution pertaining to the mode of worship." Consider too the words of the 1907 minutes of Chicago's Rodfei Zedek: "the *shul* is to remain as always—men and women [sit] together"; in addition, any services held in the basement would be "strict Orthodox —segregation."

Sometimes such language was ignored, by both those who sought change and those who sought to maintain the status quo. As a case in point, Rodfei Zedek set aside the center section of sanctuary pews for those families that wished to sit together. Men who wished to sit alone sat alongside one wall; women who wished to do the same sat in pews against the other wall or in the balcony. Sometimes traditionalists pointed out the constitutional clause and the reformers ignored it; occasionally, after a bitter dispute, the opponents of change went to civil court to prevent the synagogue from becoming Conservative. Members of B'nai Jeshurun of Manhattan had gone to court in 1875 over the decision to alter the separate seating of women and men by creating mixed seating in pews. A half-century later, Rabbi Solomon Goldman came to the Cleveland Jewish Center (1922) and began to change it from Orthodox to Conservative by similarly permitting men and women to sit together and by installing late-Friday-evening services (Rabbi Goldman, a stickler for decorum, handed a card to each person as he or she entered the synagogue with instructions about decorous behavior during worship). In 1927, a dozen men from the "largest Orthodox synagogue in Cleveland" sued the congregation in civil court. They accused it, quite correctly, of moving to conservatism. The court sided with the rabbi and against the plaintiffs.

When an Orthodox rabbi, Harry H. Epstein, came to Ahavath Achim in Atlanta in 1928, decorum became a high priority, and he would eventually move the synagogue into the Conservative movement. He was told that his predecessor, Rabbi Abraham P. Hermes, often led Sabbath services that lasted from early morning to after 2 P.M., so Rabbi Epstein set noon as the time for services to conclude.

The response was enthusiastic, unlike the outcry when he ordered the spittoons removed from the sanctuary. Much less enthusiastic were some of the members of Seattle's Herzl Congregation in 1930 when, for the first time in more than two decades, women and men sat together during the High Holy Day services. Immediately after the holy days, Rabbi Baruch Shapiro resigned, and he and his followers formed the strictly Orthodox Machzikay HaDath (meaning "holding firm to the faith"!), where Rabbi Shapiro would remain for nearly forty years.

Traditionalists and reformers at Adas Israel of Washington, D.C., struggled for years as reform-minded congregants sought to move worship from Orthodox to Conservative. There was bitter opposition among traditionalists to Rabbi Louis Judah Schwefel's attempt, in 1924, to make the services more decorous by reducing the number of times people stood during worship, to his annual attempt to eliminate the selling of honors during High Holy Day services, and to the gradual movement of wives from the balcony to seats adjacent to their husbands on the main floor. Forty-eight members signed a petition in 1927 objecting "to this breach in the Orthodox traditions of our religion." And when Cantor Louis Novick, after twenty-five years of service to the congregation, was told by reforming lay leaders to lead the services while facing the congregation, as in Reform congregations (rather than with his back to the worshipers as he faced the ark), he resigned. The congregation took its decorous instructions for proper behavior so seriously that the rules were eventually affixed to the inside front cover of the standard prayer book in use.

"Reforming" the service in Conservative synagogues tended to continue long after a congregation joined the Conservative movement. In the early 1960s, Rabbi Abraham Karp, at Rochester's Beth El, modified the Torah readings on specific occasions by reducing "long passages," abridging the daily morning service, and moving "repetitious narrations in the Torah" from the Sabbath to weekdays.

So, instead of reading Exodus 25–27 on the Sabbath on which it was scheduled, chapters 25 and part of 26 were read on Saturday morning, the rest of 26 on Saturday afternoon, part of 27 on Monday, and the rest of Exodus 27 on Thursday. The rationale was said to be "meaningfulness and interest." As we saw earlier, numerous other congregations read only a third of the standard Torah portion, choosing instead to complete the full Torah in a three-year rather than a one-year cycle, and all over the country Conservative congregations made books with the Torah portion available in Hebrew and English to worshipers who were lacking proper decorum if they could not understand the Torah reading in Hebrew.

While the 1920s represented a decade of expansion for the Conservative movement, the Depression of the 1930s caused a shrinkage everywhere. The finance committee chairman at Cincinnati's Adath Israel reported, at the end of 1930, that, "during the past year, owing to the general business depression, there was a decided loss in membership and a decrease in membership dues"; five years later, he reported that the "economic depression has lasted for over five years and hurt us in every way." In the early years of the Depression, Temple Sinai in Los Angeles reduced dues from $5 to $3.50 a month, while, at the Brooklyn Jewish Center Hebrew school, tuition and single memberships were cut in half, gymnasium membership was made free, and the raffle for the 1933 Chevy had to be canceled. At Montclair, New Jersey's Shomrei Emunah, the treasurer, as late as 1936, was trying to get congregants who had owed dues since 1930 to pay "back amounts." Temple Beth Israel of Phoenix, Arizona— Conservative until it hired a Reform rabbi in 1935—noted as early as 1930 that "pledges and funds were inadequate to cover the necessary expenditures" and thus it was necessary to borrow from the "cemetery fund." The following spring, leaders went house to house to beg members for funds "to tide the Congregation over until September 1st," and in 1932 the president declared that "we are a bankrupt institution and our temple building has been sold." Not even brotherhood "stag [without wives] parties" (1933) could put the synagogue in the black. At the Society for the Advancement of Judaism in Manhattan, the board reported a $60,000 deficit in 1931 and noted that staff members were owed thousands of dollars in back wages. Rochester's Beth El lacked sufficient funds in 1930 to pay the mortgage, after numerous congregants resigned because of "financial reverses." Banks threatened to foreclose on Seattle's Herzl Congregation in 1930 and again (on the renamed Herzl Conservative Congregation) in 1936. In Washington, D.C., at Adas Israel, the leaders reduced the salaries of synagogue employees by 10 percent in 1932–1933 and another 10 percent the following year, while relying more and more on borrowing. At the Brooklyn Jewish Center, in 1931, where the president noted the "depressing conditions now prevailing in business" and the "often threatened danger of having our doors closed for lack of financial support," he announced free tuition for the religious school and said that new members could join and make no payments for one year; annual dues were cut in half the following year for families and by 25 percent for singles.

Rabbis everywhere took salary reductions. Rabbi Louis Feinberg of Cincinnati's Adath Israel took a cut from $6,500 to $5,200 in 1930 and did not return to the earlier level until 1944; Rabbi Israel Goldfarb of Brooklyn's Kane Street Synagogue continued to reject, as late as 1940, $1,100 he was owed in salary, "to lighten the burden of debt that seems to lie heavily upon the shoulders of the congregation since the beginning of the economic depression." A Rabbi Hurwitz, at Phoenix's Beth Israel, sought a three-month advance in the summer of 1931 for his wedding and honeymoon, but the president told him this was "impossible, as the congregation has no money." By the following summer, the synagogue owed him two and a half months' salary, and neither High Holy Day tickets nor "alee-asus" (auctioning honors during the Torah service) raised these funds. Rabbi Rudolph Farber, at Temple Sinai in Los Angeles, signed a contract in 1934 for $250 a month, $100 per month less than he had earned five years earlier, and Abraham E. Halpern of B'nai Amoonah in St. Louis was paid $9,000 in 1928–1929 and, because of the economy, saw his salary decline every year until 1935–1936, when it plateaued at $6,150. Likewise, at B'nai Amoonah, the salary of the hazan, in the same period, declined from $4,200 to $2,700, as dues receipts dropped by 53 percent. Over and over, synagogue minutes reveal substantial declines in income from selling High Holy Day seats to nonmembers, significant declines in dues, and suspensions of members continually for nonpayment of dues.

Yet, not all synagogue activities were curtailed during the Depression. Conservative synagogues in the 1920s and 1930s introduced serious programs of Hebrew-language education on Saturday or Sunday mornings, as well as on weekday afternoons. Usually called *Talmud Torah*, these classes revolved primarily around the prayer book and, secondarily, the text of the Torah. Often students faced public examinations once or twice during the academic year (continuing a widespread practice in Reform congregations in the late nineteenth century) and, after completing the program, participated in a graduation ceremony. The *Talmud Torah* at the Kane Street Synagogue in 1933 had thirty-three pupils and two teachers who met one hour each day, four days a week, to study liturgy and the Torah.

Confirmation ceremonies were major events at Conservative synagogues in the interwar years. Girls made up the majority of confirmands—indeed, at Congregation Oheb Shalom in South Orange, New Jersey, every confirmation from 1926 through 1954 was exclusively female—as girls rarely had bat mitzvah ceremonies until the 1940s (they remained infrequent into the 1960s) and the boys either dropped out of religious school after their bar mitzvah or went into a separate *Talmud Torah* program. Cantatas—vocal compositions with instrumental accompaniment—were popular, especially those by Rabbi Ira Eisenstein and his wife, Judith, or by Morrison D. Bial and A. W. Binder. The confirmation ceremony, imbedded in the liturgy and Torah reading for Shavuoth, consisted of Judaica talks by the confirmands as well as numerous musical selections. Dinner dances were regular features, as well.

When the occasional bat mitzvah did take place, the young woman was not treated as were the young men in the congregation when they turned thirteen. Sisterhoods generally presented her with Sabbath candle holders, in contrast to the *kiddush* (wine) cup they gave to boys. Her ceremony was on Friday night, not Saturday morning, so there was no Torah service. She would open a Bible and chant from the *haftarah* a part of what the young man would chant the next morning, thus preparing only part of what he would do and inserting it into the service as what one rabbi in Philadelphia called a "bonus." It was not until the late 1960s here and there and then overwhelmingly in the 1970s and 1980s that the bat mitzvah of a young woman was identical to the bar mitzvah of a young man in most Conservative synagogues.

Unlike Reform congregations in these years, and notwithstanding the position of some Conservative rabbis such as Israel H. Levinthal of the Brooklyn Jewish Center ("Levinthal," his biographer noted, "kept Zionism out of the synagogue and away from the pulpit"), the "centrality of Zion," a phrase featured in a Boston synagogue's bulletins, curriculum, and sermons throughout 1926–1927, was a consistent theme in the Conservative movement. A Philadelphia Conservative rabbi titled a sermon for Rosh Hashanah in 1937 "The Most Powerful Bond is the Love of *eretz yisrael*, the Land of Palestine," and he urged his listeners to make Zionist activity a measurable part of their lives. He, like so many of his colleagues, drew widely on non-Jewish authors (Samuel Coleridge and Jack London in that sermon), as well as on Jewish sources (Heinrich Heine and Yiddish poetry). Lectures on Zionism as well as meetings of Judean boys (high school), Hadassah buds (junior high girls), Hadassah girls (high school), and Hadassah women filled synagogue calendars. And the rabbinic rhetoric, in preserved sermons everywhere, was lofty, if not elegant. Solomon Metz, during the High Holy Days of 1931, told his listeners

The Sisterhood of Rockdale Temple, Cincinnati, Ohio, 1920. Union for Reform Judaism Records (MS-72), UAHC Photo #10. Courtesy of the American Jewish Archives, Cincinnati, Ohio.

at Washington, D.C.'s Adas Israel, that "I watched the labyrinthine, hydra-headed metropolis, prostrate in the heavy sultriness of a midsummer night, and abutting this fairy-land of fanfare, there stretched the slums of the city, the empire of squalor and poverty, where undernourished, forgotten men muttered their muffled outcries of impotent rage, and envy hissed its futile protestations."

Conservative synagogues between the two world wars were busy day and night, all week. In addition to the Zionist activity, religious school on the weekend, and Hebrew school (for girls and boys) during the weekday afternoons, there were young folks league (dinners, dances, theater parties, speakers), Girl Scouts and Boy Scouts, AZA (Aleph Zadik Aleph) young men of the B'nai B'rith (before

Article on Purim Ball, *Jewish Western Bulletin*, February 26, 1937.
Courtesy of the *Vancouver Jewish Independent*.

Conservative young groups emerged), sisterhood (part of the national Women's League of the United Synagogue of America) and brotherhood activities, duplicate bridge clubs, drama clubs, Queen Esther Purim balls, fund-raisers for the American Red Cross, blood drives, and American holiday celebrations (i.e., Thanksgiving Day dinner dance). At night there were lectures, concerts, forums, and debates on Jewish and non-Jewish themes and, of course, endless synagogue committee meetings. About the only thing missing were bodies for Sabbath services, as in Reform congregations of this period. A survey of twenty-seven Boston synagogues in 1926 (mostly Reform and Conservative) noted that only 8 to 12 percent of the Jewish population above age thirteen attended the synagogue on an average Sabbath. It was no different in Cleveland, where approximately 10 percent of the total Jewish population attended a synagogue on any given Sabbath. Nearly everywhere, especially in major cities with significant Jewish populations, Jews attended worship services in very small numbers.

Orthodox Judaism

At the beginning of the interwar period, the vast majority of rabbis serving Orthodox synagogues had been born and educated in eastern Europe, spoke English as their second language (and many spoke not very much at all), and had been little influenced by either America or general culture. By the 1930s, however, a generation of Americanized Orthodox rabbis, educated at the Rabbi Isaac Elhanan Theological Seminary (RIETS) of Yeshiva University (whose origins go back to the Lower East Side of New York in 1896–1897), had begun to lead congregations and to compete for the affiliation of those Jews, largely children of immigrants, who sought to join an institution more "traditional" than a Reform synagogue. Henry Raphael Gold, the first Americanized rabbi at Baron Hirsch Congregation, a large Orthodox synagogue in Memphis, arrived even earlier than the 1930s, taking over the post in 1916. He was an immigrant who had arrived in the United States about 1908, at the age of fifteen, and who had attended Columbia University, Harvard College, and the (mostly) Conservative Jewish Theological Seminary (ordination at the JTS, as we have seen, was hardly unusual for rabbis serving Orthodox congregations before a generation of American-educated rabbis from

RIETS became available). He preached in English and in Yiddish and seemed at home in both Talmud and European literature. But he was very unusual outside New York in the years before 1920.

Sisterhoods, with dinner dances, bridge games, rummage sales, and afternoon teas, as well as Hebrew ladies aid societies, with fund-raising projects for their synagogue and community, emerged in Americanizing Orthodox congregations across the country in the 1920s, and, since most synagogues in this period could not afford caterers, these women's organizations supplied endless lunches and dinners for congregational events. By the 1930s, Orthodox rabbis conducted their confirmation, Sunday school, and adult education classes—most often, on the Talmud—in English, and they taught texts (e.g., Talmud) in English; special services took place on American holidays, such as Thanksgiving, Mother's Day, and President Washington's birthday, with non-Jewish guest speakers or the synagogue rabbi lecturing on general themes such as "The Torah and Flag Day," "How to Keep Religion and the State Separate," "Religion and the Election Campaign of 1932," "A Sermon for Thanksgiving," and "President Washington's Letter to the Jewish Community." A few decades earlier, Sabato Morais, an Italian-born immigrant preacher at traditional Mikveh Israel in Philadelphia for the entire second half of the century, had recast the American holiday Thanksgiving in terms of Jewish universalism, thanking God for providing America as an asylum from persecution. In Atlanta, Boston, Chicago, Cleveland, Columbus (Ohio), Los Angeles, and New York City, special services were held in Orthodox synagogues on Armistice Day, and there were memorial services on the deaths of President Warren G. Harding (1923) and former president Woodrow Wilson (1924). Cub Pack, Boy Scout, Brownie, and Girl Scout groups were organized at Orthodox synagogues by the 1930s; and there were even enough younger members attending colleges by that decade for many congregations to have an annual collegiate Sabbath, a special welcome that always took place during what is called in synagogue bulletins the "mid-winter vacation" for these students.

At Ohab Zedek in Yonkers, New York, Rabbi Philip Rosenberg, who was "militantly Orthodox," sported a clerical collar over a black bib with a white stripe, the mark of a European Jewish and non-Jewish clergyman. His son, Alexander, the unofficial "chief rabbi" of Yonkers's Orthodox community, served as the chaplain of the fire department. Simon Machtey, the *shochet* and *mohel*, who circumcised virtually every Jewish boy born in the town, cut a handsome figure with his Prince Albert coat, high silk hat, and silver cane. The members of the four Yonkers Orthodox synagogues plunked down their dues at weekly or biweekly meetings, and, afterward, the men played pinochle and poker.

And the content of American-educated Orthodox rabbis' English-language sermons was dramatically different from that of the (mostly) Yiddish-language sermons of an earlier generation. This was particularly true between the World Wars in New York City, where Leo Jung on the West Side and Joseph Lookstein on the East Side—self-proclaimed "modern Orthodox" rabbis—drew upon the works of Carlyle, Dickens, Freud, Goethe, Ibsen, William James, Macaulay, Shaw, Tennyson, and Whitman, as well as on the vast body of rabbinic literature, to craft sermons much like those of American-born Reform and Conservative colleagues. Keeping in mind the warning of a contemporary Conservative rabbi, Israel Herbert Levinthal, that his printed sermons were often delivered "extemporaneously" and written "out a long time after their delivery," the historian looks for typescript sermons or sermons reprinted in synagogue bulletins and the Jewish press immediately after delivery. They are abundant, and, by the 1930s, Orthodox rabbis in various places turned a Latin phrase, digested a German book on philosophy or literature, or followed the scientific arguments of the leading writers of their time as easily as they could quote from the Talmud.

These Orthodox rabbis rarely made any comments on the events unfolding on the American scene in the 1920s or early 1930s. They generally ignored race, immigration, pacifism, isolationism, the League of Nations, lynching, Sacco and Vanzetti, civil liberties, the Klan, racial segregation, industrial (textile, railroad) strikes, Einstein's theory of relativity, modern technology, modern war, Prohibition, economic warfare, Bolshevism, political events in Europe, and the Depression. Only with the rise of the Nazis and the 1939 White Paper that drastically curtailed Jewish immigration to Palestine did European events become part of their sermons. Instead, they talked about Torah (which, all Orthodox rabbis agreed, God had revealed verbally to Moses at Mt. Sinai), commandments ("word of God," they all agreed), ceremonies, customs, observances, rituals, holidays, festivals, and themes associated with the calendrical events in the Jewish/Judaic year The scientific and philosophical literature of their day was useful primarily to support the conclusions of Judaic values and beliefs.

In one area especially, Judaic beliefs and contemporary events intersected—Zionism. Nearly every Orthodox rabbi of the interwar years spoke frequently and (to the extent emotion may be read into or out of a text) passionately about Palestine. Unlike non-Orthodox rabbis, they did not speak about Zion as an idealistic endeavor or as a colonization venture or as a philanthropic enterprise or a national revival; they saw it as a "reassertion of Jewish fidelity to Judaism," a renewed effort to fulfill God's promise, what Leo Jung called "the mitzvah of *yishuv eretz yisrael*"; as a Bronx rabbi, Noah Garfinkel, put it, "the Balfour Declaration [1917] was the call of the Messiah." Orthodox rabbis took literally—as did so many post-1967 Jewish settlers in the Israeli Territories—God's promise of Zion as an inheritance to Abraham and his descendants in the Torah and the demand upon Jews in Palestine to live a life in observance of the commandments of this Scripture. The "colonization of *eretz yisrael*," the land of Palestine, as Isaac Werne of Columbus noted, "is a religious duty."

The Orthodox rabbi Harry H. Epstein, whose emphasis on decorum we noted earlier, commented repeatedly in his sermons of the 1930s that "the real aim of Israel's life in the Holy Land is holiness and service of God." For these rabbis, the Jewish claim to Palestine was not —as the League of Nations and the United Nations expressed it— the "historical connection of the Jewish people to the land" but the word of God.

If we may speak of a "Jewish" sermon, these rabbis did not, generally, deliver such talks. They did not necessarily start with a text from the *midrash* or Talmud or Scripture and expand and comment upon it, drawing lessons along the way, but were far more likely to open with comments about immortality (all affirmed what Rabbi Isaac Werne of Columbus called the "life that is eternal" and Rabbi Joseph Lookstein of New York referred to repeatedly as the "cardinal principle of our faith"), creation (most claimed to literally accept the midrashic metaphor that God created the world using the Torah as a blueprint), revelation (the belief that Moses wrote down every word of the Pentateuch as God spoke it to him), atonement, and the like.

Rabbi Israel Tabak, born in Bukovina (part of the Austro-Hungarian empire) and educated first in a traditional environment in Europe, later, in America, received his first degree (a Ph.D.!) in 1941 at Johns Hopkins University in Baltimore, where he had come to serve the Orthodox synagogue Shaarei Zion in 1931. Surrounded by more than two dozen Orthodox synagogues (most without rabbis) in the first decade or so of his twenty-five-year long Baltimore rabbinate, he preached long, intelligent, English-language sermons, especially on the High Holy Days and for other festivals on, he once noted, a "very narrow range of traditional topics." Learned in Jewish history in general and in American Jewish history specifically, he drew primarily upon a rich treasury of biblical verses, liturgical passages, Hasidic lore, medieval commentaries to the Bible, rabbinic literature (Talmud and *midrash*), the Aramaic translation of the Hebrew Bible (Targum), and modern Jewish literature. The latter, repeatedly, served to buttress traditional views about God, revelation, covenant, and theodicy. Echoing the opinion of many of his Reform colleagues about their congregants, he frequently noted that "the present generation of American Jews is largely a Torah-less generation." Eschewing non-Jewish authors of every kind, he brought traditional Jewish thought and beliefs to his followers for several decades.

Harry H. Epstein, mentioned earlier, was one of the most interesting Orthodox rabbis in America in this period. Educated in yeshivas in Lithuania and Palestine, where he was ordained, he began his rabbinic career in Tulsa (1927) and within a year was hired by Atlanta's Agudath Achim, where he would remain for fifty-five years. He has left scores of sermons in English, Yiddish, and Hebrew, and they demonstrate his interest not only in (of course) Judaica but also in the study of religion in general. He told his congregation in Tulsa, on the last day of Passover in 1927, in a sermon entitled "Judaism and Progress," that "the Torah teaches us that the Jew should drink freely at the well of culture from which modern nations derive their spiritual sustenance [and] keep up with the ranks of the progress of his times." He indeed did "keep up" his entire career, speaking on Confucianism, Jesus (in Yiddish), early Christianity, Muhammad, and Aristotle frequently. He had little sense of historical context (one of his professors at Emory, where he studied religion and philosophy as soon as he came to Atlanta, commented on one of his papers that he had an "indiscriminate coordination of men and movements widely different in time and spirit") and saw most everything through the lens of someone who deeply believed in a God who keeps track of each person's deeds (he told his congregation, on Rosh Hashanah of 1930, with no sense of metaphor, that they are "turning over their books of deeds and accomplishments to the Divine Accountant," and another Emory professor noted that "Rabbi Epstein's own religious prepossessions stand out to [sic] clearly"), but he loved to link Judaism and America in sermons that demonstrated how much he loved both. At every opportunity he would speak on "The Spirit of

Thanksgiving," "Benjamin Franklin and the Jews," "George Washington's Birthday—Symbol of Enduring Value of Courage," or "Chanukkah and Christmas." In Yiddish.

Early in his rabbinate at Agudath Achim, Rabbi Epstein noted that he would convince congregants it was okay to bring English readings into the worship service and would preach High Holy Day morning sermons in English (not done at the synagogue previously) and afternoon sermons in Yiddish, at least through the 1940s. He gave as his rationale that he was doing this not for the congregants but for their children and grandchildren. He also promptly added late-Friday-evening services, during which, over a period of six months, he gave lectures. Although he wrote that "preaching has never been considered by the rabbi to be the most significant part of his work," he gave himself a "grade" on every discourse, usually an E (excellent), G (good), or F (fair), and he noted the time it took to deliver his talks (typically, in this period, forty-five to sixty minutes [ca. 5,000 words!] on the High Holy Days). Congregants must have loved him and his message; from a membership of 75 families when he arrived in 1928, the synagogue membership grew to 1,800 families in 1978.

His Friday evening talks were on popular themes, such as "The Need for Brotherhood in the World Today" (for Brotherhood Sabbath), "Judaism and Christianity" (in late December), "A Jewish Definition of Culture," and, in October, "Columbus: Italian Inn Keeper's Son or Spanish Marrano?" In 1935, he explained to his congregation, at the start of a talk on "Babbitts": "I rarely choose a portion of the Bible as the text for my Friday evening discussions. To be frank, I do not do so because I do not wish to frighten you away. Should I discuss a biblical text for my subject, you might feel that you were getting too much religion. Even in the synagogue you wish to avoid it. Give us an interesting [sic] is the cry." Judging by the texts alone, he must have been a serious rival for the attendance of Atlanta Jews in the 1930s.

Most likely, his Friday evening book review lectures were even more popular. They ranged from novels by Jewish authors on Jewish themes (Milton Steinberg, *As a Driven Leaf*), to historical fiction by non-Jewish authors on "Jewish" themes (Thomas Mann's series *Young Joseph, Joseph and His Brothers, Joseph the Provider*, and *Joseph in Egypt*, with the enticing title of "The Story of Mann Is the Story of Man"), to fiction by non-Jewish writers without a Jewish focus (Sinclair Lewis, *Babbitt*; Boris Pasternak, *Dr. Zhivago*). Drawing on, sometimes quoting verbatim from, reviews he read on these books in the many publications to which he subscribed, he impressed numerous Atlanta Jews and non-Jews with his literary interpretations. Quoting Wordsworth as easily as the Talmud, he joined Rabbis Jung and Lookstein as a nationally celebrated Orthodox rabbi who wore his love of secular culture on his sleeve.

But, in several second-generation neighborhoods on the outskirts of larger cities (e.g., Williamsburg in Brooklyn, outside Manhattan) and even inside several cities (e.g., Baltimore and Cleveland), there were Orthodox rabbis and traditional synagogues between the World Wars that rejected the Americanization program of rabbis such as Leo Jung and Harry Epstein. Williamsburg's Mesivta Torah Vodaath was only one of several Brooklyn schools, attended by males, many of whom went on to become rabbis, that urged their graduates to dismiss secular studies beyond those required by state law. And there were Orthodox rabbis everywhere in the 1920s and 1930s, not just in Brooklyn, trained in yeshivas that remained as separate as possible from mainstream American culture, whose sermons and bulletin messages gave no indication that they read anything other than Jewish legal literature.

There were also Sephardic Orthodox synagogues where Ladino, the language Spanish and Portuguese Jews maintained for centuries after their exile, was spoken among the Western or Eastern Sephardic congregants and, occasionally, at meetings of officers. Recently arrived (before restrictive immigration legislation went into effect) Syrian, Turkish, Palestinian, North African, and Persian Jews, descendants of Spanish and Portuguese Jews, and significant numbers of non-Sephardic Jews made up the membership of these congregations, scattered from coast to coast. Almost all of them adopted the prayer book *Book of Prayers*, edited by Rabbi David de Sola Pool, by the late 1930s, and, within five years of its appearance, a second edition (1941) of the book appeared. In the 1990s and early 2000s "Sephardic" congregations became home to a wide variety of non-Sephardic Jews. In addition to a large number of members from "mixed" marriages between Sephardic and Ashkenazic Jews, there are many Ashkenazic families and/or individuals who join Sephardic synagogues because of the traditions and melodies. Around the country, one is no longer surprised to find Sephardic synagogue leadership in the hands of Ashkenazim.

Bulletins clearly reveal the extent to which the Depression hurt Orthodox synagogues everywhere. Many dismissed employees or lowered the wages of those they retained; paying utility bills, especially winter heating in the cold climates, was a continual struggle; and synagogue after synagogue lost members who could not continue to pay dues. Rabbi Chaim Williamofsky of the Durham Hebrew Congregation collected his salary by knocking on the doors of stores at closing hours; bingo games helped fund it, as well. In 1932, the president of Shaarai Torah in Worcester, Massachusetts, announced that "the shul doesn't have any money." Rabbi Epstein voluntarily took a salary reduction in 1931 and 1932. At the Baron Hirsch Congregation in Memphis, forty members were dropped from the books in September of 1930—early in the Depression—for "failure to pay dues," and two full pages of names were marked "refused to pay" or "unable to pay." Their rabbi, Morris N. Taxon, who arrived in Memphis in 1931, agreed two years later to forgo his contracted pay increase, while the cantor took a steep pay cut.

Many of these American-trained rabbis—such as Rabbi Taxon, who attended Ohio State University before seminary—grew up in Yiddish-speaking homes and spoke Yiddish as a second language.

So, at the same time that one found English sermons with references beyond the world of rabbinic literature and Judaic Studies and a concern for decorum, one also encountered a sizeable number of members who preferred the world of their fathers and mothers. This might take the form of a Saturday afternoon Yiddish lecture by the rabbi, a cultural program featuring a Yiddish singer, or even the occasional Yiddish sermon during a special Sabbath prayer service. The sisterhood or ladies aid at the Orthodox synagogue in Durham continued to conduct its meetings exclusively in Yiddish as late as World War II. Rabbi Abraham P. Hirmes of Atlanta's Ahavath Achim preached Yiddish sermons on the High Holy Days all through the 1920s, and Harry H. Epstein, his successor, continued preaching in Yiddish on Rosh Hashanah afternoon at least through the 1940s. Additionally, Orthodox synagogues in these decades sometimes used Yiddish-speaking guest speakers to make emergency appeals for Palestinian causes ("Palestinian" in these decades always referred to the *Jews* of Palestine), and both brotherhoods and sisterhoods sponsored numerous Yiddish-language activities to instill Zionist fervor and to raise money for Zionist organizations, especially Mizrachi.

The orthodoxy of this period, and well into the subsequent postwar period, was generally nonobservant or little observant in comparison with the decades after 1967. Synagogues everywhere had trouble finding ten males so that communal worship could begin; Young Israel of Parkchester, with 130 families at the end of World War II, frequently faced this challenge. Manuals produced by the national office with synagogue program suggestions for Orthodox teens emphasized cultural, social, and athletic events that had no particular connection to Judaism. Rarely was a mikveh to be found in a community—the entire county of Westchester had only one, at Ohab Zedek—and when it was there, few Orthodox Jews utilized it. Most Orthodox rabbis during these decades complained that only the occasional member used the ritual bath, and they were determined to move their congregants in the direction of greater ritual and observance. Likewise, these rabbis turned a blind eye to mixed seating in some of their Orthodox congregations by declaring that it was merely a bump on the clear road to separate-sex seating. Members of Orthodox synagogues during this period ate meals at restaurants that were not kosher—ordering with care so as to not eat shrimp, lobster, or pork—but never worrying about eating a cheese sandwich on a plate that might have previously been used for lettuce, tomato and bacon. Rabbi Herbert S. Goldstein, president of the Union of Orthodox Jewish Congregations of America, was present in 1925 when the Orthodox synagogue Beth El in Indianapolis dedicated its new sanctuary, which contained family pews and which would offer late-Friday-evening services. He installed Rabbi Isadore Goodman, who would later go from Indianapolis to the Orthodox Talmud Torah of Flatbush and then to the Orthodox Baron Hirsch in Memphis. Henry Segal, a graduate of the Rabbi Isaac Elchanan Theological Seminary of Yeshiva University, came to B'nai Israel and Talmud Torah in Washington, D.C., in 1936 and served this Orthodox congregation with mixed seating for more than twenty-five years. Orthodox women, according to sermons, kept kosher at home, lit candles to welcome the Sabbath on Friday evening, and drove to the beauty shop on Saturday morning. Orthodox rabbis all over the country discussed such patterns in their High Holy Day sermons, criticizing the laxity of observance (especially driving to the synagogue on the Sabbath—a violation of Jewish law) and pleading with their listeners to embrace more ritual and ceremony.

In these same interwar decades, late-Friday-evening services became popular in Orthodox synagogues. Rabbi Solomon M. Neches introduced them (with singing and lectures) at Shaarei Tefila in Los Angeles in 1933 "to supplement the early Friday evening [that is, sundown] services." Competing with neighboring Conservative houses of worship, they offered prayer services and lectures at 8:00 P.M. for those who could not make it to the earlier sundown worship, hoping to keep them away from the movies, boxing matches (where a plethora of Jews held titles), and the theater. Many of these "reform-ing" Orthodox synagogues—with late-Friday-evening services and lectures, organ music, and mixed seating, either throughout the sanc-tuary or in some areas—became Conservative in their affiliation as Conservative Judaism took hold in the 1920s. This, once again, sug-gests the huge variety among those synagogues that called them-selves Orthodox in this period—a number possibly equal to those synagogues that identified as Conservative or Reform combined, though without any greater precision. In larger cities, Orthodox synagogues were often so numerous in some neighborhoods that di-rectories and other local tabulations missed them, and they left no printed records, especially when they were little more than a rented storefront (e.g., in Chicago, the "Rumanian shul" or the "Douglas Blvd. shul," or, in St. Louis, the "shul on Biddle Street between Thir-teenth and Fourteenth" and the "shul next door to Hamill's stables"). This situation makes it very difficult to generalize about these syna-gogues in the 1920s and 1930s.

Nevertheless, in sermons and in newsletters throughout the 1920s and 1930s, Orthodox rabbis complained that the "old orthodoxy" would not capture the imagination and, most important, the mem-bership of the young, the children of the immigrants. It was not just the Yiddish sermons but the entire ambience of the immigrant Or-thodox synagogues that needed an overhaul. At a synagogue in Co-lumbus, Rabbi Isaac Werne took note of the fact that, while one con-gregant prayed, another engaged in conversation. The noise, the lack of decorum, the failure to, as Rabbi Leo Jung put it to his colleagues at a 1926 convention of Orthodox synagogue leaders held by the Union of Orthodox Jewish Congregations of America (the Ortho-dox Union, or "O.U."), "sell Orthodox Judaism to the children of the Jazz Age"—these were the problems. Rabbi Jung called the service at the synagogue in Cleveland he earlier served, Kenesseth Israel, "three hours of conversation, occasionally interrupted by prayer"; instead of "prayers accompanied by promiscuous conversation" and the exchanging of "jocular pleasantries" during lulls in the liturgy, and worshipers waving to each other across the sanctuary, he sought to create an "atmosphere of beauty and harmony." In that same year he described Orthodox services as "A disheartening spectacle of disorder . . . utterly unorthodox in its uncleanliness, utterly unorthodox in its lack of decorum, utterly unorthodox in the crude behavior of the worshipper." He, like the rising generation of Orthodox rabbis, saw it as his goal to eliminate "noise and indecorum" and to create "inner feelings of reverence in our boys and girls."

As in nineteenth-century synagogues, a word frequently used in sermons and bulletins was "decorum" or its adjectival form, "decorous." The liturgical changes instituted at Orthodox synagogues in Atlanta, Baltimore, Chicago, Columbus, Denver, Detroit, Los Angeles, Memphis, New York, Philadelphia, St. Louis, and Washington, D.C., included unison singing, uniform prayer books (rather than each individual bringing his own and half the congregation having Hebrew with Yiddish and the other half Hebrew with English), and periodic announcements—emphasizing the proper book—of the page being read or sung, as well as an effort at preventing worshipers from leaving during the reading of the Torah, the elimination of auctioning the honor of participating in the reading of Scriptures (usually replaced by handing the man called to the Torah a preprinted donation card), an emphasis on the proper pronunciation of Hebrew, and the introduction of responsive readings. An Orthodox worshiper in St. Louis recalled that, "when the Torah was read, it was time for intermission; everybody walked out."

The responses to this and other indecorous practices attest to the popularity of Conservative Judaism, where, as in Reform synagogues, decorum ruled the day. In Orthodox synagogues in Port Chester, Tarrytown, Peekskill, and Mamaroneck, all in Westchester County outside Manhattan, younger members found that the decorous late-Friday-evening services "on the Conservative model" offered a "refreshing alternative" to the "old-world style of worship."

At Memphis's Baron Hirsch Congregation, Orthodox worshipers began using uniform prayer books as well as head covering and prayer shawls of matching color and shapes, eliminated the auctioning of Torah honors and the announcement of contributions to "improve appearance, increase dignity, order and beauty in the service." Decorum, a number of rabbis noted, was also influenced by the emergence of Young Israel. Founded just prior to World War I on the Lower East Side of New York City to sponsor late-Friday-evening lectures and other programs in English in synagogues for young Orthodox Jews (a practice virtually unknown in 1912), as it developed into the Young Israel Synagogue Organization in the 1920s (e.g., Young Israel of Brooklyn; Young Israel of Philadelphia; Young Israel of Cleveland; Young Israel of Newark), it emphasized not only English but decorum. These Orthodox congregations, with their English sermons, abundant congregational singing, responsive readings, proper dress, and decorous services, strongly influenced an orthodoxy better able to compete with emerging Conservative Judaism for the allegiance of the children of immigrants.

Shaarei Tefila, a synagogue in Los Angeles, offers us a case study of an Orthodox congregation's activities at the beginning of World War II, that is, in the years 1939–1941. This summary is consistent with those of Orthodox synagogues of a similar size and with a full-time rabbi in Atlanta, Baltimore, Chicago, Columbus, Los Angeles, New York, and Philadelphia in the late 1930s and early 1940s. The congregation had several employees: Rabbi Dr. Solomon Neches (given an unprecedented twenty-one-year contract in 1941); a Torah reader who received $60 annually to chant the Torah on Sabbaths and festivals; a hazan; and a sexton. The latter, as elsewhere where Orthodox synagogues struggled to balance their budget, worked on commission in addition to a small monthly salary. He received 20 percent of all contributions he solicited (and collected) from members, a cut from every High Holy Day seat sold (they ranged from $3 to $7.50), and fifty cents for every name he recited on the anniversary of a death or daily for a year or so following a death.

The procedure for purchasing a seat at Shaarei Tefila was quite common among Orthodox congregations in this period. A purchaser would pay 10 percent down and the rest in eleven monthly payments —the sexton kept the records—the equivalent (in Reform and Conservative congregations) of annual dues. Every male who bought a seat in the main section of the sanctuary received a corresponding seat for his wife in the women's section and had the option of purchasing a second seat in the main section (if one was empty). A letter accompanying the receipt affirmed that the purchaser was "guaranteed that religious services must be conducted in strict Orthodox manner, as long as seven members of the synagogue so desire."

Concerns about fund-raising dominated the minutes of the synagogue as well as the content of the monthly newsletter over this two-year period. Theater parties (one with Eddie Cantor, another with the Three Stooges as entertainment), men's club events to fund Sunday school teacher salaries (about 100 students attended), fund-raisers at bar mitzvah parties ($25 got the celebrant's name in the Golden Book that in 2009 was still displayed prominently in the lobby of the synagogue), all-star shows, sisterhood dinners, festival parties (e.g., at Purim), and especially the sale of High Holy Day seats all provided badly needed funds. Only the dissemination of information about when worship took place—always a front-page item in the bulletin —took a higher priority than raising money.

Orthodox synagogues were generous in providing space for other Jewish (and some nonsectarian) organizations to use the rooms for meetings and, from time to time, publicized the activities of such organizations, especially those connected to "Palestinians" or those that helped poor, disabled, or ill local Jews. Numerous benevolent societies made appeals at Shaarei Tefila, despite its own huge needs, but the Hebrew Free Loan Association of Los Angeles took precedence.

As everywhere, decorum was a constant concern. When the High Holy Day services "went through with the greatest decorum and order," the board took note. When the "mishmash" of prayer books at worship services seemed to be a cause of "noise and inattention," the board sought to obtain a uniform prayer book for all worshipers. When the Hebrew-only Friday afternoon/sundown services were lacking "religion," the board discussed adding late-Friday-evening prayers, songs, and discourses—like those popular at Conservative and Reform synagogues—to keep people's attention. And, in 1935, the newspaper advertisements for the High Holy Day services stressed "dignity and beauty." By 1941, Orthodox, Conservative, and Reform synagogues all over Los Angeles had "Sabbath Eve Services" at 8:15 P.M.

At the same time that Orthodox synagogues and their rabbis all over America competed with congregations of other branches of Judaism for the allegiance of parents and children, some synagogues resisted this competition and held fast to what they perceived to be tradition, unchanged, for centuries. Although the majority of these congregations were small and either had (or left) no bulletins and had rabbis who either did not write or type out (or did not preserve) their sermons, there are enough materials scattered around the country for us to say something very general about the leaders of these congregations and their rabbis.

They were not especially tolerant (except on the High Holy Days, when they were an important source of income) of worshipers who did not observe Jewish ceremonies, customs, observances, and rituals and yet wanted to attend an Orthodox congregation. Those who drove to the synagogue on the Sabbath, or who attended Sabbath-morning services and then went off to their work, or who ignored the mikveh (ritual bath) in the community, or who mostly ignored kashrut (dietary laws) in public, or who violated any number of the dozens of commandments kept by the pious were not welcome.

Further, the rabbis of these congregations refused to make allowances for living in America. They continued to preach exclusively in Yiddish, interpreted Jewish legal questions from their congregants strictly, refused to participate in ecumenical activities with Reform and Conservative (sometimes even Orthodox) colleagues, rejected English readings to supplement the all-Hebrew liturgy at worship services, and joined a union of Orthodox rabbis (Agudat ha-Rabbanim), who were mostly European-born and who were dedicated to resisting the changes sweeping Americanizing Orthodox synagogues from coast to coast.

They had the greatest scorn for the numerous Orthodox synagogues with mixed seating, even when in only part of the sanctuary, and even more for late-Friday "services," whatever the term (e.g., "programs"; *oneg Shabbat* or Sabbath fun) Orthodox colleagues used. One of these rabbis, Tobias Geffen of Atlanta's Shearith Israel, noted, in a letter to Eliezer Silver, an Orthodox colleague in Cincinnati, that the "*oneg Shabbat* cause many people to violate the Sabbath." This was indeed the fundamental criticism of the late-Friday service: for some, it substituted for the required late afternoon worship, and for others it led to violations of Sabbath prohibitions. It was simply wrong.

Reform Judaism

The power of "classical" Reform Judaism did not wane much in this period. It is true that Ohabei Shalom of Brookline had a daily morning service, but the sociologist Bruce A. Phillips notes that it was "the only Reform synagogue in the United States" to do so. Yet, there were signs that changes were coming: by 1948, Rabbi Leon Feuer would state, with exaggeration, at the convention of Reform rabbis in Kansas City, that Reform rabbis had "turned our backs on so-called classical reform." But, to a great extent, Reform remained as it had been in the late nineteenth and early twentieth centuries, with the emphasis on prophetic, universal principles, "Israel's universal mission," in the words of Rabbi Feuer. "Religion consists in doing good," Rabbi Isadore Isaacson of Temple Israel of Hollywood, California, observed. Rabbis, in sermons, insisted that Judaism was a religion, nothing else, and that the public schools were the place American Jewish children belonged, never in Jewish schools ("ghetto tribalism" and "racial exclusiveness"). In bulletins, which frequently included a column by rabbis, and in sermons by rabbis all over the country, these clergymen expressed anxiety about a potential revival of Hebrew as the Palestine Jewish community grew rapidly in the 1920s. Many were scared at the thought that non-Jews might conclude that Jews were united not only by a common religion but also by a common language, as this would challenge the preeminence of the diaspora in general, and America in particular, for Reform Jews. Rabbi Norman Gerstenfeld of Washington [D.C.] Hebrew Congregation put it nicely in a High Holy Day sermon: "America is our promised land, our land of fulfillment."

No better representative of classical Reform could be found in the decades between the World Wars than Rabbi Edward Nathan Calisch of Congregation Beth Ahabah in Richmond, Virginia. He served this synagogue for more than a half-century, arriving there in 1891, and many Richmondites, including plenty of non-Jews, remembered his powerful and intelligent preaching, often without notes or a text, for decades after his death. To start, he insisted through his entire career that Jews were not a nation but a religion. Just as some people in the city were Americans of the Lutheran persuasion or Americans of the Methodist persuasion, so, he insisted, his flock consisted of Americans of the Jewish persuasion, or, as he put it once, "Americans who happened to be Jews," who no longer sought to return to Zion and establish a Jewish state, who affirmed that the Torah is for all people, not just Jews, and that one day all people will be "one," all "kneeling at the shrine of God the Father of all." Whether this meant all the world would be Jewish or that a new religion of all humanity would make all one people was never clear, but the universalism of his interpretation of Judaism was a constant theme.

It followed, for one who felt that the Torah belonged to everyone, that he rejected most ceremonies, customs, observances, and rituals. A couple could not be married in the synagogue, or elsewhere, with a *huppah* (canopy); the rabbi never wore the traditional head covering (though he did wear a silk hat on the pulpit) or provided it for worshipers; the Torah was never carried off the pulpit into the congregation; the *kiddush* (sanctification of the wine) was not chanted on Sabbath eve; confirmation replaced bar mitzvah; Hebrew was minimally used in the liturgy, making the worship service attractive to non-Jews as well as to Jews who could not read Hebrew so that members could comfortably invite non-Jewish guests (and Jews) who knew no Hebrew but loved excellent choirs, organists, and soloists, prayers that eschewed particularism and stressed universalism, and who could profit from a learned sermon on ethics or current events. In 1893, in response to a request by the board of governors and the ritual committee of the synagogue, he produced *A Book of Prayer for Jewish Worship*. The "Evening Service for Week Days" contained only sixty-three words of Hebrew before the Adoration or conclusion of the service, and there were six consecutive pages with no Hebrew. The "Evening Service for the Sabbath," twenty-eight pages in length, had nineteen pages with no Hebrew and was used for decades. And there were hymns by William Cullen Bryant, William Cowper, Gavrila Romanovich Derzhavin, Henry Wadsworth Longfellow, John Milton, and Isaac Watts, none of them Jewish. Similarly, in congregations that used the revised edition of the *Union Prayer Book* (1918), it was possible to worship with little or no Hebrew. The readings for ten Sabbath-evening services had no Hebrew, and the "Evening Service for Week-Days" included only a few Hebrew sentences.

The subjects of Rabbi Calisch's sermons were universal, citing Robert Burns and William Shakespeare far more commonly than rabbis from the classical literature of the early centuries of this era.

"Lexington and Concord, Trenton and Yorktown, New Orleans and Lake Erie, Chapultapec and Mexico, Gettysburg and Appomattox, these were names that speed the blood and melt the eyes," he intoned at places such as the University of Virginia; the Tomb of the Unknown Soldier, in Arlington National Cemetery; Mt. Vernon; the First Baptist Church of Richmond; and the Medical College of Virginia for Confederate Veterans, as well as to college and medical school graduates, Masons, and Christians. All over the country in the two decades between the World Wars, rabbis listed in their bulletins talks they had given at the Knights of Pythias, PTA meetings, Masonic lodges, hundreds of churches of nearly every Christian persuasion, Rotary clubs, and the YMCA. Frequently called Protestant ministers in their Prince Albert frock coats, they were especially proud to host interreligious forums at the synagogue. Like Rabbi Morris Lazaron at Baltimore Hebrew Congregation, these rabbis loved the designation "ambassador to the gentiles." The Reverend Henry M. Edmonds of South Highland Presbyterian Church and, later, Independent Presbyterian Church called Rabbi Morris Newfield of Birmingham's Temple Emanu-El "the best Christian I knew."

Rabbi Calisch's appeal to non-Jews was immense. He combined Old Testament and America, repeatedly, in attractive ways, such as when (in a sermon he repeated many times, with slight changes, throughout his career) he identified George Washington as a modern Joshua, Thomas Jefferson as a modern Moses, Benjamin Franklin as a modern Solomon, Andrew Jackson as a modern David, and George Mason, James Madison, and Alexander Hamilton, with "their world-embracing visions," as the seers Isaiah, Amos, and Micah. He was a great patriot and combined his Americanism ("a small American flag fastened to my desk makes my heart thrill with solemn pride") with his universal brand of religion, vaguely Judeo-Christian, in a manner that characterized many of the classical reform rabbis of this and an earlier generation. His colleague and friend Rabbi Lazaron of Baltimore was more explicit: "Judaism is essentially Christianity."

The *Union Prayer Book, Newly Revised*, was published in 1940, and, despite opposition from classical Reform rabbis ("too much Hebrew"), it was promptly adopted by nearly every Reform congregation in the United States. One rabbi after another called it something like a "fresh expression of the classic ideals of Reform Judaism," and, though they did not mean to use "classic" as a synonym for "classical," it does indeed represent the culmination of the classical period of Reform. First, it takes for granted that most Reform Jews, as Rabbi Louis I. Newman put it in 1943, "bring next to nothing to an appreciation of liturgical, ritual, and theological literature," so the "publication of a new Order of Prayer and Music will not suffice to strengthen the influence of Judaism today." He was prophetic in his prediction that a new prayer book would not, and did not, "endow our liturgy with greater vitality," as there is no evidence that this new *siddur* had much of an impact; in fact, Rabbi Newman felt it only added "to the illiteracy [of Reform Jews] regarding matters religious." This conclusion cannot be proved, but it is certain that, despite the assumption of an illiterate laity, ritually, theologically, and liturgically, the new prayer book, unlike later ones, did not seek to educate worshipers in any aspect of the liturgy and, unlike Reform worship in the last decades of the twentieth century, did not involve the worshipers. Rabbis continued to preach; cantors or choirs continued to sing; organists continued to play—and congregants continued to sit, watch, and listen passively in Reform synagogues. This was true even when the Torah scroll was removed from the ark—congregants stood quietly as the rabbi and cantor or choir read and sang, and the Torah was promptly placed on the reading table, rarely if ever taken from the pulpit and brought into the community of worshipers. This standing and sitting passively was a fundamental of classical Reform and characterized these two interwar decades.

Little Zionist activity graced Reform congregations of the 1920s and 1930s, as classical Reform was generally anti-Zionist or non-Zionist, opposed vigorously to the idea of a Jewish state in Palestine or indifferent ("neutral," many rabbis called this position, insisting that Reform Jews should not speak or teach about Zionism or anti-Zionism) to this fundamental idea. For them, as Rabbi Lazaron put it, "America is our home, and we do not [support] a philosophy or program which will jeopardize our position here." Anti-Zionist rabbis (of varying degrees) were everywhere, including Samuel Goldenson and Jonah Wise in New York City, Lazaron and William Rosenau in Baltimore, Louis Wolsey and William Fineshriber in Philadelphia, Abram Simon and Norman Gerstenfeld in Washington, D.C., Calisch in Richmond, Leo Franklin in Detroit, Sidney Lefkowitz in Dallas, Harry Ettelson in Memphis, Louis Mann in Chicago, Solomon Foster in Newark, Ephraim Frisch in San Antonio, Morris Newfield in Birmingham, Samuel Koch in Seattle, and the president of the Reform seminary, Julian Morgenstern. None went as far as Houston's Beth Israel in 1943–1944, where a full-scale attack on Zionism was launched ("Basic Principles," adopted in November 1943) and congregants agreed that a loyalty oath to America was required for membership. Beth Israel was but a bump in the road toward an acceptance of Palestine and Israel; what Zionist Reform rabbis of this period called the great folk movement of the Palestinian Jews was slowly entering the fabric of some of the congregations. Conservative synagogues virtually everywhere identified strongly with Zion, whereas Reform synagogues looked askance at this enthusiasm. This made it much harder, until Reform temple leaders changed their attitudes in the 1940s, for Reform congregations to attract the children and grandchildren of those east European immigrants who were moving away from orthodoxy. In 1930, only half the members of Reform synagogues had family origins in eastern Europe.

A significant minority of Reform rabbis vigorously supported Zionism throughout this period, not just the rabbis with national Zionist credentials, such as Barnett Brickner, Max Heller, Abba Hillel Silver, and Stephen S. Wise, but the rank and file everywhere. Support for the Balfour Declaration and the Mandate given to Britain by the League of Nations, horror at the civil strife in Palestine, Palestine as a hope for German Jewry, and the World Zionist Organization biennial congresses and the British commissions in Palestine and American Zionist activity during World War II were regular sermon topics across the land in many Reform congregations. And another sizeable group of rabbis, while not activists in their commitment to Zionism, introduced a wide variety of programs about Palestine into the synagogue. These included art, dance, drama, literature, music, and philanthropy, and, though an emphasis on the Hebrew language in worship might have been missing, activities of all sorts revolving around Palestine filled the synagogue bulletins.

These programs sometimes came at a cost, especially when a Zionist rabbi replaced one who had ignored Zion for decades in Chicago, New York, and Philadelphia. When Milton L. Grafman introduced Zionist activities at Birmingham's Temple Emanu-El in the late 1940s and early 1950s (including changing the pronunciation of Hebrew in the school from the centuries-old Ashkenazic to that of the new State of Israel, Sephardic), twenty-one members resigned and formed the anti-Zionist Temple of Judaism.

Concomitant with an interest in Zionism in the 1930s and early 1940s, there was a modest interest in restoring tradition. At the 1937 convention of Reform rabbis in Columbus, Ohio, the convention president, Felix A. Levy of Chicago's Emanuel Congregation, worried that Reform Judaism was becoming "high church" and called for a radical revision of the Reform attitude toward observance ("a code of rules for guidance in practice") as well as—a sign of how far out of touch he was with the rank and file of his movement—a joint committee with rabbis from the Conservative rabbinical association. The Committee on Resolutions took note of "the trend in Reform Jewry to restore ceremonialism and ritual to Synagog and Home" and proposed the creation of a Joint Commission (Reform rabbis and Reform lay leaders) on Synagog Activities. Although the majority of Reform Jews would have affirmed the definition of

North Shore Congregation Israel

LINCOLN AND VERNON AVENUES

GLENCOE, ILLINOIS

SUNDAY MORNING SERVICE

January 22, 1933

at 10:45 o'clock

RABBI MILTON STEINBERG

will speak on

"WANTED—A PHILOSOPHY OF JEWISH LIFE"

Cover page of the bulletin of Reform synagogue North Shore Congregation Israel, Glencoe, Illinois, 1933. North Shore Congregation Israel (Glencoe, Illinois) Records (MS-731) Box 1, Folder 4. Courtesy of the American Jewish Archives, Cincinnati, Ohio.

mitzvoth (commandments) offered by Rabbi Israel Herzog of Temple Beth El of Lynn, Massachusetts ("human relationships" and not "customs, traditions, rituals, and ceremonies"), rabbis and laypeople, as at Temple Israel of Hollywood, began to discuss both restoring discarded rituals and creating new ones. The Committee on Synagog and Community, at the 1938 rabbinical convention, took note of the "colorless[ness] and emptiness of much that constituted Reform Jewish religious life" and the "warm, colorful, helpful ceremonies and disciplines discarded by the former generation of Reform Jews."

It even recommended a "code of Reform Jewish ceremonial observance." But the idea was a generation too early, and it died quietly.

The example of Temple Israel of Hollywood illustrates those Reform congregations in the late 1920s and early 1930s whose rabbi had no anti-Zionist agenda. Isadore Isaacson served the synagogue from its founding in 1926 until his death, at age forty-six, in 1936. Like most Reform rabbis in the country, he had little interest in ritual or ceremony: the "praying shawl might have its place, but how much more important is it to see that the needy are clothed—observation [sic] of the dietary laws is proportionately less important than that the hungry be fed." When he spoke during worship services, to the brotherhood and sisterhood, to church and communal groups, at the monthly books review during Friday-evening services (as at nearby Temple Emanuel with Rabbi Ernest R. Trattner, there were no services on Sabbath mornings), and to members who studied with him, he had no anti-Zionist agenda. He rarely, if ever, even mentioned Zion. Sisterhood luncheons (with chicken salad and biscuits prepared by Mrs. Isaacson and a cookbook distributed to brides), bridge parties, Halloween suppers; brotherhood meetings every Monday night followed by games of hearts and pinochle as well as periodic dances at hotels; junior guild, Girl Scouts, Boy Scouts, Campfire Girls, young folks league (high school and college age)—these kept the synagogue busy during the week. And a Sunday school, with more than 100 students attending during these years, filled the synagogue on Sunday. Rabbi Isaacson rarely drew upon Jewish sources in his sermons or announced a title that would suggest a Jewish theme; one High Holy Day season, his sermon titles were "Prohibition and Freedom," "New Mothers for Old," "God's Gentleman," "Starting Again," and "Intuitions." Indeed, for him, rabbinic literature was a "rich source of humorous fable," little more.

Although a great many rabbis had eliminated the bar mitzvah ritual, the ceremony of confirmation was as popular and grand in this period as at other times in the history of Reform Judaism in

Sabbath School lighting of Hannukah menorah, Congregation Bene Israel, Cincinnati, Ohio, ca. 1920s. Union for Reform Judaism Records (MS-72), UAHC Photo #458. Courtesy of the American Jewish Archives, Cincinnati, Ohio.

America. Most ceremonies were cantatas, prepared by the rabbi, the cantor or musical director, the organist, and sometimes the students. These usually supplemented a prayer service; in some synagogues, they replaced the worship service. Floral offerings were commonplace, and weeks of rehearsals were needed for the students to master the words and music of the program. Grand dinner dances usually followed, especially in cities. Taking place during high school, these ceremonies added two or three years of Jewish Sunday school education for boys (by replacing bar mitzvah and the inevitable drop-out from religious school when the ceremony ended) and an extensive program for girls, for whom bat mitzvah was virtually nonexistent.

Reform rabbis of this period were generally widely read in contemporary literature, both fiction and nonfiction, and cited such reading in their sermons regularly. Lecture and book review series were especially popular; those by Pittsburgh's Rabbi Solomon B. Freehof attracted hundreds of (if not more than 1,000) townspeople and were regularly published and distributed nationally. His three lectures each year on Shakespeare were every bit as intelligent as those of professional literary critics. Rabbi Irving Reichert of San Francisco's Emanu-El gave a lecture to the graduates at the University of California, Berkeley, in 1939, and he demonstrated a sophisticated grasp of American intellectual history. For Rabbi Morton J. Cohn, in Springfield, Massachusetts, and Hamilton, Ohio, from the early 1930s until he arrived in San Diego, in 1946, Coleridge, Einstein, Freud, Gladstone, Oliver Wendell Holmes, Maugham, Niebuhr, Ruskin, and Shakespeare were constant sources of quotes. In fact, he cited non-Jewish thinkers over a fifteen year period far more frequently than those identified as Jews. High Holy Day sermon titles in Reform bulletins, in contrast to those in Conservative or Orthodox publications, rarely gave a hint of their Jewish content. Typical were these titles from Springfield, in 1931: "Measures and Values" (Rosh Hashanah evening), "Whither Bound?" (Rosh Hashanah morning), "Tolerance" (Yom Kippur evening), and "In the Heart" (Yom Kippur morning).

A pattern for Yom Kippur worship at Reform congregations became rather consistent from Boston to San Diego and from Seattle to Miami in these decades. Morning worship began at 10 A.M., with a break of about one and a half to two hours in the middle of the day, often with children's services, and resumed about 2 P.M. with the afternoon, memorial, and closing liturgies, usually finishing well before sundown and breaking the fast as soon as worship ended. Worshipers paid a premium for the "best" seats (front center and front side), either as part of their annual dues or as an "add-on" for the High Holy Days, and the manner of selling such seats occupied leaders everywhere. Generally, Reform officers felt that "selling" the seats separately took away from a "high spiritual atmosphere," but, there was agreement that, if "every Jew has a reserved seat with his name on it for the entire year, he will feel at home in the temple."

Reform rabbis in these decades (and, in most places, well after) dressed like Protestant clergy, with black robes for Sabbath worship and white robes for High Holy Day services. Rarely did they wear a head covering, though a few—in synagogue histories and on synagogue walls—are pictured with a prayer shawl over their robes. Indianapolis Hebrew Congregation eliminated the bar mitzvah and banned the wearing of head covering and prayer shawls in the interwar years. And, perhaps as with Protestant clergy, every aspect of rabbinic performance as clergy was under close scrutiny by leaders of synagogues. So, in their bulletin columns, rabbis would regularly praise their own work: "your rabbi," one wrote in 1927, "is glad to report that the attendance at public services has kept up splendidly during my ministry and much favorable comment has been evoked." No less frequently, in bulletins but especially in synagogue minutes, the officers complained about rabbis. In Baltimore, in 1934, the president of one Reform temple admitted that "the rabbi is a good man, but it seems he does not make the proper effort in the right direction. He does not awaken the interest of his people; he is too much absorbed in his personal likes; he does not unify us into a congregation. We have too many members who are antagonistic and he is not able to keep them interested in our work."

The impact of the Depression was felt just as strongly among members of Reform congregations as in the other branches. The Union of American Hebrew Congregations reported in 1933 that 84 of the 281 member congregations defaulted on their payments; in 1934, the chairman of the executive board told his board members that many small congregations have "long abandoned their payments to the Union" and that a "surprisingly large number of the larger congregations are in financial difficulties because of temples and centers which they have recently built." The president of Congregation Beth

Israel in San Diego wrote to the congregation in 1933 that "I will not speak of our financial situation, for that is bad everywhere." Rabbi Daniel Davis of Lancaster, Pennsylvania, volunteered to take a $500 pay cut in 1932 and again in 1933 at Congregation Shaarai Shomayim, and Rabbi David Marx did the same in Atlanta in 1932, where the congregation could not fill the board of trustees as members feared having to sign the recurring bank notes for the building debt. The meetings of the board of trustees at Temple Israel in Minneapolis in 1932 were, according to Rabbi Albert G. Minda, "nightmares," as "resignations from members [and] cancellation of pledges were the order of the day." He, too, "volunteered a reduction of [his] salary." At Keneseth Israel in Philadelphia, "voluntary donations," by "passing the collection box on Sunday mornings" (the morning of the main worship service), provided funds for emergency needs of congregants. In fact, it was generally the only topic to appear in synagogue records from the early 1930s more frequently than the concern about the lack of worshipers at Sabbath services ("Let us put the house of God before the movie theatre" was a constant refrain). Many families withdrew from Portland, Oregon's Beth Israel, and most of the members asked for substantial reductions in the assessments determined by a committee. By the end of 1931, 20 percent of the members owed more than $9,000 on their past-due assessments. Temple Emanu-El in New York City saw its membership decline by 44 percent during the Depression, and the federal government found that in 1936, 456 New York City Conservative, Orthodox, and Reform synagogues were owed $14 million. In Columbus, Ohio, a synagogue president noted in 1934 that "financially, we have failed terribly the last two years: we cannot borrow anymore [sic] money." And, at a Reform synagogue in Los Angeles in 1935, the president noted that "the rabbi had to leave the pulpit because we could not pay him a living salary. The new rabbi . . . is very underpaid—he and his wife must pay their own way to the Union of American Hebrew Congregations biennial as temple delegates."

Most Reform rabbis, who from the time of World War I to the end of this period described a laity sorely deficient in Judaic learning, do not seem to have made much of an impact in educating a generation or more of American Jews about Judaism. The number of hours of Jewish education the average Reform congregant received in 1920 had changed little by 1945, and the programs introduced to create a literate laity, or just a literate group of synagogue trustees, were few and fewer. Rabbi Irving Reichert of San Francisco's Emanu-El was not far off when, at the end of this period, he observed that "the number of unsynagogued Jews in America today is staggering" and added that "we have a Jewish[ly] ignorant laity. There was never a time in the history of our people when Jews knew so little about their religion and about their religious literature as in our day. Our people cannot read the Bible in the original Hebrew, and they do not read it in English."

The Synagogue-Center

Although there were a number of earlier examples, the Brooklyn Jewish Center has been called the "model Jewish Center in American Jewish life," as well as "the most well known prototype of the synagogue-center." Combining the traditional functions of the synagogue with the more modern functions of the community center (auditorium, theater, gymnasium, swimming pool), the BJC, with Rabbi Israel H. Levinthal, who arrived in 1919, became a model for numerous other congregations ("shuls with pools" was a contemporary description) that built or created synagogue-centers in the 1920s. BJC was, like so many other congregations that perceived themselves as Orthodox at that time, moving steadily in the direction of Conservative Judaism with mixed seating in the center rows (separate seating on the side) and late-Friday-evening services and lectures.

The bulletin of this synagogue-center never identified BJC as

Example of a shul with a pool. Congregation Anshe Chesed in Linden, New Jersey, circa 1960. Photograph courtesy of Congregation Anshe Chesed.

"Conservative," even as it moved steadily in that direction. But it trumpeted the benefits of praying *and* playing, with gym and bath schedules, restaurant hours (more than forty hours of service weekly), debates, operatic concerts, Monday evening forum speakers, intercenter basketball league results, roof-top golf instruction (and, in the fall, a *sukkah*), debating clubs, drama leagues, literary societies, and the like, alongside the schedule of worship, Hebrew school (ages six to fifteen), Sunday school (10 A.M. to 12 noon on Sunday), and a day school (the Center Academy) for younger children.

Shuls with pools were scattered across the country by the end of the decade of the 1920s; in 1944, Congregation B'nai Israel of Woonsocket, Rhode Island, voted to construct, when the Second World War ended, a "synagogue-center," and as late as 1955 the new building of Boston's Mishkan Tefila was called a "suburban synagogue-center" in the fund-raising literature. They were not without their rabbinic critics. Israel Goldstein, of Conservative B'nai Jeshurun of New York City, was especially vigorous in his attacks on the "building mania of our day." He called these institutions a "rabbi's folly and layman's paradise" and did not feel there was much evidence to support the thesis that "card parties and fat reducing exercises under synagogue auspices" made people any more "synagogue-minded or even more Jewishly conscious." He found them simply "banal and vulgar" and predicted that the Jewish community would conclude it had wasted enormous sums of money on a transitory fad. He was mostly right.

By the end of this period, Conservative and Orthodox Judaism had become, for the most part, distinct sectors of American Judaism, and Reform Judaism had settled into a phase of ever-so-slight movement away from its classical iteration, heading toward its eventual embrace of tradition in the 1970s. Some rabbis trained in the Orthodox tradition still served Conservative congregations, some rabbis trained at the Conservative seminary still served Orthodox congregations, and some Reform congregations continued to prohibit their rabbis from wearing head covering during worship services, but the signs of clear distinction among the branches and dramatic ritual changes were everywhere.

If one entered a synagogue sanctuary during worship services at the end of World War II, one was very likely to be able to identify the wing of Judaism. Friday-evening Conservative worship started late, contained abundant English, and always included a sermon, while Sabbath-evening services at Orthodox synagogues started precisely at sundown, rarely had English, and often just contained prayers, not a sermon. At Reform congregations, now welcoming the children and grandchildren of east European immigrants, the signs of tradition were faint but observable. Rabbis were reading prayers in Hebrew that previously had been read only in English, rabbis preached about Palestine and Zionism, a subject rarely broached in previous decades, and *kippot* could be found on the heads of men scattered throughout the sanctuary, if not yet on the rabbi conducting the worship on the pulpit. Except at the time of confirmation—graduation from the religious school program—women did not play much of a role in the sanctuary; even the bat mitzvah ceremony in Reform congregations was rare, and, in a great many, it was simply nonexistent. But, in Reform and Conservative synagogues, as the Second World War came to an end, girls, for the first time, began to enroll in Hebrew school in significant numbers, the first step toward claiming gender equality in the sanctuary. Not much would change even in the 1950s, but, with hindsight, the signs of profound transformations to come were observable everywhere.

5

Expanding Suburbs and Synagogues

The Post–World War II Years

It is estimated that there are 1,800 new synagogues being planned in the United States.

—Percival and Paul Goodman, January 1949

ON NOVEMBER 13, 1946, in Culver City—an independently incorporated city on the western side of Los Angeles County and the home of MGM Studio as well as Hughes Aircraft—three families sat around discussing the need for a West Side Reform congregation in Los Angeles as Jewish servicemen returned home and, with other Jews, began to move to the West Side of Los Angeles in significant numbers. Discussions in early 1947 focused on the availability of low-interest mortgage loans for these Jewish veterans and the confidence these families, now forty to fifty in number, had in the expansion of Jewish institutional life on the West Side. By December 1947, one hundred families (more than ninety having moved to the West Side after World War II), incorporated as Temple Isaiah of Culver City; by 1953, they had built a synagogue on the West Side of Los Angeles; and by October 1955, six hundred families belonged to Temple Isaiah (no longer "of Culver City" as the new building was outside the Culver City limits), and eight hundred Jewish boys and girls attended the religious school on Saturday or Sunday.

Nearly everywhere, congregational bulletins and trustees' min-

utes have little to say about World War II. Yes, there were occasional
dances and special Sabbath services where servicemen about to depart for Europe were the guests, sporadic news items about the war
in the newsletters, continual efforts by sisterhoods and brotherhoods
to organize activities to support the war effort, and an almost total
freeze on building because of the scarcity of materials. But the organized protests of U.S. policy (or lack thereof) concerning the Jews
of Europe, the large-scale rallies to call attention to Jewish deaths in
Nazi-occupied Europe, and the feverish debates among Zionists after
1943 over whether to give up efforts to save European Jewry because
nothing could be done and to work instead to convince Americans
of the importance of a Jewish state were largely organized outside
the synagogues of America. But the congregations of all the wings
of American Judaism would feel the impact of the returning soldiers
after the war ended, especially in the area of urban geography.

The Suburbs

As former soldiers returned from the World War II, they, and others
with growing families, increasingly settled in the rapidly expanding
suburban areas of major cities, whether inside (e.g., Atlanta, Boston,
Chicago, Columbus, Los Angeles, New York, Philadelphia) or outside the city limits (e.g., Baltimore, Boston, Chicago, Cleveland, Detroit, District of Columbia, Minneapolis, New York, Newark, Philadelphia). Urban historians and sociologists have written about the
existence of suburbs ever since cities emerged, but especially beginning in the late nineteenth century. The historian Kenneth T. Jackson
has traced the development of suburbia to the period between 1840
and 1890; the sociologist Gerald Gamm has claimed that "from the
turn of the century until the middle 1920s, the suburban center of
Boston Jewry was in Dorchester and upper Roxbury"; the sociologist
Bruce A. Phillips has argued that already in the nineteenth century,

Brookline (outside Boston) had become the "suburban ideal." But I am using the term here not only for a distant neighborhood ("streetcar suburb") inside a city (Roxbury, part of the city of Boston; Squirrel Hill, part of Pittsburgh; Riverdale, part of New York City; the West Side and North Side of Minneapolis; Palms, Mar Vista, and Cheviot Hills, part of Los Angeles; West Philadelphia and Germantown, part of the city of Philadelphia; Petworth, Brightwood, and Shepherd Park, inside Washington, D.C.) but also for those newly developing areas, beyond city borders, that were reachable mainly by train and automobile, especially after World War II. They are the *real* suburbs.

It is true, as the historian David Kaufman has pointed out, that the post–World War I period saw a "mini-boom of synagogue construction," but the scale of construction now was greatly expanded. The pent-up demand for building—unaffordable during the Depression and prohibited during the war—on cheap land, the "GI Bill of Rights" benefits for mortgages (officially, the Service Members Readjustment Act of 1944), the rapid development of expressways and freeways to the suburbs (federal funding for highway construction would culminate in the Federal-Aid Highway Act of 1956), the racial transformation of cities, and some real estate agents' attempts to create panic and to force whites to sell their homes led to large-scale population movements. The Pasadena and Hollywood Freeways, whose last sections were completed in 1953 and 1954, respectively, opened up the San Gabriel and San Fernando Valleys to residents of Los Angeles; the San Fernando Valley would more than quadruple in population during the 1950s, reaching 500,000 by 1959. The Edens Expressway, opened in 1951, helped create Skokie, north of Chicago, while expressways on the other side of Chicago allowed suburbs to the south such as Park Forest, thirty miles south of downtown, to grow rapidly. Skokie would grow fourfold in the 1950s, reaching a population of 60,000 in 1960. Park Forest, whose first residents moved there in late August 1948, had 1,800 families (8,138 individuals) one year later and 6,300 families (more than 25,000 people) by 1955. Bridges, tunnels, parkways, expressways, and the Long Island Railroad combined to link Nassau County to Manhattan and helped account for the population growth from 673,000 in 1950 to 1.3 million in 1960, 25 percent of whom were Jews. The twenty-six Nassau County synagogues of 1950 expanded to eighty-five at the end of that decade. The Jewish population of Newton, Massachusetts, quadrupled in the 1950s and early 1960s. In suburbs all over the country, houses went up block by block following the war.

The movement of blacks into previously white neighborhoods probably caused most of the Jewish (and white) migration. The South Shore of Chicago, one percent black in 1950, grew to 70 percent black by 1970. The Jews, who numbered 20,000 in the 1950s and who supported at least a dozen synagogues between 71st and 79th Streets and between Jeffrey and Yates, largely left the community by the early 1970s. Similarly, Lawndale, where as late as 1944 there were sixty synagogues—half of all in Chicago—and where blacks took over in the 1950s, emptied of Jews. In city after city, blacks moved into previously heavily white neighborhoods as the whites (including Jews) moved out, including in northeast Washington, DC; Newark, New Jersey; the North Side of Minneapolis; and New York City, where the nonwhite population increased by 41 percent between 1950 and 1957 and the white population decreased by 52 percent.

In northwest Philadelphia (Germantown and Mount Airy) in the 1960s (more than the 1950s), the black population steadily increased and the white population steadily declined. Wagner Junior High went from 17 to 90 percent black from about 1957 to 1968, while Kinsey and Rowen elementary schools, with less than one percent black enrollment in 1951, were more than 90 percent black by the 1967–1968 school year. The membership at every synagogue in the area (e.g., Ramat El, West Oak Lane, Beth Shalom, Ohev Zedek) declined precipitously (between 47 and 58 percent), as the Jewish population shrank from 50,000 at the start of this period to 20,000 at the end.

Earlier, North Philadelphia, with more than 50,000 Jews by 1930 (29 percent of the total Philadelphia Jewish population), had virtually emptied of Jews; Keneseth Israel and Adath Jeshurun members left North Broad Street and moved to the northern Philadelphia suburbs and beyond.

In the fifteen years or so after World War II, the Jews of Cleveland virtually abandoned the city (especially the Woodland and Glenville neighborhoods; the latter, with its 35,000 Jews in 1935, was about 70 percent Jewish at that time). In 1961, according to one Jewish leader, 1,000 Jewish students graduated from public high schools in the Cleveland metropolitan area (Cuyahoga County), of whom a maximum of six received diplomas from a high school in the city of Cleveland itself. And, in all grades combined, Jews constituted perhaps fewer than 250 of the 140,000 children attending the city of Cleveland's public schools. As early as 1950, this leader, Sidney Vincent, called Cleveland (with only slight exaggeration) a "city without Jews."

In Detroit, by 1941, 80 percent of the Jews lived in the Twelfth Street or Dexter (a few blocks west and parallel) neighborhoods, north of Grand Boulevard between Linwood and Hamilton Avenues, having abandoned first the Hasting Street and then the Oakland districts. At least twenty synagogues, as well as commercial, cultural, social, and philanthropic institutions, had moved from Hastings Street in the 1920s and 1930s as the Jews moved, and this process would be repeated with the next move. By 1949, 27 percent of the Jewish population lived in Northwest Detroit (62 percent still inhabited the Dexter Street area), and by 1958 that figure had more than doubled, to 62 percent (only 9 percent remained around Dexter Street). Northwest Detroit, as well as the northern suburb of Oak Park, became the new center of the Jewish population, and the synagogues once again followed the members. In 1952, Oak Park, still developing, housed only 3 percent of the area Jews, but before the end of the decade 28 percent of the Detroit area Jews lived there and only 7 percent remained near Dexter Street. Within a decade—the first blacks moved into the Twelfth Street area in 1947 and 1948—a complete racial transformation took place.

When Jews left communities such as Lawndale in Chicago or the near east side in Columbus, Ohio, and moved to suburbs either inside or outside the city, they usually abandoned their synagogues (just as white Christians abandoned their churches). Of course, there were exceptions. As the black population exploded in the Hyde Park-Kenwood area of Chicago in the 1940s and 1950s, K.A.M. made a commitment to remain in the neighborhood and worked vigorously to create a fifty-fifty balance of whites and blacks. Rabbi Jacob J. Weinstein could claim, at the end of the 1950s, that "this temple was the single most effective anchorage in holding the white people here." This was no easy task, as he also noted in a Yom Kippur sermon, for the "movement to the suburbs is, in the framework of our social and economic mores, almost as natural and instinctive as the flight of the birds to Capistrano." And, in postwar Philadelphia, rather than flee the city, Mikve Israel and Rodeph Shalom reinvented themselves and remained in the city center as their congregants (and other synagogues) left North Philadelphia for the northern Philadelphia suburbs and beyond the city limits. Such congregations, however, were the exception.

Most abandoned synagogues became black churches, and Jews, in their new communities, either built new buildings with the same synagogue name as the old or started over with new synagogues with new names. Baltimore's Temple Oheb Shalom, known as the "Eutaw Place Temple," left its grand synagogue, built in 1892 and modeled after the Great Synagogue in Florence, in the 1950s—the "Eutaw Place Temple" building still dominates Bolton Park, northwest of downtown—as did Baltimore Hebrew Congregation (1948-53) and Chizuk Amuno (1958). Park Synagogue (formerly Anshe Emeth-Beth Tefilo, or the Cleveland Jewish Center), which had already moved from its 1903 building on East 55th (Woodland) to its 1922 building on east 105th (Glenville), moved beyond the city limits to Cleveland Heights in 1950; Cleveland's Anshe Chesed Fairmount Temple, or the "Euclid Avenue Temple," moved from Woodland to Glenville in 1924 and to Beachwood in 1957; Oheb Zedek stood in Woodland in 1904 and in Glenville in 1922 and then, as the "Taylor Road Synagogue," moved to Cleveland Heights in 1955. In Boston, Mishkan Tefila, which moved from the South End to the streetcar suburb of Roxbury and built a neoclassical edifice in 1925, moved with its members from Roxbury and dedicated a new synagogue building in the suburb of Chestnut Hill, Brookline, in 1958, its 100th anniversary; Beth El, which came to the suburb of Dorchester in 1912, moved to Newton in 1955. As Roxbury and Dorchester emptied of Jews (Jewish life ended there by the completion of the 1960s), Newton—with 8,000 Jews in 1950 and 27,000 in 1960—Brookline, Brighton, and Allston thrived. In Los Angeles, Beth Jacob moved with the Jewish community from West Adams to Beverly Hills; B'nai Zion, having already moved from Vermont Avenue and then, in the late 1940s, to 79th and Western, could move no longer and closed down in the 1950s as its members departed the neighborhood. In no fifteen-year period of the twentieth century did Jews build so many synagogues, in so many areas of settlement, as in the years immediately following World War II.

Architecture

Nobody designed more synagogues than the German-born Percival Goodman (1904–1989). Goodman studied at the École des Beaux Arts in Paris and became a New York–based private architect in 1936. He lectured as a professor at Columbia University three afternoons a week beginning in 1946 and was the co-author (with his brother, Paul) of *Communitas: Means of Livelihood and Ways of Life* (1947). He was very much influenced by synagogue designs of the great expressionist architect Eric Mendelsohn (1887–1953)—the pioneer of the combination sanctuary, foyer, and assembly hall, which would enable the sanctuary to expand greatly ("flex") when needed. In 1946 and 1947, Mendelsohn designed several flex synagogues; his design for Washington Hebrew Congregation in the District of Columbia (sent by the senior rabbi to Goodman) had a 600-seat "week-day" sanctuary that could expand to 1,800–2,000 seats for the High Holy Days. Goodman studied some of Mendelsohn's designs, incorporated several of his ideas, and would design more than fifty synagogues in the first decade after World War II—a period of unparalleled church as well as synagogue construction. He was not without at least one detractor; Lou Berry, who raised money for Southfield, Michigan's new Shaarei Zedek (dedicated in 1962), noted that "Goodman did 41 bad synagogues [but] he will get everything right here."

Most of Goodman's 1950s synagogues were distinguished by the use of light ("The room is well, even brightly, lit," he wrote, "so the worshipers may see each other clearly as well as easily read their books"), elevated pulpits, choir areas, and the integration of sculpture, painting, and stained glass into the design. For the synagogue he designed in Millburn, New Jersey, he secured commissions for work by three leading sculptors, including two bronzes by Ibram Lassaw ("Pillars of Fire" and "Pillar of Cloud") chosen by the Museum of Modern Art for exhibition at the Venice Biennale of 1954, a Torah curtain by Adolph Gottlieb (on extended loan to the Jewish Museum in New York City), a lobby mural by Robert Motherwell, and a relief sculpture by Herbert Ferber. Everywhere (often without success), he pushed the fund-raisers to include an art budget equal to 5 percent of the total costs; for Beth-El in Providence, Rhode Island (perhaps his earliest design, it has a neoclassical sanctuary that evokes the Georgian architecture of Newport's Touro synagogue), he sought, unsuccessfully, Lipschitz sculptures and Chagall tapestries. His model was Italian churches; he argued that, "if the smallest congregation spent its money for a real work of art in its temple, over the years this work of art would pay for its expenditure," for "people would come to see it; travelers go out of their way to see works of art." And he would sum this argument up succinctly: "God is interested in beauty!"

But Goodman is largely remembered for the concept of a multi-use foyer and social hall that open to the sanctuary or some other innovative way to expand the normal size sanctuary when large crowds assemble on Rosh Hashanah and Yom Kippur. "It is necessary to design the social parts, the educational parts and the worship hall as a unity," he instructed, "for all our activities shall be a hymn in His praise." The synagogue he designed in Lebanon, Pennsylvania, Congregation Beth Israel, sat 200, but, when "flexed," could accommodate another 200 or even 250 worshipers, and the Goodman sanctuary at Temple Beth Emeth in Albany, New York, opened up to a great hall that expanded the seating capacity from 605 to more than 1,800. When Goodman designed Temple Beth Sholom in Miami Beach, the 700 seats with pews became 2,000 when expanded, and Temple Israel of Westport, Connecticut, had a small Goodman sanctuary that sat 200 but, when flexed, could hold 1,000. He designed a Conservative synagogue in Springfield, Massachusetts, Temple Beth El, where folding doors between the social hall and sanctuary slid apart to seat, with portable chairs, 2,000, and his sanctuary in Tulsa, at Temple Israel, when expanded, jumped the seating capacity from fewer than 300 to 900. In Providence, Temple Beth-El featured a sanctuary that sat nearly 1,000 but had a partition that could open and expand the seating to 1,600; in Lakewood, New Jersey, the synagogue (Congregation Sons of Israel) he designed expanded from 350 to 700 seats; Temple Beth El in Rochester "flexed" from 700 to 2,500 when the foyer and the social hall were opened; and when the wall comes down at the rear of the sanctuary at St. Paul's Temple of Aaron, the 456 permanent seats become 800. The sanctuary in Temple Emanuel of Pittsburgh sat 300, but, when the folding doors opened, more than 1,000 worshipers could be seated; while the sanctuary in Highland Park, Illinois's Beth El sat 365 with the doors closed, between 550

Example of a flex sanctuary designed by Percival Goodman. Temple Israel, Tulsa,
Oklahoma, built 1955. Photograph by Bernie Guzik.

and 600 (for bar and bat mitzvah ceremonies) could be accommo-
dated with the first doors open and 1,800 (for the High Holy Days)
with the walls of the social hall taken down. At Congregation Beth
Shalom in Oak Park, Illinois, Goodman designed a sanctuary that
sat 505, but, when the back walls were opened, another 900 people
took their seats. When taken down, the removable wooden wall
—huge wooden panels fit in a metal frame which took a full day
to disassemble—in Manchester, New Hampshire's Temple Adath
Yeshurun expanded the fixed pews in the sanctuary from 282 places
to 700, while the sanctuary Goodman designed in Durham's Beth El
expanded from 225 to 525 when "flexed". Out west, or as far west as
Goodman worked, Denver's Emanuel sat 950 in fixed seats but, when
the rear doors opened, that number expanded to 1,700. Perhaps the
most unusual sanctuary he designed is in the West End Synagogue
in Nashville, Tennessee, where the pulpit moves back into the social

hall when "flexed" and the 325 seats become 925. Everywhere in the 1950s (Temple Beth Sholom, Miami Beach, 1956; Temple Isaiah, Los Angeles, 1953) synagogue architects (like Philip Johnson, who noted that "the congregation comes only on the High Holy Days") imitated this "flex" style.

The wild synagogue construction boom of this period required considerable money, and both the Conservative and Reform national offices held seminars and workshops to instruct congregational campaign committees on fund-raising. One of the suggestions, widely implemented, was to hire a professional fund-raiser, who would suggest a "battle plan" heavily dependent on military terminology. The campaign committee would establish "divisions"—usually by professions, occupations, or the like (e.g., dentists, physicians, attorneys, accountants, housewives)—and make one of the dentists "captain" of the dental division. The committee would keep close tabs on the captains with letters like this one: "Captains—are you checking with your 'soldiers' and your 'lieutenants'?" The campaign committee would also "rate" as many members as possible—establish their target contribution, solicit captains with this rate in mind, and then pass the rate for soldiers along to the captains for their solicitations.

Obviously, given the number of synagogues constructed, many of these fund-raising campaigns enjoyed success, usually spurred by floods of new members. The 1950s was a decade of "belonging" —President Eisenhower urged every American to join a church and emphasized that it did not matter which one. Temple Beth Israel of Phoenix, Arizona, jumped from 300 families in 1948 to 538 in 1953 and 650 in 1958. Everywhere, not just in the Sun Belt, there were similar stories, and these new members made commitments to building funds as they joined synagogues. Temple Emanu-El in Birmingham, Alabama, began a campaign in 1955 for a $300,000 education building and dedicated it in 1956 with $285,000 in hand. Atlanta's Ahavath Achim launched a campaign in 1955 and by 1957 was able to break ground with almost $1 million confirmed. The building was desperately needed as the congregation grew steadily through the decade. Consultants told Congregation Children of Israel in Augusta, Georgia, in 1948 that they would need to raise $100,000 for a new synagogue; the members accomplished this within two years and broke ground in 1950. Other congregations, drawing upon a technique used by the federal government during the world wars, sold "bond issues" with semi-annual interest payments in exchange for loans.

Greatly aiding the solicitation efforts for new synagogues was the continuing, though modified, practice—subsequently much less common—of selling specific seats or pews. For a generous contribution, names of family members would be placed on the arm, as at St. Louis Congregation B'nai Amoona in 1952, or on the back of a seat, as at Washington Hebrew Congregation, D.C., in 1955, and ushers would make certain these places were reserved for those individuals on the High Holy Days. In both Conservative and Reform synagogues this practice often caused resentment among those who could not afford to buy permanent seats, and it resulted in considerable confusion when the original purchasers of the seats died and family members inherited the seats from their original owners. Both problems became acute when the owners of the seats failed to show at worship services, and those without permanent seats filled less desirable areas of the sanctuary (the "flexed" part behind the permanent seats) and viewed the empty seats.

Reform Judaism

We must always remind ourselves, as noted earlier, that when we discuss Reform, Conservative, and Orthodox congregants in any period, we are discussing a minority of the Jews in America. Rabbi Abraham M. Hershman of Detroit's Shaarey Zedek noted, in a 1922 address to the Phoenix Club, that most Jews were neither Reform nor Orthodox but unaffiliated. The 1950s may have been a decade of

unusually high church attendance, but Jewish religious affiliation remained low, no matter the city one studies. A population study of the
Los Angeles Jewish community in 1950 and 1951 revealed that a third
of the Jews in Los Angeles did not identify themselves as Reform,
Conservative, or Orthodox; of the two-thirds that did so, only a third
claimed to belong to a synagogue. Thus, less than 20 percent of Los
Angeles Jewry belonged to a Reform, Conservative, or Orthodox
synagogue. The Conservative Rabbinical Assembly reported in 1959
that, although 27,000 Jewish youth studied in Philadelphia religious
schools, 23,000 had no Jewish education. And, according to rabbis,
over and over and everywhere, those who did belong rarely showed
up except for the High Holy Days. Rabbi Louis Binstock of Chicago
noted, as did dozens of others in the decade of the 1950s, that, "in
spite of the boom in construction and enrollment, we are a bust in
devout prayer and regular worship. Congregations contain more and
more families, but fewer and fewer who are faithful; more *pay*-ers but
fewer *pray*-ers." He added, in another sermon, that the "emptiness of
pews" was in "inverse proportion to the rising membership rolls."

To a great extent, not much changed from earlier decades in the
Reform synagogue during the 1950s and well into the 1960s, though,
by the late 1960s, as we will see, the synagogue had become a very
different place from what it was in the 1940s and 1950s. Rabbi Joseph
Narot came to Miami's Temple Israel in 1950, eliminated head covering and prayer shawls, and frowned upon the bar mitzvah ceremony.
At Pittsburgh's Rodef Shalom, Rabbi Solomon B. Freehof put the
normative position of the early postwar period well: "We believe that
the essential of the worship of God is the ethical mandate and that
the ceremonial is incidental, if anything. That is our principle.... We
shall never make a religion for us out of all these observances. . . .
No rabbi will ever try to persuade you that God commanded you to
light lights on Friday night." The Sabbath-morning service at Temple
Beth-El in Providence began at 11 A.M., ended at noon, and included
a bar mitzvah! While not every Reform synagogue, by any means,

fit the description of "classical" Reform—there are examples of re-
trieval of tradition and of restoring customs and observances absent
from Reform services for decades (e.g., the sanctification of the wine,
the wearing of the head covering and the prayer shawl, the use of a
wedding canopy, and the construction of a *sukkah*)—the patterns of
synagogue worship, religious school, adult education, youth groups,
social activity, and social action had much in common around the
country, whether we investigate synagogues in California, Florida,
Georgia, Illinois, Massachusetts, New Jersey, New York, Ohio, Pennsylvania, Rhode Island, Texas, or Washington State. Most Reform
congregants in these years would have envied the claim by Rabbi
Maurice Goldblatt of Indianapolis Hebrew Congregation (I.H.C.)
that "more and more Christian groups found their way to the Temple." I.H.C., like so many other congregations active in interfaith or
ecumenical programs, welcomed numerous church groups to Sabbath worship services throughout the 1950s.

As an example, we can consider eight Reform congregations in
Chicago, two in Philadelphia, one in Minneapolis, one in Baltimore,
and one in Beverly Hills. With the name of the senior rabbi in pa-
rentheses they are Baltimore Hebrew Congregation (Morris Lieber-
man), Emanuel Congregation (Herman E. Schaalman), Isaiah-Israel
(H. Goren Perelmuter), K.A.M. (Jacob J. Weinstein), Kenesset Israel
(Bertram W. Korn), Rodeph Shalom (David H. Wice), Sinai Temple
(Louis L. Mann), South Shore Temple (Ahron Opher), Temple Beth
Israel (Ernst Lorge), Temple Emanuel (Bernard Harrison), Temple
Israel (Albert G. Minda), Temple Mizpah (Joseph Buchler), and
Temple Sholom (Louis Binstock). The pattern of Reform synagogue
life in these congregations in the 1950s differed not at all from that in
most other Reform congregations in America.

For Sabbath worship, the rabbis and worshipers used the newly
revised *Union Prayer Book for Jewish Worship, Part I* (Cincinnati,
1954, 1940), with either cantor or choir (sometimes both) singing
the hymns. All the hymns were marked "Choir," not "Cantor," as

the widespread use of cantors, or even soloists, had not yet arrived, though hazans had previously acted as readers or chanters of the liturgy as one of their duties. The emergence of cantors as soloists began with the emigration of numerous well-trained cantors from eastern Europe in the late nineteenth century, when, at last, there was a plethora of such men for American synagogues to hire. In most congregations, the worshipers passively listened to the choirs sing, although a number of hymns were marked "Choir and Congregation." Years of listening were not easily overcome by Reform congregants of this decade.

Rabbi Solomon B. Freehof noted, in 1963, that "a central aim" of Reform Judaism was "the restoration of the sermon to its former importance." Although there were long centuries when the regular Sabbath scriptural sermon was no longer heard in European Jewish communities, it is not completely clear to which period Freehof refers. Perhaps it is the golden age of preaching between the World Wars, when rabbis such as Barnett Brickner, Solomon Goldman, Leo Jung, Joseph Lookstein, Abba Hillel Silver, Stephen S. Wise, and others would fill sanctuaries as well as assembly halls. As we have seen, the High Holy Day schedules that appeared in their bulletins even listed the precise time their sermons would begin and end. The Baltimore, Beverly Hills, Chicago, and Philadelphia rabbis published in their bulletins a list of their sermon titles a month ahead, delivered carefully prepared manuscripts, usually typed in duplicate and read (with constant marginalia reminding them to have abundant eye contact with the worshipers), and concentrating on moral and/or ethical issues of the day or political and/or social events. Civil rights, for example, was a major issue in the last years of the 1950s; often the sermons took ethical positions on these very same current events. In the North, East, and West, where de facto but not de jure segregation existed everywhere, congregants apparently overwhelmingly approved of the strong rabbinic opposition to segregation, and Reform rabbis preached about this topic more than any other topic.

Rabbis in Baltimore, Beverly Hills, Chicago, and Philadelphia were little different. They filled their sermons with citations from the Hebrew Bible (especially the Prophets), as well as from general literature, and frequently urged their listeners—in words that seemed to convey great passion—to take an active role in the struggle for civil rights for blacks. It is notable in this regard that, according to a survey of sermon titles, rabbis generally do not seem to have similarly preached on the Holocaust at all; it took fifteen years or so for it to become a subject understood and discussed in public where children and parents worshiped together.

As we saw earlier, the Reform movement had eliminated much of the traditional liturgy and cut the reading of Scripture down to one-seventh of what was read in Conservative and Orthodox worship services on a Saturday morning. But the main sermon occasion was not the Sabbath-morning service, where a bar mitzvah usually took place, but the Friday night service, where an abbreviated liturgy and the absence of Scripture reading expanded the minutes available for the sermon. And the move of the Scripture reading platform from the middle of the sanctuary—where a preacher would have his back to much of the congregation—to the wall made it possible for a Friday evening preacher (as well as the Saturday morning Scripture reader) to face the entire congregation.

Congregants recall frequently the "rabbinic voice," suggesting that the rabbis, as many still do, had one voice for reading prayers and another voice for talking after worship services about baseball. At the larger congregations, the candidate for bar mitzvah had little intimate contact with the senior rabbi—there were too many twelve-year-old boys (sixty at Temple Isaiah in Los Angeles from September 1955 to June 1956). Bar mitzvah tutors, Hebrew school teachers, assistant rabbis, and the cantors (where they existed) were the people with whom the young men mostly interacted. Torah portions were quite short; additional Scriptural readings (*haftarot*) were also short; and every young man delivered a brief sermon about the biblical verses that he read. Receptions at homes and in the social hall were the norm; it was far more common to remain in the synagogue for a party than to go to a restaurant or hotel.

Rabbis (and choirs or cantors) rarely came off the pulpit during services, whether it was to carry the Torah or to speak. The Torah went from the ark against the pulpit wall to the nearby reading table and back to the ark; the rabbi spoke from the same podium at which he read the service; and the choir and/or cantor stayed put in a designated spot. The only movement up and down from the pulpit was by those who participated in the Torah reading (*aliyot*) with a blessing or by one of the elected officers, who might present a *kiddush* (wine) cup to the bar mitzvah lad. For most Reform rabbis, especially in the 1950s, increasing tradition made them nervous. Rabbi Morris Lieberman of Baltimore Hebrew Congregation worried that Reform Judaism was becoming more Orthodox in 1952 when he noticed an increasing number of reform men wearing "*talis* and cap" during worship services.

While the amount of Hebrew the rabbi read from the liturgy varied from place to place, it was never very much, as the *UPB* contained very little. The prayer called the *amidah* (standing), or sometimes either *tefilah* (the prayer) or *shemoneh esrey* (eighteen, because it originally had eighteen blessings), is one of the two central sections of the Jewish liturgy. The *UPB* had four services from which a rabbi could choose for a Friday evening, and only one contained it in its full Sabbath form. And many prayers, central to the liturgy, were included only in English, with no Hebrew version at all.

All of these congregations recited the Sabbath blessing over candles during the Sabbath service on Friday evening, even though it was traditionally a home ceremony, not one for the synagogue. Seemingly, most of the worshipers did not light Sabbath candles at home, so the ritual was moved into the sanctuary. When a *sukkah*, or booth, was erected at these synagogues (not very common) for the holiday of Sukkot (Tabernacles—see Leviticus 23), it was usu-

ally done on the pulpit, not outside, as is the custom. Minor holidays, festivals, and fast days were celebrated on the closest weekend
or not at all; worship services took place only on Friday evening, Saturday morning, and (in two or three cases) Sunday morning, never
on weekdays unless it was a major holiday. Holidays were celebrated
for one day—not two, as in traditional synagogues—and nearly all
the members of the synagogue attended services on either (or both)
the Jewish New Year or the Day of Atonement—thus the need for a
"flex" sanctuary or, in most cases (only a minority of congregations
could build a new edifice), rented public halls.

Plenty of sermons by the thirteen rabbis I have named survive
from the middle of the 1950s, and one is able to summarize them
in a general way. First, and most obvious, is the style—flowery and
without much in the way of textual reference. The rabbis are much
more likely to talk about applying the eternal verities of mature religious faith to the burning issues of their time—especially civil rights
—than to cite a biblical or rabbinic text, explicate the text, and use
the text and its exegesis to suggest an authority or even a strategy for
action. Their emphasis was overwhelmingly on the ethical imperatives of Judaism—the essence of Reform Judaism for them all—and
a general sense of how these ethical imperatives (e.g., the experience
of freedom from Egypt for the Hebrew slaves) might be models for
contemporary action (e.g., breaking the yoke of prejudice against
blacks). Indeed, the expansion of full rights to blacks (what Rabbi
Minda called "the progress and welfare of my Negro fellow citizens")
or civil rights was the most frequent topic of these sermons. This was
true on Rosh Hashanah and Yom Kippur (especially after citing the
verse in Isaiah, "Is this the fast I have chosen?" or Amos 9:7, "Are you
any better than the children of the Ethiopians to me, children of Israel, says God") as well as on the Sabbath; discussion of a general
theme from the Rosh Hashanah or Yom Kippur liturgy (e.g., atonement, or the Kol Nidre prayer that is sung on Yom Kippur) dominated at least one of the four or five sermons for the High Holy Days.

Nearly every rabbi preached on civil rights repeatedly, and almost every preacher acknowledged that Jews outside the South were as fearful of blacks as were white southerners, noting that congregants simply moved away when blacks approached instead of burning crosses on the newcomers' lawns. One rabbi noted that, in many non-Jewish neighborhoods, residents defended their turf against the incursion of blacks; in contrast, when blacks moved into a mostly Jewish neighborhood, "with the milk of human kindness and brotherly love for the Negro of Little Rock pumping in his veins, [the Jew] picks up his skirts and runs before the Negro." He challenged his congregants to do more than just criticize Jim Crow laws in the South.

The Reform rabbinic emphasis on civil rights was encouraged by the president of the union of Reform congregations, Rabbi Maurice Eisendrath. He was the driving force behind the creation, in 1949, of the Joint Commission on Social Action of the Union of American Hebrew Congregations and the Central Conference of American [Reform] Rabbis. He pushed Reform rabbis and congregants to "apply the precepts and practices of prophetic Jewish faith in combating all forms of injustice and bigotry." He encouraged Reform rabbis and rabbinic students to join the freedom rides in Mississippi and, especially, to participate in the 1964 Mississippi voter registration campaign, notwithstanding complaints from some Reform congregations in the South, where members feared white reprisals in an environment where their neighbors burned freedom buses and beat the freedom riders while southern police arrested the victims, not the perpetrators.

The Reform commitment to civil rights in the 1950s culminated in the establishment of the Social Action Center in Washington, D.C., in 1959, and, two years later, the Emily and Kivie Kaplan Center for Religious Action. Opened with the overwhelming support of Reform congregations everywhere, the center, from its inception, lobbied on Capitol Hill on behalf of civil rights for blacks and gave strong support to both the Congress of Racial Equality and the

National Association for the Advancement of Colored People. Eisen-drath spoke repeatedly at Reform synagogues about his commitment to social action, repeatedly urging social action programs to respond to the "vast miasma of venomous racial hatred and segregation which rises like a stink in God's nostrils." And, at the same time, he urged Reform Jews to do all they could for troubled Jewish communities around the world (in Ethiopia, Iran, Iraq, Syria, and the Soviet Union), as well as for the Jewish poor in America.

Amazingly, none of the northern and western rabbis preached on civil rights with the "tongue-lashings" of a courageous southern preacher, Rabbi Jacob M. Rothschild of Atlanta's The Temple. While the chief of police, Fred Beerman, surely exaggerated when he said that "every sermon was about integration," the latter was a constant theme as early as 1948 but especially in 1955 and 1956, when Rothschild repeatedly castigated members who hid from doing something to change the South into a "world of human equality."

A count of the people these rabbis cited most frequently in their sermons finds, in the top six, Matthew Arnold, Albert Einstein, Sigmund Freud, Martin Luther King, George Orwell, and Hasidic rabbis. Many frequently complained (while affirming their patriotism) about the mediocrity of politicians (especially when discussing the House Un-American Activities Committee and the "Red Scare"), the low level of adult Jewish literacy, the hydrogen bomb, "over-the-top" bar mitzvah receptions, the "loyalty oath" passed by the California legislature in 1953 in the face of the "Red Scare," to test the loyalty of college faculty and teachers, congregants who "sit with pressed lips and clenched teeth and never open their mouths," and how the lack of significant antisemitism in America was now actually a threat to Jewish survival (it was so easy to be a Jew in America in the 1950s that there was a great danger, as *Look* magazine would suggest a decade later, that Judaism would simply vanish). Most striking is the absence of much discussion of Israel, aside from concern during the Suez crisis and war. One or two of these rabbis described themselves as "non-Zionist," but most of them identified themselves as Zionists, as did most Reform rabbis in 1955–1956, in a shift from the interwar period. Yet, the depth and breadth of their concern for Israel, as expressed in weekly preaching, was minimal. Perhaps they felt Israel was doing quite well as it approached its tenth anniversary and that its influence on Reform Jewish life in these Reform congregations was small.

If we look at the sermons preached at these same thirteen congregations ten years later—1965–1966—we find that only a little had changed. blacks' fight was still the Jews' fight; Jews were not free if blacks were not free; and surely America was not free if either was enslaved. Civil rights ("The March on Montgomery" was the title of three of the sermons in 1965) was still the most frequent theme (of course, the urban riots across America dominated the news), but a decidedly Jewish topic had emerged, as antisemitism resurfaced in places such as Czechoslovakia, Hungary, Poland, and Rumania, affecting Jews behind the Iron Curtain in general and Soviet Jewry in particular. The American Conference on Soviet Jewry and the Student Struggle for Soviet Jewry emerged in 1964, and no rabbi in 1965–1966 failed to deliver at least one sermon on the sad situation of Jews in the Soviet Union.

The preaching, and that is the proper word for Reform homiletics of the 1950s and early 1960s, was very formal. Rarely did one of these rabbis preach from just notes, even on Friday nights; they found the time—so rare in subsequent decades as the role of the rabbi changed —to carefully prepare a full sermon typescript each week. Most of them did not appear to engage with Jewish texts, rabbinic or medieval or modern; at least, the fruits of such study (especially Talmud, *midrash*, commentaries, philosophy) was not evident in the sermons. God was certainly not absent, as rabbis periodically affirmed their belief—in rather general terms—in a living God, and, more surprisingly, given that classical Reform Judaism preferred to speak of the giving of the Torah as a metaphor, not a fact, in divine revelation at Sinai (even more vaguely). While Rabbi Morris Lieberman once claimed that "without close second or parallel, the greatest and most sublime event in the history of our people was the revelation at Sinai —the Divine Voice was heard by all the nations of the earth, coming to each in its own tongue," few Reform rabbis would make such bold affirmations. But, no matter the theology, the range of Jewish sources that would become more evident in Reform rabbinic discourse a few decades later was missing.

Finally, both Reform and Conservative rabbis (fewer typescript sermons are available from Orthodox rabbis) recycled a single sermon many times, usually (but not always!) at different locations. Rabbi Henry Berkowitz noted, in 1921, that "I have delivered the same sermon on another occasion." Like Berkowitz, it was commonplace to write on the first page of a typescript the place and date the sermon was delivered, and scores of existing texts have multiple dates and places. Perhaps the sermon preached most often was called "What Do Jews Believe?"; the rabbi who wrote this interesting text delivered it in Columbus and Starkville, Mississippi (1939), Niagara Falls (1941 and 1942), in the San Diego area at eleven different places between 1946 and 1963, and, finally, once, in 1970. His congregation heard it only three times, and, unlike Rabbi Harold I. Saperstein, "who rarely repeated the same sermon without change," the author does not seem to have ever revised it!

Supplemental Jewish education was at its peak in this period. It was usually called "Sunday school," whether it took place on Saturday or Sunday, and midweek afternoon "Hebrew school"—mostly for boys preparing for bar mitzvah—took place one or two weekdays per week. And, virtually everywhere, the Sunday school culminated with "confirmation" at the end of the ninth or tenth grade. The Reform movement published curricula materials for every grade level and dozens of subjects; textbooks, workbooks (student and teacher), posters, and magazines flowed from the education department of national headquarters. Most synagogues sought, first, Jewish teachers

from public schools, hoping that their pedagogical skills, when supplemented by modest training in Judaica, would enable them to cope
with students who would, generally, have much preferred to run
around outside or sleep in than attend religious school on a weekend
morning.

The Temple in Cleveland is fairly representative with regard to
the end of this schooling process, confirmation, except that most
synagogues ended in the tenth grade instead of the ninth, as did
The Temple. Eighth grade was pre-confirmation; ninth grade was
confirmation; and both were taught by the rabbis of the congregation. There were attendance requirements, exams, and even summer-
school make-up (e.g., for those who failed the Hebrew reading examination). Students took notes when the rabbis lectured and had
regular reading assignments. The 1958–1959 classes used William
Silverman's *The Still Small Voice: The Story of Jewish Ethics* (1955) in
pre-confirmation and Roland Gittelsohn's *Little Lower than the Angels*
(1955) in confirmation, supplemented by a study of the liturgy in the
Union Prayer Book. Rabbi Abba Hillel Silver gave the confirmation
lectures in 1958–1959.

The class was run like the most disciplined weekday schoolroom,
and bad behavior was not tolerated. Indeed, failing a class or drop-
ping out was a serious mark against someone. Buses picked students
up after school and on the weekend (the students did not, of course,
drive, and mothers were not expected to chauffeur their children),
and students dressed for weekend classes as if they were dressing for
worship services. Indeed, at every weekend class session, some time
was spent in the sanctuary in worship. Confirmation culminated
with a grand ceremony—usually written by the rabbis, who also
conducted the rehearsals and listened to the talks students prepared,
much like a high school graduation, but with each graduate showing off some of his or her Judaica learning. And, concomitantly, the
families of many of the girls hosted formal dances—mostly at hotels—to celebrate the graduation of their daughters. The girls chose

GUIDE FOR EVALUATION OF INSTRUCTION

Instructor: Miri Pinchuk	Grade: 4
Evaluator: Dr. Allen Howard Podet	
Date: 1 March 1970	Time: 9:30 A.M.
Title of Lesson: Hebrew-continuing	Type of Lesson: Knowledge
	Note: 2nd visit--See 2 Nov 69
Introduction	Warm and comfortable. Starts w/shalom song and finger-snap routine. Very warm, smiling routine. Sets tone of extreme support and non-challenge.
Presentation	See above and 2 Nov 69. Makes effective use of number games--countoff of boys and girls, counting by threes. Places 3 figures on the board, calls one in Hebrew, has other copy right one, erases the wrong 2, and asks for hands of right answers. This copy technique is designed to maximize success experiences. Constant variation of techniques. Word cards, writing, counting, underline in book. Spell-down. Copying. Fit in a selection in a blank. Pronounce as individual and as class.
Training Aids	Use of board is good. Uses word cards extensively and well. I have seen her improvise a cycle answer game around a basketball pass.
Application	Writes pointings like
Summary	Built into practice games. Whole class is structured as one game after another.
Use of Lesson Plan	One of the most highly effective examples of planning and using appropriate methodology in the school.
Questioning	Constant and relaxed. Usually only ½ directed to a specific person. Asks for hands generally.
Instructor Characteristics	Highly supportive and warm. The "accepting mother" type. No visible traces of hostility or disappointment. Very relaxed.
Assignment	Review of last exercise.

Sunday School evaluation of instruction for grade 4 Hebrew class, Temple Sinai, Bellevue, Washington, March 1, 1970. Temple Sinai (Bellevue, WA) Records (MS-393) Box 1, Folder 3. Courtesy of the American Jewish Archives, Cincinnati, Ohio.

dresses for these events as if they were selecting a dress to wear to a wedding.

The Reform umbrella organization, the Union of American Hebrew Congregations, published numerous texts and provided curriculum suggestions for every grade of religious school. Most Reform congregations used these materials, supplemented by texts published by Berhrman House, KTAV, or the Conservative movement. When fourth- through sixth-graders studied Jewish history in Reform synagogues in the post–World War II years, they made heavy use of Mordecai I. Soloff's *When the Jewish People Was Young* and *How the Jewish People Lives Today*. Rabbi Soloff wrote these texts, and the UAHC first published them, before World War II; Soloff periodically revised them a bit, and the UAHC provided students with "pupil's workbooks" and instructors with "teacher's books." An entire generation of Reform Jewish children grew up arguing over whether the title should have been *When the Jewish People* Were *Young* and absorbing Soloff's rather boring but historically quite accurate view of the Jewish past. When Soloff's texts were not used by Reform synagogues, the most popular alternatives were the Conservative movement equivalent of Soloff, Deborah Pessin's *History of the Jews in America* and *The Jewish People*, also complete with "pupil's activity books" and "teacher's guides" and published by the Commission on Jewish Education of the Conservative umbrella organization, the United Synagogue of America. Alternatively, a popular text choice was *The Story of the Jew*, by Lee Levinger (and, later, in revised editions, his wife, Elma Levinger), a history also first written and published, like Soloff's books, in the 1930s.

Students were assigned homework from these mostly dry books —pages of the text to read during the week—but few took this seriously. The few who did acquired a good background in Jewish history (and many other subjects), as the texts used throughout the curriculum in Reform synagogues during these years were informative and thoughtful. In addition, nearly everywhere, the classes convened in the sanctuary for a brief worship service (either the Sabbath liturgy, if the classes met on Saturday, or the Weekday prayer service, if on Sunday). For most students, this was their only contact with the senior rabbi—someone on a high platform who read words in Hebrew and English and gave a little talk, as well. Few students from these years recall personal contact with the senior rabbi; they remember only an elderly (no matter his age) father figure on the pulpit but also the opportunity to read and sing (and, often, learn by rote), over and over, the main parts of the worship service.

The 1950s and early 1960s were a period of considerable adult education in Reform congregations. For the first time, rabbis and other synagogue professionals began to think in terms of adult Jewish studies, and courses of all kinds filled the weekday evenings of congregational assembly rooms. The format was mostly lecture—either by the rabbi or by local people with expertise in some area of Judaica—and most courses ran for several weeks rather than consisting of a single lecture. But the latter was common as well, and single-session lectures usually were offered on Sunday mornings, as congregations continued the practice, begun before the war, of hosting a morning lecture series for adults while many of their children were in religious school. Numerous Reform congregations called their program a College of Jewish Studies, and, though there were no formal college courses or even courses with any "credits," so many of the adults in these congregations had children who were the first generation to attend college or university that the parents, too, could have a faux college experience.

Reform congregations in these years were part of a local (e.g., Southern California Federation of Temple Youth; Ohio Valley Federation of Temple Youth) and national (National Federation of Temple Youth) organization of youth groups. Individual synagogue youth groups had social, cultural, and even, occasionally, religious activities, and, a few times a year, they joined other local youth groups for weekend programs. Some of the youth group members also participated in regional programs at Reform Jewish youth camps scattered through-out the country. At the end of the 1950s, 20,000 youngsters belonged to Reform youth groups, and the synagogue was their central meet-ing place.

These were the golden years for social events at Reform congrega-tions, with brotherhood and sisterhood activities the highlight. Both organizations attracted large numbers, as endless social activities (often connected with synagogue fund-raising) dotted their respec-tive calendars. One Chicago congregation had a Brotherhood Week, regular brotherhood and sisterhood bowling teams, and a brother-hood softball team, and each of these groups hosted more than fif-teen speakers during the 1955–1956 school year. The sisterhood spon-sored a Purim carnival, an art fair, an auction, and a bingo night and sold Hanukah decorations and wrapping paper to raise funds for the synagogue, while the brotherhood supplied ushers for High Holy Day services and held a father-son barbecue to support the Sunday school. Sunday mornings, when (presumably) many fathers dropped their kids at the temple for religious school, was an especially popu-lar brotherhood activity time, while the sisterhood—packed with women who did not work—met mainly during weekdays.

The social action agenda of these Baltimore, Beverly Hills, Chi-cago, Minneapolis, and Philadelphia congregations was nearly as busy as the social calendar. Voter registration drives (probably among blacks) and fair-housing campaigns (presumably also for blacks) dominated the agenda (social action and social justice programs usu-ally meant activities on behalf of blacks). Occasionally an activity for elderly and or poor Jews is to be found listed in a synagogue bulle-tin, but (seemingly) these congregations found few needs among the Jews of Baltimore, Beverly Hills (or Los Angeles), Chicago Minne-apolis, or Philadelphia for synagogue groups to address. Rabbi Jacob J. Weinstein summed it up nicely in 1955: "We have very few poor among us."

Nationwide, only 9 percent of suburban women worked in the

1950s, and there is no evidence that this figure was different in the Jewish community. Bulletins indicate clearly that all of these congregations benefited tremendously from the attention and unpaid labor of member wives with no other places to direct their energies and ambitions in the 1950s. Overwhelmingly, the women of these congregations did not work outside the home, and synagogue volunteering, adult education classes, and sisterhood social events (the PTA, too) took up a significant part of their lives. Their daughters (and their granddaughters), to a great extent, would not have the same free time to devote to synagogues in the 1970s and beyond.

Conservative Judaism

In contrast to the interwar years, Conservative synagogues had, by the 1950s, rather clearly delineated themselves as a branch of Judaism quite distinct from orthodoxy. Membership in the United Synagogue of America meant, overwhelmingly, a rabbi ordained by the Jewish Theological Seminary, men and women seated together in the pews, a bat mitzvah ceremony (still rare), an abbreviated, late-Friday-evening service with plenty of English, a lengthy Sabbath morning "traditional" service, and the use of the common "Silverman prayer book" rather than each individual bringing his own prayer book. Few people mistook a Conservative worship service for an Orthodox service, even when some of the latter had mixed seating, by the 1950s.

For example, we can consider five Conservative congregations in Boston, two in Cleveland, one in Phoenix, and one in Los Angeles during the Jewish calendar year 1955–1956. With the name of the senior rabbi in parentheses, they are Beth El (Harry Z. Schectman), Bnai Jeshurun (Rudolph [Rudy] M. Rosenthal), Congregation Mishkan Tefila (Israel J. Kazis), Kehillath Israel (Louis M. Epstein), Park Synagogue (Armond Cohen), Temple Beth Am/Olympic Jewish Temple (Jacob Pressman), Temple Emanuel (Albert I. Gordon),

Temple Emeth (Zev K. Nelson), and Temple Reyim (Harold Kastle). The pattern of Conservative synagogue life in these congregations did not differ significantly from that of scores of Conservative synagogues elsewhere, including each rabbi's annual "sermon exchange" with a "sister congregation" (i.e., church) on a Friday evening in December.

Conservative liturgical development began in 1927 with the publication of the *Festival Prayer Book* by the United Synagogue of America. By 1950, however, nearly every congregation worshiped with the "Silverman prayer book" (*Sabbath and Festival Prayer Book*, 1946), an amazingly successful, aesthetically pleasing liturgy edited by Morris Silverman, a conservative rabbi at Emanuel Synagogue in Hartford, Connecticut, for nearly forty years (1923–1961). Silverman had developed an experimental Sabbath morning Junior Prayer Book in looseleaf format in 1933 (it appeared in book form in 1935 as *The Junior Prayer Book, Volume One, for All Sabbaths, Festivals, National and Patriotic Occasions* and in 1937 as *The Junior Prayer Book for Synagogue, School, Home and Camp, Volume Two, High Holyday Services*). Traditional in content and frequently reprinted, Silverman's book "reinterpreted" prayers "to meet present religious needs," added original English prayers and twenty supplemental services for Armistice Day, Mother's Day, and the like, generously transliterated Hebrew, and even included greatly abbreviated Torah readings. These were followed by an early version of the *Sabbath and Festival Prayer Book*, in 1936, and a *High Holyday Prayer Book* (500 pages), with new supplemental readings, in 1939.

At first, as drafts of the new *Sabbath and Festival Prayer Book* circulated among colleagues as early as 1936, everyone found something that offended him. One colleague wrote that "the prayers before the Ark are the poorest of all in the book." Another colleague—a Conservative rabbi who noted that "our synagogue is quite Orthodox" (!)—observed that a prayer for Shavuot was "so out of keeping with modern times, that a real critic of the book may taunt us for keeping it in." More than anything else, Silverman's colleagues on the Joint Prayer Book Commission of the Rabbinical Assembly and the United Synagogue debated the transliterations. Would they make it unnecessary for Conservative Jews to learn Hebrew? Or, if it were true, as Rabbi Israel H. Levinthal told Rabbi Silverman, that "it is an open admission that the Jews to whom we minister are ignoramuses when it comes to the elemental facts of Hebrew," would transliterations encourage Conservative Jews who could not read Hebrew to worship?

The Silverman prayer book, like the Reform prayer book, avoided the question of resurrection, a traditional Judaic belief, and adapted numerous innovations of the *Union Prayer Book*, but it also stayed very close to the "original" (or, acceptable) Hebrew text. It had abundant, and felicitous, English, in addition to the traditional Hebrew text, ninety pages of responsive readings and selections from Jewish literature, and eighteen pages of hymns, and it was innovative (even revolutionary) in its changes from tradition (resurrection became "keeping promise to them that sleep in the dust"). Though 655 pages, it was small and light, and rabbis in the 1950s used some of the English on Friday evenings but generally utilized mostly the Hebrew in the more traditional Sabbath-morning services. Unlike Reform Jews, for whom Friday night was the central worship service of the week and for whom the following morning was known as the "bar mitzvah service," Conservative worshipers made Saturday morning the central service; the Friday-evening service, with lots of English, consisted of a truncated and much more accessible service.

The Friday-evening service was much like a Reform service at the same period. It usually took place late in the evening (usually about 8:00 P.M.) and contained considerable cues from the pulpit and a formal sermon from the rabbi for the worshipers. Morris Silverman instituted these services to compete with those who chose to attend "all the social affairs in Hartford and become candidates for a sanitarium" with their "show and ostentation" and "overeating at so late hours." The major difference from a Reform service was the use of a cantor nearly everywhere, and, despite some English, the presence of much more Hebrew in the liturgy. Bat Mitzvahs took place on Friday evenings, beginning sporadically in the 1950s, and usually included chanting the *haftarah* (Prophets), summarizing the Torah reading a boy (or man) would do the following morning, and leading some of the service. Bat mitzvah candidates began to read from the Torah in some synagogues only at the very end of this period. On Saturday mornings the service was long—at least three hours—with nothing left out from the traditional liturgy; the primary distinction from an Orthodox service was the presence of women sitting with men throughout the sanctuary. Visitors were also struck by the informality of the service—people wandered around from time to time, and conversations were not infrequent among worshipers who had completed some individual prayers or during the lengthy Torah reading when some worshipers were unable to understand the Hebrew and were not interested in the first English-language commentary to the Torah by Jewish scholars, which was available in most pew book slots (the *Hertz Pentateuch and Haftorahs*, 1938), or were just eager to chat with friends. Nobody at a Reform service would do this—there decorum resembled that at a Protestant worship service, and conversation was reserved for the refreshments following worship—but it was an acceptable practice at Conservative worship.

And yet, throughout the 1950s, Conservative synagogues struggled with this lack of decorum. For most, Reform worship was too High Church and Orthodox services represented "chaos and anarchy" (as one Chicago synagogue put it), but Conservative services were surely in constant need of review. In one Philadelphia synagogue, a committee recommendation appeared in the Bulletin in 1957, 1958, and 1959:

> In order to maintain the proper dignity and solemnity during all Synagogue Services, the Committee on Decorum respectfully re-

quests worshipers to cooperate in the following matters: Ladies must wear hats; Gentlemen must check their hats and put on yarmulkes; Do not enter the [sic] if the Rabbi has already begun the sermon; Please refrain from talking, visiting friends or making any disturbances whatsoever; Do not smoke on Sabbath and Yom Kippur on the side walk near the Synagogue—eliminate an undesirable impression; Do not leave until the completion of the closing benediction; Uniformed [sic] Prayer Books are available to all.

The content of the sermons Conservative rabbis delivered, whether on Friday evening or during the main preaching on Saturday morning was strikingly different from that of Reform sermons of the mid-1950s. While the sermons that survive have rhetoric as flowery and elegant as that used by Reform rabbis, the primary distinction is the topics on which Conservative and Reform rabbis preached and the form of their sermons. Eschewing civil rights and the biblical Prophets, for the most part, Conservative rabbis' sermons were much more likely to highlight Jewish and Judaic themes: Israel, commandments, Jewish law (halacha), covenant, God, and prayer. They referenced *midrash*, Talmud, Maimonides (philosophy), medieval biblical commentators and modern Jewish thinkers (Martin Buber, Zacharias Frankel, Franz Rosenzweig, and Nachman of Berdichev, not non-Jewish thinkers, were most popular). Indeed, Israel H. Levinthal of the Brooklyn Jewish Center (who packed his sermons for decades with considerable thinking about rabbinic literature) argued that Jewish preaching without the use of *midrash* was not Jewish preaching. And they structured their sermons—repeatedly—around a verse from the Torah reading for that week, manipulating it, amplifying it with traditional exegesis, and drawing out homiletical possibilities that the authors surely had never imagined or intended. In short, the form and content were much more akin to the classical sermons of the early centuries of this era than to those of American Jewish preachers of the nineteenth and twentieth centuries. And few of these rabbis were guilty of what Rabbi Jacob J. Weinstein warned against—"uplifting sermons, exhortations to serenity of spirit, lullabies to peace of mind, verbal soothing syrup, or the word of God bent to the vulgar usages of the market place." Conservative rabbis continuously challenged their suburban congregants to make Jewish values—not just ceremonies, customs, observances, and rituals —a regular part of their lives. But attendance at Sabbath and festival services, as well as observance levels (what the sociologist Marshall Sklare called "the drift away from sacramentalism"), if judged by surveys, sermons, minutes, and bulletins, was modest, if not minuscule.

The religious education program, at least that for boys under thirteen, usually met on either Saturday or Sunday and on two or three weekday afternoons at the end of the public school day. Conservative educators were quite vocal about the superficiality of religious education that occupied only one weekend morning and pioneered the three-times-a-week education program. It became popular in postwar America and dominated the religious education schedule at nearly every Conservative synagogue under study. The rabbi of Temple Emanuel of Newton, Massachusetts, with 1,360 families in 1958 and 1,060 children in the religious schools, could boast that, in contrast to 1950, when 188 students attended Hebrew school three times a week as well as Sunday school on Sunday and 300 came only once a week, now 927 students came four days a week and only 133 only on Sunday. Indeed, the one-day-per-week program ended after second grade, leaving only the extended schedule.

Deborah Pessin, author of *History of the Jews in America* and *The Jewish People*, also a common choice among a minority of Reform synagogues though published by the Conservative movement, was the most popular author of Judaic Studies in these schools. Nearly everywhere, the prayer book was the primary text for study in the Hebrew school part of the religious education program. And a surprising number of schools used a terrible book by Mac Davis (who also wrote a book, used much less frequently, about Jews who fought in World War II and later went on to write many books about sports), *They All Are Jews: From Moses to Einstein*, first published in 1937 and reprinted in 1951. The sixty one-page biographical portraits are packed with misinformation (Karl Marx, one of the sixty, is identified as Jewish without comment) but are crafted to make young Jews feel good about these great heroes; Davis wrote that David Sarnoff is "one of America's leading executives and one of the most powerful figures in the world of radio."

In these years, adult education programs, often called "institutes" or "academies," flourished in Conservative congregations. The name was taken from the Conservative movement's National Academy for Adult Jewish Studies. In addition to Sunday-morning lectures, and much like what unfolded in Reform congregations, these local academics and educated laymen offered multiweek courses on subjects like "Moses Maimonides and Medicine," "Modern Jewish Thinkers," "The Structure of the Prayer Book," and "The Five *Megillot*" (the biblical books of Esther, Ruth, Ecclesiastes, Song of Songs, and Lamentations). At Temple Emanu-El in Providence, those who attended five of seven course sessions received one credit; after completing twenty-four credits (i.e., courses), students were honored at the commencement ceremony of the Institute of Jewish Studies. In many congregations, an individual might endow an annual lecture in memory of a relative, and on those occasions Louis Finkelstein, Abraham Heschel, Mordecai Kaplan, or another Conservative luminary would grace the congregation for a lecture or two.

Confirmation, with one exception, shone as brightly nationally in Conservative congregations in these years as it did in Reform synagogues. It took place on the first day of Shavuot (Pentecost), seven weeks after Passover, usually at the end of grade ten, and usually included liturgy, a Torah service, and the confirmation ceremony. At Temple Beth Am in Los Angeles, the confirmation ceremonies throughout the 1950s began with a processional and floral offering and concluded with the "Ten Commandments Pledge." A qualifying exam at Durham's Beth-El required a confirmand to explain the Talmud and kosher laws, identify great rabbis of the past, give the date (according to the Hebrew calendar) and meaning of all Jewish holidays, and answer questions on current events in Israel. The students would sing parts of the liturgy, patriotic songs (e.g., "God Bless America"), and Zionist melodies (e.g., "Zion, Our Mother"), and some members of the class would present short talks. All the confirmands (girls usually outnumbered boys three or four to one, as the former rarely had bat mitzvahs) were dressed in their finest clothing, and the first Saturday night following the ceremony was usually reserved for a fancy dinner dance.

But, in many congregations, there was no liturgy and no Torah reading, just confirmand talks crafted by the rabbi. Following a processional, Jewish and non-Jewish musical selections ("America" was sung everywhere) were woven around small, didactic essays the rabbi had written for the confirmands to recite. Typical were those of Rabbi Abraham J. Mesch of Temple Beth-El in Birmingham, Alabama. He penned brief and learned essays on some theme of Jewish history—in 1948, just following the birth of the State of Israel, the theme was "The Rebirth of Israel," with essays and talks on the First Zionist Congress, the Balfour Declaration, the Mandate from the League of Nations, the Haganah, the Hebrew University, the United Nations Special Committee on Palestine, as well as Zionist heroes —and his ninety-minute ceremonies, like others everywhere, were heavy with learned (and rather dull) historical summary.

Phoenix Beth El dropped confirmation in the mid-1950s, as an "imitation of non-Jews." In fact, the congregation eliminated the one-day-per-week Sunday school, with its "non-Jewish spirit." Instead, students attended "religious school" two or three afternoons per week and Sabbath services, celebrating a bat (rarely) or bar mitzvah at age thirteen, graduating at the end of the 8th grade or, from the "high school," after six years of study and worship.

Although the bat mitzvah ceremony remained rare at Conservative synagogues into the 1970s, when it initially took place it involved a group of girls one Friday evening, in contrast to the solo bar mitzvah, which took place on Saturday morning. Typical were Temple Emanu-El of Providence and Congregation B'nai Israel of Woonsocket, both in Rhode Island, where, on a Friday night in May, five or six girls would have a communal and much abbreviated (compared to boys') ceremony culminating their years of Hebrew school attendance and study. By the end of the decade, solo bat mitzvahs took place at some synagogues on Saturday mornings.

Like the National Federation of Temple Youth (reform) groups, the Conservative movement's United Synagogue Youth groups for junior and senior high school students began and grew at an extraordinary pace in the 1950s, with 550 chapters in seventeen regions and 22,000 members by the end of the decade. Youth group activities were much like those of the Reform synagogues; dance classes were held everywhere, and the "passion for justice and freedom and the compassion for the oppressed and disadvantaged" (as one United Synagogue Youth speaker put it in a 1965 talk on "The Moral Imperative of the Bible") was widespread, with one substantial difference—Jewish programming. The same day the teens at St. Louis's Temple Israel (Reform) had a late spring outing at a St. Louis Cardinals baseball game, the B'nai Emunah youth were at an Israeli cultural festival sponsored by the Jewish Community Center. The United Synagogue Youth groups provided the youngsters with a Jewish sleep-away camp, Ramah, which opened in Wisconsin in 1946 with ninety campers. By 1960, there were four Camp Ramahs, serving 1,200 youth.

Sisterhoods at Conservative synagogues created, stocked, and served as clerks at the gift shop, selling everything from Hanukkah gift wrapping and menorahs to Sabbath candles and candle holders. They usually had active social action (i.e., civil rights) and social (dinner dances) committees, bridge games, challah-baking workshops, game nights, rummage sales, bowling leagues, theater parties, dance classes, fashion shows, art auctions, bazaars, dessert parties, and even, as at Temple Beth Am in Los Angeles, academic guidance sessions for high schoolers, while the brotherhoods or men's club as well as young adult and couples clubs were more likely to sponsor adult athletic (bowling and golf) and cultural events and boys' athletic leagues (basketball) and to provide ushers for High Holy Day, junior congregation, holiday, and Sabbath worship.

Conservative synagogues were busy places on Monday through Thursday afternoons, not just on the Sabbath and Sunday. Typically, there were numerous Hebrew classes meeting at larger congregations (e.g., Hebrew I, II, III, and IV, as well as pre- and post-bar mitzvah and bat mitzvah classes). Most Hebrew students were required to attend junior congregation, and this took place in some places on Friday evening before the main Sabbath eve service or on Saturday morning before the main Sabbath-morning service. Attendance sheets were carefully checked and submitted to teachers.

In addition to Sabbath and festival services, Conservative synagogues everywhere celebrated national holidays (e.g., Thanksgiving) and offered special liturgies for national mourning. Like all their Reform counterparts and many Orthodox congregations, they held services of tribute following the assassination of President John F. Kennedy. In Chicago, tens of thousands attended Conservative services from Friday evening, November 22, 1963, through Sunday, November 24, 1963, and huge crowds filled the sanctuaries when synagogues added memorial services throughout the day on Monday. Everywhere, rabbis eulogized the slain president, and, almost everywhere, memorial prayers and eulogies by senior rabbis filled the next Sabbath, November 29–30, with assistant or associate rabbis delivering eulogies, as well.

As the postwar period began, the Conservative movement was generally not optimistic about either its growth or its centrality among American Jews. A national survey of 1,200 adults in 200 congregations at the end of the 1940s found that daily worship services, for three decades a mainstay of Conservative synagogues, were on the decline and "have practically disappeared" in almost half the congregations; Sabbath-morning services had become "a perfunctory affair"; the youth were mostly "missing in action"; synagogue worship attendance on Passover, Sukkot, and Shavuot had become "negligible," as had Sabbath afternoon study sessions; and, in sum, "people do not go to services, because they are, in many cases, not inspiring, not understandable, not decorous."

Rabbi Samuel Chiel of Temple Emanuel of Newton, Massachusetts, put it well in 1970, though with much humor and exaggeration (e.g., non-Jews were never counted in the quorum necessary for public worship):

> At the Bas Mitzvah and the Bar Mitzvah celebrations, one looks at a vast sea of unfamiliar faces. It would be nice to see a member once in a while. There are the Spectators (never use the prayer book and will not participate), The Farbissene (come angry and leave angrier as forced to attend a nephew's Bar Mitzvah), The Non-Jews (come on time and make up the minyan), The Schmoozers (come with small photo albums to pass around during *mussaf*), and The Silent Majority (cannot read Hebrew).

A talented group of Conservative lay and professional leaders emerged as the new decade began and dramatically resurrected the movement. As this branch of American Judaism became distinctive, clearly more acculturated than orthodoxy and clearly more traditional than Reform, the structure and content of Conservative Judaism seemed to please more Jews in the 1950s than did orthodoxy or Reform. One hundred new synagogues joined the United Synagogue of America between 1953 and 1955, and 131 joined between 1955 and 1957, bringing the national total to 642. Growth continued steadily in the late 1950s and early 1960s (736 synagogues belonged in 1961 and 778 in 1963; in 1966, a United Synagogue of America publication claimed there were "sixteen Conservative Temples in the San

Fernando Valley only"), and, by 1965, when the 800th synagogue joined the movement, Conservative Jewish leaders could proclaim the movement the largest, in the number of synagogues and of members, in the United States. Since there was no accurate count of Orthodox synagogues available, this claim could not be challenged.

Nearly every rabbi explained this amazing growth with a simple explanation: Conservative Judaism, or as many preferred to call it, Traditional Judaism, had carefully avoided issuing a platform or statement of beliefs during its entire existence, and this was the key to appealing to the widest number of Jews, of "spreading our tent wider than either of the other two branches." Solomon Schechter had called this "catholic Israel," and Conservative rabbis of the 1950s and 1960s continued to reject suggestions that the movement, as Reform Judaism had done in its platforms of 1885 and 1937, formulate its beliefs for a movement without a platform. As Jacob Pressman, of Los Angeles's Olympic Jewish Center (also known as Temple Beth Am) put it, the absence of a platform "allows for the greatest flexibility and change while remaining definite in its purpose." Whether this claim or other formulations of how the movement was committed to "tradition and change" really meant anything would occupy Conservative leaders in the following two decades.

Orthodox Judaism

A modest number of traditional rabbis and their disciples escaped eastern and central Europe and came to the United States before the Nazis began to exterminate Jews in 1941. They included Joseph Breuer, who came to New York in 1939 and started congregation Khal Adath Yeshurun in Washington Heights with a number of German refugees; Elijah M. Bloch, who arrived in Cleveland in 1941, to which he transferred, via Shanghai, the famous Telz (Telshe) Yeshiva from Russian-occupied Lithuania; and Joseph Isaac Schneerson, the sixth Lubavitch *rebbe*, who came to Brooklyn about 1940. They were joined, immediately after World War II, by a smaller number of rabbis who survived the Holocaust, including Joel Teitelbaum, the leader of the Satmar Hasidim of Williamsburg (Brooklyn), who came from Palestine. As soon as they established themselves in America, they began to shift orthodoxy to the right, affirming that all knowledge resided in the Talmud and that secular studies were of no value. They celebrated their parochialism and their resolve to remain within tightly knit Jewish communities where secular learning became a target of disdain. Rabbi Teitelbaum, who moved his congregation from Williamsburg to New Jersey and, eventually, back to New York State (in upstate Monroe), even established his own town, Kiryas Joel, in 1976.

These sectarians, however, were a small minority in the American Orthodox community. In many larger Jewish communities around the country, the pattern of synagogue distribution was much like that in the Pico-Robertson neighborhood of Los Angeles. If you lived around that intersection, there was no Reform synagogue to which you could walk and only one Conservative synagogue within a few miles. But there were at least five mainline or established Orthodox synagogues (and at least two storefront "shuls," synagogues in a rented store or in a room or two over a store, known just as "the shul on Pico near Genesee" or "the shul upstairs over the butcher shop") within walking distance. This was striking, because far fewer than 10 percent of the affiliated Jews in the neighborhood would have claimed membership in any of these Orthodox synagogues. One followed the Sephardic ritual, another the Hungarian ritual, and another accepted Polish customs. One had mostly men in their seventies, while another attracted younger Jews. At least four of the five had a bar mitzvah ceremony frequently; all had mixed seating and microphones in 1955–1956; none of them had a ritual bath, nor was there one nearby; one, Beth Jacob of Beverly Hills (with Rabbi Simon Dolgin, who had arrived in the late 1930s, when the synagogue was in a different location, still at the helm), might have been the largest Orthodox congregation in the West. At least the rabbi regularly made this claim. And this pattern repeated itself in nearly every other large Jewish community. Newark, New Jersey, the seventh largest Jewish community in the United States after World War II, had, according to its historian, forty synagogues in 1948, "many nothing more than tiny rooms, with perhaps ten to twenty congregants," and, even in 1971, when Young Israel of Springfield opened, this same historian claimed that "it merged with the remnants of sixteen [!] Orthodox synagogues that were originally in Newark." Alas, most of these small Orthodox synagogues left no print trace of their existence.

To a great extent, rare is the Orthodox synagogue with bulletins from these three decades still extant. At best, administrators or laymen saved the occasional newsletter, and rarely did anyone have a sufficient sense of history to set aside space as an "archive." For our purposes, this makes the discussion, as in that for the interwar years, both more limited (in the number of synagogues represented) and more general (in the conclusions). One Orthodox rabbi, when I expressed this concern, said to me that of course this would be true, as Orthodox members in the 1950s rarely had college degrees and hence were much less attuned to the importance of saving synagogue materials for historical purposes. But he was wrong: rare, too, were the members of Conservative and Reform synagogues in 1955 with college educations, and, in any event, a good Jewish education (which applies to a sufficient number of Orthodox synagogue leaders in 1955) should have been enough to make these officers, "people of the book," sensitive to the need to save materials in the present in order to preserve a sense of the synagogue's past.

A study of the first page of synagogue bulletins from the mid-1950s quickly reveals that the emphasis at orthodox synagogues is different from that at Conservative and Reform institutions—it is clearly on the centrality of worship. Whether it concerns High Holy Day, festival, holiday, Sabbath, or just daily worship, most bulletins devote the entire first page to details about prayer services. Of course, there were other events in Orthodox synagogues of these years—weekday afternoon and weekend religious school (frequently either Monday, Wednesday, and Sunday, or Tuesday, Thursday, and Sunday), men's club, sisterhood, adult education Judaic Studies lectures (or, at the very least, study with the rabbi)—but nothing took precedence over *tefilah*, worship. Not only was the regular worship described, but junior congregation worship (usually Saturday morning for pre-bar mitzvah age boys in a chapel or small room), father-son minyans (usually Sunday morning), practice in prayer book reading (often Saturday afternoon), children's High Holy Day services, and junior congregation High Holy Day services, along with the time that the Sabbath began on Friday afternoon (and that candles were to be lit at home) and ended on Saturday (and secular activities could begin).

Surprisingly, because Orthodox synagogue leaders are guarded about most information that is freely given to historians by Conservative and Reform congregations, the financial details of most Orthodox synagogues are readily available in bulletins. We can say, with considerable evidence available, that fund-raising was a constant concern, perhaps just below the day and time worship began. Like Reform and Conservative congregations, Orthodox institutions required that members pay dues, and these annual, semi-annual, or quarterly payments generally funded only about 25 to 35 percent of the synagogue expenses. (In contrast, Reform Temple Emanuel of Beverly Hills took in $192,000 from dues in 1967–1968, 83 percent of its $230,000 budget.) Renting seats during the High Holy Days— as everywhere—brought in another 10 percent or so, leaving a huge amount of the annual budget to be raised in less private ways. Nearly every congregation whose records I studied had at least one evening, if not more, at the home of the rabbi where (generally) the wealthiest members of the congregation (almost always exclusively male) made public gifts to the synagogue. Key gifts were solicited in advance so that, when the president stood up to pledge in the living room, the fund-raisers knew precisely how much he had privately pledged but hoped that his generous gift would up the ante for those who followed him in the room. Generally, about 40 percent of the annual budget was pledged (not necessarily paid) through this technique. The remainder of the funds needed to run the synagogue activities and to pay the professional staff came from a variety of fund-raising events, sometimes including pledging in the sanctuary on the Sabbath or a holiday. The biggest appeal in the sanctuary of nearly every Orthodox congregation took place on Yom Kippur, but it was (usually) to raise funds for Jewish philanthropy, not for the synagogue activities.

Orthodox rabbis all over the country left plenty of sermons from the mid-1950s, as they, too, typed out their addresses in full, especially those for Jewish holy days and festivals. In focusing on the following thirteen rabbis and their sermons, both typescript and published, we can generalize to an extent about Orthodox homiletics: Simon Dolgin (California), Nathan Drazin and Israel Tabak (Maryland), Louis Engelberg and Solomon Poupko (Ohio), Benzion Kaganoff (Washington, D.C.), Israel Klavan (Indiana), Bernard Poupko (Pennsylvania), Charles Chavel, Leo Jung, Joseph Lookstein, Emanuel Rackman, and Leo Stitkin (New York). There were some, everywhere, who might quote Shakespeare ("Time," says a character in "As You Like It," "travels in divers paces with divers persons"), or Proust ("Those who count by days and by years are fools—days are perhaps equal for a clock, but not for a man"), or Descartes, Euripedes, Keats, Lincoln, and Tin Pan Alley. But they were the exception. Overwhelmingly, the citations in sermons are to rabbinic literature—often difficult passages to interpret and in the original Hebrew (did very many congregants understand?—doubtful)—and, repeatedly, Orthodox rabbis, especially on the High Holy Days, chastise their congregants for lax synagogue attendance and lax observance—what Rabbi Simon Dolgin in Los Angeles called "indifference to Judaism," the title of a High Holy Day sermon, "during the year." They preached frequently, especially on the High Holy Days, about different parts of the liturgy, as well as about themes of the prayers and about ritual objects (e.g., the *shofar*), and they regularly used this occasion not only to "scold and chastise" ("You come to the synagogue for three days, offer a few prayers, beat your breast at the confessional," said Rabbi Stitkin of Rochester. "This is a faucet Judaism.") but to appeal for contributions to the synagogue, a rare occurrence in the High Holy Day sermons of Conservative and Reform rabbis.

Unquestionably, Orthodox rabbis in the mid-1950s were biblical literalists. They generally claimed to believe in the divine revelation of the Torah—that God spoke actual words that Moses wrote down and that they are what we have today in Genesis, Exodus, Leviticus, Numbers, and Deuteronomy. Many of them took other books of the Hebrew Bible literally, as well. They all revered the rabbis of the "rabbinic" or "Talmudic" period, repeatedly calling them "saintly" or describing them as "religious geniuses" who have "unique insights into the character of our people" and using their literature (e.g., *midrash*, Talmud), completely uncritically, as factual history of the past. They believed in life after death, though usually without specifics other than affirming resurrection, when the Messiah arrives, and felt certain that this was a world "where all will be rest and peace." They praised the previous generation of Orthodox Jews, "Torah-true" Jews (without any evidence), "the sturdy timber" of previous generations, the "genuine Jews" who deserve us "to sit *shivah*" (mourn), while, generally, complaining about their own congregants who made the Sabbath "movie night, card night, a day at the beach or on the golf links."

Some of them gave sermons defending mixed seating in their synagogues (whenever a more traditional colleague asked a more liberal Orthodox colleague why he was serving a congregation with mixed seating, the latter would usually answer that he was "working towards eliminating it"); others launched blistering attacks on those congregations that had mixed seating, "an erupting heresy [which] has begun insidiously to invade the citadel of orthodoxy." Most, regularly, attacked vigorously both Conservative ("an aberration") and Reform Judaism—though there is no evidence they ever attended Conservative or Reform Jewish worship services—saving their most insulting words for the latter. Typically, as Rabbi Bernard Poupko of Pittsburgh put it, "in Reform, the parchment of the Law remains within the thick walls of its Ark, distantly removed from human contact," and in place of Torah the rabbis give "flowery sermons about the universality of Judaism."

If we take a close look at Beth Jacob of Beverly Hills (the self-proclaimed "largest Orthodox synagogue outside New York") over a ten-year period, 1950–1959, we will see a very representative Orthodox synagogue of that decade. As at Reform and Conservative congregations of the 1950s, numerous auxiliary organizational meetings and activities filled the calendar. They included the sisterhood; Chevra Mikra (a study group, primarily of Mishnah and Talmud); afternoon Hebrew school (*Talmud Torah*); bar and bat mitzvah ceremonies; fund-raising committees when money was needed for a new synagogue; celebrations of both Jewish and American holidays (even when New Year's Eve coincided with Sabbath eve [January 1, 1955], a party took place [albeit in "good taste," members were warned]) —sometimes in a way that combined both traditions, such as the Purim "hoedown" of 1957; an adult institute (Monday- and Tuesday-night classes on Jewish topics, and, as at the Reform and Conservative institutes, "certificates" for those who completed 60 or 120 hours of classes); a regular new-member Sabbath; and programs on political issues ("Vote No on Proposition 16," a proposal to repeal the tax-exempt status of private schools, appeared in the bulletin in the fall of 1958). Nondenominational services, with non-Jewish guest speakers, were a regular feature on Thanksgiving and, from time to time, on Veteran's Day throughout the decade. And many of the sermon titles (the texts do not seem to have survived), like so many in that decade everywhere, give no hint that they might have drawn deeply from Jewish texts. They include (to cite some from the High Holy Days) "The Free Name," "Face the Foe," "Being a Good Person," "Microscope, Telescope, and Judaism," "Judaism Looks at Americanism," and "Religion: Advice or Device—Judaism Looks at Itself."

But many events were unique to this Orthodox synagogue, though consistent with activities at similar synagogues in Baltimore, Boston, Chicago, Cleveland, Newark, New York, and Philadelphia. One such event is the bat mitzvah ceremony, which may not have taken place on the West Coast before Beth Jacob introduced it in 1947 and which still is not ubiquitous in Orthodox congregations. It did not occur on Saturday morning, as with boys, but took place on Friday evening (or Sunday morning) as a special program when a young woman turned twelve and a half. She did not read or chant from the Torah and did not stand *on* the pulpit but began with a recitation of a creedal statement (somewhat like a confirmation ceremony), read a selection (*haftarah*) from the Prophets in Hebrew or English, sang a Jewish song or two, and delivered a talk. Girls studied with boys; the curriculum for both was overwhelmingly learning how to say the prayers for all the services (Beth Jacob teachers, as elsewhere, encouraged games to increase the speed with which the boys and girls recited the prayers). As boys approached thirteen, they went off to work privately with a tutor or even the rabbi; the girls would work with a music teacher or the like to prepare for their ceremony (often involving multiple girls).

Additionally, Yiddish, as elsewhere in the Orthodox synagogue, survived, minimally, into this decade. Beth Jacob had an annual Purim play (*shpiel*) in Yiddish, usually with words and music. Five hundred people attended the West Side Drama Group's 1951 Yiddish program, and the 1959 Yiddish performance "In the Days of Esther" appears to have drawn a large crowd, too. An attempt at a Yiddish film festival on four Tuesday evenings in 1978 was poorly attended; the majority of the audience at one film consisted of university students in their second semester of Yiddish study. And, finally, there was a regular fund-raising appeal during the Yom Kippur services. Consistently, Beth Jacob raised more than a quarter of its (large) annual budget with Yom Kippur pledges; another tenth or so came from an annual banquet and the remainder from dues.

Consistent with an emphasis elsewhere, decorum was of constant concern, as the prim and proper 1950s sometimes contrasted with the synagogue's long tradition of somewhat disorderly worship, or worship that emphasized individual, rather than congregational, worship. Before every High Holy Day service throughout the decade, the editor of the monthly *Beth Jacob Voice* instructed worshipers on proper decorum, especially the need to sit only in the seat specifically reserved. And such warnings appeared throughout the year, as well. In February 1952, he wrote about "Proper Practice," emphasizing that women should not bring a purse to Sabbath worship (they should not be carrying anything, especially money), that men should wear a head covering through the entire service, that the doors would be locked during Rabbi Simon Dolgin's sermons to prevent people from getting up and leaving, and that worshipers should "postpone all friendly visits until after the service." The latter raised the most commonly discussed problem; years later, members of the congregation recall that worshipers who had finished their individual prayers often walked over to converse with other worshipers while some were still praying. This concern would continue throughout the 1960s, 1970s, and beyond. In 1982, to cite but one of many examples, the president, in his annual report to the congregation, said that he "only wished we could devise a technique to improve decorum during services."

Additionally, the rabbi added late-Friday-evening worship, in English, to "supplement" (certainly not replace) the sundown prayers and to attract families that could not or would not attend the earlier worship. Starting at 8:15, as did Sabbath-eve worship not only in Conservative and Reform synagogues nearby but also in Orthodox congregations everywhere, they included Sabbath singing, Sabbath prayers and/or readings, a discourse by the rabbi, and refreshments at the social hour. These proved so popular, here as elsewhere, that they greatly helped Orthodox congregations maintain their membership at a time when membership in Conservative and Reform synagogues was exploding.

Judaism for the Family

No matter the branch of American Judaism, synagogue leaders— professional and lay—in these decades spoke as if only "families" constituted the membership. And, of course, this was overwhelmingly true. Bulletin and newsletter announcements were addressed to families, rabbis spoke of families in their sermons, advertisements for congregational events highlighted family fun, and membership numbers were always noted as "575 families." In 1965, 2,650 of the 2,900 members of Temple Beth-El in Providence came from families with a mother and a father living together; in addition, there were 55 single or widowed men and 195 single or widowed women. Forty percent of the members were children under the age of twenty-one. A 1957 pamphlet from Temple Beth Israel in Phoenix welcomes "new families to the temple." No pamphlet existed for any other new members. Synagogues in Denver, Portland, and Seattle—like others everywhere—began regular (once-a-month) "Family Worship Services." There were, to be sure, "Young People" cells within some larger congregations, but these were almost always for young married couples without children (who were given a one-year courtesy membership nearly everywhere). For every one of these vaguely described groups (but virtually always intended for married couples), there were ten "Couples Club" units. And the message everywhere was that the family that prayed together or did other things together at the synagogue stayed together. It was not until the 1970s that synagogue publications begin to take wide-ranging notice of "single Jews," with or without children, as the two-parent family with children (usually two) became only one of many family configurations within the synagogue communities. Synagogue leaders, by the 1980s, though remaining geared to the conventional family unit, realized that these other family configurations deserved programmatic attention.

Only with hindsight can we see that by the 1960s there were hints of the dramatic changes that were to take place in American Judaism in the following decades. For the most part, the immense transformation of Reform into a movement of considerable ritual and its effort to grapple with the presence of intermarried couples and nontraditional families was barely visible even by the middle of the 1960s. The demands of Conservative Jews for a strong statement of what the branch believes and for gender equality, both flashpoints of the 1970s, were barely discussed in 1965. And, among the Orthodox, even in the 1960s, the rigorous observance that, beginning in the 1970s, would characterize so many children of the moderate Orthodox of the 1940s and 1950s was still under the surface. Right up to the Six-Day War of 1967 and even beyond, in some ways little had changed from earlier decades. But momentous transformations were just around the corner.

6

Reinventing, Experimenting, and Ratcheting Up

Judaism after 1967

The rabbis [Eli A. Bohnen and Joel H. Zaiman] believe men should not wear sports jackets, only suits, to services and that women should wear hats.

—the bulletin of Temple Emanu-El, Providence, Rhode Island, November 12, 1968

THE SIX-DAY WAR in Israel, in 1967, and the second half of the 1960s in America initiated a transformation in all of American Judaism that is still in the process of development more than forty years later. They not only caused synagogue Jews to retrieve, in different ways, aspects of "the tradition" but also led them to experiment with new and diverse ways of expressing their religiosity: meditation centers, spiritual retreats, communes, self-improvement seminars, support groups, yoga classes, est, Esalen, and cults. Focusing on what is sometimes called "spirituality"—open talk about the divine presence in people's lives—Jews everywhere sought different ways to find spiritual satisfaction and fulfillment—to be, in the words of so many worshipers, "more religious." Together with the emergence of a fourth branch, Reconstructionism, which had been founded by the former Conservative theologian Mordecai M. Kaplan in the 1920s in New York, these seekers of spiritual fulfillment animated Judaism tremendously.

The late 1960s (the early years of the decade were much like the 1950s) found Jews of all kinds experimenting with new forms of religiosity. Among Reform Jews, this trend largely took the form of creative liturgy, thanks to easily accessible Hebrew typewriters and mimeograph machines; Conservative and Orthodox Jews found new ways to access tradition; and Reconstructionist Jews, who tended to reject the idea of a personal God while embracing Jewish values, started to experiment with bringing Jewish culture, in the broadest sense, into the synagogue. The June 1967 war in Israel, which began with real threats to Israel's existence and ended with Jews in control of "territories" that linked them to biblical events and places, also stimulated Jewish life in the diaspora. Jews noted that Israel was fighting for more than itself—it was fighting for Jewish meaning and survival everywhere. If the Jewish state could overcome those who sought its destruction, Jews everywhere should be grateful for this victory and salute the victors by renewing, in religious (and secular) ways, their commitment to Judaism.

Synagogues everywhere mobilized people to support Israel in the run-up to, and during, the Six-Day War. Mass rallies at the end of May in synagogues of all the branches raised millions of dollars with the sale of Bonds for Israel. Synagogue members formed "truth committees" to write and speak in defense of Israel. Sisterhoods and brotherhoods initiated lunches and dinners and a wide variety of programs to raise funds for Israel's defense. Youth groups sent telegrams to senators, congresspersons, and the executive branch; even Hollywood writers, directors, producers, actors, and actresses met at a synagogue to form the Committee of the Arts for Peace in the Middle East to publicize how threatened Israel felt by the calls for its destruction.

Despite all of this synagogue-related activity and creative engagement with tradition, we must again remind ourselves that every survey undertaken in these four decades indicated that "unaffiliated" is the largest (and, frequently, fastest-growing) category among American Jewry. Thus, even when we begin to discuss a fourth branch of American Judaism, those Jews who identify as Conservative, Orthodox, Reconstructionist, or Reform constitute fewer than half the Jewish population in America. The rest are what Rabbi Harold Schulweis of (San Fernando) Valley Beth Shalom in Los Angeles calls "None Jews."

Reform Judaism

By the early 1970s, the largest congregations in the Reform movement were in the Sun Belt, rather than in cities such as Boston, Chicago, Cleveland, Philadelphia, and New York. Seven of the ten largest Reform synagogue populations were in Arizona (Temple Beth Israel, Phoenix, 1,100 "families"), California (Wilshire Boulevard Temple, Los Angeles, 2,488; Temple Emanu-El, San Francisco, 1,306; Stephen S. Wise, Los Angeles, 1,300; Temple Beth Hillel, North Hollywood, 872), and Florida (Temple Beth Am, Miami, 1,150; Temple Beth El, Hollywood, 900), and an eighth (Temple Emanuel, Denver, 1,238) was far from the previous centers of Reform Jewish density. Their rabbis noted repeatedly that these were sites of "freedom" and "experimentation," "unbound," as Rabbi Isaiah Zeldin of Stephen S. Wise put it, "by old ways."

The *Union Prayer Book* continued to be used in nearly every Reform synagogue, large or small, small town or urban, well into the 1960s, but rabbis, in a variety of print forums and in discussions when they gathered, were increasingly uncomfortable with this liturgy. Although revised in 1940, it reflected in so many different ways the "classical Reform" worship experience of formal services, magnificent choral hymns, perfect decorum—basically, the worship of upper-middle-class American Protestants—so rabbis, energized by nearly two decades of a Jewish state grounded in the Hebrew language and influenced by the search, in America itself, for new forms of spirituality, desperately sought alternatives. Of course, producing a prayer book that would win acceptance by more than 1,000 rabbis and hundreds of congregations was a daunting task and would take years. In the meantime, what were everywhere called "creative services" proliferated throughout the Reform movement. At one synagogue in Columbus, Ohio, in a two-month period in 1973, creative Sabbath services replaced the *Union Prayer Book* every Sabbath. The original liturgies included "Only by love can a man hope to live: An original bar mitzvah liturgy"; "God and the Jew;" "A yearning for redemption"; "The family of man"; "An end and a beginning"; "Places I remember"; and "Light is a finite flame." Cut-and-paste jobs in most places, some of the better-quality products were not only printed by this or that congregation but also distributed, either from rabbi to rabbi or from lay leader to rabbi, and used in multiple synagogues.

"Creative" did not mean original. One who examines scores of these liturgies is struck by two things: the use of Hebrew for many of the prayers that had previously been available only in translation in the *UPB* and the use of readings that indicated the willingness to move beyond the "rational" into what may loosely be called "mystical" or, at the very least, nonrational. And these two impulses are interconnected: Reform congregants for decades had demanded that they "understand" the liturgy (as if prayer could be "understood"!), and this meant clear and simple English translations, with only occasional Hebrew, and slow reading (and singing). Each word at Reform worship services could be grasped by the mind of the worshiper, and many of the congregants did not understand that prayer was as much metaphor as "truth." By the late 1960s, Reform congregants seemed to be saying that "prayers that we do not understand [e.g., poems] and prayers in a language we do not understand [e.g., Hebrew] could be part of the worship experience." In fact, those were the words of a Reform congregant at Temple Beth Torah in Fremont, California, at a meeting of the synagogue ritual committee in 1966. Indeed, since worship was an "experience"—whether sung or read—it need not all be "understood." Cantor William Sharlin, of Los Angeles's Leo Baeck Temple, summed this concept up nicely in 1968 or 1969: "Let the Hebrew of the prayer book flow through you; whether you understand it or not, enjoy its sounds."

At the same time that experimental liturgies replaced the prayer book one Sabbath a month, twice a month, or, in some places, every week, Reform congregants demanded that worship be participatory, a "partnership," said Rabbi Beerman of Leo Baeck Temple, "of rabbi, cantor, and laymen." Congregations with operatic cantors, baritone soloists, and/or organs suddenly sought guitar-playing "song leaders" who knew Hebrew and English liturgical melodies; synagogues where the rabbi had led the singing trained congregants to be song-leading "cantors"; and, concomitantly, a generation of young Jewish composers began to produce lyrics and music (or, in many cases, just melodies for "lyrics" already in the liturgy) that could be sung by the musician *and* the congregation. Neo-Hasidic was the music of choice, what Cantor Howard Stahl of Temple B'nai Jeshurun in Short Hills, New Jersey, has called "Pete Seeger meets Rabbi Nachman of Bratslav." In 1971–1972, in three synagogues as far apart as Boston, Columbus, and Los Angeles, the same antiphonal Hebrew-English melody (BaShanah HaBa'ah—a song welcoming the new year and expressing the hope that it will be good) energized the congregations. One rabbi carried this melody from place to place to place, and for years it was a "tradition" in Reform synagogues in Ohio and in southern California. In fact, in the early 1980s, when one of the congregations tried to replace this melody, now a decade old, the song leader was told that it was an important "tradition." For Reform congregations over the past few decades, "traditions" are whatever they have been doing for a few years.

As the liturgy moved from formal (a print book) to informal (liturgies run off on a duplicating machine the week of worship services), so did dress. Although rabbis continued, in most places, to wear a coat and tie for Sabbath eve and Sabbath morning (and, of course, major holy day) services, the dress of congregants began to change dramatically in the late 1960s. Women came regularly to worship in pants, and men came without coat and tie. Being "comfortable" had the highest priority, and "casual business" (a phrase used widely by 1970 in southern California) dominated. Indeed, little changed over the ensuing four decades. At Reform Sabbath worship services in 2009 in Baltimore, Boston, Cleveland, and Philadelphia—not just in Sunbelt congregations—few men other than the rabbi wore a jacket and tie.

Together with informal dress, informal liturgies, and congregational singing mimicking summer camp, the choreography of the worship service, especially the seating, changed. In sanctuaries where chairs could be moved and in sanctuaries designed and built after 1967—even in renovated sanctuaries—moving chairs into a semicircle arrangement or other configurations gave a greater sense of involvement with other worshipers. The president of the board of trustees at the very formal Temple Emanuel in Beverly Hills noted in 1977 that "the Rabbi and Cantors are too far away from the Congregation," and he led the fund-raising for a remodeled main sanctuary. And rabbis began to come off the pulpit to read and preach (actually, "preach," as we will shortly see, is the wrong word) at the level of congregants, vigorously trying to break down the barriers, physical and psychological, between pulpit and pew. At one synagogue in Washington, D.C., the "pulpit"—something akin to the stage in an informal theater—was moved around so that one Shabbat the worshipers would see the platform and portable ark while facing east, whereas another week they would be facing south or west.

Along with the other dramatic changes came a reinvention of the "sermon," part of reconceptualizing the synagogue as a congregation of learners. Previously, for decades, and then throughout the 1950s and into the early 1960s, Reform (and Conservative) rabbis had read from typescripts, not just on Rosh Hashanah and Yom Kippur but also on the Sabbath. Most gave informal talks on Saturday mornings when there was a bar or bat mitzvah, preferring to speak directly to the youngster with modest notes, but, even these rabbis usually preached from a complete text on Friday nights. Indeed, all over the country, complete sermons by Reform rabbis are extant in the hundreds at least to the middle of the 1960s. (The scores of 1970s typescript sermons by Rabbi Meyer Heller of Beverly Hills Temple Emanuel [three to four pages for Saturday mornings; eight to ten pages for Friday evenings; and, of course, twenty to twenty-five pages for the High Holy Days] preserved at his synagogue are the exception, as note cards and outlines dominated in the 1970s, 1980s, and 1990s.) These rabbis were all too often perceived as resembling Rabbi Blinder in Philip Roth's brilliant story "The Conversion of the Jews," that is, as black-robed clergymen who delivered stentorian sermons after they read in stentorian tones from the (nearly) all-English liturgy. By 1965, rabbis began to use notes, not a complete text, and (sometimes) came off the pulpit and moved into the congregation as they delivered a talk. I use "talk" intentionally, as the tone shifted from preaching to or at the congregation to talking *with* the worshipers. Indeed, little by little, rabbis began to lead discussions of the Torah text they had just read (or chanted) and to interact with their audience instead of preaching to them. Already by 1970, the "sermon" of the past had become "old-fashioned" in many synagogues, and to be au courant one had to give the impression that one was speaking spontaneously, no matter the careful preparation. Rabbis called this, in their bulletins, "teaching" rather than preaching, and many interrupted the flow of the liturgy to "teach" something about a prayer the rabbi or congregation was about to read. Although referring to Conservative rabbis, Rabbi Abraham J. Karp of Rochester could have been describing Reform rabbis as well when he noted that "now there is less stress on *preaching* and more emphasis on *teaching*."

Great preachers were less and less common, and, unlike in previous decades, in which some rabbis had national reputations (and traveled to sold-out auditoriums in distant cities much like performers of a later generation), few rabbis were known outside their community for their sermons. Rabbinical education followed the lead, and courses in homiletics, once required annually, also became "old-fashioned." Few rabbis were more articulate than their congregants, and, in the absence of a carefully crafted and edited text, worshipers began to rank the liturgy and the music as higher priorities in motivating them to attend services.

These worshipers not only increasingly participated in discussions instead of listening to sermons but also began to take an interest in the texts that rabbis substituted for preaching. Announcements of small study groups began to appear in bulletins everywhere at the beginning of this period, as congregants attended not only the traditional guest lecture of the previous decades but also text study. And courses in beginning Hebrew suddenly appeared, making it possible for a generation of Reform Jews, who had little or no liturgical Hebrew experience to participate in worship not only in English. Concomitantly, Reform congregations announced annual retreats where congregants would have an opportunity to study a topic in depth. Jewish mysticism (also known as kabbalah) was an especially popular subject beginning in the early 1970s.

With the radical change in liturgy from book to booklet, the Reform movement hastened to prepare a new prayer book. By the middle of the 1970s, it was ready, and *Shaarei Tefillah—Gates of Prayer* (1975; revised, 1994) offered ten Sabbath liturgies, ranging from a (virtual) reproduction of the *Union Prayer Book*, the liturgy that had served Reform Judaism for eighty years, to a liturgy deeply influenced by the Holocaust, the birth of the State of Israel (it included a liturgy for Israel Independence Day, hardly a "sacred" occasion), and the rhythms and metaphors of the 1960s. It also prioritized Hebrew by interspersing it with English on every page, rather than relegating it to a page (right or left) by itself. With this format, the *UPB*, with almost no Hebrew, could not easily be replaced by a mostly English service (though some, especially older worshipers, still wished for it), as the historic language of the Jewish people could not be avoided. The book, available in Hebrew-opening and English-opening editions (in contrast to the English-only *UPB*), was quickly adopted everywhere, and, since "there are many paths to heaven's gates," rabbis had the option to vary the liturgy ("this prayer and that one") from week to week, if desired, or to mix and match in numerous ways. Some complained particularly about the lack of transliterations, as the worship service, in the 1980s and 1990s, increasingly used Hebrew, with which so many Reform Jews (and non-Jewish spouses) were unfamiliar. But this prayer book, not only because of its variety but also because it reflected both the Holocaust and the birth of the State of Israel, would remain popular with congregants for more than three decades, until, in 2008, it was replaced by *Mishkan T'filah*. With sensitivity to the equality of the sexes, the editors also eliminated masculine words for humankind. They were not quite ready to do this for God language as well, retaining words such as "he," "him," and "Lord" when speaking of the Deity. *Mishkan T'filah* completed this stylistic change; it is totally gender neutral, even when this requirement makes the writing awkward (e.g., "May Adonai grant strength to God's people; may Adonai bestow on God's people wellbeing").

A more serious problem, once a liturgy was in place that made most worshipers content, was the lack of worshipers. Much as Isaac Mayer Wise had argued (wrongly, it turned out), in 1869, with reference to the relatively recent emergence of 7 P.M. Friday-evening services, that they "will force managers of theatres and operas . . . to put off their gala evenings from Friday to Saturday evening," many rabbis argued, in the decade or so before *Gates of Prayer* appeared, that poor attendance was a direct result of deficiencies in the Reform liturgy. The *UPB* was now (as one rabbi put it) "ancient," and a new liturgy would result in more worshipers, for, so some argued, it was discomfort with having to recite liturgical passages that reflected theological positions the worshipers did not hold that kept many away. One rabbi reminded his congregation of what Samuel S. Cohon, a professor at the Reform seminary, once said of the *Union Prayer Book*: it "conveys the impression that it was especially written for a people composed of retired philanthropists and amateur social workers." But Reform Jews still came to the synagogue sanctuary—with many exceptions, of course, because of extraordinary music or gifted rabbis—in small numbers. Orthodox Jews overwhelmingly spoke of fulfilling a duty or obligation (*mitzvah*) that requires regular prayer; Conservative Jews, in far greater numbers than Reform congregants, developed a tradition of attending Sabbath morning worship more or less regularly, whereas Reform Jews preferred the cinema or theater to the synagogue on Friday evenings and plentiful alternatives to Sabbath morning worship. Communal prayer never became a defining feature of Reform Jewish life, and lay and professional leaders throughout the movement struggled with this problem.

Gimmicks appeared everywhere. In New York City, synagogue bulletins announced Sabbath-evening worship with titles such as First Friday, Fourth Friday, Tot Shabbat, Fourth Grade Sabbath, Shabbat Lite, Shabbat Alive, Jazz Sabbath, Shabbat Unplugged, Healing Sabbath, Family Sabbath, Totally Shabbat—and this list covers just one month at five Reform synagogues. In congregations where most Jews placed Sabbath worship below the cinema, theater, sports, parties, and certainly family dinners, congregations had to come up with enticements. Few motivated a significant proportion of the membership to worship on anything approximating a regular basis. Not even rabbinic gender seemed to matter much.

By the middle of the 1970s, women began to emerge from the Reform seminary as rabbis, and by 2008 the Hebrew Union College-Jewish Institute of Religion had ordained more than 500 female rabbis. While it took some adjustment for many congregants to feel comfortable having a woman conduct the funeral of their beloved or deliver a Yom Kippur sermon, Reform congregants adjusted relatively easily. And women seemed well prepared to lead this large transformation in liturgy, study, and rabbi-congregant interaction. Congregants, of course, did not have an image of a *woman* rabbi as the severe, authoritative father figure, so, as women moved into the congregational rabbinate at precisely the time that the role of the rabbi was changing, they found the new model (generally) of comfort.

There were two other dramatic changes for cantors and rabbis by the late 1960s, and both involved weddings. First, couples that had lived together before the wedding approached cantors and rabbis to officiate at their ceremony, and this meant an adjustment for these officiants who had spent their careers officiating at weddings where bride and groom had not cohabited. And, for the first time, the number of couples in which one partner was a non-Jew that requested rabbinic or cantorial officiation began, in some places, to approach the number of couples in which the man and the woman were both Jewish. There had always been plenty of Reform rabbis and cantors ready to officiate at mixed marriages—weddings where one of the two persons remained a non-Jew. Indeed, in 1937, at least a third of all Reform rabbis officiated at intermarriages, and, by the early 1970s the figure had passed 40 percent. With the number of potential intermarriages increasing steadily, more and more Jews attended such weddings. Whether this frequent rabbinic or cantorial sanctification caused wedding guests who contemplated an intermarriage to consider that they too could have a rabbi or cantor at their wedding was widely debated.

Reform rabbis everywhere debated whether to officiate at such ceremonies. How could a non-Jew say, as he or she put a ring on the finger of the spouse, without creating disbelief in all the guests, not to mention the bride or groom, "With this ring you are sanctified to me according to Jewish law"? The "rules of the game," as one Reform rabbi put it in the Reform rabbinic journal, "had changed at halftime." In contrast to those who argued that a *Jewish* wedding ceremony required two Jews, there were rabbis who made three repeated arguments. The first was that when a rabbi turned away such a couple, they got married anyway, and was it not better to have the opportunity for pre-marital Jewish counseling and a quasi-Jewish ceremony than a secular or even Christian ceremony? And what hope was there for future Jewish involvement if the rabbi (representing "Judaism" in the eyes of the couple) turned them away at this hour of need? Finally, there were those rabbis who were sensitive to what conversion meant for the non-Jew, especially when they reflected on how they felt about a Jew converting to Christianity. Rabbi Stanley Brav, who served Cincinnati's Bene Israel (the Rockdale Avenue Temple) and then Temple Sholom for several decades after 1948, put it well, like scores of others: "I find it offensive to demand that someone reared in another faith and sincerely devoted to it must . . . relinquish it in order to enjoy the benefits of Jewish clerical participation in the marriage ceremony."

Even if the rabbi or cantor of a synagogue did not officiate at a ceremony that solemnized an interfaith marriage, these couples began to join Reform synagogues in substantial numbers in the 1970s, and by the end of the decade the Reform movement was officially instituting programs to encourage their participation. Professional synagogue leaders strongly believed that a warm reception when an intermarried couple inquired about membership in the congregation played a crucial role in bringing the couple (and their children) into the orbit of Jewish ritual and ceremony, whether circumcision, Passover, or a bat mitzvah. Concomitantly, one congregation after another began the difficult process of constructing what many called "borders," deciding precisely what limits should be imposed on the non-Jewish partner. Could he or she join a synagogue committee?

Become the chair of a committee? How about chair of the rabbinic search committee? Could the non-Jewish partner read a passage from the prayer book during a worship service? Could he or she stand on the pulpit and say a blessing before or after the Torah reading? How about a blessing that links the reader to the Jewish people of the past? How about carrying the Torah or passing it from parent (Jew) to parent (non-Jew) to daughter or son? Washington, D.C.'s Temple Sinai prohibited non-Jews from four synagogue rituals: lighting and blessing Sabbath or holiday candles, leading the blessing that sanctifies wine, being called to the Torah, and carrying the Torah. Deciding whether or not to officiate at an intermarriage ceremony became the easy part; constructing rules and regulations about non-Jewish "members" (could they, in fact, be members? in Conservative and Orthodox synagogues they could not) was much more challenging. The 2000–2001 National Jewish Population Survey revealed that 40 percent of male and 40 percent of female respondents between the ages of twenty-five and forty-nine had intermarried. It was becoming rare to find an American Jewish family where there was not an intermarriage somewhere in the extended family. And once intermarriage, as Rabbi Lance Sussman of Philadelphia's Keneseth Israel put it, "had become part of the warp and woof of American Jewish life," the rules of the game did not wait until halftime to change but did so in the first quarter.

By the 1970s, middle-of-the-road Reform congregants everywhere had begun to notice gay and lesbian individuals as well as couples attending worship services. Rabbis slowly became sensitive to a vocabulary that, until that decade, had encompassed only families with a male and a female at the head. As the divorce rate soared, as well, the language of inclusion expanded, and membership committees began to encounter single-parent families as well as families with same-sex parents. This phenomenon grew steadily, and it was not long before, in larger communities with multiple Reform congregations, some synagogues developed reputations as being welcoming to and offer-ing programming for singles, gays, lesbians, and divorced mothers and fathers who wished to be active in the synagogue.

Whether the Hebrew Union College-Jewish Institute of Religion Reform seminary should ordain openly gay or lesbian rabbinic stu-dents and whether a rabbi should officiate at a "commitment" cer-emony preeminently roiled the movement in the 1970s and 1980s. By 1990, a rabbinic Ad Hoc Committee on Homosexuality and the Rabbinate had initiated conversations that led the Reform rabbinical association to affirm the right of gays and lesbians to openly enter rabbinical school and seek ordination. The decade of the 1990s wit-nessed an increasing number of rabbis who officiated at commitment ceremonies or "sanctified, intimate relationships," and, in 2000, the rabbis affirmed Jewish rituals for same-gender Jewish couples under the auspices of a rabbi, while respecting the right of every rabbi to make an "informed choice" (the watchwords of Reform) and to do what her or his conscience dictated.

Finally, Reform Jews came out of the 1960s tossing over another "tradition," that of no tradition. Minimalist in ceremony, custom, ob-servance, and ritual for nearly a century, Reform rabbis were repre-sented well by Joseph Narot of Miami's Temple Israel, who said, in 1958, of the suggestion that Reform should have a guide to recom-mend rituals and ceremonies for those who sought them, "Reform Judaism does not need and should not now adopt, either in princi-ple or in actuality, any official guide." A decade later, a generation of rabbis emerged who were comfortable wearing a head covering and a prayer shawl on the pulpit, observing some form of dietary laws, listing observances and customs that congregants might wish to try, and retrieving traditions practiced by Conservative and Orthodox Jews, which they did not describe as anachronistic. In 1972, Reform rabbis published *A Shabbat Manual*, filled with ways to "do certain things" and representing a huge step away from the rejection of "do-ing certain things" in previous decades. A decade later, the rabbis published *Gates of the Seasons* (1983), a book that provides numerous ways to observe *mitzvoth*, or rituals. And congregants slowly but steadily followed, dramatically increasing the level of ritual observance in the synagogue and in the home over the following twenty-five years.

Conservative Judaism

All of the issues that laypeople and professionals at Reform congregations discussed in this period found an echo in Conservative Judaism. It took the movement many years to become comfortable ordaining women (1985) and approving the ordination of openly gay and lesbian rabbis (2006), and the seminary (as well as member synagogues) has struggled mightily with these issues. Eventually, the movement would open itself to more than twice the number of candidates for rabbis, educators, cantors, and lay leaders by including women. And, although no Conservative rabbis officiate at weddings that do not involve a Jewish bride and a Jewish groom and although no Conservative synagogue hosts interfaith marriages, intermarried couples join Conservative synagogues in significant numbers. This development has demanded a response, and figuring out how to welcome intermarried families and encourage them to be active—especially when there is a supportive non-Jewish parent—while rejecting their marriage ceremony as Judaically invalid and excluding the non-Jewish spouse from full religious (i.e., membership) involvement has not been easy.

To a large extent, the response of Conservative synagogue professionals, especially rabbis, cantors, and executive directors, has mirrored that of Reform congregational leaders. While explaining that the non-Jewish partner could not be a "member" of the synagogue —and thus could not participate in Judaic rituals on the pulpit in front of the entire congregation or make decisions on synagogue matters—he or she could nonetheless have a rich Judaic experience in the congregational community. Realizing that the future of Jewish involvement, especially if there were children, necessitated the support of the non-Jewish parent as well as the Jewish parent (most Conservative rabbis found it much more likely that a Jewish mother and a non-Jewish father would raise Jewish children than the opposite combination), Conservative leaders made special efforts to involve the intermarried family in synagogue life.

But two other concerns dominated Conservative congregations as this period began; how to, at last, define the movement, and what to do with the increasingly outdated Silverman prayer book. The Reform movement had issued platforms in 1885 and 1937 and was preparing a centennial statement of principles for the 100th anniversary of the Reform seminary, in 1975. These activities largely dominated rabbinic discussions but remained under the radar of most Reform congregants. In fact, rare was a Reform worshiper who even saw a copy of any statement until the 1999 Statement of Principles was widely distributed in synagogue sanctuaries.

Conservative rabbis, as we have seen, had felt that the best way to remain an "umbrella" branch of American Judaism—offering a home for all—was to avoid pithy statements, as Reform rabbis had done, of God, revelation, covenant, Jewish law, authority, ritual, and the like. But, just as congregants would soon demand, following Reform Judaism, the ordination of women as Conservative rabbis, they put pressure on their leaders to tell them precisely what Conservative Judaism is and demanded to participate in the conversation. And this would involve not only a statement of principles but a careful look at the theology and language of the prayer book.

With the Reform movement's publication of *Gates of Prayer*, the Conservative leadership moved more quickly to put in print a prayer book that reflected discussions among rabbis and among laypeople since the late 1960s. Rabbi Jules Harlow edited the *Mahzor for Rosh Hashanah and Yom Kippur* (1972), but congregational rabbis were especially aware of the continual "requests for variety in the evening service for the Sabbath and Festivals." In addition, they were cognizant of the "differing practices in various congregations," the need for "a liturgical reaction to the mass murder of Jews during the Holocaust," the birth of the Jewish state, the restoration of Jerusalem after 1967 under Jewish control, and especially the desire among Conservative worshipers for "new readings, including poetry and prose of modern and contemporary writers." The "Silverman prayer book" of 1946 was quite univocal and its translations somewhat archaic (and surely dated), and, as this period unfolded, Conservative Jews sought an elegant liturgy that recognized that there are "many paths, many ways." The result was *Siddur Sim Shalom—A Prayer Book for Shabbat, Festivals, and Weekdays* (1985), a liturgy filled with "options and alternatives."

Its format is pleasing, with Hebrew text on the right and English text on the left. The English is lofty, often elegant, and a great improvement over the previous liturgy. Brief introductions to many prayers provide explanations of context and meaning (e.g., in this prayer we praise our Creator and proclaim His sovereignty over all Creation), and fifteen pages of readings for Yom Ha-shoah (commemoration of the Holocaust) and powerful readings about the State of Israel add considerable breadth to the liturgy. Congregants praised the avoidance of masculine pronouns in prayers and biblical translations (e.g., "ancestors" in place of "fathers") and complained little; the most vocal criticism, aside from the book's weight at 880 pages, was that transliterations are almost nonexistent; when they are present (e.g., for *L'kha Dodi*, a Sabbath-eve hymn), they give only the pronunciation of the chorus (a few words) and not the verses (the overwhelming bulk of the Hebrew). This liturgy won almost universal adoption in the Conservative movement and is still a favorite of worshipers after twenty years.

Some congregations utilize the book in a manner that prevents worshipers, if they close their eyes, from knowing whether the service is Orthodox or Conservative. With eyes open, of course, the differences are immediate: women are everywhere (on and off the pulpit) and in most instances are given roles equal to those of men in Conservative synagogues, and most worshipers drive their cars to and from the temple on Shabbat and, without shame, park as close as possible.

At roughly the same time that the prayer book appeared, Conservative (and, increasingly, Reform) synagogues encouraged concurrent worship and study activities on Saturday mornings. At one New Jersey Conservative synagogue, in 2008, while the main service unfolded in the sanctuary beginning a little after 9 A.M., a yoga class met at the same time in one room, a Torah study session began at 9:30 in another room, a teen service began at 10, a "learners" service started at 10:15, a meditation class (with a rabbi) commenced at 10:45, and a much more informal (and lay-led) service than the one in the main sanctuary (often called the "upstairs minyan" or the "downstairs minyan") got under way at 10.

Like congregations in other branches, Conservative observers (especially rabbis) noted the increasing informality of worshipers beginning in the late 1960s. Rabbi Eli A. Bohnen of Temple Emanu-El in Providence watched from the pulpit as men began to wear sports jackets instead of suits (and even, upon occasion, no tie) and women no longer came to worship in hats. He told the congregation in 1970 that, "when women wear hats at services a different mood prevails among the worshipers" and that there was a strong correlation between "ties, suits, hats, and decorum." Concomitantly, the leaders announced that "saving seats" was now prohibited and that (in response to a survey) there would be more congregational singing, more English reading, and more pauses during the liturgy for an occasional explanation of the next prayer. At both Tiferes Israel in Columbus, Ohio, and the Olympic Jewish Temple in Los Angeles, along with issuing instructions for parking at High Holy Day services, bulletin editors reminded congregants how to dress appropriately.

Defining Conservative Judaism was a more challenging task, for not only did plenty of rabbis (and some laypeople) prefer a movement without definition, but the very breadth of interpretations on most every major theme of Judaism—its strength—made any definition far too reductive. A creative solution to this dilemma emerged in the first, and still the only, platform of Conservative Judaism, *Emet ve-Emunah—Statement of Principles of Conservative Judaism* (1988). In contrast to the Reform platforms (the three that were in print and the fourth, which had yet to emerge), whose authors prided themselves on the brief summaries they provided of complicated theological issues, the Conservative platform included short essays on each topic. And, true to its essence, almost any position a congregant might hold found support within its pages. Take revelation as a case in point. If a worshiper believed, as the Orthodox asserted, that God spoke actual words to Moses and that Moses wrote these words down as Genesis, Exodus, Leviticus, Numbers, and Deuteronomy, that worshiper would find that view was affirmed. If a Conservative Jew denied verbal revelation but saw the Torah as the intersection of the human and the Divine, something akin to "divine inspiration," that view left him or her solidly in the Conservative ranks. And if a Conservative Jew perceived, as Reform Judaism asserted, that the Torah was a human document from start to finish, though arguably the greatest book ever written by people, Conservative Judaism had a home for them.

It was the same for a Conservative Jew's view of God or for any other topic. Refusing to yield ground to either the right or the left, to Orthodox Judaism or to Reform Judaism, the statement of beliefs put in writing what Conservative rabbis had preached and written for decades. Conservative Judaism spread an umbrella over the American Jewish community that was so wide that it offered a home to a far greater variety of Jewish beliefs and practices than either of its major rivals. For those leaning toward orthodoxy, rabbis talked to congregants about "rediscovering the power of traditional observance" and *mitzvoth* as "commandments of God." This language distanced them from Reform rabbis (and probably from at least half of their Conservative colleagues), who rarely affirmed "God's voice calling to us from the Torah." But Friday-evening services began to imitate those at Reform synagogues (e.g., English readings; hymns sung in English), and, except for synagogue *kashrut* observance, measures of Conservative Jewish identity were the same as those of Reform Jews, especially as the Reform movement, in the words of Rabbi Wolfe Kelman as early as 1967, "moved closer to creating an atmosphere in their congregations which is not different from ours" and told his Conservative colleagues that "this kind of traditional atmosphere . . . is our real competition." And, to make sure Conservative rabbis touched all the bases, they offered a home to those who might have found the newest branch of Judaism, Reconstructionism, appealing.

Reconstructionist thinkers, most of whom came out of a Conservative Jewish environment, generally rejected the idea of a personal God. For them, God was a feeling, an idea, an impulse, or, as Mordecai M. Kaplan (1881–1983), the movement's founder put it, the highest value we hold. When the Conservative statement of principles speaks of God as one who is "present when we look for meaning in the world" or as the one we find when we "work for morality, for justice, and for future redemption," it is acknowledging that Reconstructionist Jews, too, can have a home in this movement. Speaking of God as "presence" or as "not completely independent of our beliefs and experiences" is using the language of Reconstructionist theology within a document of Conservative Jewish belief.

Reconstructionist Judaism

The fourth branch of American Judaism grew more in the 1960s than it had done in any of its previous four decades of existence. Kaplan was still alive and giving it inspiration, if not, because of his age, leadership, and in that same decade the movement opened a seminary in Philadelphia and admitted its first female rabbinic student. By the late 1960s, Reconstuctionist synagogues from coast to coast, although still a mystery to most Jews because of their small memberships, had an identity that was clear. While Sabbath-morning worship less or more duplicated Conservative worship, Friday-evening services were much more informal than those of the other branches, and the movement's commitment to civilization (i.e., culture) made music, folk dance, drama, Hebrew poetry, and art an integral part of worship ("organic Jewish communities," Kaplan called this). Kaplan's most important work, *Judaism as a Civilization: Toward a Reconstruction of American-Jewish Life* (1934), already suggested this combination, and it was actualized in congregations on the East Coast and the West Coast, especially. Indeed, much of the institutional structure of American Jewry is really Kaplan's.

In Los Angeles, for example, in the late 1960s, at one Reconstructionist "fellowship" that met in a Unitarian church in the San Fernando Valley, the Rumanian-born, Orthodox-ordained, very nontraditional Rabbi Michael Roth conducted Sabbath-evening services while sitting around a group of tables arranged in a rectangle, seminar style. When he began to sing the opening hymn (the same *L'kha Dodi* referenced earlier in the discussion of Conservative Judaism), some congregants rose from their chairs at the table and began to dance around the perimeter of the large room. As the evening unfolded, the rabbi inserted a contemporary poem and a brief reading from the theologian Abraham Heschel and held up a painting in a book that he wished to discuss. The "sermon" was a discussion of some verses in the Torah (from Deuteronomy) that led to reflections on the war in Vietnam. This Sabbath-evening fellowship and worship, where Torah study, dancing, singing, and discussion took precedence over prayer, was precisely what Kaplan had in mind when he introduced this new branch of American Judaism at the

Society for the Advancement of Judaism (SAJ) in Manhattan a few decades earlier.

Reconstructionism offered not only a different form of worship from the other branches of Judaism but a different theology. *Judaism as a Civilization* is a powerful critique of revelation; Torah is a creation of the Jewish people. Its adherents were (mainly) those Conservative (especially) and Reform Jews who found their liturgy difficult to get beyond. Both Reform and Conservative prayer books —new and old—featured prayers that described a God who heard what worshipers said and who worked actively in the world, from creation to the present, if (often) in mysterious ways. Reconstructionist liturgy did not present such a God (though God language was present), and small numbers of Jews affirmed their acceptance of this credo by joining a Reconstructionist synagogue and thus proclaiming to one and all that they denied the concept of a personal God and that, in the words of Mordecai Kaplan, divine revelation was a "vestige of ancient idolatry." Probably many other Conservative and Reform Jews held similar theological beliefs but were not comfortable acknowledging them publicly. So, though it seems certain that large numbers of American Jews did *not* perceive God to be active in history and, less certainly but probably, did *not* experience God at all, they felt more comfortable in giving lip service (even if they remained at home and did not move their lips in the sanctuary) to theism. But, those willing to say explicitly that God was "the ordering force in the universe" and not the savior of the Exodus from Egypt or the author of the covenant at Mt. Sinai, found that Reconstructionist synagogues were for them.

In 1999, the Reconstructionist movement published a nearly 1,300-page prayer book for the High Holy Days, *Kol Haneshamah: Prayerbook for the Days of Awe.* Combining tradition and modernity (it includes writings by James Agee, Judy Chicago, Maya Angelou, and Annie Dillard), it not only dominated the Reconstructionist movement but was highly influential among Conservative and Reform rabbis. Building on the theology of the 1989 Reconstructionist Sabbath prayer book, *Kol Haneshamah: Shabbat Eve*, it rejects chosenness (changing the traditional "who has chosen us from among all peoples" to "who has drawn us to your service"), individual afterlife (substituting "nurturing the life of every living thing"), verbal revelation of the Torah, and (everywhere) a transcendent Deity. It included transliterations in an interlinear fashion, mixed in with the Hebrew, carefully constructed gender-neutral translations (without God as King or Lord or Shepherd), and lots of poetry. Reconstructionist thinkers insisted that the biblical concept of God is humanly constructed, legendary, and mythic. The Bible tells us nothing about God, only what its authors believed God said and did. God is not what the Bible claims but a representation of women's and men's highest aspirations, ideal, and dreams. God is the "oneness that spans the fathomless deeps of space," the "sameness in the elemental substance of stars and planets," or the "faith by which we overcome the fear of loneliness." The embracing of this pattern of belief is what distinguishes a Reconstructionist synagogue from all other synagogues.

There was never a large number of such synagogues. By 1983, there were only forty-six, and more than half were in three states: California, New York, and Pennsylvania. Twenty years later, the number had reached only 100. More and more, these "fellowship groups" (*havurot* in Hebrew) became congregations, with buildings rather than rented rooms and with full-time rabbis (the seminary has ordained hundreds of Reconstructionist rabbis) instead of lay leaders or part-time rabbis. And, while always statistically insignificant when compared to the number of Conservative, Orthodox, and Reform congregations and while often marginalized by the "major brands," these Reconstructionist communities were embraced by their members with passion and commitment. They have welcomed intermarried couples at least as long as the Reform movement (if not a bit longer), ordained openly gay and lesbian students as rabbis well before the Conservative and Reform seminaries followed suit, and had affirmed rabbinic and cantorial participation in same-sex ceremonies by 1993. Just as one should no longer speak of "Protestant, Catholic, and Jew" when describing the American religious community (Muslims now outnumber Jews), it is inappropriate to speak, as so many do, of "the three branches of American Judaism."

Orthodox Judaism

An easy way to notice the change in orthodoxy in the past few decades is to listen to sermons by Orthodox rabbis. Unlike Reform and Conservative rabbis, who often speak both on Friday night and Saturday morning, Orthodox rabbis rarely give sermons except on Sabbath mornings, late on Saturday afternoons (just before the final worship of the day), or on holidays/festivals (what are "holidays" in some Orthodox bulletins are referred to as "festivals" in others). Increasingly, the Orthodox rabbinic sermon, especially on the Sabbath, demonstrates that the rabbi has studied not only the portion of Scripture assigned for that week but the range of commentaries and other Judaic texts (ancient, medieval, and modern) that offer insight, interpretation, and analysis of passages within the Torah selection. There is usually only a perfunctory attempt to ask how this might relate to the lives of the worshipers.

The model provided by men such as Joseph Lookstein, Leo Jung, Harry H. Epstein, and other rabbis from the 1920s into the 1960s has been replaced by a model of scholarly excellence in Jewish texts. Rare is the Orthodox rabbi today who draws upon non-Jewish literature (fiction or nonfiction), popular or contemporary culture (theater, cinema, television), general academic disciplines (anthropology, sociology, psychology), or contemporary non-Jewish thinkers in philosophy and theology. Instead, the explicit assumption is that all the insight that one needs is in Jewish texts (generally, the older the better), and this parochialism stands in sharp contrast to the attitude of

Orthodox rabbis of an earlier generation who combined Torah with advanced secular education.

Of course, there were always such rabbis in the Orthodox community, rabbis who shunned secular education and culture at every level and for whom secular literature had no merit and thus could be ignored. But, seemingly, more and more Orthodox rabbis have turned inward in the past few decades, living lives—external and internal—almost exclusively within the Orthodox community. Orthodox rabbis of the interwar years and well into the 1950s and even the 1960s joined their Conservative, Reconstructionist, and Reform colleagues on boards of rabbis as well as at communal events. The Los Angeles Board of Rabbis in 1968 and 1969 had numerous Orthodox rabbis who participated in its meetings and activities and joined non-Orthodox colleagues at rabbinic forums at non-Orthodox synagogues ("Ask the Rabbis"), seemingly oblivious to the other wings or sectors their (all-male) colleagues on the board represented. Hundreds attended a program at a Conservative synagogue in Los Angeles in the late 1960s ("Can Orthodox, Conservative, and Reform Judaism Ever Merge?") with Rabbis Marvin Bornstein (C), Simon Dolgin (O), and Albert M. Lewis (R) making presentations and then responding to one another and to the audience. This changed almost everywhere beginning in the 1970s. The Synagogue Council of America (Conservative, Orthodox, and Reform) disappeared as Orthodox rabbis shunned associations with those rabbis who were not as observant as they.

Perhaps the situation somewhat paralleled the way German-American (with an emphasis on the "American") Jews felt about newly arriving East European Jewish immigrants of the late nineteenth century. Concerned over whether non-Jews would always be able to distinguish the refined and acculturated Jew from the old-world one, they kept their distance from the new arrivals. Similarly, as the other branches of Judaism ordained women (they may not become Orthodox rabbis), attracted gay and lesbian Jews (they are still not welcome in Orthodox communities), and in various ways did not match Orthodox rabbis' observance levels, perhaps the Orthodox rabbinate felt it was increasingly necessary to demonstrate that it was not like the others. Conservative, Reconstructionist, and Reform rabbis drove to and from the synagogue on the Sabbath; Reconstructionist and Reform rabbis rarely strictly observed the dietary laws in restaurants; all three non-Orthodox rabbinical associations included women, gay, and lesbian colleagues; and both Reconstructionist and Reform rabbis officiated (with varying conditions) at intermarriages, not to mention commitment ceremonies. All of this, Orthodox rabbis concluded, necessitated a clear separation.

Attending modern Orthodox and Conservative Jewish worship, as well as engaging in discussions with rabbis from each branch, confirms the impression one receives from the journals of each sector that the differences between them, other than the seating arrangements for women (separate in the former, together with men in the latter), are negligible. They both continually affirm that Jewish law has its origin in God's revelation to Moses at Mt. Sinai and that it has been interpreted continually by rabbis. Indeed, one modern Orthodox rabbi in Los Angeles noted (quite accurately) in a sermon to his congregation, "every single mitzvah requires interpretation." Modern Orthodox rabbis try to differentiate themselves from the Conservative movement by granting much less authority to one individual and his subjective interpretations, but, just as the local Conservative rabbi is the interpreter of Jewish law, modern Orthodox rabbis recognize the right of individual (albeit "great") rabbis to interpret halacha. Like Conservative Jews, modern Orthodox Jews all agree that Jewish law must be flexible. A slight difference does exist: while Conservative Judaism sees precedents as suggestive, modern Orthodox considers them binding.

By embracing the nonobservant, modern Orthodox Jews do clearly differentiate themselves not from Conservative Jews but from the right wing of the Orthodox spectrum. Jews who do not observe the Sabbath or various ceremonies, customs, and rituals, are always welcome in a modern Orthodox community ("they are family" is the common explanation of modern Orthodox rabbis) but rarely interact with the Orthodox right. And the modern Orthodox differentiate themselves in one more way, by encouraging dialogue with non-Orthodox movements. As a modern Orthodox rabbi in Potomac, Maryland, put it during a panel discussion with a Conservative and Reform rabbi, "emphasis should be placed on who we are, rather than who the other is not."

The activity calendar at a typical Orthodox synagogue may look like a Reform listing of events. At an Orthodox synagogue in Los Angeles in June 2008, the Seniors made trips to the Glendale Centre Theatre for a performance of "Singing in the Rain," to the Richard Nixon Presidential Library, to a Los Angeles Dodgers baseball game, and to the Hollywood Bowl. At the same time, Orthodox worshipers were more observant than their (Orthodox) parents (and grandparents) of the 1920s through the 1950s and 1960s. Worshipers everywhere drove to services on the Sabbath, even on Rosh Hashanah, in large numbers, in the 1950s and into the 1960s, either parking off-site to give the pretense of not driving or in synagogue parking lots. On Rosh Hashanah in 1961, worshipers around the Pico-Robertson neighborhood of west-central Los Angeles, where more than one Orthodox synagogue held services, competed for the few parking spaces available on a weekday, and a bulletin editor unabashedly alerted congregants and guests to respect the neighborhood as they went from their cars to and from the synagogue. In the past few decades, bulletin editors have assumed that worshipers walked to the synagogue. And when the congregants did not, they parked sufficiently far from the synagogue that they could plausibly seem to have walked to and from worship.

The ritual bar has also been elevated considerably in the past few decades. One Los Angeles Orthodox rabbi told a member of his congregation (Rodef Sholom) in the 1950s that a *kippah* (head covering) was "an indoor garment." Rare would be the Orthodox rabbi who makes such a statement today, and more and more Orthodox congregants keep their head covering on their head when they leave worship. A South Carolina Orthodox rabbi noted that when he came to his congregation in the 1970s, only a few women utilized the ritual bath. Premenopausal married women are required by Jewish law to use the mikveh each month after their period and before resuming sexual relations, but this practice was rarely observed between the world wars or in the decade or two following World War II. Indeed, there were many Orthodox synagogues located far from the nearest mikveh. But it has become de rigueur in most Orthodox congregations everywhere.

In the 1950s, Orthodox young men and women attended the bar and bat mitzvah ceremonies of their Conservative and Reform friends, had "sleepovers" where they might accompany their host to Sunday school, and traveled considerable distances (albeit by foot) to be guests. These same young men, after attending worship services on Sabbath mornings, walked to parks and playgrounds to compete in baseball and basketball games in the afternoon. Recently, Orthodox young men and women have restricted themselves to activities that are in the "spirit" of the Sabbath, which excludes competitive sports with their non-Orthodox friends. In fact, in earlier decades Orthodox boys joined Little League teams with Jews of all sectors, but this practice ended when they became uncomfortable when the teams served nonkosher food after games.

This ratcheting-up is also true of dietary observance among adults. A generation or two ago (sociologists change the duration of a "generation" periodically), Orthodox men and women ate at nonkosher restaurants but avoided shellfish, pork products, the mixing of meat and milk, and other foods prohibited by the Bible. The next step taken by increasingly observant Orthodox congregations was to eat at these restaurants but to avoid meat (obviously not prepared according to Jewish law) altogether and to order instead salmon, tuna, pasta, or the like. And, more recently, Orthodox congregants have tended to eat only at kosher restaurants and to avoid invitations to eat at the homes of Jews (and non-Jews) who do not observe Jewish dietary laws in a strict fashion. In sum, regular worshipers at Orthodox synagogues have become much more rigorous in their observance of ceremonies, customs, and rituals. In 2008, one Washington, D.C., worshiper told a guest that he no longer washed with a bar of soap (only a squeeze bottle) on the Sabbath, citing a prohibition against something changing its form on the day of rest.

The prayer service, too, has changed. In the 1950s, Orthodox worshipers brought different prayer books to the synagogue. Rabbis mentioned this practice in sermons, and bulletin editors frequently commented on it, as well. The most popular books were *Evening Services for Sabbaths and Festivals*, arranged by Ben Jacob (1932; frequently revised and reprinted); the 700+-page *Daily Prayers with English Translations*, edited by A. Th. Philips (1950; frequently revised and reprinted); *Prayer Book for the New Year*, edited by Philips (1931; frequently revised and reprinted); *The Standard Prayer Book*, translated by Simeon Singer (enlarged American edition, 1942); and the "Birnbaum *siddur*" (1949; frequently revised and reprinted) and the "Birnbaum *mahzor*" (High Holy Days; English and Hebrew, 1951; frequently revised and reprinted). The prayer books in use at Orthodox synagogues had Hebrew on the right and English on the left, and the service leader would ask the congregation, from time to time, to turn to this or that English reading. Today, almost everywhere, the liturgy is prayed exclusively in Hebrew, with little or no concession to the worshiper who does not read it. Thus, it is much less common for non-Jews to attend an Orthodox synagogue today than it was during the years 1920–1960, and, when they do (e.g., at a bar mitzvah), it is much more difficult for them to participate in any of the liturgy. A growing self-confidence has led orthodoxy to simply not worry about *mah yomru la'goyim* (what will the non-Jews say?).

As in the past, Orthodox bulletin editors and rabbis have worried about decorum. Rabbi Dolgin frequently expressed "strong displeasure with the decorum" during the reading of the Torah; Rabbi David Stavsky at Columbus's Beth Jacob insisted that "different ushers be appointed from the Board every Saturday to help maintain decorum," especially during a "repetitive" part of the morning liturgy (*mussaf*) near the end; a synagogue in Chicago printed and distributed on Rosh Hashanah and Yom Kippur in 2001 a "Ten Commandments of Behavior"; at a board meeting of an Orthodox synagogue in Cleveland in 1998, the president said that "reprimands regarding decorum should not come from the Rabbi from the pulpit but rather from the ushers or the president;" and a leader of Kesher Israel in Washington, D.C., told the board that "groups of young people have been organized to keep decorum in the synagogue during the High Holy Days."

Yet, decorum has not been embraced by the membership within most Orthodox synagogues. One striking difference between observing worship at an Orthodox synagogue and worship at a congregation of any other branch of Judaism is what happens when a worshiper arrives late. At a non-Orthodox worship service, the latecomer sits down, looks over at the worshiper on the right or left for the page number, and opens the book and joins the reading or singing. At a typical Orthodox service, the latecomer opens the prayer book while standing, hurriedly prays all the parts of the service already completed, and then joins the congregation. While rushing through the missed prayers, the worshiper, especially a man, uses exaggerated body movements, highlighted by bending and bowing. When asked later about this, most late-comers respond that the entire body, not just the mouth, must be involved in prayer and that one must not hold back any part of oneself. And, as the service continues, some worshipers will jump up while others sit, some will jump up and remain standing while others sit, and the worshiper on one's left and the worshiper on one's right will more often than not be reciting words that are not identical, as worshipers, for much of the service, move along at their own pace. Most agree with the worshipers who used the expressions *opschapen, opmolen, opklappen, opshalemoizen dos davnen*, all of which mean the same thing—make short work of the *siddur*, gallop across its pages in double-quick time. The Orthodox liturgy is long, and it is repetitive (albeit elegant), and worshipers tend to move as rapidly as they are able.

Recently, an Orthodox participant-observer at a small Sabbath morning worship service noticed that the rabbi and worshipers were "murmuring various prayers in Hebrew." The women, "peering through diamond-shaped holes in the *mehitza* [separation] and often questioning loudly what page the men are on," did not hesitate to chat about numerous topics during the worship service. They asked aloud "whether they are supposed to be standing or sitting for a certain prayer," why a particular woman was absent, and what page the men were on. A bit less loudly, they discussed "outfits and costume jewelry." From time to time, their conversation bothered the rabbi, and he "bangs heavily on a chair next to him." All of the conversations ended when the Torah was carried around the sanctuary, as the women moved to the front of their section to touch it. In the 1950s, at four Orthodox synagogues in the Pico-Robertson neighborhood of Los Angeles, few followed attentively (without texts or translations), as someone intoned some chapters from Leviticus. In fact, many, if not most, staged an exodus, even if the reader tried his best to outstrip the wind. At Kesher Israel in Washington, D.C., on an August Sabbath morning in 2008, twenty or so Generation X men gathered in the second-floor lobby and overflowed onto the O Street sidewalk in Georgetown during the lengthy Torah service. They discussed the Democratic National Convention, the Washington Redskins' upcoming season, and their Labor Day weekend plans. Most of the other worshipers followed the chanting of the passages from Deuteronomy with Joseph Hertz's *Pentateuch and Haftorahs: Hebrew Text, English Translation, and Commentary* (1960).

Budgets of Orthodox synagogues everywhere more and more

resemble those of the other three wings. Dues constitute a much larger share of annual income (at Beth Jacob Congregation in Beverly Hills, income from dues provided around 20 to 30 percent of the total budget in the 1950s, 50 to 60 percent in the 1970s [$125,000/ $228,000 in 1976–1977], and 70 to 80 percent in the 1990s). Banquets, appeals during Yom Kippur worship services, and auctioning honors raised an increasingly small percentage of the funds needed to meet synagogue expenses. And, as with congregations of the other branches, professional salaries now claimed the overwhelming proportion (90 percent or more everywhere) of an Orthodox synagogue budget.

In the fall of 2009, the author attended the annual meetings of two small congregations in southern California, neither Orthodox. The meetings confirmed that these conclusions about Orthodox synagogues applied to the synagogues of the "other branches," as well. Those members in attendance approved annual dues (billed quarterly) of less than $1,000 (for two adults) at both congregations and a balanced budget of less than $200,000. In both congregations, dues accounted for approximately 85 percent of the income; there had been no increase in dues—a result of the economic downturn in America—in either congregation for two years. The most striking feature of both meetings was the reports of the Long-Range Planning Committee (called the Goals and Objectives Committee in the second of the two synagogues), for short-term and long-term planning were a centerpiece of both congregations' thinking. A committee met regularly at each synagogue to reflect on where the congregation had come from, where it was in 2009, and where members hoped it would be three to five years (in the short term) and eight to ten years (in the long term) in the future. The reports of these two committees covered professional personnel, liturgy, dues structure (especially for single members), the usefulness of paying dues to the national umbrella synagogue organization, and what to do about guests who wanted to worship on the High Holy Days but did not want to buy a ticket. In all, it was an impressive display of congregational democracy.

"Dues," nearly everywhere, entitle the payer to two reserved seats for the High Holy Days (additional seats could be purchased). At a synagogue in Queens, New York, in the late 1980s, dues of $600 entitled the payor to two seats on the main floor, and dues of $400 bought one two seats in the balcony; if a couple wanted to attend supplementary services (without the featured rabbi and cantor) in an adjacent hall, the cost was only $250.

Adult study has been a serious component of Orthodox synagogue life in the past decade or two. Where more than one Orthodox synagogue serves a community, leaders often combine adult study and call it a Kollel Institute. The books of the Torah generally form the core of the curriculum, with Jewish thought, Jewish customs and ceremonies, and/or Jewish history usually featured. Everywhere, Torah is taught as oral revelation from God to Moses (who wrote it down), Orthodox thinkers are seen as traditional in terms of Jewish observances, and a rather uncritical view of the Jewish past (using rabbinic literature as historical sources) dominates the texts and lectures.

Although its influence is less visible than in non-Orthodox sectors of American Judaism, where the role of women has changed dramatically, feminism has had a striking impact in the Orthodox community. Of course, women rabbis are everywhere in Conservative, Reconstructionist, and Reform synagogues, under the *huppah*, and at the graveside; women lay leaders lead congregations and dominate boards almost as frequently as women rabbis serve on pulpits; the naming of a young girl has become as common as the *brit milah*; everywhere, the bat mitzvah ceremony takes place no less often than the bar mitzvah; and worshipers bless Sarah, Rebekah, Leah, and Rachel in the same sentence with Abraham, Isaac, and Jacob.

In the Orthodox synagogue, the changes are both architectural and liturgical or at least are quite visible in the worship service itself.

Recently built synagogues provide "sight lines"—views from the women's section of the sanctuary (usually at the same level as the men's section)—that are as "good" as those for men, whether for viewing the reading of Scripture or for seeing the man leading the worship. Tour guides (usually the rabbi) in new sanctuaries of Orthodox synagogues from coast to coast point to this change. Indeed, in Savannah, Georgia, the guide called the women's sections (on each side of the men's) "Out of the Balcony."

Within the service, the changes are no less dramatic. Bat mitzvah girls everywhere deliver a *derash* (Torah commentary) in the sanctuary, although it is placed at the end of the liturgy and thus technically is not part of the service. Some men, resistant to feminism, take off their prayer shawls to emphasize that the service is over or walk out when the young woman begins to speak. But such behavior is increasingly marginalized, and there are some congregations in which the *derash* of the boy is moved to the end of the service to demonstrate a commitment to egalitarianism.

In some synagogues, adult women give *divrei Torah* (thoughts on the Scriptural reading); women read the prayers on behalf of the State of Israel and/or the United States (which are not considered integral to the liturgy); mothers say blessings previously reserved for fathers at the bar or bat mitzvah of their child; women recite the *kaddish* prayer, which was previously reserved for male mourners; the Torah is paraded into the women's section of the sanctuary; when someone names a sick person for whom the congregation prays, the names of their father and their mother are mentioned, and women shout out names of sick people from their section just as do the men; when the Patriarchs are mentioned in the prayer for the sick, the names of their wives (the Matriarchs) are also invoked; and when a congregation has a public *kiddush* (sanctification of the Sabbath with wine) at the end of the service, women often lead it.

And, finally, although women are rarely counted in the quorum of ten needed for public worship (the minyan), many congregations have a special custom when a man or a woman is reciting the *gomel* prayer, a blessing of appreciation for surviving illness, childbirth, or danger recited publicly: women are counted in the minyan.

Postdenominational Judaism

One historian, David Ellenson, has recently made reference to his own "boundary crossings," noting that he belonged to both a Conservative and a Reform congregation for more than twenty years and asserting—more questionable—that this is "hardly unique among present-day American Jews." There is, in fact, little evidence for his conclusion about how "permeable" are the "borders for so many Jews." In fact, more than 95 percent of the members of nearly every congregation in America belong to that synagogue and no other. Hardly anyone is like Julius Blackman, who (when he left the cantorate after eighteen years) attended Conservative, Orthodox, Reconstructionist, and Reform synagogues, services at New Age congregations, at a gay synagogue, and at a number of college Hillels. If nothing else, the cost of membership prevents most Jews from joining multiple congregations, and, while there are members of one synagogue who attend worship services at another congregation, this is almost as rare as membership in two religious communities. Remember, most Jews do not attend worship services anywhere on any regular basis. And for those Jews who do, to worship elsewhere is to find "cold and boring" services that are seen as inferior to those at the member's own synagogue, which are "uplifting and spiritual." Of course, no service is either wholly cold or wholly uplifting, but such comments reveal much about the worshiper, if not the liturgy. For some, magnificent choirs singing on behalf of the congregation in grand temples are "spiritual," while, for others, a service in a room with a few worshipers chanting and reading rapidly entirely in Hebrew provides the same meaning.

So, while those who posit a "postdenomination" Judaism certainly do not mean multiple memberships, this category might refer to the emergence of synagogue communities in the past few decades that eschew the label of any of the four branches of American Judaism. There are, in fact, such groups, broadly allied together in an association (ALEPH—Alliance for Jewish Renewal) and a cantorial/rabbinic association (Ohalah—Association of Rabbis for Jewish Renewal). ALEPH and Ohalah, like the Conservative, Orthodox, Reconstructionist, and Reform synagogues and rabbis, even have a biennial *kallah*, or conference. They represent, in some ways, a tiny fifth sector, branch, or wing of the American Judaic community, with a much greater emphasis (loosely speaking) on spirituality, on ecology, on social action, and on kabbalah. They are recognizable by a consistent vocabulary in newsletters and sermons that includes words like "journey," "renewal," "replenishment," "repositioning," "spiritual awareness," and "well-being." But their services and activities are duplicated at many Reconstructionist and Reform congregations, so it is not really meaningful to speak of them as "postdenominational" or "transdenominational."

What is growing today is "nondenominationalism," the increasing number of Jews who call themselves seculars, cultural Jews, or "just Jewish." Just as significant numbers of those raised as Catholics and Protestants now define themselves as seculars and an increasing number of voters call themselves "Independents," so, too, the number of Jews raised in one of the four branches but not identifying with any of them is increasing. The number of adult Jews who would not identify themselves with one of the sectors increased from 20 to 27 percent from 1990 to 2000, and the Pew Forum on Religion and Public Life survey of 2007 found that the number of Jews following the practice continued to grow. Thus, many worry that Jews, especially those of Generation X, have abandoned community for a host of more individual alternatives. These alternatives have in common a profound interest in the self and its redemption and in one's own spiritual journey and personal fulfillment. Baby boomers (those born in the first twenty years after World War II) flooded into Conservative and Reform synagogues in the 1980s and early 1990s. Will the same be true of their children?

Conclusion

The American synagogue, like so many other institutions, was dramatically affected by the economic downturn of 2008–2010. It had a deleterious impact on almost every area of synagogue life, as budgets were cut significantly all over the land. But rabbis, arguably, felt the impact more than any other professional in the synagogue community, as congregations released, rather than renewed, assistant and associate rabbis, reduced full-time rabbis to part time, and canceled searches that were under way to provide assistants to senior rabbis.

Orthodox rabbis were less affected than rabbis of the other branches, as only a small number of those ordained had planned to enter the congregational rabbinate. But even Orthodox rabbis, especially those who wanted to make a career of teaching in Jewish schools, saw the opportunities shrinking and their career goals placed on hold. It is, however, in the other branches that the high unemployment took hold.

In the spring and summer of 2009, as Conservative, Reconstructionist, and Reform rabbis sought jobs, there were approximately three rabbis available for every opening. There were older rabbis whose congregations encouraged them to retire so that they could hire a young rabbi with a much smaller salary; there were assistant and associate rabbis whose positions disappeared when their contract expired as congregations sought to balance their budgets; and there were newly ordained and recently ordained rabbis who had not yet found jobs. When the dust settled, two out of every three non-Orthodox rabbis seeking a job in 2009 remained, at the end of the calendar year, unemployed, with little opportunity for meaningful or gainful work opportunities in the near future in their profession.

The 2009 "state of the congregation" reports delivered by presidents of congregations at annual meetings and then published on synagogue websites provide a striking summary of the impact of the economy on synagogues everywhere in the country. In addition to reducing the professional and administrative staff (rabbis dominated synagogue staffs, as it was much more common to have two rabbis than to have two cantors or two education directors), every area of synagogue administration and programming felt the cuts.

And yet, to the casual observer, the synagogue seems in good health. Bulletins and websites overflow with lists of activities of auxiliary groups (e.g., sisterhoods, brotherhoods, youth groups, seniors, social action committees), adult education programs, and Sabbath, holiday, and festival worship and celebrations. Everywhere I have traveled, Conservative and Orthodox synagogues were packed on Saturday mornings, and the few empty seats in sanctuaries could have been filled by worshipers in other parts of the building participating in alternative services of various kinds. Reconstructionist congregations were only slightly less filled, and numerous Reform congregations attracted packed sanctuaries at this or that Friday-evening service. At least in the sanctuary, the difficulties of balancing budgets were out of sight and out of mind. An Orthodox rabbi in Columbus said to me, in March of 2010, when I asked him about the impact of the economy on his congregation, that "this too shall pass."

The Zionist thinker and Hebrew-language essayist Asher Ginsberg (better known by his pen-name, Ahad Ha'am) once said that "more than the Jews have kept the Sabbath, the Sabbath has kept the Jews." If we were to paraphrase this proposition and substitute the synagogue for the Sabbath, its veracity seems highly doubtful, at least in the American experience. In most periods of the history of the Jews in the United States, fewer than half of American Jews have been members of synagogues, and surely not all of those who had memberships have participated in the religious, educational, cultural, and social activities of the institution, even after making a financial contribution.

Yet, we can say with some confidence of the American synagogue, after thinking about its history over more than three centuries, that it has been the most significant Jewish institution in the life of Jews. And, although it has offered to both young and old learning experiences in classrooms, from the early years of religious school and Hebrew school through confirmation and then in the form of adult education, and though it has provided a wide variety of ancillary activities in the form of sisterhood, brotherhood, youth fellowship, social action projects, and much more, nothing has been as central to the purpose of the synagogue as the sanctuary. Here, rabbis, cantors, choirs, and talented laypeople have used printed words (liturgies and Scripture) of all kinds, together with the spoken word (sermons, lectures, discussions) to make Judaism (call it spirituality, if you will) a part of the life of countless Jews. There is no reason to think that this will not continue, in old and new ways that blend centuries of Judaism with the American experience.

Appendix

Counting Synagogues

The claim by Solomon Schechter and Cyrus Adler that there were 1,800 synagogues in America in 1913 is most likely based on the most commonly cited—and the most erroneous—source of synagogue enumeration, the U.S. *Census of Religious Bodies.* The U.S. Census Bureau has not asked questions about religion since the 1950s, but the federal government did gather some information about religion for about a half-century before that. Between decennial censuses— 1906, 1916, 1926, and 1936 (the 1946 data have never been published) —the *Census of Religious Bodies,* by statutory creation, attempted to count synagogues (and churches). The first *Census of Religious Bodies* was conducted through questionnaires mailed to religious leaders and relied exclusively on the officers of 186 denominations grouped into twenty-seven families (e.g., Baptists). It was a failure; nevertheless, many Jewish historians (and others) used these numbers, uncritically, throughout the twentieth century. The figure 1,800 is most likely connected to the preliminary figures released before the census tabulation of 1,901 "Jewish religion organizations" in 1916.

The definition of "religious bodies" used by the census workers is one of many problems with the survey. The government counted not only synagogues but Jewish organizations, usually sponsored by Jewish religious groups, that engaged in secular activities. Mizrachi, a Zionist organization linked to the Orthodox community, is a good example; it was never a synagogue. In addition, the words alternating in the census publications for what historians simply label as synagogues were a clue as to how widely the net was cast: religious organizations, churches, synagogues, and congregations were all used interchangeably when counting "Jewish religious organizations," just as "synagogues" were listed under "churches" in numerous city directories of those same years. The intent was to count "congregations" that might not have had "synagogues" (generally, "synagogue" meant a building, whereas "congregation" meant a Jewish religious organization without its own building or "synagogue"; half the "Jewish religious organizations" in the 1916 census did not have a building of their own), but the result was to claim totals that were unimaginable if only Conservative (beginning in 1916), Orthodox, and Reform "congregations," as well as congregations that had not affiliated with one of the three large branches, were included.

The total of 3,118 Jewish congregations in 1926 is an example of the uselessness of the census. Fewer than 230 congregations belonged to the Conservative movement (the United Synagogue of America listed them all), and fewer than 280 congregations belonged to the Reform movement (the Union of American Hebrew Congregations listed them all), leaving, according to the census records, more than 2,700 Orthodox "congregations," an impossible total. Even if we grant that some Orthodox "congregations"—a group that rented a room for High Holy Day services and had nothing comparable to "membership" in a "congregation" or synagogue—were inactive except on Rosh Hashanah and Yom Kippur, it is likely that there were, at most, as many Orthodox congregations as Reform and Conservative combined. So a figure of 1,500 total synagogues in 1926 would probably be an exaggeration. And it is not at all clear that a "High Holy Day congregation" should be included in the count of synagogues.

Nonetheless, we can at least get a sense of the explosion in synagogue numbers that resulted from the mass immigration of Jews from eastern Europe from these figures: the census workers found 533 Jewish "religious organizations" in 1890 and 1,769 Jewish "religious organizations" in 1906, a more than threefold increase according to their fallacious tabulations.

Sources

This book is based largely on synagogue archival records, especially synagogue bulletins and/or newsletters, rabbis' sermons and papers, and minutes of the board of trustees/directors, as well as random materials (e.g., congregational surveys) in synagogue libraries, oral interviews, and attendance at synagogue worship. Occasionally, while investigating a synagogue's architecture or attending a meeting, I came across a random bulletin in a library or office (e.g., Congregation Shaarey Zedek [Detroit], Recorder, 28:48 [August 1, 1958]; Forest Hills Jewish Center [New York City], The Message, 14:30 [March 27, 1959]; Beth Abraham Synagogue Center [Dayton], Bulletin [November 8, 1963]); otherwise, I tried to read at least fifteen consecutive years of every synagogue bulletin/newsletter I found. The following list of bulletins includes, in parentheses, the starting year for a run. When the bulletin (or the synagogue) changed its name during the period I chose (e.g., the Olympic Jewish Temple [Los Angeles] bulletin was The Olympian from 1955 to 1961, Temple Beth Am from 1961 to 1972, Olympian from 1972 to 1978, and, recently, Kol Ha'am —Voice of the People), I have included only one name.

In addition to synagogue bulletins, most of the synagogues I visited had no official "archives," but they had boxes of sheets of papers, not catalogued or indexed in any manner. Generous synagogue administrators found a room in which I could sit and brought box after box to me. I gave as many people as possible at each synagogue a lecture on the need to catalogue the archival materials, but I doubt if a single congregation has such a project under way. There was simply no way for me to cite pieces of paper from boxes at the synagogues listed in this section and from dozens of other synagogues cited throughout the text. Thus, the list includes only synagogues whose archives I used extensively and the books I consulted to supplement the archival materials.

I divided my synagogue archival research into seven regions of the country (New England, New York–New Jersey, Mid-Atlantic, Mideast, Southeast, Midwest, and California). When an example appeared in an archival source in at least five regions, I have used "everywhere," "almost everywhere," or "virtually everywhere" within the text to indicate its prevalence. When I use "frequently," it indicates that I found an example in only three or four regions.

In addition to kind people, far too numerous to name, at the synagogues listed in this section, I am especially grateful to archivists, librarians, and other staff members who made my research at the following so enjoyable: Arizona Jewish Historical Society in Phoenix, The Ida Pearle and Joseph Cuba Community Archives of The Breman Museum of Atlanta, the Jewish Historical Society of San Diego, Leo Franklin Archives of Temple Beth El (Bloomfield Hills, Michigan), and the Ratner Center of the Jewish Theological Seminary (New York City). And, once again, I could not have written this book without the extraordinary service provided by the men and women at the Interlibrary Loan Office of Swem Library of the College of William and Mary.

Adas Yeshurun (Augusta, Georgia), Bulletin (1934)
Ahavath Achim (Atlanta), Synagogue Bulletin (1958)
Anshe Emeth Memorial Temple (New Brunswick, New Jersey), The Bulletin (1989)
Baltimore Hebrew Congregation, Baltimore Hebrew Congregation Bulletin (1955)
Beth Am (Los Altos Hills, California), Builder (2003)
Beth El (Phoenix), Echo (1952)
Beth Jacob Congregation (Beverly Hills), Beth Jacob Voice (1950)

Brooklyn Jewish Center, Bulletin (1928)
Congregation B'nai Israel (Woonsocket, Rhode Island),
    The Israel Light (1944)
Congregation Shomrei Emunah (Montclair, New Jersey),
    Bulletin (1943)
Fitzgerald Hebrew Congregation (Fitzgerald, Georgia),
    Synagogue News (1940)
Kehilath Jeshurun (New York City), Bulletin (1936)
Kehillath Israel (Brookline, Massachusetts), The Bulletin (1959)
Keneseth Israel (Philadelphia), The Weekly Bulletin (1905)
Oheb Shalom (Baltimore), Temple Topics (1980)
Olympic Jewish Temple (Los Angeles), The Olympian (1955)
Shaarei Tefila (Los Angeles), Bulletin (1933)
Shaarei Zion (Baltimore), Bulletin (1932)
Temple Beth Ami (Rockville, Maryland), Chadashot (2005)
Temple Beth El (Providence), Bulletin (1964)
Temple Beth Israel (Phoenix), News Letter (1952)
Temple Beth Shalom (Miami Beach), HaKol—The Voice (2004)
Temple Emanuel (Beverly Hills), Emanuel Bulletin (1941)
Temple Emanu-El (Providence), Voice (1964)
Temple Isaiah (Los Angeles), The Isaian (1952)
Temple Israel (Columbus, Ohio), Bulletin (1933)
Temple Israel (Los Angeles), Observer (1927)
Temple Micah (District of Columbia), Vine (2004)
Temple Sinai (District of Columbia), News (2004)
Washington Hebrew Congregation (District of Columbia),
    The Temple Bulletin (1927)

Books, Articles, Pamphlets, Proceedings, and Annual Reports

Abramovitch, Ilana, and Sean Galvin, eds. *Jews of Brooklyn* (Hanover, New Hampshire, 2002).

Ackerman, Daniel. "Early American Synagogues: Architecture and Identity in the Judeo-Atlantic World, 1732–1838." M.A. thesis, University of Virginia, 2006.

Adler, Cyrus. "President's Message." In United Synagogue of America, *Report of the Second Annual Meeting, 1914.*

Adler, Frank J. *Roots in a Moving Stream: The Centennial History of Congregation B'nai Jehudah of Kansas City, 1870–1970* (Kansas City, Missouri, 1972).

Bauman, Mark K., and Berkley Kalin, eds. *Southern Rabbis and Black Civil Rights, 1880s to 1990s* (Tuscaloosa, Alabama, 1997).

Ben-Ur, Aviva. *Sephardic Jews in America: A Diasporic History* (New York, 2009).

Berkowitz, Henry. *Kiddush or Sabbath Sentiment in the Home* (Philadelphia, 1898).

Berkowitz, Max. *The Beloved Rabbi* (New York, 1932).

Binstock, Louis. *The Road to Successful Living* (New York, 1958).

Blackman, Julius. "The Hazan—As Seen from a Seat in the Congregation," *Journal of Synagogue Music* 23:1–2 (December 1993): 37–43.

Blake, Peter, ed. *An American Synagogue for Today and Tomorrow: A Guide Book to Synagogue Design and Construction* (New York, 1954).

B'nai Jacob. *One Hundred Years: 1882–1982* (New Haven, Connecticut, 1982).

Bolkosky, Sidney. *Harmony and Dissonance: Voices of Jewish Identity in Detroit, 1914–1967* (Detroit, Michigan, 1991).

Braunstein, Susan L., and Jenna Weissman Joselit. *Getting Comfortable in New York: The American Jewish Home, 1880–1950* (New York, 1990).

Brav, Stanley. *Dawn of Reckoning: Self-Portrait of a Liberal Rabbi* (Cincinnati, Ohio, 1971).

Breck, Allen DuPont. *The Centennial History of the Jews of Colorado, 1859–1959* (Denver, Colorado, 1960).

Brener, David A. *Lancaster's Gates of Heaven: Portals to the Past: The Nineteenth Century Jewish Community of Lancaster, Pennsylvania and Congregation Shaarai Shomayim, 1856–1976* (n.p., 1976).

Brizel, Florence. *Sinai Temple* (Los Angeles, 2007).

Bronsen, Rosalind Mael. *B'nai Amoonah for All Generations* (St. Louis, Missouri, 1982).

Butler, Charles. "The Temple Emanu-El, New York," *The Architectural Forum* 48:2 (February 1930): 151.

Calisch, Edith Lindeman. "Edward Nathan Calisch: A Biography." In *Three*

Score and Twenty: A Brief Biography of Edward N. Calisch: Selected Addresses and Sermons (Richmond, Virginia, 1945), 11–21.

Calisch, Edward N. *A Book of Prayer for Jewish Worship* (Richmond, Virginia, 1893).

Caplan, Kimmy. "In God We Trust: Salaries and Incomes of American Orthodox Rabbis, 1881–1924," *American Jewish History* 86:1 (March 1998): 77–106.

Centennial: 1882–1982 [Temple Emanu-El], Birmingham, Alabama, 1982.

Cohen, Mortimer J. "The Beth Sholom Story, 1919–1969." In *Beth Sholom Synagogue: Golden Anniversary, 1919–1969* (Philadelphia, 1969).

Cohen, Simon. *Shaaray Tefila: A History of Its Hundred Years, 1845–1945* (New York, 1945).

Cole, Diane. "Joy on Eldridge Street," *Preservation* 60:2 (March–April 2008): 24ff.

Cutler, Irving. *The Jews of Chicago* (Chicago, 1996).

Cutler, Irving, et al., eds. *Synagogues of Chicago*, vol. 1 (Chicago, 1991).

Daroff, Samuel H. *History of Congregation B'nai Jeshurun: Philadelphia, Pennsylvania* (Philadelphia, 1963).

Davis, Edward. *The History of Rodeph Shalom Congregation, Philadelphia, 1802–1926* ([Philadelphia,] 1926).

Davis, Moshe. "The Synagogue in American Judaism: A Study of Congregation B'nai Jeshurun, New York City." In Harry Schneiderman, ed., *Two Generations in Perspective: Notable Events and Trends, 1896–1956* (New York, 1956).

Diamond, Etan. *And I Will Dwell in Their Midst: Orthodox Jews in Suburbia* (Chapel Hill, North Carolina, 2000).

———. *Souls of the City: Religion and the Search for Community in Postwar America* (Bloomington, Indiana, 2003).

Drachman, Bernard. *The Unfailing Light: Memoirs of an American Rabbi* (New York, 1948).

"The Earliest Extant Minute Book of the Spanish-Portuguese Congregation Shearith Israel in New York, 1728–1760," *Publications of the American Jewish Historical Society* 21 (1913): 1–82.

Ehrlich, Walter. *Zion in the Valley: The Jewish Community of St. Louis* (Columbia, Missouri, 1997).

———. *Zion in the Valley, Vol. II: The Twentieth Century* (Columbia, Missouri, 2002).

Einhorn, David. *Inaugural Sermon . . . Har Sinai . . . September 21/29, 1855.*

Translated by Rev. Charles A. Rubinstein for Centenary of the Birth of David Einhorm, November 10, 1909 (Baltimore, Maryland, 1909).

Eisenstadt, Peter. *Affirming the Covenant: A History of Temple B'rith Kodesh, Rochester, New York, 1848–1998* (Rochester, New York, n.d.).

Elman, Kimberly J. "The Quest for Community: Percival Goodman and the Design of the Modern American Synagogue." In Kimberley J. Elman and Angela Giral, eds., *Percival Goodman: Architect, Planner, Teacher, Painter* (New York, 2001), 53–61.

Ely, Carol, et al. *To Seek the Peace of the City: Jewish Life in Charlottesville* (Charlottesville, Virginia, 1994).

Endelman, Judith E. *The Jewish Community of Indianapolis: 1849 to the Present* (Bloomington, Indiana, 1984).

Enelow, H. G. *Selected Works of H[yman] G[erson] Enelow*, ed. F. Levy, 4 vols. (Kingsport, Tennessee, 1935).

Engelman, Uriah Zvi. "Jewish Statistics in the United States Census of Religious Bodies (1850–1936)," *Jewish Social Studies* 9:2 (April 1947): 127–174.

Epstein, Harry H. *Judaism and Progress: Sermons and Addresses* (New York, 1935).

Faber, Eli. "America's Earliest Jewish Settlers 1654–1820." In Marc Lee Raphael, ed., *Columbia History of Jews and Judaism in America* (New York, 2008).

Fein, Isaac. *The Making of an American Jewish Community: The History of Baltimore Jewry from 1773 to 1920* (Philadelphia, 1971).

Feingold, Norma. *Shaarai Torah: Life Cycle of a Synagogue.* [Worcester, Massachusetts, n.d.].

Feldman, Abraham J. *Remember the Days of Old: An Outline History of the Congregation Beth Israel* (Hartford, Connecticut, 1943).

Freehof, Solomon B. "The Three Groups in the Western World." In Blake, *An American Synagogue*, 47–50.

———. "What Would Grandfather Think of Us as Jews?" Sermon at Rodef Shalom Congregation, Pittsburgh, February 13, 1949.

Friedland, Eric L. "The American Jewish Prayerbook in the 19th Century: Piety and Innovation." In *The American Synagogue in the Nineteenth Century: From the Collection of William A. Rosenthall* (Cincinnati, Ohio, 1982), 19–24.

Friedman, Murray, ed. *Jewish Life in Philadelphia, 1830–1940* (Philadelphia, 1983).

Gamm, Gerald. "In Search of Suburbs: Boston's Jewish Districts." In Jonathan D. Sarna and Ellen Smith, eds., *The Jews of Boston: Essays on the Occasion of the Centenary (1895–1995) of the Combined Jewish Philanthropies of Greater Boston* (Boston, 1995), 129–164.

———. *Urban Exodus* (Cambridge, Massachusetts, 1999).

Ginsberg, Yona. *Jews in a Changing Neighborhood: The Study of Mattapan* (New York, 1975).

Gittelsohn, Roland B. *What Does It Mean to Believe in God?* Two Sermons Preached at Temple Israel of Boston, January 1958, Temple Israel Archives, Boston.

Golden Jubilee, 1931–1981: Our Jubilee Year, a Commemoration of the Founding and Growth of Temple Beth-El, Richmond, Virginia (Richmond, Virginia, n.d.).

Goldstein, Doris H. *From Generation to Generation: A Centennial History of Congregation Ahavath Achim, 1887–1987* (Atlanta, 1987).

Goldstein, Israel. "Inadequacies in the Status of the Synagogue To-Day." In *Proceedings of the 28th Anniversary Convention of the Rabbinical Assembly of the Jewish Theological Seminary of America* (Wilkes-Barre, Pennsylvania, 1929), 32–40.

———. "The Menace of Secularism in the Synagogue." In *Proceedings of the 29th Anniversary Convention of the Rabbinical Assembly of the Jewish Theological Seminary of America* (New York, 1929), 90–102.

———. *A Century of Judaism in New York: B'nai Jeshurun, 1825–1925: New York's Oldest Ashkenazic Congregation* (New York, 1930).

Goldstein, Judith S. *Inventing Great Neck: Jewish Identity and the American Dream* (New Brunswick, New Jersey, 2006).

Goodman, Paul, and Percival Goodman. "Modern Artist as Synagogue Builder: Satisfying the Needs of Today's Congregations," *Commentary* 7:1 (January 1949): 51–55.

———. "Tradition from Function," *Commentary* 3:6 (June 1947): 542–544.

Goodwin, George M. "The Design of a Modern Synagogue: Percival Goodman's Beth-El in Providence, Rhode Island," *American Jewish Archives* 45:1 (Spring–Summer, 1993): 30–71.

Gordon, Albert I. *Jews in Transition* (Minneapolis, 1949).

———. *Jews in Suburbia* (Boston, 1959).

Greenberg, Betty D., and Althea O. Silverman. *The Jewish Home Beautiful* (New York, 1941, 1958).

Grinstein, Hyman B. *The Rise of the Jewish Community of New York, 1654–1860* (Philadelphia, 1945).

Gruber, Samuel. *American Synagogues: A Century of Architecture and Jewish Community* (New York, 2003).

Grunebaum, L. H. *Perplexities of Suburban Jewish Education* (Scottsdale, Arizona, 1954).

Guest, Avery M., and James J. Zuiches. "Another Look at Residential Turn-over in Urban Neighborhoods: A Note on 'Racial Change in a Stable Community,'" *American Journal of Sociology* 34:6 (November 1971): 457–467.

Gurock, Jeffrey S. "Consensus Building and Conflict over Creating the Young People's Synagogue of the Lower East Side." In Robert M. Selzer and Norman J. Cohen, eds., *The Americanization of the Jews* (New York, 1995), 230–246.

Gutheim, James K. *The Temple Pulpit* (New York, 1872).

Gutstein, Morris A. *Frontiers of Faith: Sermons and Discourses* (New York, 1967).

———. *A Priceless Heritage: The Epic Growth of Nineteenth Century Chicago Jewry* (New York, 1953).

Harburg, Israel. "Observance of Sabbath." In *Year Book of the Central Conference of American Rabbis* 43 (1937): 342–350.

Heilman, Samuel. *Sliding to the Right: The Contest for the Future of American Jewish Orthodoxy* (Berkeley, California, 2006).

Heller, James G. *Isaac Mayer Wise: His Life, Work and Thought* (New York, 1965).

Heller, Max. *Jubilee Souvenir of Temple Sinai, 1872–1922* (New Orleans, 1922).

Helmreich, William B. *The Enduring Community: The Jews of Newark and Metrowest* (New Brunswick, New Jersey, 1999).

Hershman, Abraham M. *Israel's Fate and Faith* (Detroit, Michigan, 1952).

Hirsch, Arnold R. *Religion of the Age and of the Ages* (New York, 1953).

———. *Making the Second Ghetto: Race and Housing in Chicago, 1940–1960* (Chicago, 1998).

Hollander, David B., ed. *Manual of Holiday and Occasional Sermons* (New York, 1944).

Hornbein, Marjorie. *Temple Emanuel of Denver: A Centennial History* (Denver, Colorado, 1974).

Horvitz, David T., ed. *Temple Emanu-El: The First Fifty Years, 5684–5734* ([Providence, Rhode Island, 1975?])

Hyman, Paula. "From City to Suburb: Temple Mishkan Tefila of Boston." In

Jack Wertheimer, ed., *The American Synagogue: A Sanctuary Transformed* (New York, 1987), 185–205.

Jackson, Kenneth T. *Crabgrass Frontier: The Suburbanization of the United States* (New York, 1985).

Jastrow, Marcus. "Introduction." In *Avodat Yisrael: Israelitish Prayer Book for All the Public Services of the Year*, arranged by Benjamin Szold (Baltimore, Maryland, 1873).

Jewish Forum, vols. 6–30 (1923–1947).

Jick, Leon A. *The Americanization of the Synagogue, 1820–1870* (Hanover, New Hampshire, 1976).

Joseloff, Samuel H., ed. *The Legacy of Rabbi Morris Lieberman* ([Baltimore, Maryland?], 1977).

Jung, Leo. "Jew and Jewishness in America," *Jewish Forum* 9:3 (May 1926): 132–136.

Kaufman, David. *Shul with a Pool: The Synagogue-Center in American Jewish History* (Hanover, New Hampshire, 1999).

———. "Temples in the American Athens: A History of the Synagogues of Boston." In Sarna and Smith, eds., *The Jews of Boston*, 165–207.

Karp, Abraham J. *History of the United Synagogue of America* (New York, 1964).

Katz, Irving. *The Beth El Story* (Detroit, Michigan, 1955).

Kleeblatt, Norman L., and Vivian B. Mann. *Treasures of the Jewish Museum* (New York, 1986).

Kohler, Kaufmann. "A Biographical Essay." In K. Kohler, ed., *David Einhorn Memorial Volume* (New York, 1911), 403–455.

Krauskopf, Joseph. *The Service-Ritual* (Philadelphia, 1985).

———. *Sunday Lectures* (Philadelphia, n.d.).

Krinsky, Carol Herselle. *Synagogues of Europe: Architecture, History, Meaning* (New York, 1985).

Kruckoff, Carole. *Rodfei Zedek: The First Hundred Years* (Chicago, 1976).

Kusmer, Kenneth L. *A Ghetto Takes Shape: Black Cleveland, 1870–1930* (Urbana, Illinois, 1976).

Landesman, Alter F. "Synagogue Attendance." In *Proceedings of the Rabbinical Assembly of America of the Jewish Theological Seminary, 28th Annual Convention* (Long Beach, New Jersey, 1928).

[Landsberg, Max, ed.]. *Ritual for Jewish Worship* (Rochester, New York, 1884, 1911).

Lazaron, Morris. *Seed of Abraham: Ten Jews of the Ages* (New York, 1930).

Lazaron, Morris. *Common Ground* (New York, 1938).

———. *As I See Him* (Gerrads Crossing, Buckinghamshire, England, 1978).

LeMaster, Carolyn Gray. *A Corner of the Tapestry: A History of the Jewish Experience in Arkansas* (Fayetteville, Arkansas, 1994).

Levin, Beatrice Jackson. *Temple Judea Silver Anniversary: 1930–1955* (Philadelphia, 1955).

Levine, H., and L. Harmon. *The Death of an American Jewish Community: A Tragedy of Good Intentions* (New York, 1992).

Levinthal, Israel Herbert. *Steering or Drifting—Which? Sermons and Discourses* (New York, 1928).

———. *A New World Is Born: Sermons and Addresses* (New York, 1943).

Levy, Felix A. "President's Message," *Yearbook of the Central Conference of American Rabbis* 47 (1937): 177–193.

Lewittes, Mendell. *Beyond the Moon and Other Sermons for the Yamim Noraim and Sefer Bereishit* (Jerusalem, 1973).

"The Life and Sermons of Rabbi Israel Herbert Levinthal (1888–1982)," *American Jewish History* 87:1 (March 1999): 1–28.

Lookstein, Joseph H. *Faith and Destiny of Men: Traditional Judaism in a New Light* (New York, 1967).

Magnin, Edgar F. *The Warner Murals in the Wilshire Boulevard Temple* (Los Angeles, 1974).

Mann, Arthur. "Charles Fleischer's Religion of Democracy: An Experiment in American Faith," *Commentary* 17 (1954): 557–565.

———. *Growth and Achievement: Temple Israel, 1854–1954* (Cambridge, Massachusetts, 1954).

Marcus, Jacob Rader. *American Jewry. Documents. Eighteenth Century* (Cincinnati, Ohio, 1959).

Mayerberg, Samuel. *Chronicle of an American Crusader* (New York, 1944).

Meier, Richard. *Recent American Synagogue Architecture* (New York, 1963).

Meites, H[yman] L[ouis]. *History of the Jews of Chicago* (Chicago, 1924).

Merzbacher, Leo. *The Order of Prayer for Divine Service, 1855,* 3rd edition, revised and corrected by Samuel Adler (New York, 1864).

Miller, Israel, ed. *Manual of Holiday Sermons, 5712–1951* (New York, 1951).

Minda, Albert. *The Story of Temple Israel, Minneapolis, Minnesota: A Personal Account* (Minneapolis, 1971).

———. *Reminiscences* (Minneapolis, 1978).

Moore, Deborah Dash. *To the Golden Cities: Pursuing the American Jewish Dream in Miami and Los Angeles* (New York, 1994).

Moses, Isaac S., ed. *The Sabbath-School Hymnal: A Collection of Songs, Services, and Responsive Readings for the School, Synagogue, and Home*, 6th edition, revised and enlarged (New York, 1904).

Mumford, Lewis. "Towards a Modern Synagogue Architecture," *Menorah Journal* 11 (June 1925): 225–240.

[Narot, Joseph R.] *Sermons* (Miami, 1978).

Neches, S[olomon] N. *The Jew and American Citizenship* (Los Angeles, 1924).

———. *Children's Services, According to the Orthodox Ritual*, 3rd edition (Los Angeles, 1927).

Newman, Louis I. *Biting on Granite: Selected Sermons and Addresses* (New York, 1946).

———. *Sermons and Addresses, 1941–1954*, Vols. 1–4, 6–8 (New York, 1954).

Newmark, Marco. "Wilshire Blvd. Temple: Congregation B'nai B'rith, 1862–1947," *Historical Society of Southern California Quarterly* 38:2 (1956): 167–184.

Nodel, Julius J., and Alfred Apsler. *The Ties Between: A Century of Judaism on America's Last Frontier* (Portland, Oregon, 1959).

Nussbaum, Max, and William M. Kramer. *Temple Israel Pulpit: A Selection of Published Sermons, Speeches, and Articles* (Los Angeles, 1957).

Opher, Ahron. *Confirmation Service: South Shore Temple, Chicago, 1958* (gift to the author by Ahron Opher).

Osofsky, Gilbert. *Harlem: The Making of a Ghetto* (New York, 1968), 128–131.

Phillips, Bruce A. *Brookline: The Evolution of an American Jewish Suburb* (New York, 1990).

Pool, David de Sola. *The Mill Street Synagogue (1730–1817) of the Congregation Shearith Israel (founded in the City of New York 1655)* (New York, 1930).

Pressman, Jacob. *Dear Friends: A Prophetic Journey through Great Events of the 20th Century* (Hoboken, New Jersey, 2001).

Proceedings of the . . . Biennial Convention[s] of the United Synagogue of America.

Proceedings of the Rabbinical Assembly of America [annual].

Rabbinic Council of America. *Manual of Holiday and Sabbath Sermons, 1952* (New York, 1952).

Rabinowitz, Stanley. *The Assembly: A Century in the Life of the Adas Israel Hebrew Congregation of Washington, D.C.* (New York, 1993).

Raphael, Marc Lee. "Jewish Responses to the Integration of Cleveland

Heights, Ohio, 1960–1980," *American Jewish Archives* 44:2 (Fall–Winter 1992): 541–563.

Raphael, Marc Lee. "Rabbi Jacob Voorsanger of San Francisco on Jews and Judaism: The Implications of the Pittsburgh Platform," *American Jewish Historical Quarterly* 63:2 (December 1973): 184–203.

———. "Rabbi Leo Jung and the Americanization of Orthodox Judaism in America: A Biographical Essay." In Jacob J. Schacter, ed., *Reverence, Righteousness, and Rahamanut: Essays in Memory of Rabbi Dr. Leo Jung* (Northvale, New Jersey, 1992), 21–91.

Raskas, Bernard S. *A Son of Faith: From the Sermons of Abraham E. Halpern, 1891–1962* (New York, 1962).

Reform Congregation Keneseth Israel: Its First 100 Years, 1847–1947 (Philadelphia, 1950).

Reichert, Irving. *Judaism and the American Jew: Selected Sermons and Addresses* (San Francisco, 1953).

"Report of Committee on the Synagog and the Community," *Yearbook of the CCAR* 48 (1938): 61–75.

Roback, A. A ."The Rise of Orthodox Influences in America," *Jewish Forum* 8:8 (September 1925): 394–396.

Rogoff, Leonard. *Homelands: Southern Jewish Identity in Durham and Chapel Hill, North Carolina* (Tuscaloosa, Alabama, 2001).

Rosenbaum, Fred. *Architects of Reform: Congregational and Community Leadership. Emanu-El of San Francisco, 1849–1980* (Berkeley, 1980).

Rosenberg, Ethel, and David Rosenberg. *To 120 Years! A Social History of the Indianapolis Hebrew Congregation, 1856–1976* (Indianapolis, 1979).

Rosenthal, Frank. *The Jews of Des Moines: the First Century* (Des Moines, Iowa, 1957).

Rozenblitt, Marsha. "Choosing a Synagogue: The Social Composition of Two German Congregations in 19th-Century Baltimore." In Jack Wertheimer, ed., *The American Synagogue: A Sanctuary Transformed* (Cambridge, England, 1987).

Rubinoff, Michael W. "Charles E. H. Kauvar: A Sketch of a Colorado Rabbi's Life," *Western States Jewish Historical Quarterly* 10:4 (July 1978): 291–305.

Rubinstein, Judah,, with Jane A. Avner. *Merging Traditions: Jewish Life in Cleveland*, revised edition (Kent, Ohio, 2004).

Rudin, Jacob P. *Very Truly Yours* (New York, 1971).

Sanders, Ira, and Elijah Palnick. *One Hundred Years: Congregation B'nai Israel, 1866–1966* (Little Rock, Arkansas, 1966).

Saperstein, Harold I. *Witness from the Pulpit: Topical Sermons, 1933–1980,* ed. Marc Saperstein (Lanham, Maryland, 2000).

Sarna, Jonathan, and Karla Goldman. "From Synagogue Community to Citadel of Reform: The History of K. K. Bene Israel (Rockdale Temple) in Cincinnati, Ohio." In James P. Wind and James Welborn Lewis, eds., *American Congregations: Portraits of Twelve Religious Communities* (Chicago, 1994), 159–220.

Schulweis, Harold. "The Nature of the Rabbinate: The Fourth Son," *Proceedings of the Rabbinical Assembly* 62 (2000): 173–183.

Schwartz, Sydney. "Maintaining the Minyan: The Struggle of a Storefront Synagogue." Master's project, Yeshiva University, New York, 2005.

Seltzer, Sanford. *Worship and Ritual Patterns of Reform Congregations: An Interim Report* (Brookline, Massachusetts, 1990).

Shankman, Sam. *Baron Hirsch Congregation: From Ur to Memphis* (Memphis, Tennessee, 1957).

Shargel, Baila R., and Harold L. Drimmer. *The Jews of Westchester: A Social History* (New York, 1994).

Sklare, Marshall, and Joseph Greenblum. *Jewish Identity on the Suburban Frontier: A Study of Group Survival in the Open Society* (New York, 1967).

Sobel, Ronald B. "A History of New York's Temple Emanu-El: The Second Half Century." Ph.D. dissertation, New York University, 1980.

Stanger-Ross, Jordan. "Neither Fight nor Flight: Urban Synagogues in Postwar Philadelphia," *Journal of Urban History* 32:6 (2006): 791–802.

Stein, Kenneth W. *A History of the Ahavath Achim Congregation, 1887–1977* (Atlanta, 1978).

Steinberg, Jack. *United for Worship and Charity: A History of Congregation Children of Israel* (Augusta, Georgia, 1982).

Sugrue, Thomas J. *The Origins of the Urban Crisis: Race and Inequality in Postwar Detroit* (Princeton, New Jersey, 1996).

Summit, Jeffrey A. *The Lord's Song in a Strange Land: Music and Identity in Contemporary Jewish Worship* (New York, 2000).

Swichkow, Louis J., and Lloyd P. Gartner. *The History of the Jews of Milwaukee* (Philadelphia, 1963).

Tabak, Israel. *Treasury of Holiday Thoughts: High Holy Day and Pilgrim Festivals* (New York, 1958).

———. *Three Worlds: A Jewish Odyssey* (Jerusalem, 1988).

Taeuber, Karl E., and Alma. F. Taeuber. *Negroes in Cities: Residential Segregation and Neighborhood Change* (Chicago, 1965).

Temkin, Sefton D. *Creating American Reform Judaism: The Life and Times of Isaac Mayer Wise* (London and Portland, Oregon, 1998).

Temple Beth Israel: 1920–1970 (Phoenix, Arizona, 1970).

Temple B'rith Kodesh, 1848–1948 (Rochester, New York, n.d.).

Temple Sinai. *Ritual Policy Compendium* (Washington, D.C., 1998).

Toll, William. *The Making of an Ethnic Middle Class* (Albany, New York, 1982).

Union of American Hebrew Congregations. *Fifty-ninth Annual Report* (New York, 1933).

———. *Sixty-first Annual Report* (New York, 1935).

Union of American Hebrew Congregations Commission on Research. *Reform Judaism in the Large Cities* (New York, 1931).

Union of Orthodox Jewish Congregations of America. *Manual for Junior Groups and Orthodox Youth Leagues* (New York, n.d.).

The Union Prayer Book for Jewish Worship, revised edition, Part I (Cincinnati, Ohio, 1918).

Vorspan, Max, and Lloyd P. Gartner. *History of the Jews of Los Angeles* (Philadelphia, 1970).

Warner, Sam Bass, Jr. *The Urban Wilderness: A History of the American City* (New York, 1972).

———. *Streetcar Suburbs: The Process of Growth in Boston, 1870–1900*, 2nd edition (Cambridge, Massachusetts, 1978).

Weiner, Hollace Ava. *Beth-El Congregation: Fort Worth, Texas, 1902–2002* (Fort Worth, Texas, 2002).

Weinstein, Jacob J. *Doctrine Distilled as the Dew: Sermons at K.A.M. Temple, 1955–1956* (Chicago, 1956).

———. *Arrows from a Full Quiver: Sermons for the High Holy Days, 1958* (Chicago, 1958).

Weissbach, Lee Shai. "Community and Subcommunity in Small-town America, 1880–1950," *Jewish History* 15 (2001): 107–118.

Wenger, Beth S. *New York Jews and the Great Depression: Uncertain Promise* (New Haven, Connecticut, 1996).

Wind, James F., and James W. Lewis, eds. *American Congregations, Vol. 1: Portraits of Twelve Religious Communities* (Chicago, 1994).

Wischnitzer, Rachel. *Synagogue Architecture in the United States: History and Interpretation* (Philadelphia, 1955).

Wolf, Edwin II, and Maxwell Whiteman. *The History of the Jews of Philadelphia from Colonial Times to the Age of Jackson* (Philadelphia, 1957).

Wolfe, Gerard R. *The Synagogues of New York's Lower East Side* (New York, 1978).

Wright, Gwendolyn. *Building the Dream: A Social History of Housing in America* (New York, 1981).

Young, Toni. *Becoming American, Remaining Jewish: The Story of Wilmington, Delaware's First Jewish Community, 1879–1924* (Newark, Delaware, 1999).

Index

Abrahams, Abraham, 6
Ad Hoc Committee on Homosexuality and the Rabbinate, 182
Adas Israel (Washington, D.C.): 1930s Depression, 82; constitution, 78–79; decorum during services, 52–53, 80; denominational affiliation, 71, 80; High Holy Day sermons, 22; Metz and, Solomon, 84–85
Adas Jeshurun ("Eldridge Street Shul") (New York City), 73–74
Adas Kodesch (Wilmington, Delaware), 49
Adas Shalom (Louisville, Kentucky), 64
Adas Yeshurun (Augusta, Georgia), 45
Adath Israel (Boston), 61, 63
Adath Israel ("Avondale Synagogue") (Cincinnati), 69–70, 81, 82
Adath Jeshurun (Philadelphia), 124
Adath Jeshurun ("Blue Hill Avenue Shul") (Dorchester, Massachusetts), 66–67, 68–69
Adath Yeshurun (Manchester, New Hampshire), 17–18, 129
Adler, Cyrus, 67, 209
Adler, Liebman, 22
Adler, Samuel, 37
Agee, James, 190
Agudas Achim (Columbus, Ohio), 49, 54
Agudat ha-Rabbanim, 103
Agudath Achim (Atlanta), 92–93
Agudath Achim (Chicago), 57
Agudath Achim (New Orleans), 51
Aguilar, Grace, 60
Ahabath Emuno (Milwaukee), 17, 22
Ahavas Achim Anshei Nezhin Nusach Ho-Ari (Philadelphia), 57
Ahavath Achim ("Big Shul") (Atlanta):

architectural style, 76; decorum during services, 79–80; Epstein and, Harry H., 79–80; fund-raising campaign, 130–131; Hirmes and, Abraham P., 96; as representative Orthodox synagogue, 56; secessions from, 45; Yiddish sermons, 96
Ahavath Chesed-Shaar Hashomayim (Central Synagogue) (New York City), 61, 73
Ahavath Zion (Newark, New Jersey), 74
Alabama: Etz Ahayem (Montgomery), 72; Temple Emanu-El (Birmingham), 60, 106, 109, 130, 154; Temple of Judaism (Birmingham), 109
Albany, New York, 128
ALEPH—Alliance for Jewish Renewal, 204
American Conference on Soviet Jewry, 140
American Red Cross, 86
Americanization: Conservative Judaism, 52; Orthodox Judaism, 48–49, 88–89, 94, 103; Reform Judaism, 108
amidah, 136
Angelou, Maya, 190
Anshe Chesed (New York City), 17
Anshe Chesed, Congregation (Linden, New Jersey), 117
Anshe Chesed Fairmount Temple ("Euclid Avenue Temple") (Cleveland), 126
Anshe Emeth (Milwaukee), 17, 19
Anshe Kneseth Israel (Chicago), 56
Anshe Sephard (Manchester, New Hampshire), 17–18
Anshei Russia (Minneapolis), 45
architectural styles of synagogues, 71–76, 126–131, 201–202
Arnold, Matthew, 139

Pennsylvania (*continued*)
128; Philadelphia (*see* Philadelphia);
Rodef Shalom (Pittsburgh), 22, 132;
Shaarai Shomayim (Lancaster) (*see*
Shaarai Shomayim); Temple Emanuel
(Pittsburgh), 128
Pentateuch and Haftorahs (Hertz), 150, 199
Perelmuter, H. Goren, 133
Pessin, Deborah, 144, 152
Petersburg, Virginia, 12–13
Pew Forum on Religion and Public Life
(2007), 204
Philadelphia: Adath Jeshurun, 124; Ahavas
Achim Anshei Nezhin Nusach Ho-Ari, 57;
Beth Israel, 78; Beth Shalom (Beth Sho-
lom), 78, 123; black population, 123; B'nai
Abraham, 57; B'nai Yeshurun, 77; Emu-
nath Israel—Oheb Shalom, 57; German
Hebrew Society, 15; Jewish education of
Jewish youth, 132; Jewish population, 123–
124; Keneseth Israel (*see* Keneseth Israel
(Philadelphia)); Mikve Israel (Mikveh
Israel) (*see* Mikve Israel); Ohel Jacob, 78;
Ohev Zedek, 123; Ramat El Synagogue,
123; Rodeph Shalom (*see* Rodeph Shalom
(Philadelphia)); West Oak Lane Syna-
gogue, 123
Philips, A. Th., 197
Philipson, David, 4, 15
Phillips, Bruce A., 103, 121–122
Phoenix. *See* Beth El (Phoenix)
Pilgrims, 48
Pittsburgh, 22, 57, 128, 132
piutim (prayers), 17
Pool, David de Sola, 95
Portland, Oregon, 47. *See also* Beth Israel
(Portland, Oregon)
Portsmouth, Ohio, 55
postdenominational Judaism, 203–205
Poupko, Bernard, 162, 164
Poupko, Solomon, 162
prayer, belief in, 31
prayer books: 1860s, 37; Birnbaum *mahzor*,
197; Birnbaum *siddur*, 197; Conservative
Judaism, 40, 147, 148–149, 152, 184–185,
190; *Daily Prayers with English Translations*

(Philips), 197; Enlightenment terms, 38–
39; *Evening Services for Sabbaths and Festivals*, 197; *Festival Prayer Book*, 148; gender
neutrality, 177, 185; *High Holyday Prayer
Book* (Silverman), 148; *Junior Prayer
Book* (Silverman), 148; *Kol Haneshamah*,
190–191; *Mishkan T'filah*, 177; Orthodox
Judaism, 197; pagination, 37, 41; Reconstructionism, 190–191; Reform Judaism,
33, 37–41, 60, 107, 171–172, 176–177, 190;
Sabbath and Festival Prayer Book (Silverman), 148–149; *Shaarei Tefillah—Gates
of Prayer*, 176, 177, 184; *Siddur Sim Shalom
—A Prayer Book for Shabbat, Festivals,
and Weekdays*, 185; *Standard Prayer Book*
(Singer), 197; *Union Prayer Book* (*UPB*)
(*see Union Prayer Book*)
prayer shawls (*Talithim*): Orthodox Judaism, 49; Reform Judaism, 30, 34, 114, 132
Pressman, Jacob, 147, 158
Proctor, Bryan, 60
Proust, Marcel, 162

Queen City Congregation (Manchester,
New Hampshire), 17–18

rabbis: American-trained, 95–96; anti-
Zionist rabbis, 84; biblical literalists, 163;
Conservative Judaism, 70, 84–85, 183;
denominational affiliation, 70–71; dietary
laws, 194; dress, 114, 174; employment
prospects, 205–206; European-born, 103;
gay and lesbian rabbis, 183; head covering,
114, 118; histories written by, 4; intermarriage, 179–181; ordination of, 35–36;
Orthodox Judaism, 50, 55, 94, 97, 100–101,
102–103, 163, 193–194; Protestant ministers
compared to, 59–60; Protestant ministers
standing in for, 64; Reconstructionism,
189, 194; Reform Judaism, 59–60, 62–64,
89–95, 106, 108, 112–114, 118, 175–176,
178–180, 194; salaries, 55–56, 82–83, 95,
100–101, 115; secular studies, 94; "teaching
rather than preaching," 175–176; women
rabbis, 178–179, 183, 189
Rackman, Emanuel, 162

About the Author

Marc Lee Raphael is the Nathan and Sophia Gumenick Professor of Judaic Studies at The College of William and Mary. He is the author and editor of many books, including most recently *Diary of a Los Angeles Jew, 1947–1973: Autobiography as Autofiction.*

PEACEFUL CONFLICT

PEACEFUL CONFLICT

The Non-Military Use
of the Military

EDWARD BERNARD GLICK

STACKPOLE BOOKS

HARRISBURG, PENNSYLVANIA

To FLORENCE WOLFSON GLICK

Preface

A few years ago, I delivered a paper on the feasibility of disarmament in Latin America. My conclusion was that significant reduction of conventional forces and weapons was not feasible in the foreseeable future. I was brought to this conclusion by considerations of Latin American prestige, sovereignty, domestic order, and the internal power structure. This bothered me greatly, not because my conclusion was wrong but because it was negative. And so just before I read the paper, and in order to make myself feel better, I added a last paragraph. It argued that non-military social and economic activities by military forces "ought to be encouraged until such time as disarmament in Latin America does indeed become feasible." Later, the more I thought about the idea, the more I became convinced that I had to write about it—and in a context larger than Latin America. The result is this book.

Its objective is to present a concept, to philosophize about it, to describe its historical and present workings, to evaluate and criticize it. I have cited representative examples which, though occasionally dated, will still continue to illustrate the operation of the concept in the major geographic areas of the world. I have also tried to keep in mind that civic action, like the military profession that employs it, is much more of an art than a science. While this instrument should be used and studied and criticized as objectively as possible, it must not be blunted by rigidly codifying and then forcing the military to follow all the rules prescribed for its use. Psychological warfare and the counterinsurgency field generally suffer from overcodification and from the failure of the scholars to communicate clearly with the uniformed practitioners.

And so my emphasis is on civic action practiced more as an art than as a science, and a good deal of that emphasis is on the civic action aspects of counterinsurgency. In the latter term I include *preventive* counterinsurgency: those prophylactic measures of a social and economic nature needed to ensure that subversive insurgency does not begin in the first place.

Like all books, this one owes its birth to many people. Who are some of them? William Leavitt of *Air Force and Space Digest*, who badgered me until I had to promise that I would write the book; my publisher, who happily made it possible for me to keep my promise; Wesley W. Thomas of Stackpole Books, for his sage editorial advice; General Edward G. Lansdale, now special advisor in Vietnam and, before that, liaison officer between our Military Advisory Group in the Philippines and Secretary of National Defense Ramón Magsaysay, who talked with me one lengthy afternoon, sharing his knowledge and insights; Wynne James, Assistant for Civic Action in the Office of the Assistant Secretary of Defense for International Security Affairs, who probably knows more about this subject than any other man now in Washington; the Trustees of Temple University, for a travel and research grant to Latin America; my Temple colleagues, Profs. John C.

Donnell, Daniel J. Elazar, and Charles A. Joiner, for their manuscript suggestions; the publishers of *Orbis, Military Review, Army,* and *Background,* for allowing me to use material previously published by me in their pages; Joan Cimino, Dolores Chiolo, Andre A. Moore, Mrs. Loretta Ragni, and Linda Scherr, for their typing and proofing help; my wife, Florence, who listened, typed, and proofed, and my son, Reuven, and daughter, Marnina, who suffered my short temper.

But while the good in the book must be credited to many, the bad in it—errors of fact, of interpretation, and of style—must be blamed on only one, namely,

EDWARD BERNARD GLICK

Broomall, Pennsylvania

Contents

State Department, AID, and USIA . . . external administration: the Country Team and the host country . . . costs and commitment

TABLES

And they conspired all of them together to come to fight against Jerusalem, and to do it an injury.

And it came to pass from that day forth, that the half of my young men wrought at the work, while the other half of them were holding the spears, the shields, and the bows, and the coats of mail. . . .

And the builders had every one his sword fastened around his loins while they were building. . . .

—Nehemiah 4

PEACEFUL CONFLICT

I Conflict, Counterinsurgency, and Civic Action

W HAT is constant about international conflict is its inevitability. What is variable about it is its nature, channels, and intensity. If Russia (and someday possibly Red China) reaches a real nuclear detente or even eschews a non-nuclear general war with the West, it simply means that the Communists have made a tactical decision to alter the arenas and manner of their confrontations, even perhaps to soften conflict. It does not mean that they intend to eliminate it altogether. It means also that they wish to continue to take advantage of the political unrest in much of Africa, Asia, Latin America, and the Middle East. For the United States it means that insurgency and "liberation" wars, whether inspired locally by a non-Communist country or initiated and spurred on by Russia or China, will continue in the developing nations. And thus in many of them the expansion and use of armies and weapons and some form of unconventional warfare and counterinsurgency will go on for some time to come.

Alongside of these growing pressures of insurgency are the pressures generated by the need for disarmament and social and economic development. Is there a way of handling these opposing, even contradictory, pressures, doing justice to both, though not of course always in equal measure? Accepting armies, is there a way of making more versatile use of them? Can they be made to fulfill valuable secondary functions without degrading or destroying their ability to fulfill their primary function of national defense? In the developing countries especially, how can we utilize the energy, discipline, training, and technical capacity of the armed forces for purposes other than illegal intervention in politics and the overthrow of legitimate governments? To the extent that the military institution has been a vice—and this has not been true always or everywhere—is there a means of making the vice a bit more virtuous? In short, is there a realistic *non*-military approach to latent and active insurgency, that also carries with it important arms control and socio-economic development benefits, *using the armies themselves?*

The answers to these questions lie in the direction of the non-military uses of the military, often called in contemporary jargon military civic action or simply civic action.

The first assumption is that insurgency stems in part from the articulated dissatisfaction arising out of underdevelopment and unfulfilled expectations. If we assume this, then we can assume that counterinsurgency must relate itself to development and the fulfillment of expectations. But since—and this is the second assumption—in many of the poorer countries meaningful social and economic development cannot proceed effectively without the productive non-military use of the military forces, that is, without civic action, then counterinsurgency depends on civic action. There is, in other words, a direct relationship between social and economic development, civic action, and *successful* counterinsurgency.

This is not to minimize other ingredients in the counterinsurgency mixture—police and military force, for instance, when insurgency movements are in their more active, visible state. In such a state, they cannot be met without force—for "governments fall when their capabilities to deal with threatened violence fail"[1]—but neither can they be met solely with it. While counterinsurgency cannot succeed through civic action alone, neither can it be lastingly successful without it.

Now, what, specifically, is usually meant by civic action? Does it have the support of *civilian* leaders? What kinds of civic action are likely to bring maximum results in which stages of insurgency? And why is the military suited for it? Let us take each of these questions in turn.

In the United States, the Joint Chiefs of Staff have defined civic action officially as "the use of preponderantly indigenous military forces on projects useful to the local population at all levels in such fields as education, training, public works, agriculture, transportation, communications, health, sanitation, and others contributing to economic and social development which would also serve to improve the standing of the military forces with the population."[2] A fuller, more eloquent definition is this one by Lieutenant General Alberto Ruiz Novoa, the former War Minister of Colombia, whose country has been beset by violent insurgency:

> Military civic action has as its purpose to extend to vast sectors of the populace the government's help, especially in the field of social assistance, through the military organization of the nation. It is based on the premise that the use of military means to accomplish programs of economic and social welfare will awaken in the benefited population trust and sympathy towards the government and the military forces. These programs are developed without affecting the military efficiency of the armed institutions or compromising their principal functions.

Besides accomplishing an effective program of assistance to the people, military civic action gains the support of the populace for the legitimate and rightful regime and for its armed forces. It also helps to prove the usefulness of the army and to counter the attacks of those who see in military expenditures only a useless drain of public funds, and who deny the importance of the mission of the armed forces within the state.

Besides reaching the objective of counteracting the campaigns of the Communists among the people against the armed institutions, civic action makes known the concern of the government for the less favored and stops those who foster insurrection, by proving that welfare and social improvement can come to the people in a legal and orderly manner.[3]

Or one can speak of bilateral civic action programs as "that blend of military assistance with indigenous self-help."[4]

In recent years, national leaders in the United States and in the underdeveloped world have embraced the concept eagerly. President Johnson, in a letter to the Fifth Conference of the American Armies, pointedly mentioned civic action programs, saying:

It is not sufficient that the military protect our lands from outside interference or attack—in addition it is the responsibility of each of us to contribute to the security and well-being of our fellow citizens by working together for military and civic progress.

President Kennedy, under whom the modern American commitment to civic action took hold, told a group of Latin American diplomats that "the new generation of military leaders has shown an increasing awareness that armies can not only defend their countries—they can, as we have learned

through our own Corps of Engineers, help to build them."
Secretary of State Dean Rusk has added his voice of support,
as has Teodoro Moscoso, who, when he was United States
Coordinator for the Alliance for Progress, called civic action
"a key element of the Alliance for Progress. . . ."[5]

Abroad, President Habib Bourguiba has called civic action
involving Americans and Tunisians a "sujet de satisfaction."
Emperor Haile Selassie has told his armed forces that their
participation "with the community in building schools, drill-
ing wells and clearing roads will gain you honor and respect."
And Senator Raul S. Manglapus, Philippines Senate chairman
of national defense and security, told army officers at a
Philippines Command and General Staff School graduation:

> I am aware of the achievements of the Armed Forces in civic
> action. . . . I am aware of the rice that you have grown for
> your men, the roads and prefabricated schoolhouses that you
> have built, the relief that you have ferried, the rescues you
> have effected and the . . . photogrammetry by your airmen.
>
> I am aware of these and I must join in praise for it. [But] I
> would ask you now to reach out further, . . . beyond the
> ranks of the army, out into the people.[6]

As to the relationship between civic action and the *stages*
of insurgency, much of the literature on this subject divides
insurgency into three stages.[7] Officially, they are defined as
follows:

> a. *Phase I, Latent and Incipient Insurgency.* This phase
> ranges from circumstances in which subversive activity is only
> a potential threat, to latent or already incipient situations in
> which subversive incidents and activities occur frequently in
> organized pattern. It involves no major outbreaks of violence
> or periods of uncontrollable insurgent activity.

b. *Phase II, Organized Guerrilla Warfare.* This phase is reached when the subversive movement, having gained sufficient local or external support, initiates organized guerrilla warfare or related forms of violence against the established authority.

c. *Phase III, War of Movement.* The situation moves from Phase II to Phase III when insurgency becomes primarily a war of movement between organized forces of the insurgents and those of the established government.[8]

Each of these stages or phases appears to lend itself to a particular kind or degree of civic action. During the latent or preventive period, when the army is not tied down in physically fighting the insurgents, the emphasis should be on long-term development (often measured in years) of the social and economic environment. Literacy and vocational training for conscripts and major roadbuilding campaigns, like those being carried out by the armies of Peru, Bolivia, and Colombia, are pertinent examples. When the insurgency begins to "go active," the military objective is to prevent permanent escalation to the active stage. Therefore, the civic action emphasis must shift to shorter-term measures (months or weeks) designed to show the populace that the government (and its army) is trying to help the people even while it is busy fighting the insurgents. And so the kinds of civic action projects undertaken would be street repair, medical inoculations, temporary bridge-building, well-drilling, simple irrigation systems, etc. Finally, when insurgency is definitely active, in Phases II or III, the primary objective is to defeat it, and therefore civic action measures must be more immediate, for example, medical care for civilian wounded. Clearly, the earlier the army begins civic action, the more time and energy it has to devote to it and the higher the probability of preventing, defeating, or at least "de-escalating" subversive insurgency.

Underlying the above definitions of civic action, the verbal embraces of it by national leaders, and the discussion of insurgency phases and civic action programs is an obvious additional assumption. It is that armies *can* win public confidence and cooperation by providing, or appearing to provide, appreciated public service in the socio-economic sphere. But in order to do so they have to have certain educational, administrative, and technical capabilities. Thus the question now becomes: Do they have them, or can they be made to have them relatively quickly, and does this lead to technical progress?

Actually, most armies are skill centers. When they are not fighting they spend most of their time training, that is, "teaching and being taught. The profession views training as an essential qualification for a military leader."[9] This is true even for enlisted personnel. So important does the United States Navy consider teaching ability that it includes it among the military requirements for enlisted men in and above pay grade E-5, and the Bureau of Naval Personnel has gone to the trouble of spelling out in detail what is demanded of a good Navy teacher and teaching program. In terms of personnel administration, one can say that military institutions are essentially systems that "identify and classify . . . and train and supply manpower" for needed jobs.[10]

So it is not surprising that the average military man probably spends more time in school after formal entry into his profession than any other professional man. On any given day of the year, as many as 15 per cent of our military personnel are taking a formal course at some school somewhere. Subjects taught range from literacy to technology to doctoral-level courses. In all, defense schools give some 6500 resident and correspondence courses and prepare men for nearly 2500 different jobs, well over a thousand of which are civilian in nature. A random look at Army enlisted men's courses shows soils analysis, refrigeration, motor and generator repair, surveying, drafting, construction, motion-picture photography. The Navy prepares metal workers, dental technicians, disbursing clerks, postal clerks, musicians, patternmakers. The Air Force teaches courses in data-processing and programming, foreign languages, air traffic control, medical laboratory techniques, etc.[11]

In fact, some civilian occupations are trained for *mostly* in the military. The majority of our airplane mechanics, bakers, and medical and dental technicians have been trained in the military, and the military is an important secondary source of many of our middle-level skills: auto mechanics, electricians, meat cutters, metal workers, male office machine operators, radio and television mechanics, teachers, male typists, science technicians, utility linemen and servicemen, and welders and flamecutters.[12]

Taking all the American military services together, we find that we now require three enlisted technicians or mechanics for each ground combat specialist and that there are now actually more electronics repairmen in the services than infantrymen.[13] And this is not a sudden development stemming from the space age. A Presidential commission has produced statistics beginning with the Civil War showing the upward trend in percentage of civilian-type occupations in the enlisted service (see Table 1).

The point being made here is that the military today, even in the armies of the developing countries, needs and trains for many specialties. These are not so much "military" skills as they are skills required by the very bigness, the technology, and the complexity of modern society and of the modern

Table 1

Civilian-Type Occupations in the Military

Periods	Percentages
Civil War*	6.8
Spanish-American War*	13.4
World War I*	65.9
World War II	61.2
Korean War	69.7
1956	74.7

* For Army only.

Source: U.S. House of Representatives, 84th Cong., 2d Sess. *Veterans' Benefits in the United States: A Report to the President's Commission on Veterans' Pensions.* House Committee Print No. 236 (Washington: Government Printing Office, 1956), p. 80.

army. If these skills have civilian applicability or transferability, so much the better. Such transferability is not the reason that armies need the skills, but they can and do stress it in their drives for national support and recruitment.

Thus the main appeal in current American recruitment pamphlets is not to patriotism or to travel and adventure abroad, but to post-Army or post-Air Force or post-Navy careers. "Thousands of men have built successful civilian careers with know-how they acquired in Army Electronics," says the electronics pamphlet advertising "Choose-It-Yourself Vocational Training." The one on clerical specialties reminds its readers that "business and industry also need men with specific administrative skills" and that a "great many successful men began their [civilian] careers with training and experience in Army Clerical." An Air Force booklet entitled *Your Son's Air Force Life: What You, As Parents, Should Know* states assuringly: "Remember, too, his degree of advancement and proficiency at a trade while in the Service could well determine his qualifications for a similar occupation in the civilian world."

Small wonder, then, that some Air Force leaders, faced with increasing loss of highly and expensively trained technicians to industry, have been reported asking themselves whether their training schools were working more for industry than for the Air Force.[14] In actuality, they are working for *both*, as part of what might be called America's own internal civic action program.

But, some will argue, the United States is not Africa, Asia, or Latin America. What has the military experience of the industrialized and educated West to do with the gropings toward modernity and democracy of the countries of the developing East and South? What transferability is there from one to the other? What is the relevance or connection between the two?

First, many of the countries that are now independent but were only recently colonies received their first taste of and for technology from the military operations of the Second World War. Both France and England mobilized great numbers of native troops and in the course of doing so exposed them to technical training, organization, discipline, sanitation —in short, to modernization. This was particularly true for sub-Saharan, or Black, Africa. In consequence of this exposure and also of certain colonial failures in civilian education, the junior and middle-level officers in a number of new states today make up a large part of the "technical-executive intelligentsia."[15] The specialized schools they were trained in are superior to, and in some cases the only available substitute for, analogous civilian institutions. This phenomenon exists also in developing countries that are not new. For example, the graduates of the Peruvian Naval Academy are considered to possess the best engineering education in the nation and Peruvian seamen to be among the best technically trained. That is why General Motors, when putting up a new assembly plant near Lima, asked the Peruvian Navy to provide the names of up to 180 qualified technical people who were trained in the Navy.[16] Second, the armies of France, England, the United States, Israel, and other countries of the industrialized West conduct technical assistance programs with the armies of the developing East and South. As part of these programs, the former continue to teach and influence the latter, increasingly through civic action activities that are often publicly labelled as such.

If there is a very basic difference in the military-civilian interface in the developing as compared to the developed countries, it is this:

> In the advanced countries, the military institutions tend to follow or utilize civilian skills and technology. While much of the technology is developed for the military, it is usually done in industry or academia. The level of technical skills in the military is not necessarily superior to the rest of the society. In the developing countries, however, the level of skills in the military is substantially above the general level. This applies to educational attainment, technical skills, organizational skills, and with respect to values compatible with modernization. Being in the forefront of technical development, this institution is called upon to provide services not normally associated with military institutions in the developed countries.[17]

The new military organizations are obviously different from those in developed countries, just as the needs of the developing countries are different from those in the advanced ones. And it is precisely these differences—in outlook, problems, and time and population pressures—that make civic action worth trying before, during, and after insurgency.

But anyone studying civic action (or, for that matter, other aspects of contemporary military institutions) must first rid himself of "labelism" or "compartmentalism," that is, of the tendency to give things names and then to place them into rigid, bounded, non-transferable categories. "*This* is a military function; *that* is a civilian function. The army must do only *military* things; the rest of society, only *non*-military things." People who talk this way seem to be saying that it is the label, not the function or its worth, that is all-important. Labels can be very helpful. Indeed careful classification is the essential first step toward empirical scientific investigation. But in social affairs they can often be tyrants, especially if we let them rigidify and confuse us.

Perhaps the greatest confusion from labelism and compartmentalism is in the field of foreign aid, in particular the debate over economic *versus* military aid. For what, after all, *is* an "economic" objective, a "military" objective, or a "political" objective? Can't an objective be all three? As the Draper Committee asked in 1959,

> Were we pursuing a "military objective" when we furnished coastal patrol vessels financed from military aid appropriations for use by Burmese police forces to subdue river pirates and Red Flag Communist forces which had cut transportation on the Irrawaddy River and thus prevented the flow of teak south and the shipment of rice north? Their actions had threatened to halt some of the most essential operations of the Burmese economy and, in turn, to create chaotic conditions which might have led to a Communist takeover.[18]

Or we can get at this point another way: it is a historical fact that the United States Army performed engineering, scientific, medical, roadbuilding, and agricultural activities of use to civilians during the early settlement of our West. It did these things because at the time it was the only agency capable of doing necessary national tasks in inaccessible or inhospitable environments. Should we have said then: "These are not proper military functions, and since there are no civilians available to do them, they must not be done"?

From this type of argument it is only a short step to two others. First: civic action has virtues, but might it not lead to constant political intervention by the military? It might, but it just as easily might not. Militarism predates modern civic action, and past military dictators (in Latin America, for example) have not needed civic action to become dictators. There are contemporary military regimes that have not embraced civic action (Iraq) and non-military democracies that have (Israel). As for the second argument: Civic action may be a good thing. However, it will make the military "look good," and anything that makes the military look good, especially in the fledgling polities that have not yet learned democracy, is bad.

Now not all Western historians and social scientists would make this last statement. But enough of them, still perpetuating the *reflexive* anti-military biases of the eighteenth-century rationalists and of many nineteenth- and twentieth-century social scientists, would.[19] To them, Armies and Progress are contradictions in terms. But is this necessarily or always true? Was the progress-retarding chaos in the Congo, after her independence from Belgium, caused by too much army or too little? Was the problem that the strong Congolese Army was constantly encroaching on the civilian government or that the weak civilian government did not have under its control a well-disciplined and effective army?

It is worth remembering that armies are attributes of national sovereignty, national prestige, national power, and national insecurities. To ignore this, or their political dominance in many of the underdeveloped countries, or their needed role in counterinsurgency, is to ignore reality. Civic action provides an opportunity to bend this reality more toward national development and, hopefully, toward international good.

II Armies in History: Their Role as Nation-Builders

ARMIES have always been expensive. So maximizing their utility, minimizing their cost, and keeping their soldiers gainfully occupied in times of peace has always been a problem, even for the Ancients. While there is no evidence that they ever used their armies for educational or humanitarian tasks, the Biblical Ancients used them to explore new lands and to construct roads, forts, and public buildings. When they were not fighting, the Nubians in the army of Old Egypt built some of that country's most time-honored monuments. Etruscan soldiers built the water-supply aqueducts around Rome. And the Incan Army put down roads, irrigation systems, and colonies in Peru. Moreover, Alexander the Great is credited with creating the first specialized engineering and medical units in an army.

The Romans did these things and more in the territories that they conquered. Roman legions included in their ranks farmers, carpenters, blacksmiths, engineers, and builders of all kinds who fought and conquered, but who also built and colonized. Under a system not unlike the Nahal units of the present-day Israeli Army, troops would be stationed in virgin lands. They would establish settlements where they would farm and in other ways support themselves, and then ultimately would be discharged to live on in their colonies. Thus many of today's Rumanians are descended from Roman soldiers who settled in Dacia, and the Rumanian word for "old," *batran*, derives from the Latin *veteranus*. In Roman England, soldiers built Hadrian's Wall along the northern perimeter of Roman settlement. They also built miles upon miles of highways, many of which still exist and are traveled on today. "These roads, even more than the legionary stations and the lonely upland forts, are Rome's most enduring monument to the Great Invasion."[1]

If we turn to later centuries, we find that both individuals and units of the empire-building armies of Spain, France, and particularly England engaged in non-military activities ranging from engineering to archaeology. They made social, economic, and scholarly contributions. Of the French Army of the 1860s, a historian has written:

> No longer were the officers spoiled nobles who could parade their liquor and arrogance in peace and fumble in war; they were trained men who began their career early and included men of great learning—poets, historians, novelists, researchers, and linguists. French army officers appeared as students, archaeologists, and scientists, as they did in the English army, more rarely in the Czarist Russian army, still more rarely in other armies.[2]

As for the British, Major James Rennel of the Bengal Engineers began surveying in India in 1764. In 1788 he produced a famous map that earned him the title "Father of Indian Geography." Later, it was another military man, Colonel

George Everest, after whom Mount Everest is named, who from 1806 to 1843 surveyed the length and breadth of India, pioneering in triangulation methods of measurement. Since then, Indian map-making has largely been the work of military engineers. Such units as the Corps of Madras Sappers and Miners (organized in 1780), the Corps of Bengal Sappers and Miners (1803), the Bombay Corps (1820), and, after the Sepoy Rebellion, the Corps of Royal Engineers, pioneered, together with civilian counterparts, in building the water, communications, and transportation systems, and other civil works of India.[3] And what the British Army did in India it also did in Egypt, the Sudan, and Palestine.

British officers were the first to trace the inscription of "Pompey's Pillar" in Alexandria. This is an inscription of A.D. 292 in honor of the Emperor Diocletian. Captains C. W. Wilson and H. S. Palmer measured in 1869 the base of the Great Pyramid of Kheops (Khufu) at Giza near Cairo. In 1892 Lieutenant J. H. L'Estrange Johnstowne and a detachment of Royal Engineers worked on the Abu Simbel temples on the left bank of the Nile below Wadi Halfa, saving them from destruction.

The same Captain Wilson surveyed much of Palestine in 1864 and 1865, exploring particularly in Jerusalem near the Temple and proving conclusively that the Dead Sea was 1292 feet below sea level. Biblical Palestinologists owe a special debt to Lieutenant (later General Sir) Charles Waren, also of the Royal Engineers, who explored the Holy City between 1867 and 1870. According to Sir Walter Besant, author of *Twenty-one Years' Work in the Holy Land*:

> It is certain that nothing will ever be done in the future to compare with what was done by Waren. It was he who restored the ancient city to the world; he it was who stripped the

rubbish from the rocks and showed the glorious Temple standing within its walls, 1,000 feet long and 200 feet high, of mighty masonry; he who opened the secret passages, the ancient aqueducts, the bridge connecting the temple and the town. Whatever else may be done in the future, his name will always be associated with the Holy City which he first recovered.[4]

Still with respect to the Holy Land, it was Britain's famous soldier, Lord Kitchener, who, while still a lieutenant, finished the survey of western Palestine. In 1877 he turned over to the Committee of the Palestine Exploration Fund a survey on a one-inch scale of over 6000 miles of country as well as 26 volumes of notes, photographs, and plans, many of which he and his colleague Lieutenant C. R. Conder, also of the Royal Engineers, drew themselves. Until General Allenby's successful invasion of the area during the First World War, the Kitchener-Conder Survey remained the standard map of western Palestine.

In the Sudan, the early railways, telegraph lines, docks, canals, water systems, and roads as well as the exploration, surveying, and clearing of large tracts of land were accomplished almost exclusively by or under the supervision of the Royal Engineers. They did their work even during the upheavals of the campaign against the dervishes. In 1912 the British, using some Nuba prisoners, began to form a special Sudanese sapper section, which by 1925 became part of the Sudan Defense Force and was used in civic action.

The French, as noted, also used their military in this way. When they began their intervention in Mexico in the 1860s they needed telegraph lines from the Gulf Coast westward to the interior. Accordingly, their military engineers strung lines from Veracruz to Mexico City. For north-south communication between Durango and San Luís Potosí they tried to turn to civilian firms. However, the latter botched the job, and the French Army commander had to have it finished by a Foreign Legion company. Moreover, engineering officers of the French Expeditionary Force produced some of the very best nineteenth-century maps of Mexico and of her capital city. And at least some of the non-military socio-economic things that the French Army did in Mexico were also done by indigenous armies there and in other countries of Latin America.

In the early nineteenth century there were military normal schools in Mexico that taught commissioned and non-commissioned officers how to teach others. In 1848 the Mexican government decreed the creation of eighteen military colonies to fight Indians and protect southern settlers. From 1876 to 1910 Mexico experienced the *Pax Porfiriana*, the long military dictatorship of Porfirio Diaz. Whatever else it was, the Diaz period was a "great era of building and modernization" without which the subsequent liberalizing Mexican Revolution of 1910 would probably not have succeeded.[5] In his famous novel *El Indio*, Gregorio López y Fuentes tells of a Mexican Indian drafted into the army and taken far from his native village. When after two years his father finally learned his whereabouts, he set about buying a substitute so that his son could be released. But when the father's agent contacted the son, the latter, now a *Mexican* and not an Indian, said in *Spanish:*

> Tell my father that I am grateful for his pains and trouble to bring about my return and that I realize the effort he must have made to get this money together. But I shall not use it and I am returning it so that he may enjoy it. Tell him that . . . I have learned to read and write, I wear shoes and cloth-

ing, I hope to be promoted soon, and I would not be happy back there.[6]

Brazil possessed respectable military and naval academies, giving eight-year courses, before 1814. Even after the establishment, sixty years later, of the Polytechnical Institute, the Brazilian Military Academy produced most of the nation's civil as well as military engineers, a role it performed well into the present century. During the 1800s, Brazilian Army officers conducted most of the formal exploration and scientific observation of this vast country. The most famous of these officers was General Cândido Rondon. Every Brazilian schoolboy knows how he went into the interior in the early 1890s, befriended the Indians, and in the course of almost four decades there became one of the greatest experts in the ethnology, geography, flora, and fauna of Brazil.[7]

The Colombian Colegio Militar was so unmilitary in the early 1900s that one observer has called it "for all practical purposes a junior college where one year out of a total of five was devoted to military subjects, and where a young man with suitable political connections could acquire a free education at government expense."[8] The Peruvian Army ran an in-house educational program in 1908 and engaged in colonization and resources conservation in the 1930s. In 1936 the Cuban Army took charge of the Escuelas Rurales Cívico-Militares and taught literacy and other courses in them in order to improve the plight of rural dwellers. The Venezuelan Armed Forces established in 1937 the Fuerzas Armadas de Cooperación (FAC), which still exists. Organizationally equal to the combat services, it has engaged in conservation, communications improvement, mineral production, jail maintenance, frontier customs collection, operation of meteorological stations, illiteracy campaigns, and other rural services.[9] And military academies that were organized and/or modernized between the mid-nineteenth century and the First World War were more or less the only Latin American institutions that taught science and technology, and it happened more than once that students entered them only to learn jobs for later civilian life.

A final observation about Latin American armed forces in the context of social and economic development is in order. Viewed from the *totality* of Latin American history, the armed forces have not behaved well, and no one can deny this. But just as people can do bad things for good reasons, they can do good things for bad ones. When Latin American generals established military academies that taught science or when some of Latin America's most dictatorial soldier-presidents granted, let us say, railroad concessions to foreign companies, they were motivated more by considerations of personal power, prestige, and profit than by the overwhelming desire to develop the national patrimony. But regardless of their primary or conscious motivations, their academies after 1850 *were* more often than not the vanguard of scientific and technical education, and military dictators like Diaz of Mexico, Antonio Guzmán Blanco of Venezuela (1870–1888) and Justo Rufino Barrios of Guatemala (1873–1885), *were* among the great modernizers, though admittedly not among the great democratizers, of Central and South America. To be sure, modernizing science and technology do not by themselves bring democracy; indeed they can retard it by depersonalizing the individual and adding to the suppressive tools of totalitarians like Hitler. But, on the other hand, can we really have social and economic development (a necessary precursor and concomitant of contemporary democracy) without modernizing science and technology?

So much for historical non-military uses of the military in

countries on the lower portion of the development and modernization spectrum. What about countries on the middle and upper portion, countries like Spain, Communist China, Russia, France, England, even the United States? Their citizens often forget that each of these countries, like all currently advanced societies, was once backward or was considered to be so. Like many of the present really underdeveloped countries, they too have used their armies in disaster relief and other kinds of civic action both in the past and present.

Spain allows troops to go home for the harvest. The Spanish Air Force lends pilots and mechanics to the civilian airlines and airplane industries. Since 1875 Spain has had military factories and military trade schools whose graduates go into private industry. Many of the nation's railroad workers, professional automobile drivers, and automobile mechanics are trained in the army. The Spanish Army's engineering corps has done much construction in the Pyrenees and rebuilt a good deal of the road network destroyed during the Civil War. The Servicio Militar de Construcciones, in conjunction with civilian ministries, builds houses, roads, bridges, schools, hospitals, jails, and so on. Since its creation in 1943, this Military Construction Service has executed well over a billion pesetas of work for civilian agencies. The army also has specialized research facilities like the Pharmacy Institute and the Central Veterinary Laboratory. A particularly encouraging feature of Spanish civic action is the work with illiterate recruits. Literacy classes for them are obligatory, and the government claims that 90 per cent of those who pass through the classes can then read and write "correctly."[10]

As for the Communist Chinese, they have used civic action both before and after their conquest of the mainland in 1949. Applying it to subversive insurgency, Mao Tse-tung has written of "The Three Rules and the Eight Remarks."

The *Rules* are:

1. All actions are subject to command.
2. Do not steal from the people.
3. Be neither selfish nor unjust.

The *Remarks* are:

1. Replace the door when you leave the house.
2. Roll up the bedding on which you have slept.
3. Be courteous.
4. Be honest in your transactions.
5. Return what you borrow.
6. Replace what you break.
7. Do not bathe in the presence of women.
8. Do not without authority search the pocketbooks of those you arrest.[11]

Used by the Eighth Route Army during the conquest, this code of behavior was designed to win civilian support, or at least apathy, without terror and with very little force.

Mao has also written: "There is no profound difference between the farmer and the soldier,"[12] a statement that can be taken as the ideological justification for employing Chinese soldiers in civilian capacities. They harvest crops, work on land reclamation, build roads and railroads, and raise their own vegetables, poultry, and pork. In 1961, the army contributed 54,000 military-bred pigs to the export economy; in 1964, army-run farms reportedly accounted for 20 per cent of the total grain output of Sinkiang Province. Like other soldiers, Chinese soldiers divide their education time between military and non-military subjects. In the Chinese case, the division is as follows: purely military training, 60 per cent; political education, 25 per cent; reading and the basics of mathematics, the remaining 15 per cent.[13]

There is a history of this kind of activity in Czarist and Soviet Russia too. Sons of Russian soldiers were educated for army careers in special canton, or provincial, schools. Interestingly, during the reign of Nicholas I (1825–1855), Jewish boys from eight to twelve years of age were taught tailoring and other trades at these canton schools and then attached to Russian Army units. In Soviet times, military schools like the Kharkov Guards Armor School and the Leningrad Engineer School grant the All-Union diploma in mechanical engineering, which is of great value when officers leave the service to enter civilian life. In the words of the Soviet military newspaper *Krasnaia Zvezda,* "Soldiers of the construction units, of the engineering and railroad forces take direct part in general production; they build houses, bridges, and roads. It is a great privilege to work for the good of the people . . . and the Soviet army and navy are proud of them."[14]

Much of contemporary civic action within the Soviet Union is performed through *shefstvo,* an institution that goes back almost to the Revolution. The word means "patronage" and supposedly describes a happy civilian-military relationship in which a factory or a collective farm, for example, becomes the patron of a military unit, and the military unit or individuals from it respond by performing grateful reciprocating service. *Shefstvo* work falls into three general categories: agriculture, technical assistance, and miscellaneous. Thus the Soviet citizen will occasionally read that the personnel of an army unit helped the Lenin Kolkhoz "in planting potatoes, preparing fields for spring sowing and in hauling manure into the fields," or that the "many tractor drivers, plumbers, mechanics, etc.," in the Soviet Army sometimes "spend their day off in repairing agricultural machinery and other equipment," or that 160 "tractors were built from scrap collected by young soldiers of the Kiev military district."[15]

The Soviets even have *shefstvo* units that "ride circuit" through the countryside. Called *estafety,* or "relay teams," they are used particularly in remote parts of Siberia, along the southern borders, in the Transcaucasian military district and in areas serviced by the Pacific and Northern Fleets. One team traveled over 400 kilometers, visiting 16 places; another, 680 kilometers and 32 places; still another is reported to have traveled 4000 kilometers. These relay teams are in some ways very similar to the United States Army's Civic Action Mobile Training Teams (CAMTTs) and to the Navy's Seabee Technical Assistance Teams (STATs), which are dispatched to foreign countries.

Finally, Soviet military engineers are often used as we use our own Corps of Engineers internally. In the spring of 1964, for instance, the famed city of Samarkand in Soviet Central Asia was in danger of immediate destruction. A mountain above the city had collapsed into the Zeravshan River and created a natural dam 450–600 feet high, 1200 feet wide, and more than 2400 feet long. Millions of gallons of water pushed against this dam, suddenly among the world's largest, and threatened to break it and flood the Golden City of the Tartars and the Mongols. What the government did was to call in Soviet military engineers to blast a new channel for the rapidly rising river.[16]

As for the advanced Western countries, a recent, but typical, year in England produced these civic action facts. The forecast offices of the Army's Meteorological Service answered about 750,000 inquiries from industry, commerce, and the general public. The number of flight forecasts (both military and civil) went beyond 1,000,000. The British Army and Air Force rendered emergency assistance to famine-stricken parts of Tanganyika, to earthquake-hit Iran, to refugees in South Vietnam, to flood victims in Pakistan,

Tunisia, and Germany, to typhoon-struck Hong Kong, to storm-damaged Leeds and Sheffield, to civilian evacuees caught in the Chinese-Indian military operations, to over 60 mountain climbers at home who got into trouble, to over 250 people who had to be rescued from the sea around Britain, etc. Also, Army Apprentices Schools continued to give their three-year courses up to the City and Guilds Examination level.[17]

The army of contemporary France behaves similarly. In presenting a recent budget the Armed Forces Minister sought to demonstrate that "following national education, whose business it is, the army is, of all public organizations, that which is making the most powerful effort in behalf of the education of young Frenchmen."[18] Under the heading of La Promotion Sociale, it has a whole series of off-duty and on-duty clubs and courses to promote personal education and training in trades like masonry, plumbing, carpentry, electricity, and agriculture. In agriculture, for instance, there are about 150 clubs with about 10,000 members. Another vehicle for the education of French soldiers is the Centre Militaire de Formation Professionnelle. For overseas France, there is the S.M.A.—Service Militaire Adapté. This is meant to be specifically "adapted" to improving the social and economic conditions of the American Departments, that is, the French islands in the Caribbean and French Guiana. Units such as the Régiment Mixte des Antilles-Guyane try to raise the level of the citizenry and the economy to that of Metropolitan France. S.M.A. is civic action in the full sense. Though not very old, it has already precipitated a discussion as to whether it should be extended to France herself.[19]

Now let us turn to America, which also uses her military forces non-militarily.

III Armies in History:

The American Experience

As EARLY as 1820, Zachary Taylor could say in a letter to the quartermaster general: "The ax, pick, saw and trowel, has become more the implement of the American soldier than the cannon, musket or sword."[1] Other commanders echoed his observation, not always with approval.

From grammar-school days Americans remember the Lewis and Clark Expedition, which explored the Louisiana Purchase at the behest of President Jefferson. Meriwether Lewis and William Clark were both commissioned army officers. They traveled under War Department orders, under military discipline, and with at least thirteen regular army enlisted men in their party. That is why it can be said that the army blazed "the first clearly marked trail from the Mississippi to the Pacific."[2] A few years later, in 1805 and 1806, Lieutenant Zebulon Montgomery Pike, under commission from the commander of the Military District of St. Louis, explored west of the Mississippi and north of the Missouri River. He, a sergeant, two corporals, and seventeen privates gathered data about the Indians, the topography, and suitable military sites. Pike was also to explore the Southwest and, together with twenty non-commissioned officers and enlisted men, to note the areas around, and the sources of, the Red and Arkansas rivers.

In 1823 Major Stephen H. Long explored the Northwest from Fort Wayne to Lake Superior's northern boundary. He followed a route laid out by Secretary of War John C. Calhoun, who wrote him:

> The object of the expedition is to make a general survey of the country on the route pointed out together with the topographical description of the same, to ascertain the latitude and longitude of all the remarkable points, to examine and describe its productions, animal, vegetable, and mineral, and to enquire into the character, customs, etc., of the Indian tribes inhabiting the same.[3]

Captain Benjamin de Louis Eulalie de Bonneville spent the years between 1832 and 1835 exploring west of the Rocky Mountains, and he gave Americans their first reasonably accurate map of this area. In 1842 and 1844 Captain John C. Fremont of the Topographical Engineers explored and described in detail the Rocky Mountains and the Oregon Territory as far as Fort Vancouver. Further, history credits Lieutenant Philip St. George Cooke with opening the southern route from Santa Fe to San Diego as a result of explorations he made between 1846 and 1847. An important point about the reports of these early army explorations is that they were not stored away and forgotten in War Department files. As Prucha relates,

> . . . they almost immediately found their way into print and thus spread widely the newly acquired knowledge . . . Cartographers like Henry S. Tanner of Philadelphia, whose care-

fully drawn maps were widely circulated before the Civil War, relied heavily on the reports of exploring expeditions for areas not yet surveyed by the General Land Office. . . . By the time land-hungry pioneers advanced into the upper Mississippi Valley they had access to an imposing body of information.[4]

As for roads, railways, and other public works, the Corps of Engineers has had responsibility for internal navigation and flood control since 1816; the General Survey Act of 1824 specifically authorized the use of the Army Engineers; in 1825 soldiers built the so-called "Chicago Road" across southern Michigan; they also were involved (well into the twentieth century) in building the road, rail, and communications systems of Alaska; and between 1815 and the 1860s army officers were frequently loaned to state governments and to private railroad companies. For example, in 1827 the Baltimore & Ohio Railroad asked the federal government for technical assistance from the army, and from ten to twelve army engineers worked on the initial construction of that railroad. Other army engineers made surveys on five other lines during this same period. By 1835 at least fifteen railroads in the United States were receiving some kind of aid from the Army Engineers.

The loan of engineering officers to private railroad projects in the East ceased in 1840, but was allowed for a longer period in the West. Thus Congress appropriated $150,000 to the War Department for Pacific railroad surveys in 1853. Between that year and 1855 at least twenty engineers from the army participated in surveying expeditions for four western rail routes. When General McClellan was recalled to command the Union Armies in 1861, he was working for the Illinois Central Railroad. And in the midst of the Civil War

President Lincoln withdrew General Grenville M. Dodge from Grant's army to supervise the construction of one of the branches of the Union Pacific Railroad. Later, many of the Civil War's veterans went to work on the Union Pacific.

The history of the Army Corps of Engineers, a book-length subject in itself, includes such items as the development of the Great Lakes navigation system and the supervision of or the actual construction of the following buildings in the Washington, D.C. area: the Washington Aqueduct, the Washington Monument, the State Department, War Department, Navy, and Post Office buildings, and the Pentagon. After trying and being disappointed with civilian engineers in Panama, Theodore Roosevelt chose Major General George Washington Goethals and the Corps of Engineers to success-fully complete the Panama Canal. At the time, he is said to have remarked: "The great thing about an Army officer is that he does what you tell him to do."⁵ When the United Nations needed someone to clear the Suez Canal in 1956, it turned to General Wheeler, a former Chief of the Army Corps of Engineers.

Like their counterparts in other times and places, American soldiers in the 1800s came to the army with certain civilian skills. These men were not always top artisans, but many were competent painters, cabinet-makers, bricklayers, barrel-makers, tailors, clerks, and farmers. Because they had these skills, because civilians who also had them were un-available or could not be hired, soldiers on the frontier worked very hard indeed, usually at common labor. The normal working day was ten hours in summer, eight in winter. If a man worked for ten or more days on non-military projects he was entitled to extra pay.

At Fort Howard, Wisconsin, it was not unusual for soldiers to be assembled in work parties of almost 100 to gather fuel or hay, build bridges, shingle roofs, repair buildings, and so on. So extensive was this non-military activity that in 1826 the post quartermaster requested permission to hire a clerk to help him direct it. It apparently was denied.

In the 1830s and 1840s Washington departed from its original policy of exclusive reliance on military labor. However, an economy drive in the 1850s forced the army to revert back to it.

Military agriculture was an especially important concern on the frontier. Why this was so is not difficult to understand. The farther away from civilization the soldiers went, the farther were they from established sources of food and fodder and the more expensive and difficult it was to transport the food and fodder. Yet as they pushed farther into the wilderness they had to expend more time and energy in fighting the Indians and less in farming. The War Department wrestled with this problem for a good part of the nineteenth century, vacillating from one policy to another. In the Northwest, from 1818 to 1833 it ordered the military to farm. In 1833 it released them from this obligation except for the maintenance of kitchen gardens.[6] But in 1851 it reversed itself and mandated attempts at agricultural self-sufficiency because of increasingly lengthy and costly supply lines. And so it went.

Regardless of the necessity for using military forces in a non-military fashion, there were soldiers high and low who did not like it. There is on record the following complaint, which an enlisted man made in 1838:

> I am deceived; I enlisted for a soldier; I enlisted because I preferred military duty to hard work; I never was given to understand that the *implements of agriculture and the mechanic's tools* were to be placed in my hands *before I had*

received a musket or drawn a uniform coat. I never was told that I would be called on to *make roads, build bridges, quarry stone, burn brick and lime, carry the hod, cut wood, hew timber, construct it into rafts and float it to the garrisons, make shingles, saw plank, build mills, maul rails, drive teams, make hay, herd cattle, build stables, construct barracks, hospitals, etc., etc., which takes more time for their completion than the period of my enlistment.* I never was given to understand that such duties were customary in the army, much less that I would be called on to perform them, *or I never would have enlisted.* I enlisted to avoid work, and here I am, compelled to perform three or four times the amount of labor I did before my enlistment.[7]

A related episode took place a dozen years later in the Minnesota Territory. The probate judge of Ramsey County attempted to free eighteen soldiers from their enlistment because they complained that non-military work was not a legal part of their responsibilities. They argued that besides performing their military and garrison duties,

> . . . the additional burden of hard and laborious work at cutting rails and building fences, planting corn and potatoes, sowing oats and other grains and doing generally all other work in kind and degree appertaining to the opening of a farm (containing between three and four hundred acres) has been imposed . . . , which said additional burden of farm labor is contrary to law and the contract of enlistment and repugnant to the principles of justice and liberty.[8]

As it happened, the commanding officer of Fort Snelling, where the soldiers were stationed, refused to allow the judge's writs to be served on his post. It was lucky for the army that the judge did not press the issue, that no precedent was set, and that nothing ultimately came of it, for many of the troops were waiting for a successful outcome to secure their own discharges.

There were also general officers who deplored civic action, particularly giving soldiers ploughshares instead of swords. In 1797 General James Wilkinson damned military farming in these words:

> The Spirit of cropping which is almost everywhere to be seen, is repugnant to the principles of soldiership, destructive to the Service and disgraceful to those who indulge in it. . . . The national bounty is expended not to improve the agricultural arts, but to instruct men in the use of arms; the hoe and the plow must be laid aside, and every moment of professional duty, devoted to form, instruct, and train them in the glorious Science of War. . . . Planting and improving of corn fields is prohibited. Gardens sufficient for the accommodation of officers and soldiers are proper and necessary, and it is obligatory on all commanding officers to pay attention to this subject, the labor is however to be done by detail; the idea of an officer farming for profit is inadmissible, as it tends to neglect of duty, a relaxation of discipline, abuse of the Public Service, and the disgrace of the profession.[9]

Some years later Inspector General George Croghan bemoaned soldier farming by complaining that it

> . . . would sink the proud Soldier into the menial, & reduce him who may have gallantly led in the front of our enemies, into the base overseer of a troop of awkward ploughmen. Let the Soldier return to himself, let him no longer be able to boast of his success as a tiller of the Soil, but be encouraged to pride himself on his advancement, in the knowledge of the proud science of which he is an elected professor. He will not, he cannot, be esteemed the worst citizen, from being the more accomplished Soldier. I do not say, that a Soldier shall never

be called upon to do duties, unless such as may advance him as a Tactician—far from it. I wish him to be occupied, & desire only that such service as he may be called upon to perform, not purely military, may be considered as secondary—I would have the Soldier point to his garden, in proof of the good provision he has made during the short intervals from military exercise, rather than boastingly talk of his proficiency as a farmer, of the advantages of the *broadcast* over the *Drill*, or of the five bushels of corn per acre made by Company C more than by Company B from relying more upon the plough than upon the hoe. What has been gained by this anti-military course, to compensate for the great loss of moral strength which has been sustained? Nothing, so far as I have been able to ascertain, that is of true value to the Soldier. A few dollars may have been added to the administrative fund, but at what a cost! Look at Fort Atkinson [Nebraska] & you will see Barn yards that would not disgrace a Pennsylvania farmer, herds of cattle that would do credit to a Potomac Grazier, yet where is the gain in this, either to the Soldier or the Government? Ask the individual who boastingly shows you all this, why such a provision of hay & corn, his answer will be, to *feed* the *cattle*—But why so many *cattle*, why—to eat the *hay* & *corn*.[10]

These bold words from Generals Croghan and Wilkinson, as well as the complaints from the more common ranks, prove conclusively that non-military work in the frontier army was neither incidental nor accidental, but a regular planned activity. If it was merely an on-again-off-again secondary activity, why would they have complained? On the contrary, it was precisely because the generals and the privates feared it had become, or was in danger of becoming, a primary activity that they cried out against civic action. That the complaints were not heeded is further proof of this contention.

In sum, army posts definitely acted as an economic stimulus in the early West. They did so directly by doing work that pioneer families were unwilling, unable, or unavailable to do, in particular by providing the infrastructure in the way of protection, transportation, and communication necessary to speed civilian settlement. Later, they stimulated the economy indirectly by purchasing goods and services from the civilian communities. But the army contributed not only economically to the growth of America. It also contributed educationally, scientifically, culturally, and in the field of general welfare.

One must remember that the present in-house educational and technical capacities and contributions of our armed forces are merely an extension of past history. West Point was our first school of technology and one of the earliest in the English-speaking world, as it was also the first school in America to introduce chalk and blackboards into the classroom.[11] The standard civil engineering text in the mid-nineteenth century was the one by Dennis Hart Mahan, an officer who built the Military Academy's engineering department from 1830 to 1871. Academy graduates held the first engineering chairs at civilian universities, for example, Rensselaer Polytechnic Institute in 1824, Harvard in 1849, and Yale in 1852.[12]

So great was the Academy's reputation in engineering education that Henry Adams wrote in his *History of the United States* that American engineering "owed its efficiency and almost its existence to the military school at West Point . . . ," and President Francis Wayland of Brown University said in 1850 that the Military Academy did more "to build up the system of internal improvements in the United States than all [the other 120 some] colleges combined."[13] Adams and Wayland were only reflecting a stronger view, a prophecy, made by an unnamed observer. West Point, he said,

> . . . without considering it merely in a military point of view will be of incalculable benefit to the United States, as a *nursery for science;* for it is the only place where the higher branches of mathematics are attended to, and the education which the cadets receive is such, that if they prosecute their studies, they may vie with the scientific men of any part of the world. . . . In a short time, the United States, though with a very small army, will be able to boast of a much larger body of scientific and well-educated officers, than any other country in the world.[14]

Soldiers in the Northwest Territory were often teachers (at extra pay), and the schools at military posts were usually superior to those in the surrounding civilian communities. Civilians often asked that their children be allowed to attend, and often they were. Later, the chaplains were ordered to take charge of the post schools. Military chaplains ministered to the spiritual needs of civilians as well as soldiers, and more often than not, military garrisons became the nuclei of civilian church parishes in the adjacent areas.

The military brought into the Northwest the first good music, the first theater (for example, the Fort Snelling Dramatic Association near St. Paul and the Fort Howard Military Thespian Society near Green Bay), and the first decent libraries. To a considerable extent, therefore, army officers "conditioned the intellectual climate of the frontier." Additionally, military personnel were the first Indian agents, the first mail carriers, the first physicians to provide medical care to both white civilians and to Indians, and the first "innkeepers," for custom demanded that military commanders offer their hospitality to civilian travelers. Also, the local garrison's guardhouse was often the first county jail for non-military breakers of the civil law.[15]

Regarding the present involvement of the Department of Defense in research and research support, reasonable men can reasonably differ as to whether this is good for scholarship, for universities, for industry, for the country, or for the world. But whichever side of the argument a man is on, he cannot reasonably claim that this involvement is a new feature of American life, for history claims otherwise.

In medicine, for example, an army surgeon wrote the first American textbook in psychiatry. Another army surgeon, Dr. William Beaumont, wrote *Experiments and Observations on the Gastric Juice and the Physiology of Digestion* (1833) and earned himself a reputation as America's pioneer physiologist. He did his experiments at Fort Mackinac and Fort Crawford. Dr. Benjamin Waterhouse introduced small-pox vaccination into the United States Army in 1800, from whence the procedure spread to the civilian sector. The deeds of army surgeons Walter Reed and William C. Gorgas in typhoid and yellow fever research and elimination are well known.

Not so well known are such army research firsts as the chlorination of water, the discovery of the cause and cure of beriberi, automatic bacteria counting, the metabolic studies that led to Metrecal-type liquid diets, and the development of anthrax vaccine. The military also pioneered in synthetic rubber research, designed some of the first masks used in industry against foul or toxic vapors, discovered a means of controlling the boll weevil, discovered magnesium metal shielding, and has done impressive work in irradiation and other means of food processing and food preservation. One writer has even reminded us that the military might "be credited with hurrying the advent of mass production techniques" through its support during the War of 1812 of "the inventive Eli Whitney in his manufacture of muskets with interchangeable parts."[16]

Nowadays, both the air force and the navy have special squadrons that cooperate with the Commerce Department's Weather Bureau in hurricane hunting and other weather forecasting. But the first regular professional forecasters in the United States were *not* the employees of the Weather Bureau, which was not established until 1890, or sailors and airmen. The first forecasters were physicians in the Medical Department of the United States Army. At first, they were merely directed to take observations twice each day of air temperatures, wind directions, and general weather conditions. After 1842 the army required that they take four daily readings of the barometer, the thermometer, the direction, force, and velocity of the clouds and the winds, and of the amount of precipitation. In time, the army issued them an official handbook giving detailed instructions on how to take the various observations. Its last paragraph said:

> Connected with meteorology are many interesting subjects of inquiry, which can only be elucidated by widespread simultaneous observation. The medical officers of the army are therefore *confidently invited* to co-operate in the collection of data tending to advance the interest of science. *For the accuracy of our observations* (quoted, as they will be, both at home and abroad) *it is hardly necessary to say, the reputation of the Department is pledged.*[17]

Two other important military contributors to research that possesses non-military spillover are the United States Navy and the United States Coast Guard. Both of them have defined their research missions broadly enough to include non-naval and non-combat tasks. The navy helped to supply our early western outposts. Later, officers like Admirals Byrd and Peary pioneered in American polar explorations. Commander Matthew F. Maury, in later life professor of meteorology at Virginia Military Institute, produced the first modern wind and current charts of the Atlantic, and his *Physical Geography of the Sea* (1855) was perhaps the first classic of modern oceanography.

Interest in polar exploration and oceanography has continued unabated into the present day. The navy supported the United Nations International Geophysical Year with men, vessels, and supplies. Later, it supported such projects as ARLIS-II. ARLIS stands for Arctic Research Laboratory Ice Station and was sponsored by the Office of Naval Research. In 1965, scientists on an ice floe observed wind and ocean currents and marine biology and collected other scientific data in the Arctic Ocean. In the same year, the Coast Guard icebreaker *Northwind*, for the first time in the annals of American polar investigations, successfully entered and crossed the Kara Sea in the Soviet Arctic, obtaining oceanographic information on currents, the physical properties of the ocean, and the magnetic and gravitational fields of the earth in that area. It was proved that the southern portion of the Kara Sea, which is more than 1700 feet deep in spots, was once dry land. Another interesting development of the voyage was the knowledge that some of the currents in the Vilkitskogo Strait flowed from east to west rather than from west to east, as previously available oceanographic charts had indicated. All in all, the *Northwind* "was the first United States scientific vessel to study all of the Kara Sea, the first to investigate the currents near Vilkitskogo Strait, and the first to round the northernmost point of Severnaya Zemlya."[18]

In the summer of 1965 the press reported in great detail the exploits of Lieutenant Commander M. Scott Carpenter, who together with other navy divers and scientists lived under water for several weeks in Sealab-2, a steel cylinder lowered into the Pacific Ocean off San Diego. The Sealab-2 experiments proved that man could live and work under water for prolonged periods of time. An exciting by-product was the exploits of a porpoise named Tuffy, which the navy has been training to guard and deliver items to navy divers under sea. Commander Carpenter is, of course, the astronaut, and the navy of which he is a member has an ongoing role in America's space research program. This includes supplying astronauts, tracking them in orbit, and fishing them out of the seas when they land.

And lest it be thought that the navy's contribution to research is limited purely to physical things, we can note that *Life is with People,* the classic anthropological study of the culture of the *shtetl,* the erstwhile Jewish community of Eastern Europe, grew out of Columbia University's Research in Contemporary Cultures, inaugurated by Ruth Benedict under a grant from the Office of Naval Research.[19]

So much for the American military's involvement in research. What examples are there of its role in general welfare?

The famous Civilian Conservation Corps was in operation from 1933 to 1942, that is, roughly from the middle of the Great Depression to the early years of the Second World War. While it was the Labor Department that picked the Corps' men, and the Agriculture and Interior Departments that planned and administered the programs, it was the War Department that built and managed the camps, and fed, clothed, cared for, and disciplined the men.

The first man joined the CCC on April 7, 1933. Within a short three months, 300,000 other young men had enrolled, and 1300 camps were in various stages of completion and operation. Eventually the 1300 camps grew to 1450 and the

CCC manpower totals exceeded by far the entire authorized strength of the army itself. President Roosevelt therefore had no choice but to draw even more heavily on the three military services. "The War Department stripped regular units. Service schools had early graduation, and the Army withdrew officers from other civilian component assignments."[20] By the beginning of July 1933 almost 5500 regular and reserve officers of the U.S. Army, Navy and Marine Corps were on duty administering the CCC camps. By 1935 the enrollment in them was over 500,000 and the main burden of their administration continued to be laid upon the shoulders of over 9000 reserve officers. By June 1939, on the eve of the war in Europe, the total enrollment in the Civilian Conservation Corps went beyond three million men, with accompanying pressures on the program's military managers.

These camps had their enthusiastic supporters and violent detractors. Some thought that President Roosevelt had come up with one of the great socio-economic ideas of the century —one that positively helped to get America out of the Depression. Others were equally convinced that the CCC was a giant step toward Communism and the dissolution of the American way of life. But whatever one felt about this depression-bred measure to put idle youths to work in the civilian service of the nation, it simply could not have been done without the military personnel of the United States.

Finally, there is a state in the Union that experienced *as recently as 1965* a civic action program identical to those presently encouraged in many underdeveloped and insurgency-plagued foreign countries. What happened was this.

Early in that year, the army conducted Exercise Polar Strike in Alaska as a training vehicle for its Special Forces.[21] Part of the mission called for the dispatch of Special Forces groups and civic action teams from the John F. Kennedy

Center for Special Warfare at Fort Bragg, North Carolina, to selected villages in Alaska. Consultations between the army, the United States Public Health Service (USPHS), and the Alaska Department of Health and Welfare produced a decision that the army personnel engage in:

1. Teaching natives basic first-aid procedures, and giving general hygiene and nutritional instruction based on current publications furnished by the USPHS.

2. Advising the village council, through the village Health Aide, concerning sanitation methods and techniques.

3. Teaching, advising, and helping village Health Aides in patient care.

4. Rendering medical and dental care within the capability of the detachment medics and the Civic Action Team.

5. Consulting USPHS area physicians and dentists concerning patient management.

The villages visited, in the following priority, were Gambell, Savoonga, Teller, Shishmaref, Point Hope, Barter Island, Wainwright, and Point Barrow. Besides a medical and dental program, the army supported a veterinary civic action program in Savoonga, Shishmaref, Wales, Teller, White Mountain, Elim, Golvin, Koyuk, Shaktoolik, Stebbins, St. Michael, and Nome. Transport and logistics aid beyond the capabilities of the army teams were provided by the civil federal and local authorities in the state. Also, Special Forces personnel did research at the Arctic Aero-Medical Laboratories and the University of Alaska.

Upon arrival in a village, the team followed this standard procedure. First, it arranged a meeting with the members of the Village Council and the village teachers. At the meeting it informed the Council of the team mission, capabilities, authority, and needs. Each team member was introduced to the natives and described his particular role in the overall effort. It was especially important to make the Council aware of the team's willingness and ability to provide instruction and training in particular subjects and to let the Council know that every effort would be made to channel all activities through the Village Council. A schedule of night classes was then agreed upon. Prior to adjournment, the team requested the Council to notify the people of the village of the site, hours, and operational priorities of the civic action program. Where there was no native subprofessional dental, medical, or veterinary personnel already living within the village, the team requested the Village Council to supply candidates for on-the-job training by the army personnel.

The order of priority for medical examinations and treatment was: (1) school children, (2) pre-school children and their mothers, (3) pregnant women, (4) people over 60, and then (5) anyone who needed medical or dental care. Emergencies were of course seen at the time of their occurrence. All of the medical and dental services were given in the classrooms of the local school.

As for the training and preventive care programs, these were always within the guidelines already laid down by the United States Public Health Service and the Alaska Department of Health and Welfare. There were classes on fluoride applications and preventive dental health, purification of water, animal diseases, mouth-to-mouth resuscitation, sterilization techniques, and emergency first aid. The United States Public Health Service supplied and the civic action team showed the village three movies: "Taro's Adventures in Health," "It's Your Health," and "Dental Health: How and Why."

Before the team left each village, it had a second formal meeting with the Village Council to review the accomplishments of the visit. The team gave final instructions and made final recommendations for the continuation of the programs in the hope of expanding the self-help capabilities of each village. The Special Forces soldiers also distributed Public Health Service dental literature and posters, many of which were printed by the Twelfth Psychological Warfare Company of Fort Bragg.

For a number of reasons the veterinary civic action work during Exercise Polar Strike was especially significant. First, the livelihood of so many Alaskan Indians and Eskimoes depends upon the health of their dogs, which they must use for transportation. Second, there are no civilian veterinarians within 500 miles of Nome or north of Fairbanks. And third, animal vaccine is quite expensive for most of the natives. Consequently, the Special Forces were given a veterinary sub-mission, which was:

> To obtain information on capabilities, limitations, and utilization of dogs; to gather information on zoonotic diseases that could affect troops and/or animals deployed to Alaska; and to participate in recommended disease control and eradication civic action programs.

Most of the operational effort was directed toward a rabies inoculation program for the dogs and toward educating the people about the diseases that affect their animals. Many of the natives apparently did not understand the difference between distemper, hepatitis, and rabies, nor did they realize which vaccine was being administered to their dog or why the animal was not being immunized for all the diseases simultaneously. In an effort to clarify these points and to publicize the comings and goings of the army civic action teams, articles were written for the *Nome Nugget*. This is the newspaper which circulates throughout the Seward Peninsula, the site of many of the villages chosen for the veterinary civic action program.

Army people wrote some of them, especially the didactic articles designed to teach the readers something about the nature and effects of the diseases. Thus the *Nome Nugget* of February 3, 1965 carried an article by Captain Donald G. Tolman, the veterinarian with the Sixth Special Forces civic action team, on local animal diseases. He wrote:

> There are four diseases of major importance which affect the dog population of this area of Alaska. It is desired that the public understand some of the basic facts of these diseases because of their direct effect on the health and economy of this area. Two diseases (Rabies and Hydatid Disease) are transmissible to man, and may become significant from a public health standpoint. Two other diseases—Canine Distemper and Infectious Canine Hepatitis—are not transmissible to man but may cause considerable economic loss due to high mortality of dogs affected.

And the issue of February 5, 1965 has an article in which Dr. Tolman especially considers the required age and time sequences for vaccinating and revaccinating animals against rabies.

Some of the articles were written in a more folksy way, by local people. One began with: "We hear that Gambell hunters shot a lot of winter hair seals and that the seals are numerous whenever the men go out hunting. Here in Savoonga we have lots of walrus meat." It went on to say that "visitors arrived in Savoonga from the Lower 48 States. They were Special Forces. They had a doctor, dentist, and a vet for animals. They made examinations and gave dental care. They also gave dog vaccine." Another article heralded the arrival of the civic action team while discussing new babies, the visit of a cleric and his wife, and who was in the hospital at Nome. Many of these newspaper pieces made clear that the civic action program was possible only because of the joint cooperation of the military, the federal and state governments, and the citizenry. Thus dog owners were told that they would have to pay a nominal charge for the serum, that the army and the state health department were cooperating in actually administering the shots, and that the federal Department of Agriculture was furnishing the serum.

When one considers that in Savoonga, which is not on the mainland of Alaska but on St. Lawrence Island, it had been two and a half years since a professional dentist had last visited the village, then one can appreciate the favorable impact that army help made on the inhabitants. In one article John Kulowiyi, a local person, wrote: "We thank them for all the help they gave to the people here and we thank those who sent them here." In another, the mayor of Nome reportedly thanked "Special Forces personnel as well as local aides Bob Emmonds and Lawrence Kayoukluk for assisting in taking care of the canine welfare of our town." In a third, Bill Green, regional sanitarian for all of Alaska north of the Alaska Range, was said to have expressed "the appreciation of the State Division of Health to the Army for their cooperation." In his official trip reports, Lawrence Kayoukluk, who is the Sanitation Aide for the Seward Peninsula, wrote:

> The people of Savoonga were very receptive and cooperative and without reservations. [sic] I know that they have learned much about self-help from the Civic Action Team of the 6th Special Forces as a whole. . . . Captain Donald G. Tolman, the Special Forces Veterinarian, taught one of the local residents, the proper method of administering different vaccines

so that the residents, would be able to run their own rabies and distemper programs in the future. He followed this procedure in all villages possible, [*sic*] I feel that this practice alone was worth covering the villages since it was valuable training.

This area wide rabies innoculation program was beneficial in many ways, [*sic*] the Civic Action Team I worked with was appreciated both by the village residents and in behalf of the Sanitation Aide program of our department, by myself. It was a pleasure to work with this group dedicated in teaching our village residents to help themselves. In the villages we covered, all that will be necessary in future rabies programs, is to have the Councils order the vaccine and have the volunteers that were taught proper methods do the vaccinating.

(Mr. Kayoukluk accompanied the veterinary section to the villages. The section later reported that without his "influence and reputation, a program of this type would have taken at least three times longer and the lasting effects would have been questionable.")

A few weeks after the conclusion of Exercise Polar Strike, students of the third, fourth, and fifth grades of the state school at Teller wrote a letter to President Johnson. It began with "Dear Uncle Sam" and went on to express appreciation for the Special Forces visit. Their teacher explained that the students wanted the letter mailed to the President because he alone represented Uncle Sam. "The courtesy, kindness and efficiency of the special forces unit which was air-lifted from here today (January 27) was of the highest caliber. We hope that you can so inform their headquarters at Fort Bragg."[22]

Considering that the army stayed in each village for only a few days—too short a time in the view of the army personnel who were there—the statistical results were striking. In Gambell 95 per cent of the 400 inhabitants were examined and 8 sent to mainland hospitals. In Tetlin the dentist extracted 50 teeth, made 53 restorations, and did 35 cleanings. In Shishmaref all of the 230 inhabitants were examined and 4 sent to hospitals on the mainland. There were 126 dental extractions, 80 cleanings and fluoride treatments, 12 restorations, and 889 inoculations of dogs against rabies. Nearly 100 per cent of Savoonga's 397 people were given medical and dental examinations, and all of the children had their teeth cleaned and were given topical fluoride applications. There were 76 restorations and 326 extractions, a rather high average of 4 extractions per school child. And as for Savoonga's dog population, 120 of them were inoculated against rabies.

The Alaskan episode as well as the others that have been described proved that civic action in America and elsewhere is not new. Only its name is new. By whatever name, it has been a "prime factor in good soldiering for centuries."[23]

IV America's Civic

Action Program:

How Does It Work?

"*U.S. Forces may at times advise or engage in military civic action in overseas areas.*"

So ends the official civic action definition of the Joint Chiefs of Staff. Behind this sentence lies a structure of education and training and of economic, political, and military activity that involves more than one government department and many countries. All of it is aimed at implementing the objectives of the American civic action program abroad. What are the program's objectives and some of the landmarks of its history?

In some respects civic action is a logical and inevitable outcome of military government or, as it is now called in the United States, civil affairs. Some of the recent roots of civic action stem from ideas taught during World War II at the army's military government school at the University of Virginia, at a similar navy school conducted first at Columbia University and then at Princeton, and in the Army Air Force post-hostilities staff officers' course at Orlando, Florida. And the first American programs that were called "civic action"

67

were handled by civil affairs cadres. But by its own definition,[1] civil affairs is usually activated during and after hostilities or emergencies, whereas civic action can and should be activated in times and areas of peace as well as of war or occupation. In any case, as civic action has grown in concept, stature, organization, and use, it has outgrown Army Civil Affairs.

Though not called civic action, the Korean Civil Assistance Command and Armed Forces Assistance to Korea programs (KCAC and AFAK) were in fact the first such large-scale American activities in postwar history. KCAC served as the operational and technical staff to the American Economic Coordinator after the termination of Korean hostilities. As for AFAK's genesis, soldiers in Korea had for some time collected and contributed funds, time, rations, effort, and equipment to support destitute civilians. General Maxwell D. Taylor, the Eighth Army Commander, recognized the value of such activities and at his suggestion President Eisenhower in 1953 authorized the formal diversion of military equipment and material for civilian relief and rehabilitation in Korea. The initial amount totaled some $15 million.

In 1958 Mr. Eisenhower appointed the President's Committee to Study the United States Military Assistance Program (often called the Draper Committee after its chairman, William H. Draper, Jr.). A clear commitment to civic action flowed throughout the Committee's report. Annex C suggested that "as a matter of policy [we] encourage the use of the armed forces of underdeveloped countries as a major 'transmission belt' of socioeconomic reform and development." It recommended, for example, increased Military Assistance Program (MAP) emphasis on evening high schools at military installations, literacy training for foreign soldiers, and imparting to these soldiers basic technical skills that would have meaning for them in later civilian life. Annex D went further, recommending that the main responsibility for implementing the policy be given to the Defense Department, which would co-ordinate with agencies like the State Department and the International Cooperation Administration, the forerunner of the present Agency for International Development.

The Draper Committee introduced some caveats, however. It warned that military-taught skills with civilian applicability must not exceed the local capacity to absorb them. Second, civic action should not "unduly detract" from the primary military purposes of military forces. Third, it should not be at variance with the long-term development of private enterprise and the civilian economy in a given country. Fourth, it should be clearly in the *public* interest and not in the interests of favored individuals or groups. Finally, the general operating principle suggested was that military civic action be used primarily when labor is short, discipline needed, and working conditions bad.

In presenting its conclusions to President Eisenhower, the Committee recalled that the Mutual Security Act of 1959 already directed military assistance administrators to encourage the use of military units in underdeveloped countries for public works and economic development. The Committee reaffirmed this encouragement and recommended the continuation and expansion of civic action. Specifically, it urged much greater MAP emphasis on training and education of foreign personnel, particularly that "military training assistance be extended beyond narrowly technical matters to broad orientation and schooling in leadership, managerial and executive skills. . . ."[2]

While the Draper Committee, whose members and staff included military men, was researching and deliberating, the military agencies themselves were also busy.[3] In March 1959 the Army Chief of Staff directed the Chief of Civil Affairs to conduct a study of the Armed Forces Assistance to Korea program to determine whether and how its lessons were applicable to other countries in the underdeveloped world. The study concluded that the AFAK concept was indeed applicable, whereupon the army sought approval for the expansion of civic action from the Office of the Secretary of Defense. This approval was given in early May 1960 subject to these main conditions. First, no more than a total of six training teams could be dispatched overseas. Second, civic action must not interfere with the more traditional military capabilities of the armies involved. Third, civic action requests and programs must be sanctioned by the American ambassador to the country concerned. And fourth, they must be funneled through the channels of the military assistance advisory groups and the Unified Commands.

The policy was formally communicated to the field in mid-May 1960 in a joint Defense Department–State Department–International Cooperation Administration message. In June 1960 the Department of the Army notified its military assistance personnel abroad that civic action training teams were now available and, upon request, could be furnished to help formulate specific programs in specific countries.

Thus by the spring of 1960 military assistance missions and groups were being quite actively encouraged to promote civic action. They began to do so in earnest in 1961, the year in which Congress confirmed and strengthened the basic authority for military civic action by including Section 505(b) in the Foreign Assistance Act: "To the extent feasible and consistent with the other purposes of this part [of the Act], the use of military forces in less developed friendly countries in the construction of public works and other activities helpful to economic development should be encouraged."

The Foreign Assistance Act of 1961 was passed in September. In December, National Security Action Memorandum No. 119 was issued. It is one of the key civic action directives because in it President Kennedy related civic action to the stages of subversion:

1. In countries fighting active campaigns against internal subversion, Civic Action is an indispensable means of strengthening the economic base and establishing a link between the Armed Forces and the populace.

2. In countries threatened by external aggression, forces should participate in military Civic Action projects which do not materially impair performance of the primary military mission.

3. In countries where subversion or external attack is less imminent, selected indigenous military forces can contribute substantively to economic and social development, and such a contribution can be a major function of these forces.

As originally conceived by American planners, civic action was supposed to be on a no-cost or low-cost basis. Each project was to be funded by the host government with little or no monetary expenditure by the United States. On this basis, the first civic action training team went out to Guatemala in November 1960. While it discovered many desirable projects that could be undertaken, because of the no-cost, low-cost doctrine, the team was unable to recommend their implementation. Another team, which was sent to Ecuador at the beginning of 1962, found itself faced with the same problem. Nevertheless, it produced a detailed program for implementation whenever funds would become available.

It so happened that in April 1962, Major Ben Safer, the

chief of the civic action training team returning from Ecuador, and Secretary Robert S. McNamara found themselves at the same time at the Canal Zone Headquarters of the Southern Command. Mr. McNamara became so interested in what the major told him that he directed the chief of the Southern Command to submit a complete civic action plan for Ecuador. This was done, and on May 8, 1962, Mr. McNamara approved its implementation. Ten days later the Joint Chiefs of Staff authorized for the Ecuadorean plan a "one-time world-wide priority" over all other military assistance programs and requests. The Defense Department earmarked $1.5 million from MAP funds and arranged with the Agency for International Development for the latter to contribute a half-million dollars to what was essentially the pilot program of contemporary American civic action overseas.

This monetary sharing between the Defense Department and the Agency for International Development in the Ecuador program was made bureaucratically possible because in February 1962 the two agencies had agreed upon a funding formula, which has more or less continued to the present day. Under it, the Defense Department, through the Military Assistance Program, pays for the purchase and maintenance of military equipment employed in civic action and in any training connected with it. AID pays the cost of consumable items like lumber, cement, gasoline, and oil, which the military use in training for or actually doing civic action.

Assume a decision has been made that a telecommunications system is a practical and feasible civic action project in country X. The Defense Department will pay for the team that studies the project and for expendable military supplies for its installation *if* such supplies will *improve* a military unit's ability to *install* the system. Anything that is actually part of the system itself, for example, wire, batteries, switchboards, telephones, poles, etc., will be paid for by the Agency for International Development.

Perhaps the final legitimization of contemporary military civic action came in September 1962 and March 1963. In the first month a Civic Action Branch was organized within the Army's Civil Affairs Directorate, which is located in the Office of the Deputy Chief of Staff for Military Operations. In the latter month the Joint Chiefs of Staff officially redefined counterinsurgency as "those military, paramilitary, political, economic, psychological, and *civic actions* taken by a government to defeat subversive insurgency."* Civic action, like counterinsurgency, was now "in" doctrinally.

Just as American counterinsurgency doctrine postulates that we cannot really fight other peoples' counterinsurgency battles for them, but only help them in this task, our civic action doctrine assumes that we should merely advise or support in what are essentially host country programs (see Chapter VII for some reasons why civic action fails where this principle is ignored, as in Vietnam). Thus the activity flow is not supposed to be from the American soldier to the foreign civilian, but from the American army to its foreign counterpart and from the latter to its people. Second, the civic action training given to both United States and foreign personnel teaches that armies should work *with* civilians on projects which *they* need and have helped to choose. Armies should not work *for* civilians. Third, the American military is not supposed to be competing with other American organizations like the United States Information Agency or AID, nor are foreign armies supposed to be competing with the civilian ministries of their country. Rather they are envisaged as spearheads until American or indigenous civilian agencies can do the jobs properly themselves. Fourth, it is always

---

* Italics added by author.

assumed and taught that the military usefulness of friendly foreign forces and equipment will not be degraded by civic action. And fifth, ultimately civic action will lessen the dependence of these friendly foreign forces on United States military personnel and United States aid.

With these objectives and principles in mind, the United States Army Civil Affairs School began teaching civic action courses in April 1963. They are open to officers about to be assigned to military missions and advisory groups, to Special Forces personnel, to foreign military officers and to officials of American civilian agencies. Civic action is also taught at the army's School of the Americas in the Canal Zone, at the Inter-American Air Forces Academy (formerly the Air Force School for Latin America), which is also in the Canal Zone, and at the Special Warfare Center at Fort Bragg, North Carolina, where personnel learn and demonstrate various types of civic action in a simulated Vietnamese hamlet. By now, nearly every army service school whose subject has any relevance at all to civic action or counterinsurgency is required to include instruction in these areas in the curriculum.

How is civic action actually presented in the training manuals and institutions of the United States military? FM 31-22, the army's field manual on counterinsurgency forces, has an appendix that lists 27 different examples of civic action from well-digging to ambulance service to temporary provision of primary school teachers. It also suggests that civic action may be applied by airborne special forces groups, army aviation companies, civil affairs detachments, and engineer construction battalions, among others. An appendix entitled "Guidelines for Advisors and Members of MTT's [Mobile Training Teams]" says: "Continually stress the advantages of good military/civilian community relations; these are civic action at its best." It also advises: "Don't hesitate to begin a project because you won't be in a country long enough to complete it. Get it started and sell your successor on completing it."

The Civil Affairs School's *Common Subject Lesson Plans: Civic Action* considers civic action "a prophylaxis where insurgency is probable and therapy where it exists." Its teaching of civic action is based upon the requirements of (1) desire, (2) equipment, (3) supplies, (4) personnel, (5) opportunity, (6) time, and (7) continuity. The School's Lesson Plan 5135, "The Concept of Civic Action," teaches it around the phrase "Armies Serve For Social Reform," the first letter of each word standing respectively for Advice, Supplies, Facilities, Services, and Relationships. It tells the students to ask these questions when they are called upon to evaluate the feasibility of a proposed civic action project:

1. Does proposed action conform with national policy and community desires?
2. What requirements will exist to accomplish the job?
3. What capabilities exist, both civilian and military, to accomplish the job?
4. Will the effect to be obtained be sufficiently rewarding in terms of effort expended?
5. Can the project be maintained when military support is withdrawn?

Annex I of *Command and Staff Guidelines for Civic Action* suggests a detailed model plan for constructing an air strip and 28 kilometers of road on the outskirts of a mythical town for an estimated $18,000, to be shared equally by the Military Assistance Program and the Agency for International Development. This plan is reproduced in this chapter as "Example of a Civic Action Program."

Another noteworthy text is the *Counterinsurgency Plan-*

Example of a Civic Action Program

FUNCTIONAL AREA—PUBLIC WORKS
TASK: IMPROVE ROAD AND AIR COMMUNICATIONS
REFERENCE: ANNEX G, CIVAC/MAPLAN FY
PROJECT NR. PW-5   TITLE: ROAD AND AIR STRIP CONSTRUCTION VIC MERALDA

(1) PROJECT SITE	(2) DESCRIPTION (Objective)	(3) ITEMS REQUIRED (Nomenclature)	(4) QTY REQ	UNIT	(5) COST PER UNIT	(6) TOTAL COST		
						MAP	USAID	USIS
Outskirts of city of Meralda Tacama Air Strip	This project consists of the construction of 28 kilometers of connecting road and an air strip 1800 x 45 meters on the outskirts of the city of Meralda. See attached TAB A for Map of Area for Construction Sites (omitted).							
		Diesel Oil	1200	Gals	$ .20		$ 240.00	
		Gasoline, 80 Octane	8000	Gals	.24		1,920.00	
	POL, at rate of 7,000 miles per year per motorized equipment. To be contracted for by local Esso distributor.	Oil, wt 10	100	Gals	2.20		220.00	
		wt 20	400	Gals	2.80		1,120.00	
		wt 30	150	Gals	3.20		480.00	
	Culvert and bridge construction. Concrete structure reinforcement. Hand tools for labor force.	Portland Cement	1000	Sacks	1.10		1,100.00	
		Steel rods ½"	50	Tons	80.00		4,000.00	
		Shovel, D-Handle	100	Ea	2.70	$ 270.00		
		Shovel, Long-Handle	25	Ea	2.40	60.00		
		Mattock, Pick (5-lb)	100	Ea	3.50	350.00		
		Wheelbarrow	50	Ea	11.65	582.50		
		Bar, Digging	25	Ea	5.00	125.00		
		Ax, Single Bit, (4-lb)	20	Ea	3.10	62.00		

Example of a Civic Action Program, Continued

FUNCTIONAL AREA—PUBLIC WORKS
TASK: IMPROVE ROAD AND AIR COMMUNICATIONS
REFERENCE: ANNEX G, CIVAC/MAPLAN FY
PROJECT NR. PW-5   TITLE: ROAD AND AIR STRIP CONSTRUCTION VIC MERALDA

(1) PROJECT SITE	(2) DESCRIPTION (Objective)	(3) ITEMS REQUIRED (Nomenclature)	(4) QTY UNIT REQ	(5) COST PER UNIT	(6) TOTAL COST		
					MAP	USAID	USIS
	U.S. Army Technical Assistance Support.	3 NCO's 18-MTT-102	For 370 days at $15.00 per diem	$5,550.00			
			Cost of Travel	375.00	$5,925.00		
		2 NCO's 18-MTT-02	For 120 days at $15.00 per diem	1,800.00			
			Cost of Travel	250.00	2,050.00		
			Totals		$9,424.50	$9,080.00	
			GRAND TOTAL		$18,504.50		

Example of a Civic Action Program, Continued

FUNCTIONAL AREA—PUBLIC WORKS
TASK: IMPROVE ROAD AND AIR COMMUNICATIONS
REFERENCE: ANNEX G, CIVAC/MAPLAN FY ____ TITLE: ROAD AND AIR STRIP CONSTRUCTION VIC MERALDA
PROJECT NR. PW-5

(7) HOST COUNTRY MILITARY PARTICIPATION (Pers—Equip—Materials, etc.)	(8) CIVILIAN COMMUNITY PARTICIPATION (Labor—Equip—Materials)	(9) U.S. MILITARY PERSONNEL REQUIRED	(10) ESTIMATED STARTING DATE	(11) ESTIMATED COMPLETION DATE	(12) REMARKS (Tasks–Priorities– Benefits)
EQUIPMENT Major MAP items of equipment will be furnished by 113 Engineer Battalion and will be located on site, consisting of: 2 Tractor, TD-20 1 Tractor, Whl 1 Scraper, MTD 6 Truck, DP, 2½ T 1 Roller, Sheepsfoot 1 Roller, TWD, PNEU 1 Rooter, MTD 2 Grader, Road, MTD 1 Compressor, Air 210 1 Air Hammer 1 Distributor, Water, TRK-MTD 2 Pumps, Centrifugal 1 Crane, Shovel 20T, TRK-MTD 1 Crushing and Screening Plant PERSONNEL Cudan Army to supply project officer (Eng), equipment operators, mechanics, labor team supervisors, supply personnel, and truck drivers.	Meralda Community is supplying 400-man labor force (volunteers). To be compensated only by payment in kind by Cudan Govt. using U.S. PL 480 surplus foods. Two local civilian doctors will support project with free medical care in the Meralda Dispensary. Sand and gravel locally available in unlimited quantities from River Rimar.	3 U.S. NCO's (Constr Eng), supervisors from 18-MTT-102, FY ____. 2 U.S. NCO's (Hvy Eng Equip Maint) from 18-MTT-103, FY ____.	1 Jan ____	30 Dec ____	Meralda, a fertile but isolated farming area of great potential will be able to market its produce in the heretofore unreachable capital of Ito. May encourage mechanization of farming, and offer market for manufactured products from local industries.

ning Guide of the United States Army's Special Warfare School. In education, for example, it says that

> . . . if the area study of the region revealed a literacy rate of 10–15 percent, it can be assumed that educational help is required. In order to determine necessary corrective action in this instance, the answers to the following or similar questions would be required:
>
> (a) Are there compulsory attendance laws?
> (b) Are there prescribed curricula?
> (c) Is education a local or national effort?
> (d) Is there a school budget?
> (e) Are teachers available?
> (f) Are teaching materials available?
> (g) How many school-age children are there?
> (h) What facilities exist?
> (i) Is the area secure?
> (j) What is the attitude of the populace toward education?
> (k) What is the social structure?
> (l) What are the immediate needs?
> (m) What agencies are concerned?

It also includes a work sheet as a means of accomplishing the educational and other evaluations (see Table 2).

For overall civic action plans, the *Guide* suggests this format:

CIVIC ACTION PLAN FORMAT

TASK ORGANIZATION: List military organizations that are to be included in the execution of the plan. Task organization may be shown as an annex if sufficiently large.

1. SITUATION.
    a. *General.* A statement of the situation as it exists within the country concerned.

Table 2

COUNTERINSURGENCY PLANNING GUIDE

WORK SHEET--CIVIC ACTION ESTIMATE (EXAMPLE)

(Complete by indicating affirmative or negative response with detailed explanatory notes attached as necessary)

Classification	Proposed course of action	Will it gain population support for government?	Will it contribute to the stabilization of society?	Will it improve local relations between local military and population?	Will it promote democratic processes?	Will the population accept it?	Is it amendable to publicity exploitation?	Will its psychological effects be favorable?	Will it have immediate impact?	Will other agencies react favorably to our nations?	Can we start on it immediately?	Will government support efforts?	Will military support efforts?	Will population support efforts?	Will other agencies support efforts?	Are all necessary skills available?	Are labor, materials, and equipment available?	Does it conform to local custom?	Can it be supported by current programmed funds?	Will it provide maximum return on investment and effort?	Will it avoid serious interference with other missions?	Does it avoid duplication with other agency efforts?	REMARKS
A. Area																							
B. Education	Build Schools																						
	Train Teachers																						
	Provide Texts																						
	Etc.																						
C. Public Health	Immunization Program																						
	Train Village Medics																						
	Create Dispensaries																						
	ETC.																						
D. Agriculture																							

Source: U.S. Army, Counterinsurgency Planning Guide, p. 166.

b. *Insurgent forces.* Summary of insurgent forces.

c. *Friendly forces.* Summary of assets available to support civic action mission including military units or organizations.

d. *Assumptions.* Assume the current or future situation to be true in the absence of positive proof. Assumptions must be logical and reasonable and should be used to state conditions that must exist for the plan to be used.

2. MISSION. State the task and its purpose, for example, "To conduct civic action activities in _____, to effect economic and sociological improvement in support of national objectives."

3. OBJECTIVES. List all objectives that the military is to support.

4. TASKS. . . .

a. *Concept of operations.* This is a statement of the anticipated conduct of the entire operation. It should clarify the purpose of the operation and be stated in sufficient detail to enable subordinates to fully understand their roles. The concept of operations may be included as an annex as necessary.

b. *Subsequent subparagraphs (c, d, e, etc.) should list those courses of action proposed to achieve the objective.* Depending on the military organization in the country, tasks may be assigned to units, listed by service, or given as tasks peculiar to a local area.

5. COORDINATION. State specifically the arrangements made to insure coordination between military organizations, and between the military and other government agencies. Levels of coordination, extent of coordination, and responsibilities for coordination should be shown.

6. SUPPORT REQUIREMENTS. List any support requirements that are beyond the current capability of the military. This should in-

clude additional funds (to include administrative handling
of these funds), equipment, and personnel.

7. COMMAND. Identify responsible command elements and show
   location as necessary. Clarify command channels for implementation of plan.

There are also army texts that seek to teach actual tech-
nological know-how. For example, the *Village Water Well
Project* was published by the Thirteenth Psychological Warfare Battalion both as a training mission and as a manual for
teaching how a serviceable well could be dug by three people
for about twenty-five dollars. The *Village Technology Handbook* is a Civil Affairs School reprint of an Agency for International Development book containing fifty articles on how
to help villagers to make tools and acquire useful work techniques. It contains tables on weight, length, and temperature
conversions, and material on how to construct things like
hand pumps for irrigation, water boilers, bailing buckets,
latrines, bamboo poultry houses, chicken brooders, grain
cleaners, evaporative food coolers, hand-operated washing
machines, solar water heaters, silk screen printing presses,
and the like. The *Manual for Rural Community Health
Worker (Thailand)* is a Civil Affairs School reprint of a
handbook originally written by an American cultural an-
thropologist and an American health educator on the staff of
the United States Operations Mission in Thailand, with the
help of two Thai health educators from the Thailand Department of Health.

Finally, one of the most illuminating army primers for the
conduct of good civic action is a memorandum by Lieutenant
Colonel John T. Little, former chief of the White Star Mobile
Training Team in Laos. Among its "field-tested" ideas are
these:

Always make the villagers share the workload. Let them know that all these projects are village projects, not US help for the helpless. Once you do one project all by yourself the villagers will forever after expect this from your team. Do not give them something for nothing. For example, a good approach could be "I will try to get a tin roof for this school house if you will build the school and furnish all the other materials and labor."

Try to present your ideas to the Chao Muong [village headman] in such a fashion as to make him think it was his idea in the first place. Let him win full credit for the completion of any project. Do not issue orders to him or demand an instant decision. . . .

Do not start anything you cannot fully support. Never promise anything. Remember you can be moved out at a moment's notice. Have all the materials on hand before you start any project. Check it out with your superiors before you begin.

General Lansdale, when he was Assistant to the Secretary of Defense for Special Operations, thought the Little memorandum so important and relevant to civic action and counterinsurgency beyond Laos that he had it widely circulated.[4]

Bureaucratically, how does the civic action program work? It is one of the most interdepartmental foreign programs we have. At the Washington level, the Department of Defense, the Military Assistance Program, the United States Army, Navy, and Air Force, the State Department, the United States Information Agency, the Agency for International Development, and the Food for Peace Program are all involved. Food for Peace is involved because Title II of the Agricultural Trade Development Assistance Act (Public Law 480) authorizes the transfer of food and other agricultural commodities acquired by the Agriculture Department's Commodity Credit Corporation for disaster relief and economic development including military civic action. Title II permits the use of agricultural products as wage payments to people in the poorer countries who work on military civic action programs. Thus a recent report of the Food for Peace Program cited a civic action community development program in Ecuador which employed 377 workers for six months, and to whom 67 tons of flour, bulgur, butter oil, cornmeal, and milk were contributed as partial payment for their labors. In all, approximately 1900 people benefited.[5]

At the local level, all United States agency heads (who comprise what is known as the Country Team) are encouraged to plan, use, and contribute to feasible military civic action programs in the countries to which they are posted. It is the Country Team, headed by the American ambassador, that is supposed to request and monitor a civic action program in country X. The formal request procedure is generally as follows. If the ministry of foreign affairs of country X wishes to have American civic action aid, it will approach the American ambassador (or its defense ministry will approach the chief United States military representative) and request it. If the Country Team believes a military civic action program is in order, it will pass the request, with any necessary modifications, to the appropriate Unified Command (such as the Southern Command for Latin America). From there it will go sequentially to the Office of the Assistant Secretary of Defense for International Security Affairs, to the Joint Chiefs of Staff, and if approved, to the Department of the Army, Navy, or Air Force for implementation. In most cases, it will be the army that does the implementing. For of all the services, it contributes between 75 and 95 per cent of the American personnel and equipment that support existing programs.[6]

If the American representatives already in country X do

not themselves have military civic action capability, they will call for the dispatch of temporary duty specialists to come there in the form of a Civic Action Mobile Training Team (CAMTT). The team can be either an interagency, inter-service, or single service unit. Most often it is from the army.

Normally, each team consists of from one to four people (who can be augmented). They are trained or experienced in governmental affairs, engineering, medicine, public health, sanitation, psychological operations, agriculture, and public relations. Each specialist advises in his area of competence, trying always to help the local people help themselves to achieve a self-sustaining momentum after he has gone. The engineer, for example, advises in such matters as insect and rodent control; fire protection; the building, maintenance, repair, and operation of public utilities, roads, railroads, waterways, bridges, culverts, etc. The specialist in medicine, public health, and sanitation advises on hospital and dispensary needs, preventive medicine programs, basic sanitation, first aid, personal hygiene, food inspection, and the care and use of medical equipment. The education member of the CAMTT advises on the requirements for school buildings, school equipment, school instructors, literacy campaigns both within the foreign army and among the surrounding civilian population, and basic education and technical training courses in useful civilian occupations. The agriculture member shares his experience and knowledge in crop improvement, pest control, irrigation and water storage, prevention of crop destruction, and so on.

Since engineering and construction forms a large part of civic action, the United States Navy is also involved, though not as heavily or with as much formal structure as the army. Often its principal function is to provide resources to agencies like AID or a Military Assistance Advisory Group. The typical navy instrument for civic action implementation is the STAT, or Seabee Technical Assistance Team, formed from the CBs, the Construction Battalions of World War II fame.

There are some inherent differences between navy STATs and the analogous CAMTTs fielded by the army. Unlike their army counterparts, who may or may not be engineers, the officers in charge of a STAT are members of the naval Civil Engineer Corps and are graduate engineers with practical experience in fields like civil, electrical, and mechanical engineering. As for the enlisted members of the team, each man possesses from eight to eighteen years of construction experience (which is equal to the "journeyman" level) in a building trade, as well as training and experience in at least a second one. The normal team consists of two equipment operators, two construction mechanics, a construction electrician, two builders, a steelworker, a utilities man, an engineering aide, and, where appropriate, a hospital corpsman. Together, they represent the following skills: automotive equipment, diesel equipment, carpentry, cement work, demolition, heating and ventilating, diving, draftsmanship, electricity, plumbing, sheet metal work, steel work, surveying, and first aid and subprofessional medicine.

Seabee Technical Assistance Teams are usually self-contained, carrying practically all of their equipment with them wherever they go. They can therefore *do* as well as show and teach. Thus if the civic action objective is to bring water quickly to villages of country X, then the Seabees may be called in to dig wells as rapidly as possible and leave. However, if the objective is to teach the villagers how to dig wells themselves, then the chances are that an army group will be ordered to do the job.[7]

Several years ago Costa Rica suffered a serious flood control problem stemming from a volcanic eruption. A United

States Navy team was rushed to the scene. When it arrived, one of its members remarked that the mud had "the density of cake batter and the speed of flood water with giant rocks riding on top." When it left, a high Costa Rican official said: "Without the Seabees we would have had a real catastrophe on our hands."[8]

Aside from the Seabees and STATs, the navy engages in more generalized but less structured kinds of civic action through its People to People Program, especially Project Handclasp. Handclasp transports foods, drugs, clothing, and other items given by American individuals, organizations, and businesses. In 1964 the navy assisted Ambassador Julius C. Holmes in visiting the Persian Gulf area of Iran. The U.S.S. *Bache* stopped at ports in remote southern Iran which would have been difficult if not impossible for him to reach overland. These included Abadan, Bushire, Kharg Island, Bandar Lengeh, Bandar Abbas, and Hormuz Island. According to the *Department of State Newsletter*,[9] which reported the trip, "at each of the ports where the U.S.S. *Bache* put in, personnel of the ship engaged in their 'Operation Hand Clasp Activities,' presenting medical supplies, playground equipment and other gifts. At Bandar Abbas a large group of dignitaries of the port were entertained on board ship at a reception, and a party was held for 70 children."

An example of civic action under the People to People Program is the work of Lieutenant (j.g.) Philip Wyne. During a six-month tour of the attack transport *Monrovia* in 1964, he "made himself something of a legend among the people of the Mediterranean" by repairing revered clocks in churches and orphanages in Greece, Malta, Italy, and Spain.[10]

The air force also participates in civic action, particularly in Latin America. For example, it has in Panama a Preventive Medicine Training Program. Each participating Latin American country sends a team of 5 airmen to a 5½-month course in (1) hygiene and public sanitation, (2) human, animal, and crop disease detection and isolation, (3) laboratory techniques, (4) first aid, and (5) inoculation procedures. The chief of each team is a pilot, qualified in light aircraft, who can fly the team and its portable dispensary to far-away areas where civilian medical assistance is not available.

What, in sum, are some of the key statistical indicators of American involvement in contemporary civic action? Between 1950 and 1959 (before civic action as it is known today was fully accepted or functioning) the United States Army spent some $5 million on mobile training teams abroad, and a third of this money was for non-military progress and skills.[11] The Military Assistance Program began to formally engage in civic action in 1961, supporting it in nine countries in fiscal year 1962, in twenty-four countries in fiscal year 1963, and in more than twenty-five countries in fiscal year 1964. Since then, American-aided civic action has been going on in more than thirty countries with some thirty others supporting their own programs.[12] Table 3 shows how much the Military Assistance Program spent on civic action between fiscal years 1962 and 1966. Table 4 shows the amounts spent by USAID for civic action during fiscal year 1965 and its estimated spending in that field for fiscal years 1966 and 1967.

It is obvious that America is heavily—and financially— committed to civic action overseas. This being the case, what kind of civic action commitment do other countries have, especially those in the major geographic divisions of the underdeveloped world? The following three chapters will help to answer this question.

Table 3

U.S. Military Assistance Funds for Civic Action Programs, Fiscal Year 1962
Through Fiscal Year 1966[1]

(In thousands of dollars)

	Fiscal year 1962	Fiscal year 1963	Fiscal year 1964	Fiscal year 1965	Fiscal year 1966
Latin America:					
Argentina			298	1,253	539
Bolivia		1,817	397	239	114
Brazil	2,200	2,156	2,097	2,386	1,961
Chile	860	2,019	1,279	391	634
Colombia		1,488	1,655	550	696
Costa Rica			222	13	(2)
Dominican Republic		596	59	64	122
Ecuador	1,500	323	709	476	104
El Salvador		534	145	99	65
Guatemala		863	567	133	343
Honduras		84	20	240	71
Mexico				8	20
Nicaragua		59		3	
Panama			2	44	22
Paraguay		840	1,111	596	576
Peru	1,135	2,794	1,271	2,411	2,871
Uruguay		546	431	286	103
Venezuela			23	47	59
Region					72
Area total	5,695	14,119	10,286	9,239	8,372
Far East:					
Cambodia		792			
Indonesia		2,887		69	
Korea	3,140	385	1,084		45
Laos			8	25	35
Philippines		930	22	32	19
Thailand		3,617	851	1,866	1,082
Vietnam	3,900	35,343	1,132	25	32
Region	750				
Area total	7,790	43,954	3,097	2,017	1,213
NESA and Africa:					
Congo (Leopoldville)				(2)	
Ethiopia			167	6	5
Greece			10		5
Guinea				783	152
Iran	1,221	404	668	6	
Jordan	198	1,276	174	61	6
Liberia		463	66	88	9
Libya			6		
Mali			5	230	162
Pakistan		7			
Senegal		183	66	276	306
Sudan			(2)		
Tunisia			2		
Upper Volta				8	8
Area total	1,419	2,333	1,164	1,458	653
World totals	14,904	60,406	14,547	12,714	10,238

[1] Fiscal year 1962 was the first year that civic action assistance was so identified in MAP. Fiscal year 1967 is estimated to have a worldwide total of $11,810,000.
[2] Less than $500.

Source: U.S. Congress, House of Representatives, 89th Cong., 2d Sess., *Foreign Assistance Act of 1966: Hearings before the Committee on Foreign Affairs.* Part 7 (Washington: Government Printing Office, 1966), p. 1040.

Table 4

USAID Expenditures for Civic Action Programs

(In thousands of dollars)

	Actual, fiscal year 1965	Estimated, fiscal year 1966	Estimated, fiscal year 1967
Latin America:			
Bolivia	125	790	604
Colombia	317	287	290
Dominican Republic	1	....	....
Ecuador	55	80	100
El Salvador	70	50	50
Guatemala	74	....	....
Peru	48	254	1,778
Uruguay	....	65	100
Total, Latin America	690	1,526	2,922
Near East and south Asia:			
Iran	108	100	....
Jordan	436	....	....
Total, Near East and south Asia	544	100	....
Far East:			
Indonesia	261	....	....
Thailand	195	433	593
Vietnam	....	2,500	2,500
Total, Far East	456	2,933	3,093
Total, civic action	1,690	4,559	6,015

Source: U.S. Congress, House of Representatives, 89th Cong., 2d Sess., *Hearings before a Subcommittee of the Committee on Appropriations.* Part 2 (Washington: Government Printing Office, 1966), p. 85.

ADDENDUM TO CHAPTER IV

22 March 1962

MEMORANDUM

SUBJECT: Civic Action and Counter-Insurgency

What should an American military man do when stationed in a native village during a counter-insurgency campaign?

John T. Little, Lt-Col Inf., came up with an impressive answer last year when he was in Laos. He commanded a Mobile Training Team of Army Special Forces, whose officers and men were stationed with Lao military units throughout the country. Taking a number of standing instructions and the lessons learned in Laos, the Philippines, and Vietnam, he compiled a set of instructions on Civic Action for his officers and men in simple, every day language.

Although these instructions are tailored to conditions in Laos, they contain many points worth heeding elsewhere. With Lt-Col Little's permission, I am passing these instructions along. They deserve wide reading and understanding by all U.S. military men concerned with counter-insurgency.

> EDWARD G. LANSDALE
> Brigadier General, USAF
> Assistant to the Secretary of Defense
> (Special Operations)

Attachment

HEADQUARTERS
WHITE STAR MOBILE TRAINING TEAM
Vientiane, Laos

22 September 1961

SUBJECT: Civil Assistance

TO: Commanders
        All Field Training Teams
        White Star Mobile Training Team
        Military Assistance Advisory Group to Laos

1. In an insurgency condition, the guerrilla is dependent on a sympathetic population. Counter-guerrilla operations must, therefore, have as one objective winning the population's cooperation and denying the enemy their sympathy. This can be done by psychological operations in many forms.

2. An imaginative program of village assistance properly backed in the military and civil authorities is one form of psychological operation which will contribute significantly toward this objective and achievement of U.S. goals in Laos.

3. The attached outline for a civil assistance program which can realistically be applied by operational detachments is for-

warded for team use in establishing a positive civil relations program. The ideas expressed have been field tested and are practical. Use them as a guide for your actions in this field. Start at once.

4. You are not in competition with other U.S. agencies; USIS and USOM; you are the spearhead of these activities and a focal point for injection of these activities until Laos civil assistance teams are trained and in use. Your primary mission is training and operations with FAR [Armed Forces of the Kingdom of Laos]; this is secondary to that mission but has an important impact on it.

5. Those teams operating from villages in which USIS and USOM representatives are not permanently represented are expected to initiate action in this field and keep this headquarters informed of progress.

s/ John T. Little

John T. Little
Lt. Col., Inf.
Commanding

1 Incl
   Outline of a Civil Assistance
      Program
Copies furnished:
   Chief Each Military Region
   American Embassy

OUTLINE OF A CIVIL ASSISTANCE PROGRAM

1. Actions prior to commencement of civil assistance program in Lao villages.
   a. Become acquainted with key members of the district. These include:
      (1) The Chao Muong—political boss of the district (has absolute authority over villagers).
      (2) The High District Judge and his staff—this official is second in authority to Chao Muong.

(3) The Chief Buddhist (Bonze) of the district.
(4) The Police Captain and his staff.
(5) The Village Headmen.
(6) The Schoolmaster and School Teachers.
(7) Leading business men including shop owners and restaurant owners.

b. Gather background data on key personnel of district to include:

(1) Nationality.
(2) Date and place of birth.
(3) Education and Religion.
(4) Knowledge of foreign languages.
(5) Special skills or abilities.
(6) Military service.
(7) Travel background.
(8) Past activities in government.
(9) Present job and salary.
(10) Details of family—how many wives and children.
(11) Character and personality—is he honest, is he loyal, is he a doer and not just a talker, does he have initiative, drive, imagination?
(12) Is he pro-FAR, pro-American, pro-French?

c. Gathering this information will be a continuing process. Record it and pass it on to the succeeding team.

2. Recommend activities for civil assistance program.

a. Medical Support: Have team medic assist village doctor in sick call. If there is no doctor, team medic should run sick call himself. Team medic will visit all villages in area and make occasional visits to remote villages out of the area. From among the more intelligent of the young villagers the team medic should choose an assistant aid-man with the object of training him to eventually become the village doctor. The village should be persuaded to build a hospital with the theme, "this will be for your village and your people. If the people want continued team medical support tell them to build a hospital."

Note: Doctors are paid by government so team need not worry about depriving village doctor of livelihood.

b. Aid to Education: By the team encouraging and helping the children the parents can be made aware of the importance of education. School supplies to be furnished include blackboards, chalk, erasers, pencils, pencil sharpeners, writing paper, tablets, multiplication tables, rulers, books, globes, atlases, charts on anatomy, chemistry, physics and biology and nature subjects. Get the material in front of the children. Teach the schoolmaster to be responsible and accountable for the equipment—to take the books up at the end of the semester and reissue them at the beginning of the term. Use the school aid program as a lever to get the village to repair and expand the school. Require the village to send all their children to school. This can be done through the Chao Muong. The children must be taught the world is not flat, that Laos is not the only country, that America is a powerful friend and what the Communists are.

c. Sanitation: This field offers the greatest possibilities for achievement and improvement. Persuade the people to police the streets, cut the grass, burn and bury the rubbish, rake under the houses. Encourage village authorities to destroy homeless, vicious and unwanted dogs. Start a DDT program. Teach the natives how to use the sprayers and mix the solution. Put rat poison in village, placing it high enough to be unreachable by children and chickens. Start a war on bed bugs. Use oil to stamp out mosquito breeding areas. Put the villagers on chloroquin. In the dry season have family latrines dug. Instruct natives on covering waste. Get villagers to dig wells for drinking water. Instruct families on fly control—distribute swatters. Action should be taken to prevent livestock from overrunning living areas. Work all projects through the Chao Muong. When he issues the order the people will take action.

d. Aid to Agriculture: Get assistance from USOM. To start program persuade a few farmers to try crop rotation, proper spacing, fertilizing and spraying. This is a long-range project taking patience, time and skillful persuasion. A Lao farmer puts all his earnings into his crop and he is very hesitant about making experiments. But once he has been shown the results of this new method of rice growing he will be an eager participant. In many areas the irrigation system could be improved, small streams could be dammed, etc.

e. Transportation Improvement: All roads in Laos need improvement. Get villagers to build bridges, repair washouts, fill holes, make detours. Use whatever labor is available whether it is three men or three hundred men. Have village construct an airfield. Sell Chao Muong on the advantages in trade and business. Have villagers construct flat-bottom boats to haul goods on the rivers.

f. Children's Playground: This represents an opportunity to influence, educate, and take part in raising children for a better Laos. Stock the playground with swings, teeter-totters, sliding boards, monkey bars, parallel bars. Set up volley ball, basket ball, soccer, baseball and just plain ordinary tag ball. Set up relay races, obstacle races and jumping contests. Teach them sportsmanship, teamwork, how to win and how to lose. Teach them fair play and get them in top physical condition. To help all this the team captain could write to his favorite town in the United States informing them that the Lao village where the team is stationed wants to be a sister city with them and learn about the American way of life. Through civic organizations in the US town many items for the children could be obtained such as clothes, candy, toys and educational games.

g. Special Tools: Through USOM try to borrow, lease or directly obtain a circular saw. All lumber is cut by hand. This takes hours of time and delays the building pro-

gram. In addition to the saw, obtain fuel, lubricant, extra
blades and maintenance instructions. Also a chain saw is
ideal for clearing land.

h. Market Place: If the market place is in a typically rotten
condition, interest the Chao Muong in building a new
one. Get it centrally located for the people. If you furnish
tin for the roof you can demand that they clean the
market up after each day's use.

i. Movies: You can obtain a generator and projector from
USIS and show Lao and American movies. There are
many excellent propaganda movies in the USIS ware-
houses. Show American films also—particularly those with
a simple direct theme showing us at our best. (e.g., war
pictures, cowboy pictures, adventure pictures and light
comedies. Avoid films which degrade us or are extremely
sophisticated and complex.). The villagers love to watch
American films even when they cannot understand a
word. A portable PA speaker which would enable the
interpreter to give the general plot line would be a big
asset when showing US films.

j. Electric lights: Interest the Chao Muong in trying to
start a light plant if one is not in operation. Possibly the
better-off citizens can be persuaded to pool their money
to finance the operation, particularly if they can see how
they can make a profit in the future. Get USOM help on
this one.

k. Local Restaurants and Markets: Try to get the local bars
and restaurants to clean up their kitchens and their premises and dispose of their food waste in sanitary fashion.
This can be handled through the Chao Muong. Do not
patronize below-standard places. If it is a small town try
to interest the local people in building new buildings and
attracting more people and more business.

l. As a final word on these recommended activities remember that any program you undertake will be secondary to
your mission of training FAR. The time for project plan-

ning and team participation is at night and during off duty time. Before starting any work see the people at USOM and USIS and find out what kind of support they can actually give you. These civic projects will take up many hours but they will be hours well spent in the achievement of the United States objectives of building a greater and stronger free Laos.

3. Tips on conduct of a civil assistance program.

    a. Upon arrival in the village pay a courtesy call on the Chao Muong. Do not talk shop on the first meeting, just make friends.

    b. Deal directly with the Chao Muong. Do not work through his subordinates. Always work through one man—the chief.

    c. Make a statement on graft. Let the Chao Muong know that under no circumstances will you tolerate graft and if you detect it all aid will stop. If corruption starts the villagers will tell you. You do not need to search for it.

    d. Do not stockpile supplies—get them distributed promptly. You must have a system of control. Make the Chao Muong sign for everything you give him and see that he signs out the equipment to his subordinates. Since it is impossible for everyone to have a pick, shovel, grub hoe and axe, the tools should be issued from a central point on a loan basis. When a farmer finishes with a piece of equipment he returns it to the village chief. The chief must be taught how to run this system.

    e. Always make the villagers share the work load. Let them know that all these projects are village projects, not US help for the helpless. Once you do one project all by yourself the villagers will forever after expect this from your team. Do not give them something for nothing. For example, a good approach could be "I will try to get a tin roof for this school house if you will build the school and furnish all the other materials and labor."

    f. Try to present your ideas to the Chao Muong in such a

fashion as to make him think it was his idea in the first place. Let him win full credit for the completion of any project. Do not issue orders to him or demand instant decision. When you approach him with an idea let him have a night to think about it. But the next day be sure to gently push him toward a decision.

g. Do not start anything you cannot fully support. Never promise anything. Remember you can be moved out at a moment's notice. Have all the material on hand before you start any project. Check it out with your superiors before you begin.

h. Initially your weapon is talk. It must be interesting, arousing, intelligent. You are a master salesman for the United States. Some pitfalls for newcomers: drinking too much at social functions (keep your mind clear for business), getting involved with the native women (creates jealousy and hate and makes you a setup for anti-US propaganda), being arrogant, sarcastic or belittling in your conversation (these people are hypersensitive and proud and you will come to a dead end if they dislike you). Some positive tips are: avoid anything that reminds the people of French control. For example the French required that every man in the village contribute one day's work or a couple of pieces of lumber to each building project. The Lao do not even like to talk about it. Maintain the proper team attitude of good-natured willingness and endless patience in the face of resentment to change and complete apathy. Be tactful, be tolerant. Show exceptional kindness to the children and the very old. Be courteous, be relaxed and do not be in a hurry.

i. Do not worry if they do things differently from what you propose. If they achieve the end result that is all that counts.

j. For success on this mission observe the native customs. For example when you are visiting a different village inform the villagers that you are coming so that the people can assemble. The district headman (the Chao Muong) always makes a political speech on these occasions. Never force your way into a village where the broken branches across the trail indicate a closed celebration. Follow the native custom of removing your footgear when going into a village house. Learn the customs of your region.

k. Make sure the United States gets credit for all U.S. items distributed. If possible equipment should be stamped with a U.S. flag. When the Chao Muong makes a speech to the citizenry about the tools and supplies they are to receive make sure he tells the villagers that the equipment comes from America.

l. Do not give away U.S. items for nothing. For example, if you give picks demand they dig a well or ditch the streets. If you give school supplies, make them either build a school or repair the old one.

4. In conclusion: The sky is the limit in what you can achieve. You cannot make a new Laos in one day but it only takes one day to start. Now is the time to start beating the enemy at his own game—the winning of men's minds, emotions and loyalty to the concept of freedom, justice, individual human rights, equality of opportunity and a higher living standard.

V Acción Cívica Militar:

Latin American Armies

in Social and Economic

Development

THE DEFENSE DEPARTMENT has compiled the following cost comparison for building twenty kilometers of road through a mountainous Latin American forest. According to it, civic action units can build the road for $2500 less than a foreign contractor's price merely for *studies,* and the road would cost *four* times more if done by a local contractor than by army civic action units advised by two United States mobile training teams.

If the comparison is valid and typical of Latin America, then it is a strong economic argument for military civic action. But even if it is not, it is quite significant. For it indicates what American military people publicize and believe (or would like to have believed) about military civic action, particularly in Latin America.

Whatever the actual case, the United States is currently supporting civic action in all Latin American countries except Cuba and Haiti. More than half of the total number of countries in the world whose civic action programs are American-assisted are in Latin America, which about 500 United

Table 5
Civic Action Cost Comparison

Projects: Two 10-km sections on a Latin American road projection as part of a penetration route through mountainous rain forests into a colonization area.

Comparative Costs: (U.S. dollars as computed from local money exchange rate of September 1963):

1. Local Contractor		$132,000
2. Foreign Contractor (studies only)		$ 36,000
3. Civic Action Units		$ 33,454
a. Materials	($18,560)	
b. Troop pay, including food and uniforms	($ 5,202)	
c. Depreciation of equipment	($ 7,035)	
d. U.S. Mobile Training Teams (2)	($ 2,657)	

Representative Costs:

	Civilian Contractor	Military Unit
1. Excavation (per cubic meter)	$0.60	$0.46
2. Structural excavation (per cubic meter)	1.06	0.79
3. Reinforced concrete (per cubic meter)	100.00	100.00
4. Cyclopean concrete for foundation, 50% rock enlarging (per cubic meter)	15.67	14.67
5. Transportation of materials (per ton/km)	*	0.13

*Included in above costs

Source: U.S. Department of Defense, International Security Affairs (1965).

States military personnel visit each year as members of mobile training teams.[1] It is also true that, while the Latin Americans and the North Americans agree on the need for civic action both in socio-economic development and counterinsurgency, in many countries *they* stress the development and *we* the counterinsurgency. This difference comes up again and again in military assistance negotiations.

In some countries—for example, Venezuela and Colombia, where urban and rural violence is a continuing problem—the primary motivation is to improve internal security. In others, it is indeed to use the armed services for social and economic

Official Emblem of Civic Action in Guatemala

improvement. Brazil has a civic action tradition almost as old as our own; Haiti is new and relatively untried at it. Whereas Haiti's commitment is informal and minimal, Guatemala's is formal and full. Guatemala is a country where civic action has been recognized by Presidential proclamation and where troops may be seen laboring under the official emblem of "ACCION CIVICA MILITAR—SEGURIDAD Y PROGRESO." Moreover, some Latin American countries have created interministerial agencies to plan and direct civic action. Others have "special military bodies" devoted only to civic action tasks.[2] In the rest of them, the regular military organizations or analogous groups such as Costa Rica's Guardia Civil perform civic action as part of their duties.

Colombia exemplifies the interministerial approach, with a Presidentially established National Committee on Military Civic Action. The Committee's Secretary is the War Minister, and the other members are the Ministers of Government, Education, Health, Agriculture, and Public Works, as well as additional public or private persons. The Committee has its counterparts at lower levels of government too, and former Colombian War Minister General Alberto Ruiz Novoa has said of this type of cooperation:

> Military civic action requires coordination among the different government levels and is carried out by committees composed of military and civilian authorities; ecclesiastic authorities are also invited to participate, as well as all those individuals and groups who desire to collaborate. The task of the committees is to promote the cooperation of the civilian population through campaigns of social, educational, and communal action for the betterment of the population.

The Colombian experience has shown the excellent results that are obtained through the establishment of these committees, and which are evident in the cooperation that all the citizens have offered in the actions accomplished.[3]

Though other branches also perform civic action, Chile's Military Work Corps illustrates an independent civic action body under the army commander in chief. It carries out projects in conjunction with national or municipal agencies, the cost being charged to the latters' budget. Honduras is an example of a country where civic action is planned and co-ordinated by and within the regular armed forces through an Office of Civic Action.

Further, there is an essential difference between present-day and earlier civic action in Latin America. In earlier days, a great deal of the non-military use of the military was un-planned and uncentralized, with no continuity and no follow-through. Much of its operation and success depended upon the enthusiasm and competence of individual, often isolated, commanders. And even they considered it a by-product, not a regular function, of the military. Today the opposite is true in many countries of the hemisphere. What is more, there are Latin American officers who are deeply committed to the concept, speak up for it, and devote energies to implementing and improving it. One of them is Julio Sanjinés Goytia. He is now Bolivia's Ambassador to the United States. Before that, however, he was a colonel in the army in charge of his coun-try's civic action program. While he was still with the pro-gram, he wrote a pamphlet in English called *Civic Action: Role of the Armed Forces in the Social and Economical* [sic] *Development of a Country,*[4] which merits some discussion.

Sanjinés Goytia is very conscious of the continuing migra-tion to the cities (a Latin American as well as a worldwide phenomenon) and of the growing "unemployed urban pro-letariat" that it produces. He therefore argues that it is not enough for armies to teach their Indian and other conscripts to read, to write, and to eat and dress properly. They must also teach them a trade that can be used gainfully in the countryside. It is, in other words, the responsibility of armies to make the rural areas more productive and satisfying. "If this sort of education is not provided . . ., the only thing that may have been obtained, after an artificial period of life, is that the subject individual [the army conscript] may abandon the country and turn to the cities," where because of competition and other factors he may increase "the worthless and negative population." Consequently, he suggests that nearly every army post should be an "agricultural instruction center," where each soldier would learn, aside from military things, "better farming methods, community development techniques and cooperativism."

Education is very important to Sanjinés Goytia. Since teachers in many rural areas are overworked or non-existent, he suggests that the army select a special group from conscripts who have completed high school and give it an intensive three-month course emphasizing sanitation and agriculture. After the course, they would serve out the remainder of their military service as auxiliary rural teachers. The army can also help with rural schools. Aided by local people and locally available construction materials, *any* eight-man squad with its commander can, he feels, complete a school for thirty or forty children equipped with water, sanitary facilities, a teacher's room, a sports field, and a small experimental farm. In his opinion, this can and must be done within three months because no single military unit should be put on a non-military task for a greater length of time lest its military preparation and performance be impaired.

Sanjinés Goytia is very much concerned about making Latin American armies and police civic action conscious. (While not every town has a military garrison, there is hardly one without a policeman.) He is not too hopeful about older army officers, who are "highly oriented towards the traditional aspects of war." What is required, then, is a reorganization of military academy education, making it more balanced so that newer, younger officers will be more receptive to the non-military uses of military forces. He argues that technically trained officers are more receptive to civic action than are those whose education has been largely in the humanities and military tactics.

This last argument requires a caveat against the downgrading of social and humanistic studies. Admittedly, civic action cannot be performed without technology; and soldiers, in order to perform it, must learn technology. But they also need a social orientation without which they may never be able to perceive problems and provide civic action solutions within the context of proper civilian-military relationships.

As regards civic action solutions to problems, Sanjinés Goytia distinguishes between long-range (six months or longer) and short-range programs. In the first category, he includes the construction of roads and airstrips, river navigation, the preparation of what he calls the National Map, agriculture, colonization, industry, sanitation, and literacy campaigns. In the second, he lists rural school and dispensary construction, teaching programs, recreational programs, rural road maintenance, and the supply of water systems to local communities. He asks visiting foreign technical assistance experts to take into account the planning and development organizations that already exist within many Latin American armies. With (for an officer) rare candor and understatement, he points out:

It is characteristic of the majority of the South American countries, that the military authorities exercise political and administrative control on most activities either in urban, suburban or rural centres. Their organizations and discipline can therefore guarantee the success of any program.

Finally, Sanjinés Goytia comes very close to the doctrine of preventive counterinsurgency. For he believes that the army must get to a village or town *before* the Communists or other extremists, and its job must become "one of reducing frustration by creative and visible product." If the villages and towns are overrun in a future conflict, then those people who have had an intimate civic action relationship with their nation's soldiers will be more likely to offer permanent resistance to the enemy and constitute a fifth column and intelligence source for the beleaguered regime.

With the foregoing discussion as background, what are some of the presently operative civic action programs in Latin America?

Agriculture

Many armed forces promote the breeding and raising of horses, mules, and cattle. Their veterinary corps and institutes cooperate in caring for animals and in developing and providing vaccines to the civilian sector. The Chilean Army, for example, has a General Department for the Promotion of the Breeding and Raising of Horses. It distributes studs from the National Horse Farm, controls private horse-breeding organizations, and enforces the national laws relating to mule and horse production. Also, the army has for almost a quarter of a century been conducting tractor operator courses for conscripts. Half of the graduates go into agriculture, the rest to public works projects.

As far as actual farming is concerned, Venezuela's army and air force have a military farm, described by a United States civic action mobile training team as "one of the most outstanding examples of agriculture training for military conscripts in Latin America."[5] The Honduran Air Force has one that raises pigs and poultry, training army personnel to do this in later civilian life. It supplies quality pig and poultry breeding stock to isolated villages in the country. The air force has also planted fruit trees, which will later be airlifted to villages. Bolivia, for her part, now has fourteen army farms, eight of them managed by civic action units. The one at Yerba Buena runs the only poultry-raising and -processing industry in the entire country. Yerba Buena will perhaps in time be a classic example of civic action cooperation between the military and the civilian population. Hopefully, the army will purchase grain from the local peasants for feed with which to produce eggs, and then will supply the peasants with chicks for their own chicken and egg production.

In Nicaragua, the air force is planning a flying school to train crop duster pilots and the Guardia Nacional, the Nicaraguan army equivalent, has trained, with technical aid from our Agency for International Development, enlisted men in artificial insemination of cattle. They are now working with civilian cattle raisers in seven different regions of the nation. Recently, the graduating class of the Military Academy enrolled in a 23-week course at the National Agricultural College. The purpose was to given new officers some knowledge of agriculture, livestock, and agricultural economics, so that they can be of help to the peasantry in the remoter regions. In this same vein, the armed forces of El Salvador regularly print farm information in their military periodicals, and their farms train men in the use of fertilizers, seed selection, planting, soil conservation, and so on. "The armed force spares no effort," says an El Salvadoran document, "in making each soldier a useful and trained grower of corn, rice and beans, the basic elements of the peasant diet."[6]

The army of the Dominican Republic has an interesting agricultural civic action project. When the Ministry of Agriculture reported that small rice farmers were losing up to 50 per cent of their annual rice crops to rats, the army organized a rat extermination program. Government agronomists taught pest control to army engineers. The latter were then organized into a civic action team, which is now going about the countryside issuing bulk poisons to rice farmers and teaching them how, when, and where to use them. In Castro Cuba, it is already a tradition to use army units to harvest coffee, sugar, and other crops.

Finally, forestry problems concern a number of Latin American armies. In Honduras, for instance, 40 per cent of the pine trees are afflicted with pine beetle plague, a very serious disease. So the Honduran government has called for foreign aid, and West Germany, the United Nations, and the United States have responded. Our Forestry Service has provided a survey team; our navy, helicopters; and our Agency for International Development, funds. The Honduran Air Force uses the helicopters to detect the plague, having been instructed in this (and in forest fire fighting) by the Forestry Service team.

Colonization

Bolivia and Peru are examples of military participation in internal colonization. In both of them the armed forces have primary responsibility for opening the trans-Andean regions to the east. A civic action company works in the Alto Beni region of Bolivia. Its soldiers assist the Bolivian Development Corporation and other civilian organizations to clear the woods, plant the first seeds, and build the first houses for the first permanent settlers. As for Peru, before 1959 special army detachments, with very little coordination with civilian agencies, had the mission of establishing farms to be settled by discharged veterans. Between 1959 and 1962 Army Colonization Units were established, and there was more coordination on the national and interministerial levels. The trend during this period was in the direction of providing help to already established colonists. Since 1962 the army, air force, and navy have been collaborating with civilian agencies in colonization. There has been progress, but not "great progress because of the high costs."[7] Nevertheless, the armed forces and the government are increasing their efforts. Four large settlements are planned for the regions of Nazareth, Tocache, Atalaya, and Manu. Among the special responsibilities of the army here will be helping to determine the areas of colonization, classifying and clearing the lands selected, constructing and operating the provisional installations, transporting the civilian colonists and Army Colonization Units to the projected settlements, and supporting the colonists in every aspect except credit and financing.

Industry

The armies of at least four Latin American countries—Argentina, Brazil, Chile, and Peru—engage in industrial activities that in other countries are performed either by private enterprise or non-military agencies of government. In the case of Argentina, the military has justified its involvement with four arguments. First, "the technology of weapons brought a constant need to increase the installations for their maintenance, repair, and salvage. The civilian sector, with its incipient industries and shops, was not capable of giving the required support, and consequently the increase was accomplished within the structure of the armed forces." Second, the military has not only increased production in a number of old and new fields but is responsible for "the creation of numerous small workshops [and] . . . a network of small subsidiary industries." Third, production in excess of military requirements has been offered to the civilian consumer. And fourth, "when civilian activity . . . [reached] a high degree of interest and development, the [military] factories [e.g., tractors, motorcycles] were offered for sale . . . and acquired at public auction by civilian companies. . . ."[8]

Whether one accepts these justifications—and military control of non-military industries can be a very dangerous kind of civic action—it is a fact that the Argentine military is heavily involved here, owning some of the largest industrial enterprises in the nation. The army has its Dirección General de Fabricaciones Militares (DGFM), the navy its Astilleros y Fábricas Navales del Estado (AFNE), and the air force its Industrias Aeronáuticas y Mecánicas del Estado (IAME). The army's DGFM currently directs the mining of iron ore, beryllium, copper, manganese, and sulfur, as well as the country's first blast furnace. Its goal is to possess Latin America's largest steel industry. DGFM also produces electrical motors, steel plates, farm machinery and tools, nitric acids, sulfuric acids, zinc compounds, and other chemicals for civilian and military use. The air force's IAME makes railroad equipment and rolling stock, as do the industrial establishments of the other two military branches. IAME was Argentina's first manufacturer of airplanes, trucks, tractors, motorcycles, and cars. In recent years it has been selling off some of its smaller automotive plants to civilian car manufacturers, keeping only the main plant in Cordoba. Finally, AFNE has built vessels both for the navy and for Argentine civilian shipowners, although not to the same degree as Brazil.

The Rio naval shipyard builds truck ferries and cattle barges, and its industrial shops devote about a third of their man-hours to private industry. Merchant vessels take up half of the approximately 15 million ton-days of work averaged each year in the naval drydock. AID has approved a $200,000 loan to the Brazilian Navy for rehabilitating two floating drydocks. They are to be used at the naval bases at Belem and Natal, where commercial fishing boats and coastal steamers are regularly repaired.

Research

Brazil may also be cited as a Latin American example of military participation in industrial and other research. The United States Southern Command credits Brazil's Naval Research Institute with "contributing to the development of industrial standards in Brazilian Industry" and with working on research projects of benefit to industry.[9] One such project is fish-finding sonar to help particularly the fishing industry in the depressed Northeast. Other industrially related research tasks of the Brazilian military include the preparation of maps, the preparation and dissemination of meteorological and navigational information to civilian users, aerial surveys of lands that may be expropriated, hydrography, oceanography, and scientific studies for port selection. Because of military-aided surveys of the north channel of the Amazon River, Brazil was able to construct the port of Santana in the Amapá territory, through which come annually 80,000 tons of valuable manganese ore.

The Peruvian Navy's Instituto del Mar must also be noted. One of its most immediately practical projects is the study of the characteristics, locations, and fluctuations of the anchoveta population. As one of the world's leaders in fish catch, particularly of anchovies, Peru's need for this kind of scientific information is obvious.

Education

After medicine, education is the most practiced civic action activity in Latin America today. This is hardly surprising when one remembers the illiteracy figures. In Argentina 13 out of every 100 adults cannot read or write, nor can 66 out of every 100 Hondurans. In Haiti the illiteracy rate soars to 89 per cent. This is why at least eight of the republics have educational civic action programs ranging from adult "alphabetization" to school construction, school lunch programs, vocational training, and military support of primary, secondary, and university level curricula.

Brazil has seven military colleges that provide primary and secondary educations to an estimated 40,000 students from both military and civilian families. Over half of the graduates go directly to higher civilian schools or occupations. At the university level, Brazil has her Instituto Militar de Engenharia, which produces graduates in physics, mathematics, geography, metallurgy, communications, chemistry, electronics, and civil, mechanical, electrical, automotive, and nuclear engineering. The entering military students are graduates of the army and air force academies, while the civilians are generally secondary school graduates who have spent two years in the Institute's pre-engineering course and then enrolled in its professional three-year course. In one recent year enrollment was 168, of whom 26 were civilians and 60 enlisted men.

Peru, by using 90 primary schools in various military units, aims to teach 6000 soldiers a year how to read and write, as well as to produce an additional 6000 literacy instructors from among men to be discharged. The Colombian Army claims that the literacy rate of men passing through its induction centers has risen from 40 to 85 per cent. Venezuela teaches literacy to soldiers in so-called Popular Culture Centers and Collective Centers for Literacy. But it is Guatemala that has one of the most organized military literacy campaigns in Latin America.

Guatemala's is a cooperative effort by the Ministry of Education, the United States Information Agency, the National Television Education Commission, the Guatemalan-American Foundation for Educational Television, the press, the Army Literacy Service, the army's Acción Cívica Militar, and the Army Publication Section. The latter, for example, has printed more than a million copies of the "Juan" series of primers. The newspaper *Prensa Libre* has carried literacy booklets as a Sunday supplement. With the help of the army, eighty lessons for teachers and students have been kinescoped in the studios and laboratories of the USIS and are broadcast over commercial television. Organizations like the Guatemalan-American Foundation for Educational Television donate TV sets to expand reception. And Acción Cívica Militar has functioning army literacy centers at the brigade, zone, base, and reserve command levels.

The Guatemalan results have been impressive. Of the 70,000 people (many of them migratory farmers) who enrolled in military-sponsored classes in 1963, 35 per cent completed their courses. In 1964, 658 literacy instructors and 57,028 new literates were trained in over 2400 centers. By 1966 the number of centers reached 4500. Most of the new readers and writers are civilians.

Guatemala also represents one of the best examples of military participation in a national school lunch program. Coordinated by the military but with the cooperation of the American relief organization CARE and the Guatemalan

Ministries of Defense, Education, Public Health, and the Treasury, the program gives needy students milk, precooked cereal, bread, cheese, and soybeans. Over 300,000 hot lunches are given *each day* to young scholars in over 3000 primary schools.

As for school construction, military participation has in many cases been literally from the ground up. Troops have built the schools, "built furniture for the classrooms, delivered it to the site, and seen to its installation within the classroom."[10] Thus Honduran military units, cooperating with local communities, the Ministry of Education, and the Alliance for Progress, have helped to build some 53 schools, to repair an equal number of schools, and have donated some 900 school desks. The desk-building program is multilateral cooperation at its best. For the money to buy the saws that were used to build the desks was provided by the United States Southern Command. Honduran business men sold the saws without profit, and the Honduran Air Force flew them from Miami to where they were needed. The local people provided the wood, and Honduran soldiers cut it and fabricated the desks.

Like the rest of the underdeveloped world, Latin America suffers heavily from unemployment and from a lack of people trained in needed vocations. What contributions is civic action making here?

Civilian firemen from all over Argentina are taught fire and damage control at the Puerto Belgrano Naval Base near Bahia Blanca. Fishermen and sailors, radio operators, machinists, pursers, and pilots for the merchant marine are trained by the Brazilian Navy. The Rio de Janeiro navy yard trains carpenters, electricians, machinists, metalsmiths, etc. for private industry. In Ecuador the United States military mission provides technical assistance to a three-months school for training soldiers in such tasks as culvert installation, road resurfacing, and road repair. The Peruvian Army has industrial training centers that teach mechanical drawing, electric motor rewinding, heavy equipment operation, steel work, tailoring, shoemaking, sanitation, welding, locksmithing, cooking, pipefitting, electricity, bricklaying, and carpentry. Peruvian industry eagerly seeks the graduates of these centers. It is hoped that at the completion of the current five-year plan these military industrial centers will be training 10,000 Peruvians a year. Also, the Colombian armed forces train conscripts in such fields as baking, diesel motors, accounting, lathe operation, typesetting, welding, automobile repair, cabinet-making, and building construction. The army's goal is to train 5000 conscripts each year. It hopes to do so with the continuing cooperation of Colombia's National Apprenticeship Service, established in 1957 by the International Labor Organization, whose experts still assist the Service.

Similar activity goes on in Fidel Castro's Cuba. Besides employing draftees for harvesting agricultural products, the regime teaches them how to use the advanced equipment being received from the Soviet bloc. Under a law that went into effect in 1964, the draft is used as an educational device, giving "special attention" to men who are not employed or not doing well in school. While many young people in Cuba react negatively to it, others view their three-year tour of duty as a way of getting vocational training and improving their job prospects after military service. The government is encouraging this view with slogans such as "Join the Army and Learn a Trade." Writing from Havana, *New York Times* correspondent Juan de Onis tells the interesting story of a fifteen-year-old boy named Efraim who lied about his age at the time of registration so that he could be called up next year. One of six children in a rural farm family, he said: "I know all about cutting cane and yoking oxen. What I want to learn is a trade, and they will teach me that in the army. I'll go next year for sure."[11]

Transportation and Communications

Practically all of the Latin American nations use their armed services to support and expand civilian transportation and communications. One approach is for the air force to carry civilian passengers and cargo on a regular basis. Thus Ecuador has her TAME, or Ecuadorean Military Air Transport organization. At the time of writing this book, its schedule is 57 flights a week, the passenger traffic being largely between Quito and Guayaquil. It employs civilian clerks, ticket agents, and stewardesses, and charges lower fares. It thus very definitely violates one of the basic civic action precepts, for it competes directly with commercial aviation. A better case in this regard is Colombia's SATENA.

SATENA was started a few years ago by air force commander Brigadier General Mariano Ospino Navia, an acknowledged civic action advocate. It serves the isolated 57 per cent of the country in which less than 3 per cent of the people live. Each month some 3200 passengers are carried, and 320 tons of bananas, beef, rice, corn, and other items are taken to the lucrative Bogotá market. *Newsweek's* chief Latin American correspondent has compared a flight on SATENA to "a bus ride in Mexico. Chickens flop under the seats, bags of fruit block the aisles, and the passengers frequently break forth into song." One of the regular stops is at Tres Esquinas, a remote river town. When the Colombian Air Force decided to reopen the airbase there a few years ago, it sent a hundred airmen and civilians to build a road from the base to the territorial capital of Florencia, some 70 miles away. It gave settlers part-time jobs while they cleared their land and planted crops. The base bought all of the corn grown by the settlers, who were encouraged with government loans to buy cattle. What is the result? SATENA now flies 6600 pounds of Tres Esquinas beef to Bogotá each week, not to mention what is sent downstream by boat.

The Peruvian and Brazilian air forces are other cases in point. The former flies passengers and cargo largely in the commercially unattractive Amazon regions. The latter estimates its civic action flight time at over 1000 hours per month. Moreover, Brazil's air force maintains the nation's airports and landing strips, with as much as 80 per cent of its yearly budget going for activities that in the United States are the responsibility of civilian bodies like the Federal Aviation Agency.

What do Latin American navies do for civilian transportation and communications? The Argentine Navy Meteorological Center prepares weather forecasts that are broadcast to commercial aircraft. The navy also carries cargo and passengers to and from the remote and frigid southern regions. As far as the remote south of Chile is concerned, the Chilean Navy annually transports some 5000 tons of wood, wool, and sheep from Navarino Island to Punta Arenas, and 10,000 tons from the Baker River estuary to Punta Arenas. Somewhat farther north, it provides transportation for the people, sheep, and agricultural products of the Chiloe Island region. In the Chilean Pacific, the navy regularly supplies transportation for the people and products of Easter Island, and the islands of Mocha, Santa Maria, and Juan Fernandez. It also maintains the more than 300 lighthouses and lighted buoys that dot the Chilean coast. Similarly, the Ecuadorean Navy regularly delivers water to towns along Ecuador's arid coast. The

Peruvian Navy has at least three tankers assigned to transport oil and oil products to some of the coastal ports of Peru. The Uruguayan Navy also transports fuel regularly, saving freight costs and foreign exchange.

As for the Latin American armies, Peru's is building roads and doing other chores in an effort to open up 3.5 million unused, but usable, acres. To this end, the Export-Import Bank lent her $4 million, part of the money going to equip engineer battalions building "penetration highways" through the Andes to the eastern slopes. Bolivian military civic action has engineer battalions assigned to the construction and maintenance of up to 5000 kilometers of national highways. Civic action units are also building landing strips that will not only interconnect the country, but will also permit the marketing of more products abroad. Chilean units have recently built or repaired 340 kilometers of highways, 172 meters of bridges, and 23 meters of canals. Much the same kind of figures can be given for Colombia, whose army now has 128 kilometers of highways under construction and has recently built 8 wooden bridges, rebuilt 135 kilometers of roads, and done 14,300 square meters of paving. The Paraguayan Army has 1200 men engaged in road and bridge construction within the country. Many of these engineer personnel were trained in the Canal Zone and in the United States. Lastly, in June 1964 an engineering battalion of the Guatemalan Army completed the first overland passage from the distant jungled department of El Peten to Guatemala City. This is extremely important, for the department and its products can now be tied to the national body politic and economic. Comparing the work of the army to that of the Instituto Nacional de Transformación Agraria (INTA), the United States Southern Command says: "Construction by

INTA is slow and inferior to that being done by the Battalion."[12]

This account of civic action in transportation cannot end without mentioning Brazil, in many ways unique. Military construction engineer battalions work *under contract* to civilian ministries and departments, the army getting paid as it completes sections of the railroads and highways it is building or repairing. Besides military engineers, it uses civilians hired in the work localities. Where necessary, the latter get specialized on-the-job training. Under these arrangements, the construction engineer battalions are building a 1700-kilometer railroad between the states of Rio Grande do Sul and Parana. In this same southern area, they are also building, maintaining, and repairing some 770 kilometers of roads. Moreover, a railroad battalion will presently begin joining Brasilia, the national capital in the center of the country, to the existing communications and transportation network along the Atlantic coast.

In the vast poverty-stricken Northeast, other construction engineer battalions have been busy for about ten years. The cooperating agencies are the Ministry of Communications and Public Works, the Brazilian Army, the Directorate of Transport, and the Superintendency for the Development of the Northeast (SUDENE). The civilian bodies supply the overall direction, program specifications, and money, while the army's First Engineering Group does the work, with its own men (or civilian hirees), equipment, and vehicles. The military and civilian agencies also exchange personnel on a temporary basis.

To date, the Brazilian Army has received over a billion cruzeiros for roads, almost 2.5 billion for railroads, and 187 million for irrigation. It has constructed 1356 kilometers of railroads, 272 kilometers of roads, an irrigation system with a water volume capacity of 52 million cubic meters, and 5 public dams. In addition to its primary highway- and railroad-building tasks, the First Engineering Group has provided civilians with sports facilities, schools, residential housing, apprenticeship and farm training, elementary school education, X rays, vaccinations, and medicine.[13]

Health and Hygiene

The reference to the medical activities of the Brazilian Army's First Engineering Group is a reminder that military involvement in preventive medicine, disease control, environmental sanitation, and the like is the most common kind of civic action. In some Latin American areas, civilians had never seen a doctor until the arrival of military physicians, who now treat them on a regular basis. In other areas the permanent medical facilities of the military are available to civilians. Where medical problems exceed local capabilities, military transport carries patients to the larger, better equipped centers. What are some specific country examples of medical civic action?

In Ushuaia, the world's southernmost city, the only medical facility belongs to the Argentine Navy. It is freely available to ill civilians, who, if need be, are evacuated to Buenos Aires for better care. Similarly, Colombia's Leguizamo Naval Hospital, supplied with essential equipment by the American Military Assistance Program, is the sole medical facility available to civilians of Colombia and nearby Ecuador and Peru living in a large jungle area accessible only by water or air. The other military hospitals in Colombia also try to care for needy civilians, with drugs supplied by the Ministry of Health. Colombian civic action has, in addition, established dispensaries in twenty interior towns. Each possesses a jeep ambulance, an electric dental outfit, a 10-kilowatt capacity electrical plant, twenty-four stretchers, forty-eight blankets, and a permanent $40,000 drug stock. Two floating naval dispensaries serve the medical needs of people living along the banks of the Magdelena and Putumayo rivers.

The Honduran Air Force, with the cooperation of the Health Ministry, the United States, local village committees, and private industry, has embarked upon "Alas para la Salud." This "Wings for Health" program provides drug, medical, and dental service, plus medical evacuations. Students from a dental school pitch in, too, receiving course credit. The local agent of the Colgate-Palmolive Company supplies sample tooth paste, tooth brushes, technical help, and dental educational materials. A West German drug firm does the same thing by donating medicines for the so-called medical journeys that the Guatemalan armed forces regularly undertake in the Peten jungles. As for Brazil, her Air Medical Unit Service has since its founding in 1956 taken more than one million X rays and given more than four million treatments to civilians in the interior. In Bolivia, a United States mobile medical team from the Eighth Special Forces helped to successfully combat hemorrhagic fever, a rodent-borne disease that can kill in eight days. Finally, the Bolivian Army's civic action program has been building rural community water systems. The recently completed one in Achacachi has a large filtration tank, two pumps, a large storage tank, and a complete network for distributing potable water to the homes of 6000 people.

Most of Latin America is not yet actively insurgent. An exception is Colombia, gripped for almost two decades by a violence that has taken at least 200,000 lives. There are parts of the country, such as the "Independent Republic of Marquetalia," that have not been under effective government control for years. Carved out of the departments of Tolima and Northern Huila, Marquetalia is the domain of Pedro Antonio Marin. He gets his passive local support through force, and his active support from the discontent generated by poverty, disease, and deprivation. Obviously, Marin and Marquetalia embarrass and anger the central government in Bogotá.

Colombia's violence is unique in that it is mainly the result of banditry, not Communist-inspired insurgency. And the government's response is likewise unique because of its heavier than usual emphasis on civic action. Some years ago, the Colombian representatives of CARE reported this episode:

> Belen de Umbria is located in the rich coffee highlands of western Caldas. Its population of 28,000 severely felt the ravages of the violence during the years of Colombian civil strife. . . . In Belen de Umbria lived several score of "violence widows," women with children to support whose husbands had been slain during the war years. They lacked roof and home, a place of their own. Colonel [Alvaro] Valencia [chief of Battalion Ayacucho], visited them, asked them what their greatest needs were. All of them answered, "a home." With that in mind, the military garrison in Belen de Umbria was ordered to start helping these widows build their own homes. Local municipal and church authorities pitched in, too, and the CARE Mission in Colombia was asked to supply construction tools and Cinva-Ram block-making presses.
>
> That was over a year ago. Today, more than twenty houses have been constructed in urban Belen de Umbria, and the Church and a private philanthropic group have been able to take over the house construction project. This leaves the soldiers and officers of Battalion Ayacucho free to work in the rural veredas, where the campesino has begun to organize himself to reconstruct school and home.[14]

Early in 1964, Colombia began a $30 million program in Marquetalia. "The Government is ready," said the War Minister on the eve of the program, "to occupy the region to attend to its needs and bring it all the things we have been unable to give it, such as schools, health posts, roads, and principally legitimate authority."[15] The key elements are the army engineers who, with AID backing, are putting roads into the area, connecting it for the first time with the rest of the country. Marin's reaction was immediately to seize and presumably slay a local police inspector. He then issued a communiqué from the "Revolutionary Command of Marquetalia," saying that, while *military* operations would never be tolerated, civic action units would. The bandits have not always adhered to this distinction, however. In one instance they tried to assassinate a civilian who had cooperated with civic action units.

There has been progress in building health stations, roads, and schools, and the feeling in Washington and Bogotá is that the Colombian Army is beginning to win the peasants' confidence. Thus in Latin America a little bit of insurgency (or the fear of it) may be a blessing in disguise, especially if it forces armies into civic action and soldiers and civilians into mutual understanding and cooperation for the public good.

VI Civic Action
in the Middle East
and Africa

T HE OLD TESTAMENT'S BOOK OF NEHEMIAH relates how King Artaxerxes allowed the Israelites to return and rebuild their Holy City. When the "Arabians, and the Ammonites, and the Ashdodites, heard that the walls of Jerusalem were restored, and that the breaches began to be closed up, . . . it displeased them greatly." They therefore decided to "come in the midst of them, and slay them, and so stop the work." And according to the Bible, the Israelite response was:

> Those that built on the wall, and those that bore burdens, with those that loaded,—every one with one of his hands wrought on the work, and with the other hand held a weapon.
>
> So we labored at work, while the half of them were holding the spears from the rising of the morning-dawn till the stars appeared.
>
> Likewise at the same time said I unto the people, Let every one with his young man lodge within Jerusalem, so that they may be in the night a guard to us, and during the day for the labor.

Israel

What was true for the ancient Israelites is truer still for the modern Israelis. They too have returned to Jerusalem, and their current neighbors, like their earlier ones, are greatly displeased. And their youth, as in olden times, have been trained to work simultaneously with the builder's tools and the soldier's weapons. Just as one can read in the Bible that the Israelite "builders had every one his sword fastened around his loins while they were building" Jerusalem, so can he read in the modern press about the Israeli settlement of Almagor. Many of its settlers are "military personnel, young men and women who have chosen to serve the state by turning a few more acres to grapes, tomatoes and egg plant." When they leave, "civilians will take over and another Israeli community will have been established on the frontier."[1]

Israel has, in fact, the most highly developed internal civic action program in the world. Except for the United States, she is the biggest "exporter" of civic action help abroad and the biggest "importer" of foreign civic action trainees. Egypt (in Yemen), West Germany (in Ecuador), and France (in Black Africa) are other civic action-helping countries, but none of them comes close to the Israeli involvement.

Israel's immigration—she has quadrupled her pre-independence population—has created special problems of absorption and integration. This is especially true for the more than 50 per cent of her citizens who hail from oriental countries and who have levels of skill, education, and culture far below those of Jews from the West. At the same time, her security needs have made it necessary to draft both men and women. Surrounded by states sworn to her destruction, Israel constantly calls her youth to the colors, be they educated or uneducated, skilled or unskilled, native-born or immigrant, and fluent or unlearned in the Hebrew language.

Besides defending the state, the defense forces have been given the task of fusing within their ranks the *vatik* (old-timer) and the *oleh hadash* (newcomer). Where necessary, the military begins or expands the process of making educated people out of uneducated ones and skilled people out of unskilled ones. All conscripts who need it are given training in Hebrew, history, geography, and the three R's.

The usual arrangement for a conscript without a primary school diploma is to post him to Camp Marcus on Haifa's Mount Carmel.[2] There, he completes a three-month course taught by lady soldiers, who are graduates of teachers' seminaries. At first, the army gave the course immediately upon induction and the experiment was "disastrous." The new, undisciplined recruits "nearly wrecked the camp and drove their teachers to the verge of hysteria."[3] Why? Their earlier school failures had left scars that were painfully reopened at Camp Marcus. Second, the sex of the teachers also caused resentment. Said one of them: "It isn't easy for an oriental—and most of our students come from Islamic countries—to have a woman in authority."[4] Now the course is given at the end of the recruit's period of service, when he is older, more mature, and certainly more disciplined.

The Israelis are quick to remark that in three short months they cannot possibly give their illiterate or semi-literate soldiers all they need. The basic aim is to give them a start, defeat hopelessness, and encourage them to go on after their release. The army's chief education officer, Colonel Mordechai Bar-On, claims that 85 per cent of the "maturer soldiers" are happy to make up for missed schooling, with the rest dragging along "unwillingly."[5] As one of the maturer students in the course put it:

> Sure, every one who's seen a movie wants to get on in life, but there [at a new development town in the north where he lived on relief work], I didn't know how to go about it. Once I joined the carpentry course, but it was no good. . . . Not without Hebrew and doing sums quickly. . . . I gave up and thought that was it. . . . Well, now I won't give up. I may not be a scholar when I leave but I can already read an easy newspaper and understand a textbook that isn't too difficult.[6]

Another army experimental program is designed to help school dropouts achieve a university diploma. Israeli soldiers from oriental communities study ten hours a day at one of Israel's universities. The program is sponsored by the university, the Ministry of Defense, the Ministry of Education, and two American Jewish benefactors of Sephardic extraction, Marco Mitrani of Bloomsburg, Pennsylvania, and Colonel G. R. Elyashar of New York City. The university organized and administers the course. The Ministry of Education pays two-thirds of the cost of tuition and books, with Mr. Mitrani and Colonel Elyashar paying the other third. As for the students' living expenses, these are paid either by the Ministry of Defense or the Ministry of Education. If paid by the former, the student must agree to serve as an officer upon graduation; if by the latter, he must become a teacher in a so-called development area.

It is the soldiers of Chen, the Women's Army, who largely staff the army's educational program both internally and externally. Each year 100–120 girls are graduated from the army's teacher seminary. After the two-year course, a one-year stint in border villages or slum areas, and a written thesis, they are recognized as certified teachers. In the

Morasha quarter of Jerusalem, one of the slums of the capital, Chen members teach and help children with their homework. This is part of a formal "adoption" of the schoolchildren in the area by the army men and women of the Jerusalem District Command. Besides teaching, the army is training a cadre of youth leaders from among the children and increasing sports and club activity.

The saga of Corporal Itta Szabo illustrates Chen's work in the remoter regions of the land. During her military service, she was sent to Zimrat, in the southern desert near the Gaza Strip. Most of Zimrat's inhabitants come from a backward area of Tunisia, and more than half of them—the women, to be more precise—could not read or write. As the local postman put it: "The women here all used to sign for their mail with their fingerprints. Now they all insist upon signing with pencils." The credit for this must go to Miss Szabo. When she left the village, it was with the knowledge that the Ministry of Education had awarded certificates to forty-three women for completing the first stage of their studies, and that practically every adult under fifty years of age could read Hebrew and write simply.

Miss Szabo was replaced by other soldiers, who have attempted to advance the adult pupils to simple arithmetic, geography, social studies, the Bible, and the sciences. These soldiers are part of a contingent of women sent by the army to teach in settlements in the Negev, the Galilee region, and the Beisan Valley. Their work's importance cannot be exaggerated. For 10 per cent of Israel's population, even in the larger cities, are illiterate in any language, but in villages like Zimrat "the illiterates set the cultural levels."[7]

Another example of Israeli civic action—less structured and formal than those already cited—is the work of Sergeant-Major Hazi Ovadiah of the army's Reception and Classification Base. More than a decade ago, he took it upon himself to "adopt" the mental hospital at Be'er Yaakov, south of Tel-Aviv. First, he spent a month working in the hospital so that he could learn something of the patients and their needs. Then he organized entertainments for them. Now he and his fellow soldiers conduct a variety of activities at the hospital including performances by the base orchestra on festive occasions.

Any discussion of Israel's socio-economic use of her military forces must dwell upon Gadna and Nahal. They are the two most important civic action institutions in the country. Gadna is an abbreviation of the Hebrew words "Ge 'dudei Noar" (Youth Battalions), and Nahal comes from "Noar Halutzi Lohem" (Fighting Pioneer Youth).

Actually, Gadna is not new. It existed before the Jewish state was recreated, training the signalers for the Haganah, the fighting arm of the official Zionist underground during the British mandate. Though it is under military command, Gadna is today the joint responsibility of the defense and education ministries. Its aim is to train young people for pioneering and the study of specialized military and technical skills. It operates in over 140 secondary schools, 35 technical schools, 21 agricultural schools, and 250 social clubs. Additionally, Gadna has a farm at Be'er Ora, which prepares people for Nahal; an acclaimed symphony orchestra, which regularly performs abroad; weekly radio programs; a fortnightly magazine called *Ba'mahane Gadna* (In the Gadna Camp); and a regularly appearing wall newspaper, *Be'ohalei Gadna* (In the Tents of Gadna). It has several branches: marksmanship, signals, sea, and air. Air-Gadna members learn to fly gliders and light aircraft. Successful sea students can go directly to petty officer status when they enter the navy.

Gadna's members are all volunteers between the ages of fourteen and eighteen, drawn from the schools, the youth movements, and the immigrant villages. In a recent typical year, some 29,000 boys and girls received Gadna training. Nearly 25,000 competed in athletics; over 27,000 went on Gadna-sponsored hikes; 2700 trained at a Gadna base; and 4000 did two weeks of national service in border settlements.[8]

Gadna has been both successful and publicized. It has therefore captured the attention of foreign leaders. Students have come to Israel from such Latin American countries as Bolivia, Ecuador, Costa Rica, Colombia, Peru, and Venezuela, and from the two Congos (Brazzaville and Leopoldville), the Central African Republic, Togo, Malagasy, Nigeria, Liberia, Ghana, Singapore, Sierra Leone, the Ivory Coast, and Tanganyika to enroll in Gadna courses given in English, French, and Spanish.

At the same time, Israel has dispatched her own military men abroad to advise on Gadna-like projects in places like Latin America, the Ivory Coast, the two Congos, Ghana, the Central African Republic, Liberia, and Tanganyika. One of her early problems was the age disparity between her officers and those elsewhere. The average age for Israeli military instructors at home is twenty-two for lieutenants and twenty-six for majors. Equivalent officers in Africa, Asia, and Latin America, "whom they were supposed to advise, teach, and instruct, were old enough to be their fathers. . . . They feared losing face by accepting the younger men as their teachers."[9] A resourceful people, the Israelis solved the problem by making thirty-five the minimum age for foreign assistance assignments, a solution which also opens up the ranks for promotion of younger officers at home.

Tanganyika (now part of Tanzania) is a good illustration

of Gadna foreign aid. In the early 1960s, while Tanganyikan students were still in Israel completing military-sponsored youth and agricultural training courses, an Israeli team was sent abroad to advise the Tanganyikans in the setting up of a pilot program of their own. In short order, the Israelis produced a printed plan for a pioneer youth training center at Rugemba. It was based

> . . . on the premise that the rural communities which constitute the vast majority of Tanganyika's population must furnish the nucleus from which a flourishing national culture will grow as the basis for the national economy. The village shall serve as a catalyst in the process of national revival and pass its pioneering spirit to the urban population as well.

The fields to be served were:

> 1. Auxiliary agricultural training and organization in rural areas.
> 2. Home industry and vocational training for women.
> 3. Training of community leaders and instructors.
> 4. Youth leadership and training in organization.[10]

The blueprint discusses the selection of candidates, study tours and field work for the students within Tanganyika, scholarship programs for advanced students in Israel, training aids, the role of women in the community, the work-study day, and suggestions for establishing a model family-sized farm. It also details plans for organizing and managing the center, including its budget, the estimated investment and operating costs, and detailed lists of the quantities and kinds of materials needed for the students, their living quarters, the dining room, kitchen, pantry, classrooms, staff rooms, lounges, halls, laundry, women's workshops, carpentry tools, plumbers' tools, machinists' tools, dispensary, and office equipment.

This kind of effort by Israel has brought her testimonials by Africans. For example, when the Central African Republic's Ambassador to Israel presented his credentials, he said:

An experiment, tried out successfully in Israel, has permitted the establishment in the C.A.R., with the invaluable assistance of Israel's experts, of an organism designed to further civic and technical education: the National Pioneering Youth is the crucible in which the national and civic sentiments of our young generation are being forged. . . .[11]

Earlier, Chief S. P. L. Akintola, the late Prime Minister of West Nigeria, said:

I see in the *Gadna* Youth Corps hope for Nigerian youth. Africa is one geographically and physically, but has been divided through the imperialistic machination. It is our duty to unite the entire continent and *Gadna* is a stepping-stone toward this future greater unity.[12]

Soon after Israel's independence, her parliament passed a Special Law on Military Service, which contained these paragraphs:

1. Agricultural training will be an integral part of military service (but the Ministry of Defense has the right to exclude certain units from this training in accordance with its program).
2. Special kinds of equipment and of service will be established so that groups of young people who are organized in one of the youth movements with the goal of establishing themselves on the land can maintain maximum unity during their period of military service and can realize their objective, namely, establishing themselves on the soil.[13]

The first paragraph legitimized and institutionalized Nahal; the second permitted its special kind of organization and recruitment. In the early years, *all* army recruits were given farm training and socialist indoctrination in the ways of the *kibbutz* and the *kvutza*, Israel's cooperative and collective settlements. "Because there was non-socialist resistance to the use of universal military service as an agency for propagating socialism, Nahal was transformed, in the mid-1950s, from an obligatory into a voluntary instrument."[14]

Boys and girls may be posted to it as individuals. For example, agricultural school dropouts are very often put in that branch of the service. But the normal pattern is for groups of Israeli youths who are planning to establish agricultural and other settlements to join Nahal *en masse*. This has at least two advantages. It prevents the breakup of these valuable groups, and it permits their *esprit de corps* to be transferred and used during their period of military service. Upon the completion of that service, the group permanently joins an existing settlement or creates a new one of its own.

Generally speaking, how does Nahal function? Israeli men are usually drafted for a period of two and one-half years. For the first three months, a Nahal recruit gets his basic military training. During the next twelve, he and the other members of his group are sent to an agricultural settlement, to Nahal's own agricultural college, or, in the case of soldiers slated to study agronomy, to the civilian Rupin Agricultural College.

Though always under military jurisdiction, he is essentially a farmer or farm trainee by day and a soldier and military trainee by night and on weekends. His second fifteen months is divided sequentially into five months of advanced military training and ten of agricultural work on the frontier or in a labor-short area.

The very latest Nahal innovation is industrial groups, one of which is Ogen Arad, to be set up in the Negev city of Arad. After their discharge, its members will create a co-operative for metalwork, mechanics, and carpentry. In the initial period, the men will work in various industrial shops in town and the women at the local hotel. Upon hearing of the establishment of Ogen Arad, Israeli Prime Minister Levi Eshkol wrote:

> Just as in the past we expected the communal and coopera-tive villages to build up Jewish agriculture, so we expect the Nahal industrial groups to grow into thousands and devote themselves to the country's industrial development. This will be a most valuable contribution to our country, both nation-ally and socially.[15]

The success and number of Nahal industrial groups remain to be seen. The more traditional agriculturally oriented groups have already proved themselves. More than 50 per cent of their enrollees have remained with their original youth groups and are living in rural settlements. Nahal can point to at least five training farms, fifty-six settlements all of whose members came from Nahal, and ninety-eight Nahal "reinforced" settlements.

Nahal has attracted foreigners perhaps even more than has Gadna. Latin Americans, Africans, and Asians have come to Israel from over thirty countries to study Nahal, and Israelis have gone to their countries to advise in the establishment of Nahal-like units and programs. Ecuadoreans, Peruvians, Venezuelans, Colombians, and Bolivians have participated in Nahal courses in Israel. When the first Peruvians returned, the Peruvian Army established its Colonization Office. As for Ecuador, her Defense Minister has observed agricultural and irrigation methods in Israel, and a team of Israeli water resources and agronomy experts, headed by an army major, spent two years in Ecuador's Manabi region. Further, Israeli officers in Bolivia were once paradoxically responsible for a temporary civic action delay. According to a United States Army report, the program of the Bolivian Army's dehydrated food production plant "was set back because of the unexpected departure of Lt Col Paz Soldan, the Chief, to Israel for three months." The same report also notes that the supervision of the Bolivian Army farm at Chirapaca was turned over to the Israelis.[16]

Much of the same thing can be reported concerning cooperation between Israel and Afro-Asia. For instance, a Nahal mission in Ghana helped to establish the Builders Battalion and the Young Pioneers. In Burma,

> . . . the military early developed an interest in and a rapport with their opposite numbers in Israel, . . . being especially interested in the colonization activities of the Israeli army. . . . The Burmese military were interested in the colonization of sparsely settled areas near their borders not only for national security reasons, but also to create employment opportunities and to minimize potential unrest among discharged soldiers who might otherwise swell the insurgents' ranks.[17]

The insurgents being referred to could be the White Flag Communists, the Karen rebels, the Kachins, or some other dissident minority. In any case, Burma sent army officers and ex-servicemen to Israeli settlements. Upon their return home, they established cooperative villages under Israeli supervision in the Namsong region of northern Burma.

Now what about other countries in the region, besides Israel?

The Rest of the Middle East and North Africa

At least nine other countries—Afghanistan, Algeria, Egypt, Iran, Jordan, Morocco, Libya, Tunisia, and Turkey—use or have used their armed forces to foster economic and social development. Israel's neighbor, Jordan, suffers from aridity and chronic water shortages. One such shortage in the Jerusalem-Bethlehem area was particularly severe. So Jordanian Army engineers, using American Army surplus quick-coupling pipe, laid pipelines from wells not far from Hebron to Solomon's Pools, connecting them to locally built lines to Jerusalem. As a result, over 300,000 gallons of water now flow each day into the Bethlehem-Jerusalem area through this pipeline.

Further, Afghanistan has for some years had a military Labor Corps, which has built arterial roads and permanent bridges. Article 8 of Algeria's Constitution alludes to civic action by saying that the army "assures the defense of the territory of the Republic and participates in the economic and social activities of the nation. . . ." As for *French* Algeria, some observers estimate that 30 to 60 per cent of the French military effort during the rebellion was devoted to civic action.[18] That the final outcome was unfavorable to the French cannot be blamed on civic action. By the time they instituted it, the minimal political demands of the Arabs were beyond the reach of civic action, no matter how intrinsically worthwhile.

The same can be said for Egyptian civic action in Yemen. Besides their more military contributions to the Yemeni civil war, Egyptian troops have supplied pumps, tractors, seeds, money, schools, sports, and youth programs to villages under their control. But here again, by itself civic action cannot possibly overcome the intense violence between the Yemeni rebels and royalists, or the fact that Egyptian help to one side is considered foreign intervention by the other.

In Ottoman Turkey, there was no modern educational system. The "first stirrings of modern political interest occurred among teachers and students of technical subjects in military academies, which were in fact the only indigenous modern educational institutions of that great Empire."[19] Nowadays, the Turks continue to use

> . . . the army as an instrument for general cultural development in the immediate areas surrounding major army installations. The location of the First Army headquarters in Erzurum has stimulated the effort to develop that city as the cultural center of eastern Turkey. Among the specific reasons cited by Turkish authorities for the establishment of a new university in Erzurum was the existence there of large numbers of military children, who would be likely candidates for university education. The impact of such an educational enterprise on eastern Turkey may be considerable. In recent years, the growth elements in these areas—the more educated and the more wealthy—had been lured increasingly into Ankara and Istanbul by the more comfortable life and greater intellectual companionship to be found in these cities. Those parts of the country most in need of their dynamic elements were thus deprived of them. The army now tends to reverse this flight from the rural east and to provide a new dynamism that is likely to speed modernization by using public resources to build institutions that are educative, egalitarian, and functional.[20]

But Turkey has another problem. Nearly 40,000 villages are without schools and 60 per cent of the adults and at least 50 per cent of all draftees can neither read nor write. So one of the largest civic action efforts is the eradication of illiteracy, which the army has attacked in several ways. First, male teachers can fulfill their military obligation to the state by teaching instead of actually entering the armed forces. Second, officer candidates have often been sent out to villages to teach for as much as eighteen months. (Eleven thousand did so in 1962). Third, men already officers can be ordered to active duty to teach in primary schools. (This happened to several thousand in 1960.) Fourth, the Turkish Army, with the advice and help of the United States, has established literacy training centers from which 10–12 thousand soldiers graduate every two months. After graduation, they go on to finish their military service.

The hopes of the Turkish military literacy training program may be summed up in the words of one of its graduates: "Two months ago, when I came to this camp, I could read and write only two words—my first and last names. Now I am reading to you a speech which I have written myself."[21]

Turkey's neighbor to the east, Iran, has one of the largest civic action programs. Though not so comprehensive as Israel's, it ranks with some of the best in Latin America. It operates in seven fields: engineering, sanitation, agriculture, education, vocational training, communications, and transportation. Besides subcommittees that carry out specific projects and an Executive Committee of national agency representatives who plan and direct these projects, there is a Permanent Committee at the ministerial level that supervises the overall effort. The members of that Permanent Committee are the chief of the Supreme Commander's Staff of the Imperial Iranian Armed Forces, the director of the national Plan Organization, the director of the Red Lion and Sun Society, the director of the Imperial Organization Society Services, and several ministers of the national government. What are some of the things that are done?

In the areas of the Persian Gulf and the Gulf of Oman, the temperature reaches 130 degrees and the humidity 80 per cent. There is little rain, many locusts, few medical facilities: in short, a situation generally conducive to misery. The Iranian Navy is the only government agency with capabilities and responsibilities suited to the reduction of the misery. It is the only reliable communications channel along a coast whose hinterland has few land links. Thus it attempts to care for the medical needs of the civilian population. It regularly carries drinking water to humans and animals in danger of dying of thirst. Suitable drinking water is a problem in interior Iran as well. In 50,000 villages the water is unclean. Consequently, each army brigade has a standing order to cover the polluted springs in its region and install water pipes in at least three villages each month.

The Iranian Army also teaches agriculture and tractor driving in some 14 military garrisons, and the Extension Corps of about 500 men teaches modern farming methods to civilian farmers. The army has at least six vocational training centers at which 200 conscripts learn trades and skills in their final three months of military service. Training is offered in masonry, welding, carpentry, plumbing, metalwork, tailoring, mechanics, electricity, leatherwork, and shoe repair. There is also a Health Corps composed of 1100 high school and university graduates (including over 100 physicians and 300 medical technicians), who move about the countryside giving medical care, establishing clinics, and teaching sanitation.

Perhaps the army's most successful civic action is in literacy training. It claims that 50,000–75,000 illiterate inductees leave the army two years later able to read and write the

Farsi language. Outside of the army proper, there is the heralded work of the Literacy Corps, now numbering over 17,000 men. Draftees who can qualify take three months of intensive special training and then complete their military obligation as uniformed teachers in the villages. By 1965 they were instructing 69,667 boys, 14,687 girls, 32,294 adult men, and 1928 adult women.

Finally, there is the Iranian Air Force. It is engaged in the typical kinds of activities already discussed for other countries. For example, it uses modified air transports to ferry insecticides in the continuing anti-locust war. It detects and fights forest fires. It transports and drops food, fodder, and other supplies to flooded and snowed-in areas. And it engages in general disaster relief and rescue.[22]

This mention of relief and rescue recalls an episode in the Zagros Mountains of Iran. It started as a rescue of Americans and ended also as a civic action project for Iranians. An American aircraft had crashed at an altitude of over 15,000 feet, and a Special Forces team was sent to recover the airmen's bodies. The mission succeeded where two earlier tries had failed, apparently because the American soldiers obtained the help of the local tribesmen through an offer of medical care. As the surgeon of the John F. Kennedy Center for Special Warfare phrased it: "Even in this desolate area, apparently almost uninhabited, there soon came to this aid station, operating from the rear of an ambulance, a sick call of 80 patients a day. Medicine has this appeal for those who have not had it available."[23]

The rebuilding of the rail bridge at Khledia, in Tunisia, is still another example of Middle Eastern civic action. The original bridge was destroyed by flood in 1964. Its destruction was felt immediately because it was the only route to iron, phosphate, and other mines, from whose extracted ores the Tunisians earned $1.5 million each and every month. When the government discovered that ordinary and completely local efforts would mean a construction time of 90 days (and a loss of $4.5 million), it turned to the United States.

The original bridge was destroyed in October. (See Table 6 for a chronology of events in the Khledia Bridge project.) By November 12, the liaison officer of the American Seventh Engineer Brigade was already on the scene. On November 23, the government of Tunisia and AID officials signed the project agreement. The first American C-130 aircraft with bridge parts and an advanced army engineer party arrived on November 25. The assembling of the bridge began December 1. The United States portion of the bridge was completed by December 7, the same day on which the Tunisian Railway installed the rails. All work on the bridge was completed by December 9, and the formal dedication took place two days later. Thus, the entire rebuilding took *less than a month*. When it was finished, the American government presented the new bridge to the Tunisians as a gift.

The Khledia bridge is an excellent example of joint American-local civic action projects. United States Army engineers did the work together with their counterparts in the Tunisian Army and with the Tunisian Public Works Ministry, and the Agency for International Development supplied the funds for the first AID-supported civic action project on the continent of Africa.

Sub-Saharan Africa

Black Africa south of the Sahara Desert is, relatively speaking, at the bottom of the civic action totem pole. This ought to surprise no one. After all, they are the newest sovereignties, with the newest, smallest, and least trained armies. Yet the pressure for them to engage in military civic action is great. In Liberia, for example, both private local and foreign construction contractors are reluctant to take on projects outside of Monrovia. Why should they face the problems and dis-

Dedication Sign Appearing on Khledia Bridge (*U.S. Army photograph*)

Table 6
Chronology of Events, Bridge Project,
Khledia, Tunisia

12–14 Nov: Liaison visit by Major Hutchins, 7th Engineer Brigade.

19 Nov: Tunisian Railway and Public Works begin preparation of pier foundations.

20 Nov: Major Komoto, Bridge Project Officer, 7th Engineer Brigade, arrives.

21 Nov: Final approval for project received from Washington.

23 Nov: Project agreement signed by USAID and GOT [Government of Tunisia] officials.

25 Nov: First C-130 aircraft with bridge parts and advance party arrives from Co B, 293d Engr Bn, 24th Engr Gp (Const).

26 Nov: Second C-130 arrives. Thanksgiving meals for advance party in homes of Capts. Banda, Bonner and Mr. Stiles, AID. Capt Rosenthal, 7th Brigade Medical Officer, arrives.

27 Nov: 3rd, 4th and 5th C-130 arrive.

28 Nov: 6th thru 11th C-130 arrive. All remaining B Co personnel arrive.

29 Nov: 12th thru 15th C-130 arrive. Job site is prepared and all unloading is completed. Col Wilson, 24th Engr Gp and Lt Col Rufavoid [?], CO 293d Engr Bn arrive.

30 Nov: Col Banks, CO 7th Engr Brigade, arrives. Bridge center line laid. Painting of components is started.

1 Dec: Bridge assembly started. Painting continues. Pier construction started.

2 Dec: Piers 55% complete, painting and assembly continue. Reception given by Lt Col Spiece, USARMA.

3 Dec: Weather interferes with welding but construction continues. Press visits site. Reception given by Mr. Goldberger, Chief Industry Div, USAID, Tunis.

4 Dec: Final preparations for launching of bridge. Unfavorable weather continues.

5 Dec: Bridge is launched.

6 Dec: Bridge lowered to bearings. Track being laid.

7 Dec: US portion of bridge construction completed. Rails installed by Tunisian Railway.

8 Dec: Rail work completed. Engineer officers, Embassy, USAID, OUSARMA [Office of the United States Army Military Attaché] officials involved in project received by President Bourguiba in his Carthage palace.

9 Dec: Work completed on bridge. US troops given tour to Kairouan, Sousse and Hammamet by Tunisian officials.

10 Dec: Load testing of bridge completed.

11 Dec: Dedication of bridge by Secretary of State for Presidency and National Defense Bahi Ladgham. . . . Reception by Tunisian officials for US troops in Amilcar Hotel. C-124 arrives for departure of US personnel.

12 Dec: Departure of US Engineer troops by US military aircraft.

14 Dec: Departure of EUCOM PIO [European Command Public Information Office] representatives by civil air.

Source: U.S. Department of Defense, International Security Affairs (1965).

Table 7

Persons Associated with Khledia Bridge Project

Mr. Francis H. Russell—Ambassador, US Embassy

Mr. Leo G. Cyr—Deputy Chief of Mission, US Embassy

Lt. Colonel Donald C. Spiece—Army Attaché, US Embassy

Captain Norman R. Banda—Military Assistance Program Logistics Officer, OUSARMA [Office of the United States Army Military Attaché], Tunisia

Captain Laurence D. Bonner—Military Assistance Program Training Officer, OUSARMA, Tunisia

CWO Stuart D. Van Ostrand—Administrative Officer, OUSARMA, Tunisia

SP-7 Edward F. Small—Administrative Assistant, OUSARMA, Tunisia

Sgt E-6 Judson D. C. Bailey—Military Assistance Program Logistics NCO, OUSARMA, Tunisia

Sgt E-6 Lloyd H. Peterson—Military Assistance Program Training NCO, OUSARMA, Tunisia

Mr. Daly C. Lavergne—Director, USAID, Tunisia

Mr. Benjamin H. Goldberger—Chief, Industry Division, USAID, Tunisia

Mr. William J. Baker—Acting Deputy Director, USAID, Tunisia

Mr. Winthrop Stiles—Engineer, USAID, Tunisia

Mr. William Astill—Information Officer, USIS [United States Information Service], Tunisia

Mr. James Pettit—US Peace Corps Engineer assigned to Tunisian Ministry of Public Works

Mr. Robert Farrel—US Peace Corps Engineer assigned to Tunisian Ministry of Public Works

President Habib Bourguiba—President of Tunisia

Mr. Bahi Ladgham—Secretary of State to the President and for National Defense

Mr. Habib Ben Ammar—Chef de Cabinet, Tunisian Defense Ministry

General Habib Tabib—Chief of Staff, Tunisian Army

Colonel Bechir Hamza—Chief of Engineers, Tunisian Army

Major Mahmoud Gannouni—Commander of El Aouina Caserne

Captain Chine—Engineer Officer, Tunisian Army

Captain Abdelhamid Lejouad—Engineer Officer, Tunisian Army

Mr. Mustapha Dellagi—President Director General of the Tunisian National Railroad

Mr. Mokhtar Latiri—Chief Engineer, Roads & Bridges, Tunisian Ministry of Public Works

---

Source: U.S. Department of Defense, International Security Affairs (1965).

comforts of heavy work in the interior, with its high costs and low profits? Why should they go to the provinces when work awaits them in the capital? Because they will not, public agencies must do so. Often this means the military. For despite their own lacks, they usually have a slight edge over their civilian brethren in education, skills, administrative know-how, discipline, and national outlook.

Thus we find that Ethiopian units are building new schools and roads, jointly with civilians and with the encouragement of Emperor Haile Selassie. Guinea and Mali, like the already mentioned Ghana, have paramilitary builders' or workers' brigades for "veterans and unemployed youths." This is a method of human resources mobilization that "will undoubtedly be emulated by an increasing number of the governments of other new states, partly because of the imperatives of rapid economic development, and partly because of the growing gap between the large numbers of youths leaving primary school and the limited number of career opportunities in the society."[24] Further, half of the military tour of duty of the Ivory Coast conscriptees is devoted to public work projects, and she and her other partners in the Conseil de l'Entente (Niger, Upper Volta, and Dahomey) engage in the more classical kinds of military civic action: road repair, land clearing, sanitation, and air field maintenance. But Dahomey has had an unusual program centered around the reward of housing.

Military dependent housing in Dahomey has been "superior to that of the local civilian community, not so much better that it elicited an invidious response, but good enough to excite a desire on the part of the local population to emulate." Military families who want to continue to reside in this superior housing must therefore obey these rules:

(1) Houses must be kept clean by 20th century standards.

(2) Dependents had to avail themselves of the modern medical facilities (i.e., no witch doctors, etc.).

(3) Children had to attend school.[25]

If not—if, for example, their children go around naked in public or their homes are indecorous—they face the risk of losing their homes. While the major benefit of this program obviously goes to the military community, the civil population is at least exposed to the example of better sanitation practices, social behavior, school attendance, and the like.

Finally, there is a current French experiment, tried largely in the former African colonies, that might well be repeated by other "givers" of foreign aid. Mature young soldiers between twenty-two and twenty-seven (who in most cases took their college and professional degrees under draft deferments) are being sent out to teach, do engineering work, and engage in other technical assistance activities. More than 60 per cent of the men are in teaching. Wearing civilian clothes, they teach abroad for the school year, returning to France for basic military training. In the future, they may be allowed to spend their entire sixteen months of military service as teachers.

The program began in 1963 with 300 men. It had 1300 in 1964 and approximately 1800 in 1965. Its director hopes that the draftees will soon fill one-third of the 10,000 French technical assistance jobs in Black Africa. Perhaps they will. Already one-third of the military teachers have signed agreements to stay on at their posts when they become civilians.[26]

Like all good bilateral agreements (whether in business or diplomacy), this one must be maximally beneficial to both sides. The benefits to the Africans and to French foreign policy are obvious. But there are also internal benefits to

France for at least two reasons. As the *New York Times* stated them:

> The first is cost. Privates are lower-paid employees than civilians, especially in posts requiring a high degree of specialized training.
>
> The second reason is that the Government can assign soldiers to teaching posts abroad without arousing domestic criticism. There is a teacher shortage in France.[27]

VII   Civic Action in Vietnam

and the Far East

"U.S. SOLDIERS IN VIETNAM SERVE CIVILIANS
ALONG WITH MILITARY"
"U.S. MEDICS ASSIST VIETNAM TRIBESMEN"
"G.I. 'DOCTOR' AIDS VIETNAM VILLAGES"
"MARINES IN VIETNAM GET 10 INSTRUCTIONS
ON MAKING FRIENDS"
"A U.S. ARMY TEAM IN VIETNAM HEALS SICK
AND AIDS HOMELESS"
"AMERICANS USE CIVIC ACTION PROGRAMS TO
COUNTER VIETNAMESE PEASANTS' FEARS"

T HESE HEADLINES from Philadelphia and New York newspapers relate to only a few of the articles printed about military civic action in South Vietnam. From them many readers may have got the impression that Asian civic action has been an affair confined to Vietnam. But neither for the present nor the past is this a correct impression.

In the early 1900s the American War Department established the free public school system of the Philippines, and American soldiers taught reading, writing, and arithmetic to Filipino children. After the Second World War, United States military government in Okinawa, in addition to normal occupation duties, used agricultural equipment to condition the soil for crops. Currently, SEATO, the South East

151

Asia Treaty Organization, includes civic action in its military exercises. In both the Air Boon Choo and Ligtas exercises of 1964, the participating forces built bridges and roads and gave medical care to civilians, water pumps and tanks to villages, and writing materials to school children. SEATO also has its Military Technical Training School in Thailand, which gives a three-year course.

As for individual countries, almost a dozen of them besides South Vietnam use or have used their armies in a civic action capacity. Nor is South Vietnam the only Far Eastern country that worries about insurgency. India has her dissident Naga minority and worries about infiltration from Pakistani Kashmir. Burma has her Shan, Kachin, and Karen rebels. The Filipino Huks are down but not entirely out. And Thailand is nervously watching her restless Lao-related minority in the Northeast. So, while the overriding interest in Vietnam demands a discussion of that country, fairness and completeness require a discussion of civic action in other countries of the region as well.

These can be divided into three categories. They are: (1) insurgency-absent countries, or countries that have had little or no Communist subversive insurgency, (2) insurgency-passed or dormant countries, that is, places that have suffered and survived Communist subversive insurgency, (3) insurgency-active countries, those presently facing the threat.

Insurgency-absent Countries

Here are included South Korea, India, and Pakistan. As noted earlier, the American Armed Forces Assistance to Korea (AFAK) program was the genesis of America's post-war overseas civic action involvement. As the American troops remained in Korea, so did the commitment to AFAK and to civic action. By the end of 1955, AFAK had, with $15 million worth of American materials, completed 2914 construction projects. Their estimated value to the Korean economy was nearly $50 million. By the beginning of 1959, the projects totaled 3780, the worth of American materials was over $20 million, and the economic value to Korea was $66 million. By the fall of 1960, the number of projects had risen to 4000, and by July 1963 to 4500. In concrete terms, these 4500 projects meant 2000 schools, 250 churches, 350 orphanages, over 400 civic buildings, 350 public health facilities, and a myriad of bridges, public utilities, flood control systems, and so on. The 1964 program included 286 classrooms, besides the 3745 built since 1954, and materials for school kitchens, sewer systems, hospital additions, and mobile medical clinics.[1]

The now defunct Korean Civil Assistance Command must also be noted. For it suggests an important justification for civic action: the United States government turned to this military agency only when (and as long as) it had difficulty recruiting American civilians for foreign aid work in Korea. Second, it also illustrates military civic action phaseout: as soon as the predecessor agency of AID succeeded in recruiting its own organization, KCAC functions were turned over one by one without interruption.

An interview with the Indian Military Attaché in Washington proved again that in civic action, as in other matters, people often use different words to describe essentially the same thing. When asked whether the Indian Army engages in civic action, Brigadier M. M. Nath pointed to a gigantic map of India's northern frontier and said: "With frontiers like that to be kept, we can't be involved with civic action. It will detract from the army's primary function of defending the country." But when he was asked if the army had an education program in the ranks, he said: "Yes, Yes, Yes," telling how the army teaches Hindi to all entering recruits who do not know it. And finally, when he was asked: "Isn't that civic action?", he smiled and produced a document describing the work of the Indian Army Educational Corps. It says:

> . . . the army is the largest single organization in the country dealing with Adult Education. And what goes on in the army educational field has naturally far-reaching effect. . . . The training as a whole [that] Jawans [Indian G.I.s] get changes the whole concept of their life. When they go back to the village on leave or on retirement they bring about a change in the atmosphere of the village community; through them the education they receive in the army filters down to the village population. And of course they set an example, standing for a national approach to problems and bringing to bear on problems an objective outlook free of parochial loyalties . . . [Within the army itself, the soldiers] speak the same language. Hindustani or simple Hindi is the common language of the army and it has proved to be the greatest single factor in the spread of a common language in India.

In the northern part of West Pakistan there is a mountain-surrounded area known as the Gilgit Agency. Until 1958 the only land access to its principal town, also called Gilgit, was a mule track that the Army Corps of Engineers had built ten years earlier via the Kaghan Valley. But the 14,000-foot pass through which the track went was open for only three months of the year. Thus, for practical purposes the area was commercially inaccessible. Consequently, in 1956 the Central Public Works Department planned an all-weather road along the Indus River. In addition to linking Gilgit to the rest of West Pakistan through Swat State, the project called for reducing the distance to Rawalpindi by 50 miles. This was to be done by building a new road between Besham Qila and Abbottabad, avoiding the 7300-foot-high Shangla Pass, which is snowbound during part of the winter. The estimated cost of this construction was 60.6 million rupees. But since so great an amount was not then available to the Public Works Department, it was decided to involve the army at a revised cost of 30.5 million rupees. "This by itself was a major contribution, because this saving could be utilized on other civil development projects."[2] And so the Indus Valley road is being built by two agencies: the Army Corps of Engineers and the civilian Public Works Department. The first is responsible for the 158 miles between Karora and Chilas; the second for the 187 miles between Chilas and Gilgit.

How many people are employed on the project? Approximately 750 military engineers and 1000 locally hired civilian laborers. One might suppose that in a poor country like Pakistan, getting workers would be no problem. But actually it is not at all easy to get civilian laborers. During the summer months, local people move from lower to higher ground looking for pasture, or they prefer to work for timber contractors at higher wages. While more job-seekers are available during the winter, the weather is cold and the work is hard and dangerous. Men must go along cliff sides that frighten mountain goats. The slightest misstep may send one falling into the river, hundreds of feet below. And, in fact, some twenty civilians and soldiers have already lost their lives through accidents.

Despite these conditions, over 118 miles, or about half, of the road is done. When completely finished, it will give Gilgit a dependable all-year, all-weather road. Products brought into the area should be cheaper. It will be easier to transport heavy equipment and machinery needed to develop the area's mineral and forest resources. Great sums of government money now being spent on subsidizing the transportation of food grain by air or through the 14,000-foot-high Babusan Pass will be put to new use.

Insurgency-passed or Dormant Countries

Indonesian army and air force officers have played a large role in the nation's administration ever since the independence and postindependence struggles. This may explain why Colonel William Swarm, civil affairs officer of United States Pacific Headquarters in 1960, concluded after a visit that "there is little Americans can teach Indonesia about civic action." But on the other hand, the *New York Times* reported later that Americans and other Westerners in Indonesia were "disappointed by the army's recent lack of initiative in using its transport and manpower to help people in the critical areas."[3]

Between these two extremes of observer judgment there are some facts to go on. In 1963 Indonesia requested, and the United States sent, two civic action mobile training teams. Between fiscal years 1963 and 1965 the Military Assistance Program and the Agency for International Development contributed $5 million to Indonesian civic action. Under one part of the program, Indonesian officers attended American universities, where they studied management, finance, and related subjects. Under another, MAP contributed Indonesian currency to help pay for the army's public works and farm improvement programs. AID developed special corn in Indonesia and planted pilot plantings for what the army there calls its "battalion farming program." Additionally, American military engineers have trained their counterparts to use heavy equipment, and in West Java the latter have been fixing roads, buildings, small dams, and rice irrigation systems. Finally, the Indonesian Army has reportedly begun to change one-third of its infantry battalions from combat to civic action functions.[4]

What about Indonesia's neighbors, Malaya (now part of Malaysia) and the Philippines? So far, they have been the most successful (and most written about) Western reactions to aggressive Communist insurgency. In Malaya, civic action played its *small* part, particularly when it was decided to resettle the so-called Chinese squatters in "New Villages." British and Commonwealth troops helped to build them. Infantry units often adopted individual new villages, giving them protection from the CTs (Communist terrorists) and some social and economic amenities as well. Military medical men and facilities were made available to civilians, and military engineers supplied roads, bridges, and sanitation.

But one cannot really claim that the success of Malayan counterinsurgency was largely due to civic action. True, there was excellent cooperation among the military, the police, and the civil administration. While crucially necessary for successful counterinsurgency, this is not what is usually meant by civic action. Second, almost 100 per cent of the guerrillas were of Chinese extraction. They were thus easily identified from the racially different Malays, Indians, and Europeans. Third, there was no common international frontier between Malaya and an insurgent-aiding state, so that there was almost no infiltration of foreign men and supplies. Fourth, the ratio of government to rebel forces ranged from 8 to 1, to 17.5 to 1.[5] And fifth, the British had a powerful political and psychological trump card: they could promise (and later grant) independence through peaceful negotiations. The use of such a trump card against the rebels was obviously impossible in already independent South Vietnam and the Philippines.

If civic action did not play an important role in the Malayan counterinsurgency, it did in the Philippine response to the Huk Rebellion, one of the most nearly successful Communist insurgencies in postwar history. It was *nearly* successful, rather than successful, because Ramón Magsaysay, first as Secretary of National Defense and then as President, relied heavily on unconventional military tactics, including civic action. But to do so, he first had to change this image of the military that a retired Filipino colonel described at a seminar at Fort Bragg:

> As I recall those days, it was very normal for a company commander in the field to dispatch a patrol from squad to platoon size to serve a warrant of arrest in an isolated village. This patrol would reach the village, locate the individual (if he were surprised and found there) and would return to town without further action. Junior leaders of these formations did not attempt to stay long enough in this village to get friendly with the people, find out what were their problems, and if their patrol could assist them in any manner. . . .
>
> Another important factor which entered into our failure and which I still cannot forget, was the poor support we received from higher echelons. Particularly significant was the inefficiency of our logistics system. Support was so poor that troops in the field were often forced to live off the country. As you know, gentlemen, when there is no other way for the troops to eat, commanders are virtually forced to tolerate troopers going to the villages and demanding food. It's either they go hungry or we go hungry. That was the theory of the average government trooper in the field. This, of course, worsened matters. . . .
>
> That general situation was bad enough. Even worse, there

were, as might be expected, instances of officers involved in matters definitely unworthy of one who is by definition an officer and a gentleman by the act of our Congress. Instances, including demanding bribes for the performance or non-performance of duty, occurred in all ranks. Each, of course, was magnified by Huk propagandists and their sympathizers. Few of the offenders were punished appropriately and publicly. We had quite a few big scandals in Central Luzon during this period. In a general statement, we can say that troop behavior was so low that it cultivated an antipathy by the masses for the man in uniform.[6]

Since the Huk insurrection moved rapidly from Phase I to Phase II (see the description of phases of insurgency in Chapter I), the Filipino government and army had no choice but to meet illegal force with legal force. This was the first priority. But Magsaysay also made civic action a command responsibility. If there was anything that soldiers could do for the people without seriously jeopardizing the execution of armed action against an armed enemy, they were to do it. To a remarkable extent, they did. Units on patrol regularly carried medicines to share with any civilians they encountered. Troops built roads, schools, and *barrios* (villages). They escorted the Agriculture Department's extension agents into combat areas so that peasants could be helped with their farming problems. Magsaysay also sent the army's legal officers into the courts to serve as free lawyers for tenants engaged in litigation. But the most spotlighted piece of civic action during the Huk insurrection was the work of EDCOR, the Economic Development Corps of the Army Engineers.

EDCOR was originally conceived as a scheme for giving land to conscripted and discharged servicemen and for ensuring food for the military forces. But Magsaysay soon saw it

as a means of making the Huks' slogan "Land for the Landless" boomerang against them. So he put EDCOR to work in
counterinsurgency, giving it three immediate tasks:

1. The taking over of surrendered or captured dissidents,
who are neither indicted or convicted by civil courts, for the
purpose of resettlement and re-educating them in democratic,
peaceful, and productive ways of life.

2. The resettlement of selected ex-servicemen, ex-guerrillas,
and ex-trainees, and other selected Filipino citizens, in ED-
COR farms as a means of utilizing them as a stabilizing influence in the re-education and reformation of ex-dissidents taken
over by EDCOR as settlers.

3. The training of surrendered or captured dissidents in
the various trades and occupations for the purpose of enabling
them to pursue gainful occupations.[7]

His more long-range objectives for EDCOR were the following:

1. To rehabilitate both socially and economically the great
masses of our people who need a new start.

2. To populate large, uncultivated tracts of land in order
to distribute population from the congested to the less congested areas.

3. To embark on an agricultural progress geared to the
needs of the resettlement project with the end in view of re-
covering in whole or in part money invested in the resettlement project.

4. To solve the peace-and-order problem by establishing
peacefully law-abiding towns.

5. To organize model communities in many parts of the
Philippines peopled by peaceful progressive citizens.

6. To give landless persons a chance to own a piece of land
at low cost through their own efforts.

7. To produce new money crops to hasten our economic self-sufficiency.

8. To pioneer in the establishment of new home industries.

9. To provide training in agriculture for trainees while undergoing military training.[8]

The first EDCOR project was its Rehabilitation Center. This was essentially a small carpentry shop in an army warehouse. The workers built furniture for army barracks, sharing whatever profits were made. A second EDCOR activity was the transplantation of entire economically depressed villages, such as San Luis, in the province of Pampanga, the home *barrio* of Luis Taruc, the Huk military chief. The third activity was the setting up of EDCOR farms on vacant government land. In time there were four of them—three in Mindanao and one in Luzon, on the edge, but not in, the area of Huk activity. Before the settlers would arrive, the army would complete houses for them and quarters for itself, clear the land for cultivation, and provide an administration building, a school house, roads, electricity, and medical care. Later, it was normal to add a church, a library, a cooperative store, an airfield, a nursery, and shelter for the farm animals and fowls. The army also provided free transportation to the farms, schooling, farm supervision, general administrative services, help in securing land titles, and, of course, protection.

What were the settler's obligations? He had to sign a contract with the army under which the town and farm lots were provided him free. But he had to promise to pay for his house, his tools, his animals, and his initial food allowances out of his future earnings. He had to promise, too, that he would be law-abiding and that he would live on and work his land, not becoming a tenant.

How successful was EDCOR, and from which or from whose viewpoint? It did apparently give the settlers a national outlook and it added an increment to their experience in local self-governance. Said Simeon Gonzales, a former Huk commander in Panay: "As soon as a settler coming from Luzon and Visayas gets inside the premises of the EDCOR townsite, he is no longer a Papangan, Tagalog, Ilongo, or Waray-Waray. He is already an EDCOR citizen with obligations to fulfill as a member of the community."[9]

EDCOR sites also stimulated adjacent areas. Not only did the army give protection and security to the EDCOR settlers, but also to the surrounding non-EDCOR families. It helped them clear their land titles, just as it helped the EDCOR settlers. It gave them technical, agricultural, and medical advice, just as it did to the EDCOR settlers. At least half of the civilian patients at EDCOR installations came from outside, as did more than half of the pupils at one EDCOR school, and almost one-third at another.

A third point to be made is that both the soldiers and settlers liked being in EDCOR. The army had more volunteers for the Corps than it was able to employ, and only 6 per cent of the civilians quit or were dismissed. Another measure of EDCOR's impact was the violent reaction of the Huk leaders. They tried to destroy the first farmsite and they ambushed engineers en route to another. In their propaganda, they pictured the settlements as concentration camps, telling their followers that they would either be liquidated on their arrival or murdered by the Moros when the army withdrew.

Yet, whether Huks surrendered because of EDCOR is questionable. Interviews of ex-Huks indicated that less than half had even heard of it before deciding to give up. Most of them surrendered because of hardships in the mountains, harsh Huk discipline and failures, government promises, and family pressures, in that order. EDCOR did not significantly change the socio-economic profile of the Philippines. It helped not more than 1000 families, and only about a quarter of them were Huks.[10] EDCOR's value lay in its symbolic and publicized proof that the government, through its army, was willing and able to aid civilians in the midst of armed turbulence.

Unfortunately, the Philippine Army viewed civic action primarily as a weapons system against insurgency, to be discarded when the latter subsided. By the last quarter of 1953, spare parts and gasoline to operate EDCOR equipment were in short supply. Ration allowances were cut. Pending projects were deferred. By February 1959, EDCOR's military strength was reduced to augment other army units. Yet poverty and Huks (and therefore the need for military civic action) remain in the Philippines, as does this moving plea by a Filipino senator, speaking to a group of army officers:

Out there, outside the fences of your army station, are people —Filipinos sorely in need of change—change in their lives— and, most important, change in their thinking. . . .

In the Philippines, only a handful of citizens have learned to use windmills. . . . May not the soldier reach out to our farmer, teach him to make a servant of the wind? . . .

The Armed Forces have now available in disposal yards a considerable amount of mechanical gear not in use. With this, trainees could receive instruction in the basic construction and maintenance of gasoline motors, in soldering and welding, in iron casting and electrical work. This same equipment could be based in centers around the country to be used in the training of local farm people.

A large part of the technical air [aid?] received by the

Philippines is consigned to the Armed Forces. How much of this may be used by the Armed Forces in applied research, to supplement the basic researches of the National Science Development Board?

How much collaboration are the Armed Forces involved in [in] our rural and urban housing program? Has your potential been considered in the operation of the Central Luzon–Cagayan Valley Authority, the Mindanao Development Authority, the Bureau of Reclamations, the Bureau of Public Works and the National Irrigation Administration?[11]

Insurgency-active Countries

In this category are Burma, Laos, Thailand, and Vietnam. It is frankly not easy to discuss civic action in contemporary Burma, whose government is a military dictatorship. On the one hand, the Burmese Army has an archeological section, and the Army Engineers are constructing highways, buildings, and civilian water supply systems. Burma also has her Defense Service Resettlement Program, which attempts to settle retired soldiers and their families in the far Northeast. The colonization there is similar to that of Israel and some of the Latin American states. There is also the Central Services Training School at Phaunggyi, which teaches agricultural, technical, economic, and administrative subjects to candidate Assistant Security Officers of the People's Police Force and Assistant Township Officers.

But on the other hand, the Burmese military is so comprehensively involved in the economy that it far exceeds anything discussed with regard to, let us say, Argentina's military industry. Through such devices as the Defense Services Institute, later the Burma Economic Development Corporation, and now the governing Revolutionary Council of generals and colonels, the military not only operates government departments, but also "a huge economic complex which [has] comprised banking, department store merchandising, road construction, ocean shipping, fishing, shoe manufacturing, radio assembling, restaurant operation, coal and coke imports, and still other commercial activities." The price that Burma has had to pay for this is an atmosphere of fear and discrimination against resident aliens and Burmese minorities. "In such a climate, physical progress might be made." But it is doubtful whether "real development, the economic, political, social, and cultural flowering of a people . . . can take place."[12] Burma thus exemplifies a degree of military involvement in the economy of a nation that goes beyond the usual meaning of civic action, illustrating the dangers of what may be termed "runaway civic action."

Next to Burma is Laos. She is close enough to Vietnam to be involved in that insurgency and poor enough to need civic action. In fact she has suffered from a surfeit of civic action organizations. At various times, often simultaneously, there have been five-man United Nations teams, three-man teams organized by the United States Operations Mission (AID), six-man teams fielded by the Royal Laotian Army, ten-man civilian teams sent out by the central government, teams of Filipino doctors and medical technicians, United States Army mobile training teams, and American Special Forces units. Only in the villages serviced by the Special Forces was there any measure of success, and even this dwindled after they left because of the lack of follow-on direction by local and national Laotian officials.

The Commissioner General of Civic Action, that is, the head of the overall national effort in Laos, was Brigadier General Oudone Sananikone. He has described the program and its shortcomings in a frank article in *Military Review,* making a number of interesting comments:

1. It is necessary to have at least one member of the team from the same general area, but it is not a wise move to send a team of local people back to their own villages or to adjacent areas where they are well known. They may not be respected and may have difficulty in exerting any influence.

2. . . . it is of major importance to the success of the team mission to include at least one minority member if the team is to work with minority groups. This must be done even at the expense of accepting a less qualified team member, as his knowledge and information concerning these groups will more than compensate for reduced technical skill.

3. . . . former monks made particularly good trainees and this source should not be overlooked, even though some of them may not have the required educational background.

4. Many volunteers did not have the special skills for which they were recruited; others were well qualified on a theoretical level, but lacked the practical experience necessary to pass information on to the villagers.

5. If the program were to start again, it would be preferable not to give the trainees officer status or provide them with uniforms. While this had the advantage of providing easy identification of civic action members, it also closely identified them with the military and the government—a factor that the *Pathet Lao* tried to exploit.

6. [It should be stressed] constantly that the civic action people [are] . . . in no way competing or attempting to reduce the local officials' influence.

7. It may be very necessary to convince the women as well as the men before a village will support a project.

8. Crash civic action programs had a tendency to cause confusion and problems in other ministries of the government.

9. Where civic action was begun in an area relatively un-

poisoned by propaganda or irresponsible political promises, the idea of self-help took hold quickly. . . . In areas previously dominated by the *Pathet Lao* there was sometimes a demand for showy improvements at the expense of more modest long-range benefits.

10. The problem of an enlightened central government is to improve living conditions and standards without destroying the cohesive influence of village life. Civic action is a reasonable first step because it builds on what is there, *but tangible results are not likely to be dramatic.*[13]

Next to Laos is Thailand, and though the government there is more stable than that of Laos, it is beset by some of the same problems of insurgency. If measured by the spectrum ranging from Phase I to Phase II to Phase III, described in Chapter I, then Thai insurgency is somewhere between Phases I and II. Civic action efforts are proceeding accordingly.

American Army mobile training teams have given instruction in civic action to Thai officers and enlisted men, members of the Border Patrol Police (BPP), and local civilian officials. American Navy STATs (Seabee Technical Assistance Teams) have built dams and reservoirs, bridges, roads, schools, and playgrounds, and they have trained Thais in the operation and repair of heavy construction equipment. The 809th and 538th Engineering Battalions of the United States Army, working twelve-hour days and six-day weeks, have been building a bypass road around Bangkok and a highway linking the country's northeastern frontier to the Gulf of Siam. Aside from the military and physical impact, this construction has a psychological impact, for the "Army engineers are creating a new image for Americans in Southeast Asia, letting the Thais see white men working with their hands to help develop their country."[14]

As for the Thais themselves, their two principal civic action instrumentalities are the Border Patrol Police and the Mobile Development Units. The Border Patrol Police have established 150 village schools, 134 of which have BPP teachers who teach both children and adults. Each teacher tries to be "a one-man civic action project, serving as teacher, doctor, sheriff, farm advisor and general information man."[15] The BPP also introduces new crops, fertilizers, farm tools and machinery, and new strains of chickens and pigs. It engages in medical, sanitation, and first aid programs as well. The Mobile Development Units, whose leaders are army officers, move about the countryside advising or supporting in road construction, well-digging, rice-growing, medical care, animal care, etc. Their success, especially in countering insurgency in the Northeast, remains to be seen. As one American observer has said:

> One trouble with the Mobile Development Unit is that it is too mobile. The technicians and propagandists come in for a year, raise everybody's expectations, then move out. The provincial governor has no resources to follow up, so you get a letdown and resentment.[16]

Both North and South Vietnam proclaim and participate in military civic action. In his book, *People's War, People's Army*, General Vo Nguyen Giap, victor over the French at Dien Bien Phu, and North Vietnam's Minister of Defense and Army Commander in Chief, mentions the ninth point of his army's Oath of Honor:

> In contacts with the people, . . . follow these three recommendations:
>
> To respect the people
>
> To help the people

> To defend the people . . . in order to win their confidence and affection and achieve a perfect understanding between the people and the army.

He also has this passage:

> Our army has actively taken part in stepping up agricultural cooperation as it did formerly in land reform. Through the struggle against famine, drought and flood and the building of construction sites and factories, etc., it has shown itself a faithful servant of the people, as President Ho Chi Minh has always reminded us. In recent years, in response to the Party's call, tens of thousands of officers and men volunteered to go to remote areas on the frontier to break virgin lands, to set up army farms, to accelerate the socialist construction of the Fatherland.[17]

In South Vietnam the Vietnamese and Americans are trying to implement the Honolulu Declaration's pledge "to build while we fight," particularly in the rural areas. The latest program for doing this is Rural Reconstruction or Rural Pacification. This is the present version of what in earlier years was the New Life Hamlet Program (1964–1965), the Strategic Hamlet Program (1962–1964), the Civic Action Program (of the 1950s), etc.[18]

The current program is built around Rural Reconstruction Teams of fifty-nine South Vietnamese. About half of each unit is the Political Action Team. These armed propaganda workers are supposed to protect the entire team from enemy attack, secure the village, train the peasants in defense, and engage in the kinds of agitation and propaganda that the North Vietnamese and Viet Cong use so effectively. The remaining members are divided into three subteams: a "census grievance" team, a civil affairs team, and an economic development team.

The "census grievance-ers" try to learn and correct the peasants' complaints, hoping thereby to break the Viet Cong hold on them and to improve the very bad South Vietnamese military intelligence situation. The civil affairs team must essentially set up loyal local governments in areas that lack them or assist government hamlet officials already on

Table 8
South Vietnamese Rural Reconstruction Teams

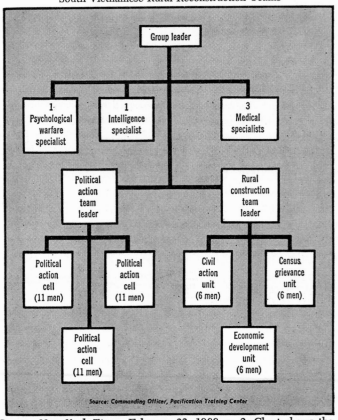

Source: Commanding Officer, Pacification Training Center

Source: New York Times, February 22, 1966, p. 2. Chart shows the organization of each 59-man group in South Vietnam.

the scene. It also strives to organize the inhabitants into government-sponsored organizations. The economic development team engages in rudimentary economic and health improvement programs until such time as better-trained teams on the provincial level can take over as the area is pacified. At this writing, 431 pacification teams are operating in South Vietnam, fewer by far than the number anticipated or needed. When they operate in already secured areas, there is *some* success. Elsewhere, there is practically total failure. There are many reasons for this, the primary one being this vicious circle: civic action (or rural reconstruction, development or pacification) is required to permanently pacify a given insurgency-ridden area. Yet a precondition for such civic action is the military security of that area. However, the South Vietnamese Army has neither understood, welcomed, or protected these teams, and the American Army prefers to use its men against the fighting enemy, and not in the protection of South Vietnamese pacification teams.[19]

One may therefore wonder whether the current program will be any more successful than its failed predecessors, whether American and South Vietnamese soldiers, shooting and being shot at, can or will give it the *field* support that their superiors are giving it verbally in Washington and Saigon, whether the average South Vietnamese or American fighting man really understands and cares about civic action. Where the South Vietnamese Army has engaged in civic action it has taken the "form of public works by special . . . units and not as a performance expected of every soldier."[20] Much the same can be said for American troops. How else can one explain the need to issue these "Ten Commandments" to Marine Corps units "involved in a pacification drive" near Da Nang:

1. Wave to all Vietnamese.
2. Shake hands when meeting people, whether it be for the first time or upon subsequent meetings.
3. Respect graves, tombs, and other religious buildings or shrines.
4. Afford normal courtesies such as deference and respect to elders, respect for authority of the village and hamlet officials.
5. Give the right of way (on the road and paths) whenever possible.
6. Treat women with politeness and respect.
7. Recognize that hand-holding among Vietnamese males is a custom of comradeship in South Vietnam and is not an indication of homosexual tendencies subject to ridicule and mockery.
8. Keep your word. Be slow to make promises, but once they are made, do your best to keep them. Remember, though, that promises involve a command decision. Your commander must be given an opportunity to rule in such a matter.
9. Enter into the spirit of bartering without abuse, and respect the local methods for conducting business.
10. Return what you borrow, replace what you break and avoid unnecessary "liberation" of local items for your personal or unit's use.[21]

(How strikingly similar to Mao Tse-tung's "Three Rules and Eight Remarks.")

Second, whatever real military civic action there is in South Vietnam is largely the product of United States forces. They help in disasters, such as the terrible floods of November 1964, when army helicopters ferried families and food in mountainous central Vietnam. When Saigon was faced with a cholera outbreak, the navy sent out a medical team from Taiwan to Saigon. There is also the informal civic action of an army or navy medic and the formal programs under such rubrics as CAMTT (Civic Action or Civil Affairs Mobile Training Team), STAT (Seabee Technical Assistance Team), MEDCAP (a joint U.S.–Vietnamese Medical Civic Action Program), and ECAD (Engineering Construction Advisory Detachment), and of course Army Special Forces.

This leads to a third reason for doubt. Excellent explanations exist for the fact that American rather than Vietnamese forces are doing most of the civic action. The former have more capabilities than the latter. Often they suffer from an impatience that leads them to do something themselves rather than patiently teach the Vietnamese to do it. A former AID official has said of this:

> It is difficult being an advisor in Asia; every instinct shouts for immediate personal intervention whenever some seemingly logical and necessary project gets shunted off into oblivion because it conflicts with a local religious, political, or purely personal interest. Americans by tradition and inclination seem much better fitted to get things done themselves than hopefully offer advice to others. Here in Phu Bon there were not enough Vietnamese officials to do the work, even if they were all efficient and dedicated.[22]

But is this what military civic action is supposed to be about? The theory says that civic action should flow from the foreign army to the indigenous army and from the indigenous army to the indigenous people. It is not supposed to flow from American soldiers to South Vietnamese civilians, but from the Vietnamese military to the Vietnamese people. And until it does, it is difficult to see how, in the words of the Joint Chiefs of Staff definition, civic action can "improve the standing of the local military forces with the population."

Fourth, both American and South Vietnamese troop levels have reached the point where the real or imagined *military* requirements of counterinsurgency contradict (or at least overshadow) the *non*-military requirements of civic action. Military attacks on villages and civic action treatment of their wounded inhabitants are getting in each other's way. There are simply not enough medical personnel in South Vietnam for *both* civilians and soldiers, and to do a proper medical civic action job we would have to draft many more physicians and train many more medics than we are now doing. In other words, successful civic action in a Phase III insurgency demands enough men *and* will to fight and build simultaneously. So long as this mix is absent in South Vietnam, civic action will not work.

VIII The Problems
and Promise of
Military Civic Action

W HAT CATEGORIZATIONS AND CONCLUSIONS emerge from this study of the non-military use of military forces? In countries like Brazil, Iran, Israel, and Peru civic action is systematic and continuous. In others, such as El Salvador, Pakistan, Thailand, and Ethiopia, it is still formal but rather idiosyncratic. As for the *ad hoc* activities represented by disaster relief, all of the world's armies engage in this kind of civic action. Some countries—the United States, Israel, and France—are civic action exporters, receiving foreign trainees and sending advisors and funds to underdeveloped lands, who are the civic action importers. Countries such as Colombia, the Philippines, Thailand, and South Vietnam illustrate insurgency-generated civic action: they are serious about civic action only when pressured by real or anticipated insurgency. Others, like Brazil, Israel, Iran, and nineteenth-century America, illustrate non-insurgency-oriented civic action. Then, of course, there is the civic action-counterinsurgency equation: the earlier and more massive the civic action and the lower the stage of insurgency, the more flexible, useful, and successful is civic action's role in countering the insurgency.

A second set of conclusions relates to civic action's problems. At the research level, there is the overall problem of objective criteria and empirical evaluation. More work has to be done here. Perhaps we shall then find that the criteria for deciding when to start and use civic action revolve around such questions as: What is the level of unemployment or underemployment in country X? What are its internal security problems? Which institution can best build the country and at the same time handle these security problems? Who can do a specific development task cheaper, faster, better, and at what social, economic, or military cost? Perhaps we shall also find that at least one of the criteria for *stopping* civic action is the point at which the private sector begins to show anxious interest in a previously unattractive area now made more attractive (or safer) by military civic action. This happened more than once in the history of the opening of the American West.

We also need answers to a set of questions raised by Prof. Lyle N. McAlister with respect to Latin American armies, but which can also be raised for others. These are:

> How many functional literates have the Latin American armed forces (or any one of them) actually produced? How many technicians have they in fact contributed to the national pool, and what have these men actually done with their skills? How many volunteers and conscripts have returned to civilian life with a new image of the nation and of themselves as citizens? How many manufactured goods have in fact been produced as a consequence of the military's interest in industrialization? Even more fundamental, how do the contributions of the military in these areas compare qualitatively and quantitatively with the work of civilian agencies? Or if the armed forces had not done these things would they have

been done at all? . . . If proportionate amounts of military budgets had been transferred to Departments of Education, Industry and Commerce, and Agriculture, would the accomplishments have been greater or less?[1]

Moreover, we still do not know how strongly the American public (largely unaware of the program's existence) supports the use of American troops in civic action programs abroad, especially in non-insurgency contexts. Nor do we really know (at least from the open literature) whether and the extent to which foreign civilians in country X have changed previously negative attitudes toward their government and army because of a period of civic action.

On the technical and administrative levels, there is the problem that military units in some countries may not be located where development projects are needed most, and it may not be an easy, quick, or cheap job to redeploy them. Also, the technical caliber of soldiers in some countries (in Africa, for instance) may be far too low to be of much help to the civilian population for quite some time. Where the technical caliber of soldiers is high, there may be just too few of them to contribute meaningfully to solutions of their nation's socio-economic problems.

Even America's civic action support program is confronted by a greater demand for technical specialists than the military is now willing or able to make available.[2] An American soldier or sailor who can do, may not be able to teach. If he can teach, he may not be able to teach in a foreign language. If he can teach in a foreign language, he may have a personality or political orientation that prevents him from teaching and doing well in a particular country. Yet the American commitment to civic action is likely to increase. Perhaps one way of meeting it is to increase Seabee participation. Unlike their army and air force counterparts, navy

Seabee Technical Assistance Teams are logistically self-contained, carrying their own men, material, and equipment wherever they go. Greater use should also be made of the navy's capability to launch and maintain hospital ships, floating "institutes of technology," floating power plants, and so on.

There are other administrative and technical questions. Can civic action and the traditional (but often still necessary) military function always be carried out simultaneously without the former degrading the latter? Both Vietnamese and American military forces in Vietnam are having great difficulty in doing so. Can military personnel really be shuttled back and forth, easily and quickly, between civic action and non-civic action duties? After civic action has been operating for a while, exactly *how* does one make the crossover from civic action by the military to the same non-military duties performed, as is usually the case, by civilian departments of government?

Once started, civic action may be very difficult to stop. This may be true even where its military practitioners lack any political ambitions and are completely loyal to the civilian government. One can easily imagine the following danger in a new country that has early embraced civic action: the Army Medical Corps has become so efficient, effective, and respected by the people that it completely atrophies or destroys that country's embryonic Ministry of Health. Even in older countries, and with the purest of military intentions, a certain amount of opposition can be expected from the civilian bureaucracy, especially in departments dealing with such matters as health, education, labor, welfare, communications, and transportation. Being human, civil servants may perceive civic action, especially if done successfully, as a threat to their egos and their jobs.

What are some of the psychological problems of civic action? There are undoubtedly both civilians and soldiers who consider it beyond the proper pale of the military. Harry F. Waterhouse, a former officer in Army Civil Affairs, who strongly supports civic action, believes that the American military's commitment to it is more ephemeral than permanent, more verbal than real, that it is little understood, and even less liked. "Military forces," he says, "harbor an inherent reluctance to engage in projects which appear to be only remotely linked to national security."[3] Unless and until military officers are convinced (as they are *not* now convinced) that a successful career in civic action will not lessen their chances of "making general," it will be impossible to attract and retain dedicated men with the special talents that civic action requires. Further, some civilian "doves," sincerely troubled by militarism and the expansion of military activities, oppose civic action, as do many civilian "hawks," but for a different reason. Already some of the latter in Congress have criticized our counterinsurgency programs for developing a "social-action rice-raising army instead of 'fighting' men."[4]

As for some foreign military establishments, the Argentine Navy is reluctant to engage in more civic action because it wishes to avoid criticism for performing jobs usually associated with the civilian sector, and the Venezuelan Defense Ministry reports that while military-sponsored vocational training courses have greatly reduced the "natural allergy" of young men to military service, many of the recruits are taking courses that they are not really interested in.[5]

At the social-psychological level, there are the problems associated with the transmission of ideas across class lines. During the Huk Rebellion, officers working in the Philippine Army's Economic Development Corps (EDCOR) often found that civilian settlers stiffly resisted their advice—in agriculture, for example—even when the officers were experienced in that field. A sociologist who studied the problem comments:

> The fact that . . . instruction came from an officer and a member of another social class made it sound like foreign and unreliable advice. . . . When the administrator [of an EDCOR farm] gave an order backed by force it was, of course, obeyed without question. When he attempted to instruct the settlers, however, they became suspicious and often chose to disregard the advice. The task of imparting information across class lines, in an atmosphere of confidence and understanding, can be surprisingly difficult. The class lines themselves tend to destroy confidence. The problem is not the difficulty of the ideas but the barriers created by social class.[6]

Even when military men wholeheartedly accept civic action, they may be doing so for reasons unacceptable to its civilian advocates. Some military officers may perceive it as simply and *only* another weapons system, as a means of "buttering up" the population in order, for example, to obtain better intelligence information. "The acts which the troops perform," Major General Alva R. Fitch, Assistant Chief of Staff for Intelligence of the United States Army, told a conference of Latin American military officers, "create the psychological climate which nurtures cooperation with military intelligence and the public security forces."[7] Other military men may be much too much concerned with the public relations aspect of civic action, that is, with its shadow and not its substance, with its reflection and not its reality. Says a United States Army document on psychological operations: "In undertaking civic actions we must plan appropriate publicity on local, regional, and national levels to exploit its image of progress." Similarly, at the same conference addressed by General Fitch, another officer called the circulation of information about civic action "a weak link in the civic action chain" and urged more "appropriate dissemination, through all communications media? . . ."[8]

There are also psychological problems on the receiving end of civic action. Non-repeatable civic action can be worse than no civic action at all. Let us assume that an army medical officer, while on a temporary mission, learns of a little girl who is seriously ill. Informally, he treats and cures her, earns her family's gratitude, and then leaves. Other families in the neighborhood whose children are also ill will resent their having been left out. Change the word "family" to "village" and one has the same problem writ larger.

Or the military begins a formal civic action program. Later, for one reason or another, the program lags or is stopped entirely. This has already happened more than once. But to be effective, a nation's commitment to civic action must be total and continuous, not just a temporary response to a temporary stimulus or ephemeral bandwagon psychology. Once civic action takes hold in a given region, the government and its military must be prepared to expand it in inkblot fashion. In other words, to raise the population's expectations and then to dash them is, to say the very least, counterproductive. Only the *sustained* endorsement of civic action by a nation's highest civilian and military leadership and by the civilian bureaucacy will avoid or minimize this problem.

There are also problems associated with the flow of civic action support from one country to another. Theoretically, it is supposed to be from the foreign army to the local army and from the local army to the local civilians. But in practice it often turns out to be from the foreign army to the local civilians. Because Americans are impatient people, judging themselves and others by the ability to get quick results, there is great pressure on American military personnel working in civic action to *do* rather than to teach or advise. This is especially true in insurgency-ridden areas like South Vietnam.

Let us assume that in village Y of South Vietnam (or elsewhere) the American Army performs civic action. It does it well and the villagers appreciate it very much. But the more and better the American civic action, the worse does the South Vietnamese Army suffer by comparison in the villagers' eyes. It may happen, if it has not already happened, that the villagers will begin to say: "The Americans have an army that not only knows how to fight, but also cares about us and helps us. That's a real army! *Our* army is absolutely good for nothing!" Even when the local army and government aren't good for nothing, civic action may still backfire if it is oriented (or perceived to be oriented) solely toward counter-insurgency. For then the people may well say: "Sure, you are taking care of our medical and other needs now, but you are doing it only because of the Viet Cong. Where were you yesterday, before the Viet Cong, and where will you be tomorrow, after they are gone?"

The economic questions associated with civic action and military-sponsored development range from "How do we find and allocate the funds to build that road in province Z?" to "How much of our country's resources should we channel away from long-range development projects and toward short-range immediate-impact projects?"[9] Within this range, there are subsidiary problems. For example, some military officers in some Latin American countries perceive civic action as a kind of cheap labor. Conversely, in a country like Peru there has been open complaint that military engineering construction units interfere with the operation of the private economy. In this vein, a United States naval officer (who desires anonymity) claimed in a conversation that the Sea-bees had to stop building military housing in the Aleutians when the labor unions complained. This is the same reason, he said, that Seabee well-drilling trainees are not permitted to drill wells in this country in competition with commercial drillers. If actual or potential unemployment is a problem in the United States, how much more is it one in the under-developed lands, where carelessly integrated civic action can be disastrous?

On the matter of civic action and education, it cannot be denied that in certain highly technical fields the military competes with the civilian economy for scarce skills. This is true in the United States, where the air force and the aerospace industry compete strongly for electronics-trained people. It is perhaps truer in a country like Pakistan where "the military is a heavy consumer of its own trained person-nel. . . . Therefore, the contribution of the military to tech-nical training, while important, should not be exaggerated."[10]

Military civic action planners must also guard against training recruits for jobs that are not available, or in the use of tools they will not find in their civilian environments. An army officer acquainted with Turkey bemoaned privately how Turkish recruits were trained to type and then returned to villages where there are no typewriters. This is, of course, also a problem for planners in the civilian manpower training field. In the Canadian North, for example, Eskimos who had been trained in the basics of the white man's education have found "nothing to do after such training. . . . Meanwhile, they have not had time to learn the means by which their own people make a living."[11]

But it is in the political arena that civic action arouses the most misgivings. Porkbarreling, favoritism in the location of projects, outright misfeasance, politically motivated decisions to furnish civic action equipment to technically incompetent units and armies are all possible. In one Latin American country, military dentists regularly treat peasants who work on a hacienda owned by the commander of that country's air force!

Since civic action is meant to directly benefit the population, "it logically has a decided impact on their affections and allegiances. Quite naturally, therefore, there will be a direct political dividend accruing to the [military] persons who appear to be responsible for the program."[12] This may well plant political ambitions in soldiers now without them or increase such ambitions in soldiers that already have them. A possible solution here is to have the civic action program sponsored by and associated with the civilian head of state as often as possible. If the civilian leadership and civil service in a nation is not civic action- and development-oriented, then the military forces by themselves will not be able to accomplish much.

This raises the question of the propriety of American soldiers engaging (and advising foreigners to engage) in overseas socio-economic activities in order to achieve political and military objectives. The American officer is taught to be non-political and nurtured in the tradition of civilian control of the military. But his counterpart in most underdeveloped countries of the world has *not* been nurtured in that tradition and is often already involved in politics. Is America's task to condemn the population of these countries to social and economic oblivion just because their military establishments are not politically neutral? Or is it rather to make the foreign military more *responsibly* involved, more *humanely* involved, and in time, hopefully, more *democratically* involved?

Despite its problems, civic action holds out great promise. First, it brings government and civilization to remote areas, where often there are no other actual or symbolic representations of national authority and national development. The non-military use of military forces is particularly called for in areas that are inaccessible, inhospitable, unhealthy, unprofitable, and unsafe. More than once has the Agency for International Development had difficulty getting technically qualified Americans to work in far-off dangerous and tropical countries. Why should they, when wages at home are good, loved ones are nearby, and physical dangers are few or absent?

Second, civic action gives the anti-militarist a practical opportunity to "subvert" the military institution. It enables him to put it to good use, to do something more effective about militarism than merely damning it, and helplessly longing for its destruction. To the advocate of foreign aid, civic action proves that under proper conditions money spent by or for the military *can* simultaneously be spent on education, economic development, and social and cultural betterment. To the arms controller and disarmer it suggests a way of engaging the military in peaceful and productive pursuits until true disarmament can come about in this world.

Third, civic action definitely has a role in counterinsurgency. It removes some of the grievances and helps destroy the cooperation between civilians and guerrillas, which the latter need for support and success. How much of a role and how effective it will be depends on the stage of the insurgency. Precisely because civic action is hampered as insurgency escalates, more, not less, attention must be paid to peoples and places outside of Southeast Asia. The involvement in

Vietnam must not blind America to the probability that civic action is now a better bet in Latin America, Africa, and the Middle East.

Finally, neither as a concept nor as a process must civic action depend upon insurgency or counterinsurgency. It is strong enough to stand on its own feet. It is worthy of experimentation in the *developed* as well as underdeveloped countries that are as far away from rebellion and aggression as one might possibly imagine. In the underdeveloped countries, the option is often this: needed roads, schools, or hospitals will be built by military civic action *or they will not be built at all.* In the industrialized countries, military civic action has applications in campaigns against illiteracy, school dropouts, delinquency, poverty, and unemployment.

Even the United States may benefit from more internal use of civic action. The Indians and Eskimos helped by Special Forces medical and veterinary teams in Alaska in 1965 are still there. They still need such help, as do others in the remote corners of that state. The disadvantaged Indians on the reservations of the Southwest can benefit from the kinds of teaching and working that the Seabees do so well. Why not use Army medical reserve units to aid the overburdened hospitals of America?[13] Just as in the poorer countries, civic action in the wealthier ones might be a temporary alternative to demobilization, which by definition quickly turns soldiers into civilians, raising the work force and often the unemployment level.

These are only some of the possibilities of domestic civic action. More will emerge from the continuing national debate about the draft and its relation to other forms of national service. To those who worry more about civic action's dangers than its promise, one might say that it is like fire and radium. Uncontrolled, fire destroys people and property.

Controlled, it heats, cooks, and comforts. Uncontrolled, radium causes cancer. Controlled, it saves countless lives from cancer. The fact that fire and radium can have contradictory results has not prevented society from using them. Similarly, the dangers of civic action—and they are there—are not so great that we should fear employing or at least experimenting with it.

The essential fact about armies is that they exist. They will not, and, in most cases, should not go away. Military civic action thus permits the use of these forces-in-being in the (hopefully) peaceful conflict for the social and economic betterment of mankind.

Notes

Chapter 1

1. H. L. Nieburg, "The Threat of Violence and Social Change," *The American Political Science Review*, LVI (December 1962), 868.

2. *Dictionary of United States Military Terms for Joint Usage*, U.S. Joint Chiefs of Staff Pub. 1 (Washington: Government Printing Office, 1964), pp. 90–91.

3. *Final Report: Fourth Conference of the American Armies* (Fort Amador, C.Z.: Southern Command Headquarters, U.S. Army, 1963), p. 70. Cited hereafter as *Fourth American Armies Conference*.

4. Colonel Truman F. Cook, quoted in Julio Sanjinés Goytia, *Civic Action: Role of the Armed Forces in the Social and Economical Development of a Country* (La Paz: Centro Audio Visual, USAID, Bolivia, 1964), p. 2 of prologue.

5. *Fourth American Armies Conference*, p. 118.

6. Quoted respectively in *La Presse* (Tunis), December 9, 1964, p. 2; Lieutenant Colonel Anthony J. Auletta, "Ten-Nation Progress Report," *Army*, XIII (July 1963), 56; and the *Manila Times*, March 25, 1964, as reproduced in *Civil Affairs Trends* (Fort Gordon, Ga.: U.S. Army Civil Affairs School, August 1964), p. 21.

7. See, for example, Seymour J. Deitchman, *Limited War and American Defense Policy* (Cambridge, Mass.: M.I.T. Press, 1964), pp. 35–37; Edward W. Gude, *Internal Dynamics of Conflict and Change: Arms Control and Internal Warfare*, BR-2526 (Bedford, Mass.: Raytheon Company, August 1, 1963), pp. 18–24; *Counterinsurgency Planning Guide*, ST 31-176 (Fort Bragg, N.C.: U.S. Army Special Warfare School, 1964), p. 14, cited hereafter as *Counter-*

insurgency Planning Guide; and *U.S. Army Counterinsurgency Forces,* Field Manual FM 31-22 (Washington: Department of the Army, 1963), p. 8.

8. *Counterinsurgency Planning Guide,* p. 14.

9. Morris Janowitz, *The Military in the Political Development of New Nations* (Chicago: University of Chicago Press, 1964), p. 81. "Measured in terms of numbers of individuals involved, time consumed, effort devoted, and dollars expended, training is one of the most important undertakings of the armed services." John W. Masland and Laurence I. Radway, *Soldiers and Scholars: Military Education and National Policy* (Princeton: Princeton University Press, 1957), p. 51.

10. Masland and Radway, *op. cit.,* p. 51.

11. Harold F. Clark and Harold S. Sloan, *Classrooms in the Military: An Account of Education in the Armed Forces of the United States* (New York: Columbia University, 1964), pp. 6–7, 32–33, 36–39, 107–109.

12. Mary Bedell and Roger Bowlby, *Formal Occupational Training of Adult Workers,* Manpower/Automation Research Monograph No. 2 (Washington: Manpower Administration of the Department of Labor, December 1962), p. 12.

13. Harold Wool, "The *Changing* Pattern of Military Skills," *Employment Security Review* (July 1963), p. 1.

14. Albert D. Biderman, "Sequels to a Military Career: The Retired Military Professional," in Morris Janowitz (ed.), *The New Military: Changing Patterns of Organization* (New York: Russell Sage Foundation, 1964), p. 329.

15. Edward Shils, "The Military in the Political Development of New States," in John J. Johnson (ed.), *The Role of the Military in Underdeveloped Countries* (Princeton: Princeton University Press, 1962), p. 23.

16. *Civic Action Projects Report, 1 Mar 1964–1 Jan 1965* (Quarry Heights, C.Z.: United States Southern Command, 1965), p. 151.

17. Gude, *op. cit.,* p. 10.

18. John G. Ohly, "A Study of Certain Aspects of Foreign Aid," Annex G of *Supplement to the Composite Report of the President's Committee to Study the United States Military Assistance Program, Annexes,* II (Washington: Government Printing Office, 1959), 283.

19. This point is made strongly and well in Lyle N. McAlister, "The Military," in John J. Johnson (ed.), *Continuity and Change in Latin America* (Stanford, Calif.: Stanford University Press, 1964), p. 155; and Lucian W. Pye, "Armies in the Process of Political Moderni-

zation," in Johnson, *The Role of the Military in Underdeveloped Countries*, pp. 69, 86–87.

Chapter 2

1. Leonard Cottrell, *The Great Invasion* (New York: Coward-McCann, Inc., 1962), p. 209. The discussion of Rome is taken from *ibid.*, pp. 35, 63, 209; "Counter-Guerrilla Operations in the Philippines, 1946–1953," a U.S. Army seminar on the Huk Campaign held at Fort Bragg, N.C., June 15, 1961, p. 55; Brigadier General Edward G. Lansdale, "Soldiers and the People," lecture at the U.S. Army Special Warfare School, Fort Bragg, N.C., August 30, 1962, p. 1; Harry F. Waterhouse, *A Time to Build* (Columbia: University of South Carolina Press, 1964), pp. 39–41; and "Rumania," *Encyclopaedia Britannica* (1947 edition), XIX, 638.

2. Jack Autrey Dabbs, *The French Army in Mexico, 1861–1867: A Study in Military Government* (The Hague: Mouton & Co., 1963), p. 16.

3. Waterhouse, *op. cit.*, pp. 43–45.

4. Quoted in Lieutenant Colonel E. W. C. Sandes, *The Royal Engineers in Egypt and the Sudan* (Chatham: Institution of Royal Engineers, 1937), p. 509. The discussion of the British Army in Palestine, Egypt, and the Sudan is based on *ibid.*, pp. 503–504, 507, 509, 511, 518, 521, and Waterhouse, *op. cit.*, pp. 46–47. The material on the French Army in Mexico comes from Dabbs, *op. cit.*, pp. 242–244.

5. John J. Johnson, *The Military and Society in Latin America* (Stanford, Calif.: Stanford University Press, 1964), p. 78.

6. Quoted in McAlister, *op. cit.*, p. 138.

7. Johnson, *The Military and Society in Latin America*, pp. 197–198.

8. J. Leon Helguera, "The Changing Role of the Military in Colombia," *Journal of Inter-American Studies*, III (July 1961), 352.

9. For further details on FAC, see Venezuela, Ministerio de la Defensa, *Acción Cívica Informe* (Caracas: Comandancia General del Ejército, n.d.), pp. 27–28, 44–46, 52.

10. The material on Spain is taken from Brigadier General Donald G. Shingler, "Contributions of Military Resources to Economic and Social Progress," Annex D of *Supplement to the Composite Report of the President's Committee to Study the United States Military Assistance Program, Annexes*, II, 129; and Spain, Junta Interministerial Conmemoradora de los 25 Años de Paz Española, *El Ejercito*, Volume III of *El Gobierno Informa* (Madrid: Editora Nacional, 1964), pp. 51–52, 129–130, 138–139, 142–150, 173–174.

11. Mao Tse-tung, *Guerrilla Warfare*, trans. by Brigadier General Samuel B. Griffith, USMC (Ret.) (New York: Frederick A. Praeger, 1961), p. 92.

12. *Ibid.*, p. 73.

13. Chalmers Johnson, "How Sharp Are the Dragon's Teeth?", *New York Times Magazine*, February 28, 1965, pp. 22, 86; *New York Times*, May 5, 1964, p. 5; and O. Edmund Clubb, "The Sino-Soviet Frontier," *Military Review*, XLIV (July 1964), 9.

14. Quoted in R. Kolkowicz, *The Use of Soviet Military Labor in the Civilian Economy: A Study of Military "Shefstvo,"* RM-3360-PR (Santa Monica, Calif.: RAND Corporation, 1962), p. 23. The ensuing discussion of *shefstvo* is based entirely on this document.

15. Quoted in *ibid.*, pp. 8, 9, 11.

16. *Washington Post*, April 28, 1964, p. A-1.

17. Rear Admiral H. G. Thursfield (ed.), *Brassey's Annual: The Armed Forces Year-Book* (New York: Frederick A. Praeger, 1963), pp. 306–308, 333–334, 339.

18. Quoted in Edgar S. Furniss, Jr., *DeGaulle and the French Army: A Crisis in Civil-Military Relations* (New York: Twentieth Century Fund, 1964), pp. 171–172.

19. For more on contemporary French civic action, see *ibid.*, p. 170; "La Promotion Sociale dans Les Armées," *Bulletin d'Information des Armées*, No. 24 (June 18, 1964), pp. 1–7; J. Y. Perchat, "Education et Promotion Sociale," *Revue Militaire d'Information* (June 1963), pp. 46–49; General Nemo, "A Propos de la Réforme du Service Militaire," *Revue de Défense Nationale* (February 1964), pp. 193–202; "Le Régiment Mixte des Antilles-Guyane," *Frères d'Armes* (October 1964), pp. 13–22; "Le Service Militaire Adapté Aux Antilles-Guyane," *T.A.M.* ["Terre, Aire, Marine"] (June 10, 1964); and General Nemo, "Terres Françaises D'Amérique: Le Service Militaire Adapté," *Revue de Défense Nationale* (January 1962), pp. 53–64.

Chapter 3

1. Quoted in Francis Paul Prucha, *Broadax and Bayonet: The Role of the United States Army in the Development of the Northwest, 1815–1860* (Madison: State Historical Society of Wisconsin, 1953), p. 104. Most of the historical examples dealing with the non-military activities of the American Army on the frontier relate to the Northwest and are taken from this book, to which I am highly indebted.

2. James Ripley Jacobs, *The Beginning of the U.S. Army, 1783–1812* (Princeton: Princeton University Press, © 1947), p. 323.

3. Quoted in Prucha, *op. cit.*, p. 189.

4. Prucha, *op. cit.*, p. 195.
5. Quoted in Waterhouse, *op. cit.*, p. 78, n. 42.
6. "In a large garden back of the fort, the soldiers cultivated all the corn, potatoes, turnips, onions, etc., which they required. They cut and piled up near the fort all the wood that was consumed, and in marshy spots on the prairie secured the hay necessary for keeping our livestock through the long winters; these duties, together with those more directly in the military line, kept them constantly on the go through the short summers."—John Bliss, recalling his boyhood at Fort Snelling, quoted in Prucha, *op. cit.*, p. 120.
7. From *Army and Navy Chronicle* of May 17, 1838, quoted in Prucha, *op. cit.*, p. 105.
8. Quoted in Prucha, *op. cit.*, p. 102, n. 30.
9. Quoted in Jacobs, *op. cit.*, pp. 197–198.
10. Quoted in Prucha, *op. cit.*, pp. 108–109.
11. Masland and Radway, *op. cit.*, pp. 77, 227. The military, incidentally, have continued their pre-eminence in the design and use of classroom teaching aids to this very day.
12. *Ibid.*, p. 78; and Shingler, *op. cit.*, p. 102.
13. Shingler, *op. cit.*, pp. 102, 105.
14. Quoted in Prucha, *op. cit.*, p. 190. Italics added.
15. *Ibid.*, pp. 94–95, 186, 204–213; and Jacobs, *op. cit.*, pp. 256–258. For an interesting account of the long career of a recent professional army musician, who was principal of the Army Music School and who wrote marches and scholarly works on music history and musicology, see the obituary of Chief Warrant Officer William C. White in the *New York Times*, October 10, 1964, p. 33.
16. Waterhouse, *op. cit.*, p. 66.
17. Quoted in Prucha, *op. cit.*, pp. 196–197. Italics added.
18. *New York Times*, October 17, 1965, p. 74.
19. See Mark Zborowski and Elizabeth Herzog, *Life is with People: The Culture of the Shtetl* (New York: Schocken Books, 1962), especially p. 14. This was originally published in 1952 by International Universities Press, Inc.
20. Waterhouse, *op. cit.*, p. 61. The ensuing discussion of the CCC program is taken from this book.
21. Except for the next notes, this discussion, including quotations, is taken from U.S. Army, Civic Action Team, Exercise Polar Strike, 6th Special Forces Group (ABN), 1st Special Forces, *Civic Action Team After Action Report* (*Alaska, 2 January 1965–22 February 1965*), with memorandum and attachments from Major Robert W. Sweet to the Surgeon, U.S. Army, John F. Kennedy Center for Special Warfare (Fort Bragg, N.C., 1965).

22. Quoted in "Alaskan Children Thank 6th SFGA," *Veritas,* IV (March 24, 1965), 3. This is the official organ of the John F. Kennedy Center for Special Warfare at Fort Bragg.

23. Brigadier General Edward G. Lansdale, "Civic Action," lecture, Counter-Guerrilla School, Special Warfare Center, Fort Bragg, N.C., February 24, 1961, p. 8.

Chapter 4

1. Civil affairs is defined officially as: "Those phases of the activities of a commander which embrace the relationship between the military forces and civil authorities and people in a friendly country or area, or occupied country or area when military forces are present. Civil Affairs include, inter alia: Matters concerning the relationship between military forces located in a country or area and the civil authorities and people of the country or area usually involving performance by the military forces of certain functions or the exercise of certain authority normally the responsibility of the local government. This relationship may occur prior to, during or subsequent to military action in time of hostilities or other emergency and is normally covered by a treaty or other agreement, express or implied." *Command and Staff Guidelines for Civic Action,* Special Text ST 41-10-90 (Fort Gordon, Ga.: U.S. Army, Civil Affairs School, 1964), p. 3.

2. See Shingler, *op. cit.,* pp. 98–99, 121; Foreign Policy Research Institute, "A Study of United States Military Assistance Program in Underdeveloped Areas," Annex C of *Supplement to the Composite Report of the President's Committee to Study the United States Military Assistance Program, Annexes,* II, 55–56; and The President's Committee to Study the United States Military Assistance Program, *Conclusions Concerning the Mutual Security Program* (Washington: Government Printing Office, 1959), pp. 42–43, 45.

3. The remainder of this historical summary of civic action's organizational growth is based on the following U.S. Army texts: *Command and Staff Guidelines for Civic Action,* pp. 7–13, D3–D4; *Basis and Directives for Civic Action,* Lesson Plan 5140, Civic Action Course 41-G-F7 (Fort Gordon, Ga.: U.S. Army Civil Affairs School, 1964), pp. LP6–LP12; and *The Concept of Civic Action,* Lesson Plan 5135, Civic Action Course, 41-G-F7 (Fort Gordon, Ga.: U.S. Army Civil Affairs School, 1964), p. LP2.

4. The full text of Colonel Little's memorandum, given to me by General Lansdale, is appended to the end of this chapter.

5. U.S. Food for Peace, *The Nineteenth Semi-Annual Report on Activities Carried on Under Public Law 480, 83d Congress, as*

Amended, Outlining Operations under the Act During the Period July 1 through December 31, 1963 (Washington: Government Printing Office, 1964), pp. 63–65.

6. The lower figure is Wynne James's, given in an interview on January 6, 1965. He is Assistant for Civic Action in the Office of the Assistant Secretary of Defense for International Security Affairs. The higher figure is from U.S. Army text, *Command and Staff Guidelines for Civic Action*, p. 46.

7. For more details on STATs, see U.S. Navy text, *Seabee Technical Assistance Teams: An Existing Counter Insurgency Force* (n.p., n.d.).

8. Both quotations are taken from the *New York Times*, August 23, 1964, p. 35.

9. Of May 1964, p. 48.

10. *New York Times*, December 6, 1964, p. 146.

11. Shingler, *op. cit.*, p. 111.

12. Wynne James, "The Military as an Aid to Development," address to the panel on "The Military: Deterrent or Aid to Development?" Seventh World Conference of the Society for International Development, Washington, March 11, 1965, p. 2.

Chapter 5

1. According respectively to Wynne James in an interview on January 6, 1965, and the *Washington Post*, August 19, 1965, p. F-3.

2. Inter-American Defense Board, *Military Civic Action in the Economic and Social Development of the Countries*, Document T-255 (Washington, September 23, 1965), p. 2. Cited hereafter as IADB, *Military Civic Action*. Unless otherwise indicated, the material in this chapter is based on this document and on the *Civic Action Projects Report* of the United States Southern Command for the periods March 1–August 1, 1964 and March 1, 1964–January 1, 1965. Page citations are given for quotations only.

3. Quoted in *Fourth American Armies Conference*, p. 70.

4. (La Paz: Centro Audio Visual, USAID, Bolivia, 1964).

5. *Civic Action Projects Report, 1 Mar 1964–1 Aug 1964* (Quarry Heights, C.Z.: United States Southern Command, 1964), Inc. 17, Venezuela, Sec. I, p. 1. Cited hereafter as USSC, *CAP Report, 1964*.

6. "Sumario de las actividades desarrolladas por Acción Cívica Militar de El Salvador," p. 1. Attachment to a letter from Colonel Carlos Urrutia S., Military and Air Attaché of El Salvador in Washington, January 26, 1965.

7. IADB, *Military Civic Action*, p. 11.

8. "Programa de Acción Cívica de las Fuerzas Armadas Argentinas," pp. 2–3. Attachment to a letter from Colonel Rudecindo P. Nadal, Assistant Military Attaché of Argentina in Washington, February 1, 1965.

9. *Civic Action Projects Report, 1 Mar 1964–1 Jan 1965*, p. 37. Cited hereafter as USSC, *CAP Report, 1965*.

10. *Fourth American Armies Conference*, p. 102.

11. *New York Times*, March 31, 1964, p. 10.

12. USSC, *CAP Report, 1964*, Inc. 10, Guatemala, Sec. I, p. 1.

13. This discussion is based largely on an interview on June 10, 1964 with Lieutenant Colonel Newton Correa de Andrade Mello, Assistant Military Attaché of Brazil in Washington, and on two internal working papers he was kind enough to provide: "Emprêgo das Unidades de Engenharia na Região Sul do País," and "Informes sobre Projectos e Programas de Desenvolvimento da Comunidade."

14. Quoted in Lansdale, "Civic Action," pp. 6–7 (see note 23 to Chapter 3).

15. Quoted in my "The Nonmilitary Use of the Latin American Military: A More Realistic Approach to Arms Control and Disarmament," *Background* (since renamed *International Studies Quarterly*), VIII (November 1964), 168.

Chapter 6

1. *New York Times*, May 2, 1965, p. 18.

2. The camp is named after Colonel Mickey Marcus, an American graduate of West Point who fought with the Israelis during their War of Independence. He died in it. Not knowing Hebrew, he replied to a sentry's challenge in English and was shot accidentally. In view of the tragedy, the naming of this army educational institution after him symbolizes the determination of the Israeli government to teach its disadvantaged citizens the national language, the national culture, and needed skills.

3. *New York Times*, April 26, 1964, p. 16.

4. Quoted in Alisa Levenberg, "Camp Marcus: Model School for Adults," *Pioneer Woman*, XL (January 1965), 8.

5. *New York Times*, April 26, 1964, p. 16.

6. Quoted in Levenberg, *op. cit.*, pp. 8, 22.

7. According to Itzhak Navon of the Israeli Ministry of Education, quoted in the *New York Times*, November 1, 1964.

8. Mordekhai Nurock (ed.), *Israel Government Year-Book, 5722 (1961/62)* (Jerusalem: Government Printer, 1962), p. 120.

9. Leo Heiman, "Military Assistance by Small Nations," *Military Review*, XLIV (March 1964), 17.

10. *A Pioneer Youth Training Centre for Tanganyika* (Jerusalem: Israel, Ministry for Foreign Affairs, Department for International Cooperation, 1962), p. 2.

11. Quoted in "Three Envoys Present Credentials," *Israel Digest,* VIII (December 3, 1965), 3.

12. Quoted in Israel, Ministry for Foreign Affairs, Information Department, *Israel-Africa: A Story of Cooperation* (Jerusalem: Hadassah Apprentice School of Printing, n.d.), p. 26.

13. Quoted in *Les Defenseurs D'Israel: Nahal, les Fermiers Combattants* (Tel Aviv: Editions "Eshel," n.d.), pp. 8–9.

14. J. C. Hurewitz, "The Role of the Military in Society and Government in Israel," in Sidney Nettleton Fisher (ed.), *The Military in the Middle East* (Columbus: Ohio State University Press, 1963), p. 96.

15. Quoted in "Nahal Industrial Cooperative in Arad," *Israel Digest,* VIII (December 31, 1965), 5.

16. USSC, *CAP Report, 1964,* Inc. 1, Bolivia, Sec. III, pp. 1, 29.

17. Louis J. Walinsky, "The Role of the Military in Development Planning: Burma," paper presented to the Conference on Economic Planning in Southeast Asia, Honolulu, February 1–5, 1965, p. 4.

18. Shingler, *op. cit.,* p. 129. For favorable accounts of French civic action in Algeria, especially the work of the Army's Special Administrative Section (SAS), see Waterhouse, *op. cit.,* p. 53; and *Civil Affairs Trends* (August 1964), pp. 58–59, published by the U.S. Army Civil Affairs School, Fort Gordon, Ga.

19. Shils, *op. cit.,* p. 53.

20. Daniel Lerner and Richard D. Robinson, "Swords and Ploughshares: The Turkish Army as a Modernizing Force," *World Politics,* XIII (October 1960), 38.

21. Quoted in Auletta, *op. cit.,* p. 55. The rest of the data on Turkish civic action are from Brigadier General Edward G. Lansdale, "The Free Citizen in Uniform," talk to the U.S. Army Civil Affairs School, Fort Gordon, Ga., November 1, 1960, p. 3; Sidney Nettleton Fisher, "The Role of the Military in Security and Government in Turkey," in his *The Military in the Middle East,* p. 33; IADB, *Military Civic Action,* pp. 85–86; and Janowitz, *The Military in the Political Development of New Nations,* p. 82.

22. This discussion on Iran is taken from Lee Griggs, "When He Wills It, Things Happen," *Life,* LX (January 14, 1966), 42; Drew Pearson's column in the *Washington Post,* November 14, 1964, p. D-45; and two different documents with an identical title: Iran, Supreme Commander's Staff, J-3, *Civic Action Program for Imperial Iranian Armed Forces* (1963). One document is in English and the

other is in English and Persian, and they were prepared for "The First CENTO Professional Military Development [Civic Action] Seminar."

23. Lieutenant Colonel Richard L. Coppedge, *The Role of Medicine in Counterinsurgency* (Fort Bragg, N.C., n.d.), p. 26.

24. James C. Coleman and Belmont Brice, Jr., "The Role of the Military in Sub-Saharan Africa," in Johnson, *The Role of the Military in Underdeveloped Countries*, p. 397.

25. *Common Subject Lesson Plans: Civic Action,* USACAS-03 (Fort Gordon, Ga.: U.S. Army Civil Affairs School, 1965), pp. 9–10. See also, Waterhouse, *op. cit.,* p. 109.

26. *Les Jeunes Militaires Français et l'Oeuvre de la Coopération,* DCT/CT.RM (Paris: France, Ministère de la Coopération, Direction de la Coopération Culturelle et Technique, November 1964), pp. 1–2; and the *New York Times,* October 18, 1964, p. 15.

27. *New York Times,* October 18, 1964, p. 15.

Chapter 7

1. Shingler, *op. cit.,* pp. 132–133; Waterhouse, *op. cit.,* p. 77; Auletta, *op. cit.,* p. 53; and U.S. Defense Department, OASD (PA) News Release No. 223-64 (March 16, 1964), p. 2.

2. Colonel Mian Ijaz Ahmad, "Pakistan's Concept of Military Civic Assistance," paper presented by Pakistan to the CENTO Central Treaty Organization Seminar on Military Civic Action Programmes (n.p., n.d.), p. 5. The discussion of the Indus Valley Road Project is taken from this document.

3. Waterhouse, *op. cit.,* p. 92; and the *New York Times,* March 29, 1964, p. 9.

4. According to "Civic Action: The Military Role in Nation Building," *For Commanders—This Changing World,* III (January 15, 1964), 3.

5. Roger Hilsman, in his foreword to General Vo Nguyen Giap's *People's War, People's Army: The Viet Cong Insurrection Manual for Under-developed Countries* (New York: Frederick A. Praeger, 1962), p. xiii, says the English had 65,000 men to the insurgents' 8000. Waterhouse (*op. cit.,* p. 51) gives the ratio as 100,000 to 10,000. Deitchman gives it as 175,000 to 10,000 (*op. cit.,* pp. 210–211).

6. Colonel Napoleon D. Valeriano, in "Counter-Guerrilla Operations in the Philippines 1946–1953," a U.S. Army seminar on the Huk Campaign held at Fort Bragg, N.C., June 15, 1961, pp. 28–29.

7. Quoted in Alvin H. Scaff, *The Philippine Answer to Communism* (Stanford, Calif.: Stanford University Press, 1955), p. 154, n. 24. This

entire work is devoted to a study of EDCOR, and I have relied heavily upon its factual information. However, Scaff is uncritically favorable to EDCOR, sometimes leaving one with the impression that it was the government's single most effective weapon against the insurgency.

8. *The EDCOR Plan* (Camp Murphy, Quezon City: Philippine Department of National Defense, Office of the Chief, Economic Development Corps, n.d.).

9. Quoted in Scaff, *op. cit.*, p. 97.

10. *Ibid.*, pp. 75–77, 103–105, 123–124.

11. Quoted in the *Manila Times*, March 25, 1964, as reproduced in *Civil Affairs Trends* (Fort Gordon, Ga.: U.S. Army Civil Affairs School, August 1964), p. 21.

12. Walinsky, *op. cit.*, pp. 7–8.

13. "Laos—Case Study in Civic Action: The Royal Lao Program," *Military Review*, XLIII (December 1963), 52–54. Italics added.

14. The *Washington Post*, June 29, 1965, p. A-8.

15. IADB, *Military Civic Action*, p. 86.

16. Quoted in *New York Times*, July 16, 1966, p. 2.

17. (New York: Frederick A. Praeger, 1962), pp. 56, 125.

18. George K. Tanham, *et al. War Without Guns: American Civilians in Rural Vietnam* (New York: Frederick A. Praeger, 1966), p. 35, n. 2. For a discussion of the Civic Action Program of the 1950s, and how it was "all but destroyed by bureaucratic rivalries," see John D. Montgomery, *The Politics of Foreign Aid: The American Experience in Southeast Asia* (New York: Frederick A. Praeger for the Council on Foreign Relations, 1962), pp. 70–72, 179–181.

19. See the *New York Times*, September 19, 1966, p. 4; September 25, 1966, p. 6, sec. 4, and November 8, 1966, p. 6.

20. Major General Edward G. Lansdale, "Viet Nam: Do We Understand Revolution?", *Foreign Affairs*, XLIII (October 1964), 85.

21. Quoted in the *New York Times*, November 28, 1965, p. 3.

22. Tanham, *op. cit.*, pp. 91–92.

Chapter 8

1. McAlister, *op. cit.*, pp. 141–142, 144.

2. For instance, the United States Southern Command reported that a "billet . . . for a full-time U.S. Naval officer advisor to the [Brazilian Naval Research] Institute . . . is vacant at present due to delays in acquiring a fully qualified officer." USSC, *CAP Report, 1965*, pp. 337–338.

3. *Op. cit.*, pp. 5, 125 *ff.*

4. According to the syndicated columnists Robert S. Allen and Paul Scott, in the *Northern Virginia Sun*, January 18, 1965, p. 4.

5. See respectively USSC, *CAP Report, 1965*, p. 10; and Venezuela, Ministerio de la Defensa, *Acción Cívica Informe*, pp. 49–50.

6. Scaff, *op. cit.*, pp. 91–92.

7. *Fourth American Armies Conference*, p. 23.

8. *Psychological Operations Planning for Counterinsurgency Operations*, Lesson Plan P 9.01403 (Fort Bragg, N.C.: U.S. Army Special Warfare School, June 1964), p. 11; and *Fourth American Armies Conference*, p. 108.

9. "The limitations . . . on the diversion of resources from economic development or from an economy of scarcity to defense, or the trade-off between investments in defense and in development, are little understood at present." H. Roberts Coward, *Military Technology in Developing Countries*, Report C/64-5 (Cambridge: Center for International Studies of the Massachusetts Institute of Technology, 1964), p. 15.

10. Janowitz, *The Military in the Political Development of New Nations*, p. 76.

11. According to Dr. Roger West, a physician who treats Eskimos in the Arctic, as quoted in the *New York Times*, August 1, 1965, p. 35. See also the article "Korean Jobs Few, Graduates Many," *ibid.*, February 27, 1966, p. 8.

12. *A Review of the Civic Action Program*, attachment to Lesson Plan 5135 (Fort Gordon, Ga.: U.S. Army Civil Affairs School, July 1964), p. AS-A-9.

13. For a comment by the originator of this idea, see Michael O. Finkelstein's letter to the *New York Times*, September 21, 1966, p. 42.

Bibliography

I. PRIMARY SOURCES

A. Unpublished Materials

1. Documents

Argentina. "Programa de Acción Cívica de las Fuerzas Armadas Argentinas." Attachment to a letter from Colonel Rudecindo P. Nadal, Assistant Military Attaché in Washington, February 1, 1965.

Brazil. "Emprêgo das Unidades de Engenharia na Região Sul do País." Supplied by the Brazilian Military Attaché in Washington, June 10, 1964.

Brazil. "Informes sobre Projectos e Programas de Desenvolvimento da Comunidade." Supplied by the Brazilian Military Attaché in Washington, June 10, 1964.

El Salvador. "Sumario de las actividades desarrolladas por Acción Cívica Militar de El Salvador." Attachment to a letter from Colonel Carlos Urrutia S., Military and Air Attaché in Washington, January 26, 1965.

Guatemala, Servicio de Relaciones Públicas, Cultura y Acción Cívica, Ejército de Guatemala. "Descripción del Emblema de Acción Cívica Militar." Attachment to a letter from Dr. Carlos Garcia-Bauer, Guatemalan Ambassador in Washington, July 29, 1965.

India. Untitled memorandum on the Army Educational Corps. Supplied by Brigadier M. M. Nath, Military Attaché of India in Washington, May 16, 1965.

Lansdale, Edward G. "Binh Hung: A Counter-Guerrilla Case Study." n.p., February 1, 1961.

Lansdale, Edward G. "Civic Action and Counter-Insurgency."
Memorandum, March 22, 1962.
Lansdale, Edward G. "Civic Activities of the Military, Southeast
Asia." Working paper of the Anderson–Southeast Asia Subcommittee of
the Draper Committee, March 13, 1959.
Little, Lieutenant Colonel John T. "Civil Assistance." Memorandum.
Vientiane, Laos: Headquarters, U.S. Army White Star Mobile Training
Team, September 22, 1961.
Waskow, Arthur I. "The Strategy of Demilitarization." n.p., n.d.

2. Correspondence (letters to the author)

Ackerman, Major H. L., Office of the Military Attaché of South
Africa in Washington, April 20, 1965.
Albright, W. F., Emeritus Professor of Semitics, The Johns Hopkins
University, January 22, 1965.
Auletta, Lieutenant Colonel Anthony J., Assistant Chief, Plans and
Policy Division, Civil Affairs Directorate, Office of the Deputy Chief of
Staff for Military Operations, Department of the Army, February 26,
1965.
Bar-On, Hanan, Counselor of the Embassy of Israel in Washington,
June 19, 1964.
Bekhti, B., Press Division, Embassy of Algeria in Washington,
January 8, 1965.
Blumenson, Martin, Senior Historian, Office of the Chief of Military
History, Department of the Army, September 20, 1964.
Brasart, Lieutenant Colonel Pierre, Assistant Military Attaché of
France in Washington, February 9, 1965 and June 8, 1965.
Coloma, Colonel Francisco, Military Attaché of Spain in Washing-
ton, April 20, 1965.
Dannaud, Jean Pierre, Director, Department of Technical and Cul-
tural Cooperation, French Ministry of Cooperation, December 4, 1964.
Garcia-Bauer, Carlos, Ambassador of Guatemala in Washington,
June 24, 1965 and July 29, 1965.
Gardner, Hugh N., Staff Historian, United States Army Forces,
Southern Command, Fort Amador, Canal Zone, November 6, 1964.
Goytia, Julio Sanjinés, Director, Civic Action, USAID-Bolivia, June
15, 1964.
James, Wynne, Assistant for Civic Action, Office of the Assistant
Secretary of Defense for International Security Affairs, April 23, 1965,
May 3, 1965, May 14, 1965, January 18, 1966, January 21, 1966,
February 8, 1966.
Kashmoula, Colonel M. T., Armed Forces Attaché of Iraq in Wash-
ington, April 5, 1965.

Kramish, Arvin M., Staff Assistant, Arms Control Directorate, Office of the Assistant Secretary of Defense for International Security Affairs, November 27, 1964.

Leeflang, Major A., Office of the Military Attaché of the Netherlands in Washington, June 1, 1965.

Legters, Major Llewellyn J., Deputy Surgeon, John F. Kennedy Center for Special Warfare, Fort Bragg, N.C., March 15, 1965 and May 12, 1965.

McAlister, Lyle N., Director, Center of Latin American Studies, University of Florida, February 27, 1964.

Mellish, Nicholine, Assistant to the Press Counselor, Royal Afghan Embassy in Washington, December 31, 1964.

Moll, Brigadier G. T., Armed Forces Attaché of South Africa in Washington, March 17, 1965.

Nadal, Colonel Rudecindo P., Assistant Military Attaché of Argentina in Washington, February 1, 1965.

Nath, Brigadier M. M., Military Attaché of India in Washington, May 16, 1965.

Peal, S. Edward, Ambassador of Liberia in Washington, March 9, 1965.

Platig, E. Raymond, Director of Studies, Carnegie Endowment for International Peace, July 17, 1964.

Sannon, Major Moussa, Military Attaché of the Ivory Coast in Washington, March 1, 1965.

Urrutia S., Colonel Carlos, Military and Air Attaché of El Salvador in Washington, January 26, 1965.

Walinsky, Louis J., Economic Development Consultant, Chevy Chase, Md., January 28, 1965.

Wool, Harold, Director for Policy Planning, Office of the Assistant Secretary of Defense for Manpower, February 16, 1965.

Wright, Colonel Jay W., Acting Commandant, U.S. Army Civil Affairs School, Fort Gordon, Ga., June 18, 1965.

Yarborough, Major General William P., Commandant, United States Army John F. Kennedy Center for Special Warfare, Fort Bragg, N.C., January 5, 1965.

3. Persons Interviewed

Andrews, Commander J. E., Regional Affairs Officer, United States Southern Command, August 8, 1966.

Arámbula Durán, Brigadier General Marcos, Military Attaché of Colombia in Washington, June 10, 1964.

Cornejo, Colonel Carlos Humberto, Director General of the Policia de Hacienda of El Salvador and Chief of Civic Action, August 24, 1966.

Correa de Andrade Mello, Lieutenant Colonel Newton, Assistant Military Attaché of Brazil in Washington, June 10, 1964.

Crócamo, Lieutenant Abraham, Chief, Civic Action Section, Panamanian National Guard, August 12, 1966.

James, Wynne, Assistant for Civic Action, Office of the Assistant Secretary of Defense for International Security Affairs, January 6, 1965.

Lansdale, Major General Edward G., special advisor in Vietnam, April 30, 1965.

Laue, Lieutenant Colonel Albert R., Local Affairs Officer, United States Southern Command, August 8, 1966.

Legters, Major Llewellyn J., Deputy Surgeon, John F. Kennedy Center for Special Warfare, Fort Bragg, N.C., March 11, 1965.

Moger, Lieutenant Commander Jack, Civil Engineer Advisor, United States Naval Forces, Southern Command, August 9–10, 1966.

Molina Pizarro, Colonel Emilio, Military Attaché of Bolivia in Washington, June 9, 1964.

Nath, Brigadier M. M., Military Attaché of India in Washington, February 17, 1965.

Porter, Jr., General Robert W., Commander in Chief, United States Southern Command, August 17, 1966.

Ron, Colonel Ram, Military Attaché of Israel in Washington, March 11, 1965.

Sine, Lieutenant Colonel Robert, Operations and Training Staff Officer, Special Warfare and Civil Affairs Group, U.S. Army Combat Developments Command, Fort Belvoir, Va., January 22, 1965.

Swarm, Colonel William, former Commandant, United States Army Civil Affairs School, February 20, 1965.

Watson, Lieutenant Colonel Francis M., Jr., Operations and Training Staff Officer, Special Warfare and Civil Affairs Group, Combat Developments Command, Fort Belvoir, Va., January 22, 1965.

4. Speeches and Lectures

Ahmad, Colonel Mian Ijaz. "Pakistan's Concept of Military Civic Assistance." Paper presented by Pakistan to the CENTO Seminar on Military Civic Action Programmes, n.p., n.d.

Coppedge, Lieutenant Colonel Richard L. "The Role of Medicine in Counterinsurgency." Fort Bragg, N.C.: John F. Kennedy School of Special Warfare, n.d.

James, Wynne. "The Military as an Aid to Development." Address to the panel on "The Military: Deterrent or Aid to Development?"

Seventh World Conference of the Society for International Development, Washington, March 11, 1965.

Lansdale, Edward G. "Civic Action." Lecture, Counter-Guerrilla School, U.S. Army Special Warfare Center. Fort Bragg, N.C., February 24, 1961.

Lansdale, Edward G. "The Free Citizen in Uniform." Talk to the U.S. Army Civil Affairs School, Fort Gordon, Ga., November 1, 1960.

Lansdale, Edward G. "The Insurgent Battlefield." Talk at Air Force Academy, May 25, 1962.

Lansdale, Edward G. "Soldiers and the People." Lecture, U.S. Army Special Warfare School, Fort Bragg, N.C., August 30, 1962.

Lansdale, Edward G. "Southeast Asia." Lecture at the Army War College, December 3, 1958.

Walinsky, Louis J. "The Role of the Military in Development Planning: Burma." Paper presented to the Conference on Economic Planning in Southeast Asia. Honolulu, February 1–5, 1965.

B. Published Records and Documents

Bedell, Mary and Bowlby, Roger. *Formal Occupational Training of Adult Workers.* Manpower/Automation Research Monograph No. 2. Washington: Manpower Administration of the Department of Labor. December 1964.

Foreign Policy Research Institute. "A Study of the United States Military Assistance Program in Underdeveloped Areas." Annex C of *Supplement to the Composite Report of the President's Committee* [Draper Committee] *to Study the United States Military Assistance Program, Annexes,* Volume II. Washington: Government Printing Office, 1959.

France, Ministère de la Coopération. Direction de la Coopération et Technique. *Les Jeunes Militaires Français et L'Oeuvre de la Coopération.* DCT/CT.RM. Paris, November 1964.

Inter-American Defense Board. *Military Civic Action in the Economic and Social Development of the Countries.* Document T-255. Washington, September 23, 1965.

Iran, Supreme Commander's Staff, J-3. *Civic Action Program for Imperial Iranian Forces.* n.p., 1963.

Israel. *Air-Gadna.* Tel Aviv: Ministry of Defense, 1963.

Israel. *Nahal: Pioneer Fighting Youth.* Tel Aviv: Ministry of Defense, 1963.

Israel. *A Pioneering Youth Training Centre for Tanganyika.* Jerusalem: Ministry for Foreign Affairs, 1962.

Israel, Ministry for Foreign Affairs, Information Department. *Israel-Africa: A Story of Cooperation.* Jerusalem: Hadassah Apprentice School of Printing, n.d.

Livni, Yitzhak (ed.). *Nahal.* Tel Aviv: Israel Ministries of Defense and Foreign Affairs, 1962 (in French).

Nurock, Mordekhai (ed.). *Israel Government Year-Book, 5722 (1961/62).* Jerusalem: Government Printer, 1962.

Ohly, John G. "A Study of Certain Aspects of Foreign Aid." Annex G of *Supplement to the Composite Report of the President's Committee* [Draper Committee] *to Study the United States Military Assistance Program, Annexes.* Volume II. Washington: Government Printing Office, 1959.

Philippine Department of National Defense, Office of the Chief, Economic Development Corps. *The EDCOR Plan.* Camp Murphy, Quezon City, n.d.

Sanjinés Goytia, Julio. *Civic Action: Role of the Armed Forces in the Social and Economical Development of a Country.* La Paz, Bolivia: Centro Audio Visual, USAID, 1964.

Shingler, Brigadier General Donald G. "Contributions of Military Resources to Economic and Social Progress." Annex D of *Supplement to the Composite Report of the President's Committee* [Draper Committee] *to Study the United States Military Assistance Program, Annexes,* Volume II. Washington: Government Printing Office, 1959.

South-East Asia Treaty Organization. *SEATO Report, 1963–1964.* Report of Konthi Suphamongkhon, Secretary-General. Bangkok, September 8, 1964.

South-East Asia Treaty Organization. *Skilled Workers for the Armed Forces.* Bangkok: SEATO Military Technical Training School, n.d.

South-East Asia Treaty Organization. *Training Workers for Developing Industries: A Survey of the SEATO Skilled Labour Project.* Bangkok, n.d.

Spain, Junta Interministerial Conmemoradora de los 25 Años de Paz Española. *El Ejercito.* Volume III of *El Gobierno Informa.* Madrid: Editora Nacional, 1964.

U.S. Agency for International Development. *The Foreign Assistance Program: Annual Report to the Congress for Fiscal Year 1963.* Washington: Government Printing Office, 1964.

U.S. Agency for International Development. *The Foreign Assistance Program: Annual Report to the Congress for Fiscal Year 1964.* Washington: Government Printing Office, 1965.

U.S. Agency for International Development. *Proposed Mutual De-*

fense and Development Programs, FY 1966: Summary Presentation to the Congress. Washington: Government Printing Office, 1965.

U.S. Agency for International Development and Department of Defense. *Proposed Mutual Defense and Assistance Programs, FY 1964: Summary Presentation to the Congress.* Washington: Government Printing Office, 1963.

U.S. Agency for International Development and Department of Defense. *Proposed Mutual Defense and Development Programs, FY 1965.* Washington: Government Printing Office, 1964.

U.S. Air Force. *Information and Guidance on Military Assistance.* 8th ed. Washington: Department of the Air Force, 1964.

U.S. Air Force Recruiting Service. *Your Son's Air Force Life: What You, As Parents, Should Know.* Washington: Government Printing Office, 1964.

U.S. Army. *Basis and Directives for Civic Action.* Lesson Plan 5140. Civic Action Course 41-G-F7. Fort Gordon, Ga.: Civil Affairs School, 1964.

U.S. Army. *Civil Affairs Trends.* Fort Gordon, Ga.: Civil Affairs School, August 1964.

U.S. Army. *Command and Staff Guidelines for Civic Action.* Special Text ST 41-10-90. Fort Gordon, Ga.: Civil Affairs School, 1964.

U.S. Army. *Common Subject Lesson Plans: Civic Action.* USACAS-03. Fort Gordon, Ga.: Civil Affairs School, 1965.

U.S. Army. *The Concept of Civic Action.* Lesson Plan 5135. Civic Action Course 41-G-F7. Fort Gordon, Ga.: Civil Affairs School, 1964.

U.S. Army. *Counterguerrilla Operations.* Field Manual FM 31-16. Washington: Department of the Army, 1963.

U.S. Army. *Counter-Guerrilla Operations in the Philippines, 1946–1953.* A Seminar on the Huk Campaign held at Fort Bragg, N.C., June 15, 1961.

U.S. Army. *Counterinsurgency Planning Guide.* ST 31-176. Fort Bragg, N.C.: Special Warfare School, 1964.

U.S. Army. *Final Report: Fourth Conference of the American Armies.* Fort Amador, C.Z.: Southern Command Headquarters, 1963.

U.S. Army. *Manual for Rural Community Health Worker (Thailand).* Special Text ST 41-30-1. Fort Gordon, Ga.: Civil Affairs School, 1962.

U.S. Army. *Military Civic Action Troop Topics.* DA PAM 360-207. Washington: Government Printing Office, 1964.

U.S. Army. *Program of Instruction for 41-1-F7: Civic Action.* Fort Gordon, Ga.: Civil Affairs School, July 1964.

U.S. Army. *A Review of the Civic Action Program.* Attachment to Lesson Plan 5135. Fort Gordon, Ga.: Civil Affairs School, July 1964.

208   PEACEFUL CONFLICT

U.S. Army. *U.S. Army Counterinsurgency Forces.* Field Manual FM 31-22. Washington: Department of the Army, 1963.

U.S. Army. *Village Technology Handbook.* Special Text ST 41-10-93. Fort Gordon, Ga.: Civil Affairs School, 1963.

U.S. Army, Civic Action Branch, Civil Affairs Directorate, Office of the Deputy Chief of Staff for Military Operations. *Military Civic Action.* Washington: Department of the Army, 1963.

U.S. Army, Civic Action Team, Exercise Polar Strike, 6th Special Forces Group (ABN), 1st Special Forces. *Civic Action Team After Action Report (Alaska, 2 January 1965–22 February 1965).* Fort Bragg, N.C.: John F. Kennedy Center for Special Warfare, 1965.

U.S. Army Special Warfare School. *Civic Action Advance Sheet.* C6. F2206-C3. F2204. Fort Bragg, N.C., February 1965.

U.S. Army Special Warfare School. *Civic Action Lesson Plan.* C6. F2206-C3. F2204-6120. Fort Bragg, N.C., June 1964.

U.S. Army Special Warfare School. *Psychological Operations Planning for Counterinsurgency Operations Lesson Plan.* Fort Bragg, N.C., June 1964.

U.S. Army Special Warfare School. *Role of the U.S. Army Forces in Counter-Insurgency Operations.* Lesson Plan C6. F2403-C9. F2403. Fort Bragg, N.C., January 1965.

U.S. Army, 13th Psychological Warfare Battalion. *The Village Water Well Project.* Fort Bragg, N.C.: John F. Kennedy Center for Special Warfare, n.d.

U.S. Congress, House of Representatives. *Foreign Assistance Act of 1964: Hearings before the Committee on Foreign Affairs on H.R. 10502,* 88th Cong., 2d Sess. Washington: Government Printing Office, 1964.

U.S. Congress, House of Representatives. *Foreign Assistance Act of 1966: Hearings before the Committee on Foreign Affairs,* Part 7. 89th Cong., 2d Sess. Washington: Government Printing Office, 1966.

U.S. Congress, House of Representatives. *Foreign Operations Appropriations for 1965: Hearings Before a Subcommittee of the Committee on Appropriations,* Parts 1 and 2. 88th Cong., 2d Sess. Washington: Government Printing Office, 1964.

U.S. Congress, House of Representatives. *Hearings before a Subcommittee of the Committee on Appropriations,* Part 2. 89th Cong., 2d Sess. Washington: Government Printing Office, 1966.

U.S. Congress, House of Representatives. Committee on Veterans' Affairs. *Veterans' Benefits in the United States: A Report to the President by the President's Commission on Veterans' Pensions, Parts I and II, Findings and Recommendations.* House Committee Print No. 236. 84th Cong., 2d Sess. Washington: Government Printing Office, 1956.

U.S. Department of Defense. *President Kennedy's Statements Relating to Civic Action.* Washington, n.d.

U.S. Eighth Army. *Troop Topic.* Number 3-62. March 1, 1962.

U.S. [Executive Office of the President]. *The Budget of the United States Government, Fiscal Year Ending June 30, 1964.* Washington: Government Printing Office, 1963.

U.S. Food for Peace. *The Nineteenth Semi-Annual Report on Activities Carried on Under Public Law 480, 83d Congress, as Amended, Outlining Operations Under the Act During the Period July 1 through December 31, 1963.* Washington: Government Printing Office, 1964.

U.S. Forces Korea. *Civil Relations, Government Affairs: Armed Forces Assistance to Korea (AFAK) Program.* Policy Directive No. 5-12. October 25, 1962.

[U.S. Navy] *Seabee Technical Assistance Teams: An Existing Counter Insurgency Force,* n.p., n.d.

U.S. Navy, Bureau of Personnel. *Education and Training.* NAVPERS. 10827-B. Washington: Navy Training Publications Center, 1964.

U.S. Navy, Office of Naval Research. *Contract Research Program.* ONR-1. Washington: Department of the Navy, 1964.

U.S. President's Committee to Study the United States Military Assistance Program [Draper Committee]. *Conclusions Concerning the Mutual Security Program.* Washington: Government Printing Office, 1959.

U.S. President's Committee to Study the United States Military Assistance Program [Draper Committee]. Volume II. *Supplement to the Composite Report: Annexes.* Washington: Government Printing Office, 1959.

United States Southern Command. *Civic Action Projects Report, 1 Mar 1964–1 Aug 1964.* Quarry Heights, C.Z., 1964.

United States Southern Command. *Civic Action Projects Report, 1 Mar 1964–1 Jan 1965.* Quarry Heights, C.Z., 1965.

Venezuela, Ministerio de la Defensa. *Acción Cívica Informe.* Caracas: Comandancia General del Ejército, n.d.

II. SECONDARY MATERIALS

A. General Works and Special Studies

Ashford, Douglas E. *The Elusiveness of Power: The African Single Party State.* Ithaca, N.Y.: Center for International Studies of Cornell University, 1965.

Beers, Henry Putney. *The Western Military Frontier, 1815–1846.* Philadelphia: University of Pennsylvania Press, 1935.

Center of Latin American Studies. *Statistical Abstract of Latin America, 1963.* Los Angeles: University of California Press, 1963.

Clark, Harold F. and Sloan, Harold S., *Classrooms in the Military: An Account of Education in the Armed Forces of the United States.* New York: Columbia University, 1964.

Cottrell, Leonard. *The Great Invasion.* New York: Coward-McCann, Inc., 1962.

Coward, H. Roberts. *Military Technology in Developing Countries.* Report C/64-5. Cambridge: Center for International Studies of the Massachusetts Institute of Technology, 1964.

Dabbs, Jack Autrey. *The French Army in Mexico, 1861–1867: A Study in Military Government.* The Hague: Mouton & Co., 1963.

Les Defenseurs D'Israel: Nahal, Les Fermiers Combattants. Tel Aviv: Editions "Eshel," n.d.

Deitchman, Seymour J. *Limited War and American Defense Policy.* Cambridge, Mass.: M.I.T. Press, 1964.

Fisher, Sidney Nettleton (ed.). *The Military in the Middle East.* Columbus: Ohio State University Press, 1963.

Foster, Robert J., et al. *Human Factors in Civic Action: A Selected Annotated Bibliography.* Alexandria, Va.: Human Resources Research Office of George Washington University, 1963.

Furniss, Edgar S., Jr. *DeGaulle and the French Army: A Crisis in Civil-Military Relations.* New York: Twentieth Century Fund, 1964.

Georgetown Research Project. *Castro-Communist Insurgency in Venezuela: A Study of Insurgency and Counter-insurgency Operations and Techniques in Venezuela, 1960–1964.* ARPA Project No. 4860; Contract No. SD-215. Alexandria, Va.: Atlantic Research Corporation, 1965.

Georgetown Research Project. *A Historical Survey of Patterns and Techniques of Insurgency Conflicts in Post-1900 Latin America.* ARPA Project No. 4860; Contract No. SD-215. Alexandria, Va.: Atlantic Research Corporation, 1964.

Giap, General Vo Nguyen. *People's War, People's Army: The Viet Cong Insurrection Manual for Under-developed Countries.* New York: Frederick A. Praeger, 1962.

Goetzman, William H. *Army Exploration in the American West, 1803–1863.* New Haven: Yale University Press, 1959.

Gude, Edward W. *Internal Dynamics of Conflict and Change: Arms Control and Internal Warfare.* BR-2526. Bedford, Mass.: Raytheon Company, August 1, 1963.

Guevara, Che. *On Guerrilla Warfare*. New York: Frederick A. Praeger, 1961.

Hill, Forest G. *Roads, Rails, and Waterways*. Norman: University of Oklahoma Press, 1957.

Jacobs, James Ripley. *The Beginning of the U.S. Army, 1783–1812*. Princeton: Princeton University Press, © 1947.

Janowitz, Morris. *The Military in the Political Development of New Nations*. Chicago: University of Chicago Press, 1964.

Janowitz, Morris (ed.). *The New Military: Changing Patterns of Organization*. New York: Russell Sage Foundation, 1964.

Johnson, John J. *Continuity and Change in Latin America*. Stanford, Calif.: Stanford University Press, 1964.

Johnson, John J. *The Military and Society in Latin America*. Stanford: Stanford University Press, 1964.

Johnson, John J. (ed.). *The Role of the Military in Underdeveloped Countries*. Princeton: Princeton University Press, 1962.

Kolkowicz, R. *The Use of Soviet Military Labor in the Civilian Economy: A Study of Military "Shefstvo."* Memorandum RM-3360-PR. Santa Monica, Calif.: RAND Corporation, November 1962.

Lieuwen, Edwin. *Arms and Politics in Latin America*. New York: Frederick A. Praeger, 1961.

Maass, Arthur. *Muddy Waters: The Army Engineers and the Nation's Rivers*. Cambridge, Mass.: Harvard University Press, 1951.

Mao Tse-tung. *Guerrilla Warfare*. Trans. by Brigadier General Samuel B. Griffith, USMC (Ret.). New York: Frederick A. Praeger, 1961.

Masland, John W. and Radway, Laurence I. *Soldiers and Scholars: Military Education and National Policy*. Princeton: Princeton University Press, 1957.

McCardle, Catherine. *The Role of Military Assistance in the Problem of Arms Control: The Middle East, Latin America, and Africa*. C/64-24. Cambridge: Center for International Studies of the Massachusetts Institute of Technology, 1964.

Montgomery, John D. *The Politics of Foreign Aid: American Experience in Southeast Asia*. New York: Frederick A. Praeger for the Council on Foreign Relations, 1962.

Pauker, Guy J. *Notes on Non-Military Measures in Control of Insurgency*. P-2642. Santa Monica, Calif.: RAND Corporation, 1962.

Prucha, Francis Paul. *Broadax and Bayonet: The Role of the United States Army in the Development of the Northwest, 1815–1860*. Madison: State Historical Society of Wisconsin, 1953.

Pustay, John S. *Counterinsurgency Warfare*. New York: Free Press, 1965.

Pye, Lucian W. *Military Development in the New Countries.* C/62-1. Paper prepared for the Smithsonian Institution. Cambridge: Center for International Studies of the Massachusetts Institute of Technology, 1961.

Ramati, Lieutenant Colonel Shaul. *The Israel Defence Forces.* "Israel Today Series," No. 4. Revised ed. Jerusalem: Jerusalem Post Press, 1961.

Sandes, Lieutenant Colonel E. W. C. *The Royal Engineers in Egypt and the Sudan.* Chatham, England: The Institution of Royal Engineers, 1937.

Scaff, Alvin H. *The Philippine Answer to Communism.* Stanford, Calif.: Stanford University Press, 1955.

Spaulding, Oliver L. *The United States Army in War and Peace.* New York: G. P. Putnam's Sons, 1937.

Tanham, George K. *et al. War Without Guns: American Civilians in Rural Vietnam.* New York: Frederick A. Praeger, 1966.

Thursfield, Rear Admiral H. G. (ed.). *Brassey's Annual: The Armed Forces Year-Book.* New York: Frederick A. Praeger, 1963.

Valeriano, Colonel Napoleon D. and Bohannan, Lieutenant Colonel Charles T. R. *Counter-Guerrilla Operations: The Philippine Experience.* New York: Frederick A. Praeger, 1962.

Waterhouse, Harry F. *A Time to Build.* Columbia: University of South Carolina Press, 1964.

Zborowski, Mark and Herzog, Elizabeth. *Life is with People: The Culture of the Shtetl.* New York: Schocken Books, 1962.

B. Articles

"Alaskan Children Thank 6th SFGA," *Veritas,* IV (March 24, 1965), 3.

Alba, Victor. "The Stages of Militarism in Latin America," in Johnson, John J. (ed.). *The Role of the Military in Underdeveloped Countries.* Princeton: Princeton University Press, 1962, pp. 165–183.

"American-Vietnamese Medical Team: SF Doctor Leads Fight Against Disease," *Veritas,* IV (March 24, 1965), 6.

"Army Trains Teachers," *Israel Digest,* VIII (January 29, 1965), 3.

Auletta, Lieutenant Colonel Anthony J. "Ten-Nation Progress Report," *Army,* XIII (July 1963), 53–59.

Baldwin, Hanson. "Winds of Change Stir the Academies," *Think,* XXXI (January–February 1965), 28–32.

Bentz, Major Harold F., Jr. "Psychological Warfare and Civic Action," *Army,* XIII (July 1963), 62–65.

Biderman, Albert D. "Sequels to a Military Career: The Retired

Military Professional," in Janowitz, Morris (ed.). *The New Military: Changing Patterns of Organization.* New York: Russell Sage Foundation, 1964, pp. 287–336.

Black, Colonel Edwin F. " 'Dragon's Teeth' of Freedom," *Military Review,* XLIV (August 1964), 20–25.

Blumenson, Martin. "Some Thoughts on Professionalism," *Military Review,* XLIV (September 1964), 12–16.

Burke, Major Robert L. "Military Civic Action," *Military Review,* XLIV (October 1964), 62–71.

"Civic Action: The Military Role in Nation Building," *For Commanders–This Changing World,* III (January 15, 1964), 1–4.

Coleman, James S. and Brice, Belmont, Jr. "The Role of the Military in Sub-Saharan Africa," in Johnson, John J. (ed.). *The Role of the Military in Underdeveloped Countries.* Princeton: Princeton University Press, 1962, pp. 359–405.

"Colombia: The New Look," *Newsweek* (August 17, 1964), p. 47.

Duffy, Colonel John J. "Signpost: Success in the Philippines," *Army,* XIII (July 1963), 60–62.

Eagleburger, L. S. "FSOs Learned Engineering to Help 'Quake' Victims," *Department of State Newsletter,* No. 37 (May 1964), pp. 54–55.

Fisher, Sidney Nettleton. "The Role of the Military in Society and Government in Turkey," in his *The Military in the Middle East.* Columbus: Ohio State University Press, 1963, pp. 21–40.

Forstmeier, Commander Friedrich. "Academic Education for Bundeswehr Officers," *Military Review,* XLIV (May 1964), 36–45.

Francis, Michael J. "Military Aid to Latin America in the U.S. Congress," *Journal of Inter-American Studies,* VI (July 1964), 389–404.

Ginsburgh, Colonel Robert N. "The Challenge to Military Professionalism," *Foreign Affairs,* XLII (January 1964), 255–268.

Glick, Edward Bernard. "Alaskan Civic Action," *Military Review,* XLVI (December 1966), 57–61.

Glick, Edward Bernard. "Conflict, Civic Action and Counterinsurgency," *Orbis,* X (Fall 1966), 899–910.

Glick, Edward Bernard. "The Feasibility of Arms Control and Disarmament in Latin America," *Orbis,* IX (Fall 1965), 743–759.

Glick, Edward Bernard. "The Nonmilitary Use of the Latin American Military," in Bailey, Norman A. (ed.) *Latin America: Politics, Economics, and Hemispheric Security.* New York: Frederick A. Praeger for the Center for Strategic Studies of Georgetown University, 1965, 179–191.

Glick, Edward Bernard. "The Nonmilitary Use of the Latin American Military: A More Realistic Approach to Arms Control and Economic Development," *Background* (since renamed *International Studies Quarterly*), VIII (November 1964), 161–173.

Griggs, Lee. "When He Wills It, Things Happen." *Life*, LX (January 14, 1966), 42, 47.

Halpern, Ben. "The Role of the Military in Israel," in Johnson, John J. (ed.). *The Role of the Military in Underdeveloped Countries*. Princeton: Princeton University Press, 1962, pp. 317–357.

Halpern, Manfred. "Middle Eastern Armies and the New Middle Class," in Johnson, John J. (ed.). *The Role of the Military in Underdeveloped Countries*. Princeton: Princeton University Press, 1962, pp. 277–315.

Hanegbi, Yehuda. "Awakening of the Arava," *Land and Life*, XX (September 1964), 4–7.

Heiman, Leo. "Military Assistance by Small Nations," *Military Review*, XLIV (March 1964), 14–18.

Helguera, J. Leon. "The Changing Role of the Military in Colombia," *Journal of Inter-American Studies*, III (July 1961), 351–357.

"Historic Finds at Massada Dig," *Israel Digest*, VII (May 8, 1964), 1, 4.

Hurewitz, J. C. "The Role of the Military in Society and Government in Israel," in Fisher, Sidney Nettleton (ed.). *The Military in the Middle East*. Columbus: Ohio State University Press, 1963, pp. 89–104.

"Impressive Independence Day Parade at Beersheba," *Israel Digest*, VII (April 24, 1964), 1, 4.

"Jerusalem's Soldiers Adopt Slum Area," *Israel Digest*, VII (May 8, 1964), 8.

Johnson, Chalmers. "How Sharp Are the Dragon's Teeth?", *New York Times Magazine*, February 28, 1965, pp. 22, 85–87.

Johnson, John J. "The Latin American Military as a Politically Competing Group in Transitional Society," in his *The Role of the Military in Underdeveloped Countries*. Princeton: Princeton University Press, 1962, pp. 91–129.

Johnson, John J. " 'New Armies' Take Over in Latin America," *New York Times Magazine*, March 8, 1964, pp. 14, 97–99.

Kirk, George. "The Role of the Military in Society and Government in Egypt," in Fisher, Sidney Nettleton (ed.). *The Military in the Middle East*. Columbus: Ohio State University Press, 1963, pp. 71–88.

Ladd, Lieutenant Colonel Jonathan F. "Some Reflections on Counterinsurgency," *Military Review*, XLIV (October 1964), 72–78.

Lansdale, Major General Edward G. "Viet Nam: Do We Understand Revolution?", *Foreign Affairs*, XLIII (October 1964), 75–86.

Lerner, Daniel and Robinson, Richard D. "Swords and Plough-shares: The Turkish Army as a Modernizing Force," *World Politics*, XIII (October 1960), 19–44.

Levenberg, Alisa, "Camp Marcus: Model School for Adults," *Pioneer Woman*, XL (January 1965), 7–8, 22.

Levine, Yehuda. "Long Twilight: The Jews of Finland," *Congress Bi-Weekly*, XXII (March 1, 1965), 10–12.

Lieuwen, Edwin. "Militarism and Politics in Latin America," in Johnson, John J. (ed.). *The Role of the Military in Underdeveloped Countries*. Princeton: Princeton University Press, 1962, pp. 131–163.

Lieuwen, Edwin. "Neo-Militarism in Latin America: The Kennedy Administration's Inadequate Response," *Inter-American Economic Affairs*, XVI (Spring 1963), 11–19.

Mans, Lieutenant Colonel Rowland S. N. "Victory in Malaya," in Greene, Lieutenant Colonel T. N. (ed.). *The Guerrilla—and How to Fight Him*. New York: Frederick A. Praeger, 1962, pp. 115–143.

Martínez Codó, Enrique. "The Military Problems in Latin America," *Military Review*, XLIV (August 1964), 11–19.

McAlister, Lyle N. "Civil-Military Relations in Latin America," *Journal of Inter-American Studies*, III (July 1961), 341–350.

McAlister, Lyle N. "The Military," in Johnson, John J. (ed.). *Continuity and Change in Latin America*. Stanford, Calif.: Stanford University Press, 1964, pp. 136–160.

McNamara, Robert S. "The Military Assistance Program for 1965," *The Department of State Bulletin*, L (May 4, 1964), 705–715.

Nemo, General. "A Propos de la Reforme du Service Militaire," *Revue de Défense Nationale* (February 1964), pp. 193–202.

Nemo, General. "Terres Françaises D'Amérique: Le Service Militaire Adapté," *Revue de Défense Nationale* (January 1962), pp. 53–64.

Nieburg, H. L. "The Threat of Violence and Social Change," *The American Political Science Review*, LVI (December, 1962), 865–873.

Perchat, J. Y. "Education et Promotion Sociale," *Revue Militaire d'Information* (June 1963), pp. 46–49.

"La Promotion Sociale dans Les Armées," *Bulletin d'Information des Armées*, No. 24 (June 18, 1964), pp. 1–7.

Pruck, Colonel Erich F. "Officer Training in the Soviet Army," *Military Review*, XLIV (July 1964), 61–66.

Pye, Lucian W. "Armies in the Process of Political Modernization," in Johnson, John J. (ed). *The Role of the Military in Underdeveloped Countries*. Princeton: Princeton University Press, 1962, pp. 69–89.

Pye, Lucian W. "The Army in Burmese Politics," in Johnson,

216   PEACEFUL CONFLICT

John J. (ed.). *The Role of the Military in Underdeveloped Countries.* Princeton: Princeton University Press, 1962, pp. 231–251.

Rattenbach, Lieutenant General Benjamin. "The Military Sector of Society," *Military Review,* XLIV (July 1964), 81–86.

"Le Régiment Mixte des Antilles-Guyane," *Frères d'Armes* (October 1964), pp. 13–22.

Rosson, Major General William B. "Understanding Civic Action," *Army,* XIII (July 1963), 46–47.

Rostow, Dankwart. "The Military in Middle Eastern Society and Politics," in Fisher, Sidney Nettleton (ed.). *The Military in the Middle East.* Columbus: Ohio State University Press, 1963, pp. 3–20.

"Rumania," *Encyclopaedia Britannica* (1947 edition), XIX, 638.

Sananikone, Brigadier General Oudone. "Laos–Case Study in Civic Action: The Royal Lao Program," *Military Review,* XLIII (December 1963), 44–54.

"Sergeant-Major Adopts Mental Hospital," *Israel Digest,* VIII (January 29, 1965), 3.

"Le Service Militaire Adapté aux Antilles-Guyane," *T.A.M.* [Terre, Aire, Marine] (June 10, 1964).

Shils, Edward. "The Military in the Political Development of the New States," in Johnson, John J. (ed.). *The Role of the Military in Underdeveloped Countries.* Princeton: Princeton University Press, 1962, pp. 7–67.

Singlaub, Colonel John K. "Special Warfare Training in 7th Army," *Military Review,* XLIV (March 1964), 54–61.

Slover, Colonel Robert H. "This Is Military Civic Action," *Army,* XIII (July 1963), 48–52.

Smith, Major William A., Jr. "The Strategic Hamlet Program in Vietnam," *Military Review,* XLIV (May 1964), 17–24.

"Soldier Students Learn to Learn," *Israel Digest,* VIII (December 31, 1965), 6.

Stockell, Major Charles W. "Laos–Case Study in Civic Action: The Military Program," *Military Review,* XLIII (December 1963), 55–63.

"Technical Cooperation with Latin America," *Israel Digest,* VIII (November 19, 1965), 8.

Theikpa, Maung. "Training Tomorrow's Civil Service Officers," *Forward,* IV (October 1, 1965), 16–21.

"Three Envoys Present Credentials," *Israel Digest,* VIII (December 3, 1965), 3.

Topping, Seymour. "Next on Peking's Hit Parade?" *New York Times Magazine* (February 20, 1966), pp. 30–31, 76, 78–79.

"U.S. Department of Defense Military Assistance Program," *Army Research and Development*, V (April 1964), 14–15.

Wool, Harold. "The *Changing* Pattern of Military Skills," *Employment Security Review* (July 1963), pp. 1–6.

Yannay, Ya'acov. "Technical Cooperation Between Israel and the Developing World," *International Development Review*, VI (September 1964), 10–15.

Index